THEODORA, A NOVEL

BY DOROTHEA DU BOIS

CHAWTON HOUSE LIBRARY SERIES
Series Editors: Stephen Bending
                  Stephen Bygrave

TITLES IN THIS SERIES

The Histories of Some of the Penitents in the Magdalen-House
edited by Jennie Batchelor and Megan Hiatt

Stéphanie-Félicité de Genlis, *Adelaide and Theodore,
or Letters on Education*
edited by Gillian Dow

E. M. Foster, *The Corinna of England*
edited by Sylvia Bordoni

Sarah Harriet Burney, *The Romance of Private Life*
edited by Lorna J. Clark

Alicia LeFanu, *Strathallan*
edited by Anna M. Fitzer

Elizabeth Sophia Tomlins, *The Victim of Fancy*
edited by Daniel Cook

Helen Maria Williams, *Julia*
edited by Natasha Duquette

Elizabeth Hervey, *The History of Ned Evans*
edited by Helena Kelly

Sarah Green, *Romance Readers and Romance Writers*
edited by Christopher Goulding

Mrs Costello, *The Soldier's Orphan*
edited by Clare Broome Saunders

Sarah Green, *The Private History of the Court of England*
edited by Fiona Price

Translations and Continuations: Riccoboni and Brooke, Graffigny and Roberts
edited by Marijn S. Kaplan

Sydney Owenson, *Florence McCarthy: An Irish Tale*
edited by Jenny McAuley

Frances Brooke, *The History of Lady Julia Mandeville*
edited by Enit Karafili Steiner

Ann Gomersall, *The Citizen*
edited by Margaret S. Yoon

Eliza Haywood, *The Rash Resolve and Life's Progress*
edited by Carol Stewart

Mary Brunton, *Self-Control*
edited by Anthony Mandal

Eliza Haywood, *The Invisible Spy*
edited by Carol Stewart

Isabelle de Montolieu, *Caroline of Lichtfield*
edited by Laura Kirkley

Mrs S. C. Hall, *Sketches of Irish Character*
edited by Marion Durnin

Sophie Cottin, *Malvina*
edited by Marijn S. Kaplan

Charlotte Dacre, *The Confessions of the Nun of St Omer*
edited by Lucy Cogan

Mary Brurton, *Discipline*
edited by Olivia Murphy

Marguerite Blessington, *Marmaduke Herbert; or, the Fatal Error*
edited by Susanne Schmid

Elizabeth Hays Lanfear, *Fatal Errors*
edited by Felicity James and Timothy Whelan

THEODORA, A NOVEL

by Dorothea Du Bois

Edited by Lucy Cogan

LONDON AND NEW YORK

First published 2022
by Routledge
2 Park Square, Milton Park, Abingdon, Oxon OX14 4RN

and by Routledge
52 Vanderbilt Avenue, New York, NY 10017

Routledge is an imprint of the Taylor & Francis Group, an informa business

© 2022 selection and editorial matter, Lucy Cogan; individual owners retain copyright in their own material.

The right of Lucy Cogan to be identified as the author of the editorial material, and of the authors for their individual chapters, has been asserted in accordance with sections 77 and 78 of the Copyright, Designs and Patents Act 1988.

All rights reserved. No part of this book may be reprinted or reproduced or utilised in any form or by any electronic, mechanical, or other means, now known or hereafter invented, including photocopying and recording, or in any information storage or retrieval system, without permission in writing from the publishers.

Trademark notice: Product or corporate names may be trademarks or registered trademarks, and are used only for identification and explanation without intent to infringe.

British Library Cataloguing-in-Publication Data
A catalogue record for this book is available from the British Library

Library of Congress Cataloging-in-Publication Data
Names: Du Bois, Dorothea, 1728–1774, author. | Cogan, Lucy, editor.
Title: Theodora : a novel / by Dorothea Du Bois ; edited by Lucy Cogan.
Description: Abingdon, Oxon ; New York, NY : Routledge, 2021. | Series: Chawton House Library. Women's novels | Includes bibliographical references. | Summary: "This scholarly edition of Du Bois's 1770 novel, Theodora, A Novel, introduces readers to a unique voice in women's writing of the eighteenth century that has been undeservedly dismissed by literary history for far too long"–Provided by publisher.
Identifiers: LCCN 2021016725 (print) | LCCN 2021016726 (ebook) | ISBN 9780367714215 (hardback) | ISBN 9781003150794 (ebook)
Classification: LCC PR3429.D25 T48 2021 (print) | LCC PR3429.D25 (ebook) | DDC 823/.6—dc23
LC record available at https://lccn.loc.gov/2021016725
LC ebook record available at https://lccn.loc.gov/2021016726

ISBN: 978-0-367-71421-5
eISBN: 978-1-003-15079-4

DOI: 10.4324/9781003150794

Typeset in Times New Roman
by Apex CoVantage, LLC

CONTENTS

Acknowledgements viii
Introduction ix
A brief chronology of Dorothea Du Bois and the contested
  inheritance of 6th Earl of Anglesey's Estate xix
A note on the text xxi

THEODORA, A NOVEL
Vol. I. 1

THEODORA, A NOVEL
Vol. II. 85

Appendix A "A True Tale" from *Poems on Several*
  Occasions (1764) 185

Appendix B *The Case of Ann Countess of Anglesey, Lately*
  Deceased . . . (1766) 194

Bibliography 213

ACKNOWLEDGEMENTS

Many thanks to all of those who gave me their help and support in the making of this edition. My particular thanks go to my fellow travellers Laura Kirkley, Deborah Russell, Bryan Radley, and Michelle O'Connell, as well as my UCD colleagues Porscha Fermanis, Sarah Comyn, and John Brannigan. I'd also like to thank Ian Campbell Ross, Moyra Haslett, Aileen Douglas, and Andrew Carpenter, who helped spark my interest in this topic. I am grateful to Ciara Durnin most particularly for allowing me to pick her brains on the quality of Du Bois' legal arguments. I'd also like to extend my particular gratitude to the staff of the library at University College Dublin, the National Library of Ireland, the Bodleian Library, Oxford, and the British Library. Thank you to Stephen Bygrave and Stephen Bending, the editors of this series, for seeing the potential in this project. Thanks to Agnes for your patience and Richard for the pleasant distractions when needed. And a special thanks to Bess, who is the best.

INTRODUCTION

In the summer of 1770, *The Monthly Review* cast its critical eye over a recently published novel, *Theodora*, by the Irish female author Dorothea Du Bois. The reviewer alludes to the outlandish story of Du Bois' recent family history in a manner that assumes the reader's familiarity with this context:

> The story is founded on the strange, romantic, but true and well-known incidents of the Anglesey family, of which the Writer is an unfortunate branch; and who, being in necessitous circumstances, has industriously endeavoured to mend them, in some small degree, by telling and embellishing her hapless tale. This is not the first time of her soliciting the attention of the public; which she has occasionally done, not in prose only, but also in verse: but, poor Lady Dorothea is not a very correct writer. She has, however, laudably endeavoured to render her work (to use the words of her previous advertisement): useful, as well as entertaining, by placing Virtue in her loveliest dress, and marking Vice with every feature of deformity.
>
> (43: 66)

From the vantage point of the present, what precisely is meant by the "correctness" or otherwise of *Theodora* is not immediately apparent, though by declaring "poor Lady Dorothea's" work beyond critical reproach, the author of the review implies that the novel does not merit serious attention.[1] To the readers of the day, however, the writer's implication would have been quite clear. For Du Bois' extended family had been embroiled in a rolling, multi-layered scandal that had been playing out in the courts and in the press of Britain and Ireland for decades by that point, and to this great pile of commentary, she had added her own explosive contribution. Perhaps one of the criteria by which the reviewer judges her writing to be "incorrect" was Du Bois' unusually frank portrayal in *Theodora* of the infamously wild behaviour of the Irish nobility in the period, which was informed by her own personal experience.[2]

Theodora is an entertaining and frequently shocking tale of a young woman's efforts to regain her position in high society after her aristocratic father's abandonment of and denial of marriage to her mother. Beyond this the novel includes an account of a "ravishment" and forced marriage, several instances of bigamy, extortion, more than one kidnapping, forgery of legal documents, slanderous accusations of "crim con," as well as domestic abuse and multiple instances in which women must defend themselves against violent male predation, sexual and otherwise. Throughout these trials the protagonist of the work, the eponymous Theodora, is presented as an unfailingly virtuous young woman, but she is also far more spirited than is common for the heroine of a mid-eighteenth-century novel. This resilience would be remarkable in a purely fictional character, but it is all the more so since the events of the novel are drawn from Du Bois' own life; she was, as Andrew Carpenter says of her, "the seriously wronged daughter of an Irish nobleman" (298–99). Central to the narrative of *Theodora* is the powerlessness of women in the face of a system, moral, social, and legal, that was designed to enshrine and protect patriarchal interests. In this manner *Theodora* – though Du Bois was no radical – exposes the gross injustices of eighteenth-century society with regard to gender that more mainstream works of the era typically softened or elided, making her work an important corrective to more typical examples of women's writing from the period.

The Right Honourable Lady Dorothea Du Bois

In the advertisement to *Theodora*, Du Bois engages in what may appear to be the formulaic disavowal of ambition and pride expected of a female author in the period: "AS I am impelled, *by more pressing motives* than a vain desire of applause, to subject these volumes to public inspection, I trust I shall meet with that indulgence, to which my sex, and unhappy circumstances may *unambitiously intitle me*" (5). The "unhappy circumstances" Du Bois delicately gestures towards here were rather more extraordinary than the conventional phrasing might suggest. The assertion that she intended the novel to place "VIRTUE in her loveliest dress, and mark VICE with her every feature of deformity" similarly had a particular resonance, since the narrative had its basis in the well-known scandals that had consumed her family for three decades. The novel represents just one prong of what was a very public campaign to assert what Du Bois believed was her rightful place among the nobility of Ireland and Britain, which included musical entertainments, a collection of poetry, and other works alongside numerous legal cases. On the title page of *Theodora*, the author styles herself with the impressive honorific "the Right Honourable Lady Dorothea Du Bois," and the text was conceived in large part to validate the lofty name the writer claims for herself.

Born in Ireland in 1728 as Dorothea Annesley, Du Bois was the eldest child of Richard Annesley, who became Lord Altham that same year and Earl of Anglesey in 1737, and Ann Simpson, who was the daughter of a wealthy Dublin merchant. Around 1740–1, Du Bois' father threw the family into chaos when he left her mother and, finding his efforts to obtain a divorce thwarted, declared that they had never been married. This had the effect of rendering his three daughters by

INTRODUCTION

Simpson illegitimate at a stroke, a degradation Du Bois would fight against for the rest of her life. To support his assertion, Annesley revealed that he had been married in 1715 to a woman named Anne Prust or Phrust of Devonshire, though he appears to have abandoned her soon after. Prust died in 1741, but the overlap in time made his marriage to Simpson bigamous and therefore void. Annesley's mistress and later wife, Juliana Donovan, would claim after his death that he had married her in 1741 on Prust's death, despite a public ceremony not being held until 1752. Indeed, it also emerged that the earl had married yet another woman, Anne Salkeld, in London in 1742.

The notoriously debauched earl's marital entanglements were a further complicating factor in what was the already knotty issue of who the rightful heir to the earldom of Anglesey really was. Soon after he had been made Lord Altham in the late-1720s, Annesley had arranged to have his nephew, a rival claimant, bundled off to the American colonies as an indentured servant, a story which inspired a chapter of Tobias Smollett's *Peregrine Pickle* (1751) and Robert Louis Stevenson's *Kidnapped* (1886).[3] A decade later, in the 1730s, Annesley fought off a cousin in the courts to retain his earldom. Given the contested nature of the earl's position in life and the question of which, if any, among his children could be considered his legitimate heir, it is unsurprising that numerous claimants emerged to assert their right to his titles upon his death in 1761. Amid the miasma of claim and counter-claim, Du Bois worked tirelessly to have her rights and privileges, as well as those of her mother (who died in 1765) and her sisters, reinstated. However, as a woman, she was at a serious disadvantage. Du Bois' literary career originated as part of her effort to see her mother, and by extension herself, vindicated in the eyes of the law or at least, if that should prove impossible, in the eyes of the public.

The narrative of *Theodora* begins with a thinly veiled account of Du Bois' parents' marriage and separation, and through the remainder of the two volumes the author traces the devastating impact of that schism and its aftershocks on their daughter's life into adulthood. Along the way Du Bois provides many glimpses of the misbehaviour of the upper classes in Ireland and Britain, sparing no blushes in exposing the endemic immorality of many of those who moved in the most fashionable circles of the age. The reader is inevitably left wondering, how much of this is true? Sifting through contemporary newspaper reports, magazine articles, and court records reveals that, in its broad strokes, much of the narrative has a strong basis in fact, with some "embellishments" as *The Monthly Review* puts it. A glancing knowledge of the cases that were regularly splashed across the newspapers of the period would have made the identification of the major characters relatively straightforward. The owner of the British library copy from which this text is taken, William Musgrave, a keen collector of biographies, was even able to name many of the minor players from the representations of their fictional counterparts in his annotations. Du Bois also helpfully covered the same ground in multiple fictional and non-fictional works, two examples of which appear in the appendices, which provide contrasting perspectives on the main events of the text, as well as illuminating the shading she gave to those events depending on which formal strategy she was employing.

INTRODUCTION

A useful point of comparison for *Theodora* is Du Bois' poem "A True Tale," published as part of her *Poems on Several Occasions by a Lady of Quality* (1764), which contains another version of her mother's story and is presented here alongside the text of the novel as Appendix A. The poem also recounts an infamous incident that occurred in late 1760, which Du Bois claims had been used by her enemies to discredit her, when she attempted to visit her dying father and was assaulted by her half brother and his servants. Then in 1766 came the non-fiction text *The Case of Ann Countess of Anglesey*, which appears in this edition as Appendix B. *The Case* sets out, in a legalistic register that was highly unusual for a female author in the period, the positive case for her parents' marriage and her own legitimacy.[4] Again, *The Case*, in the form of an introduction, includes a retelling of the same disastrous visit of 1760 Du Bois made to her ailing father. *Theodora* was, therefore, part of what was a sophisticated attempt to influence public perception both of the cases before the courts and of Du Bois herself. In the years after the publication of *Theodora*, there followed further theatrical works entitled *The Magnet: A Musical Entertainment* (1771) and *The Divorce: A Musical Entertainment* (1771) that echo the same themes of infidelity and marital breakdown.

Du Bois used the paratextual material that accompanied her *Poems* of 1764 to assert her place among the great and the good of British and Irish society. As well as styling herself by her noble honorific on the title page, she lists among the subscribers the names of some powerful supporters. The Earl of Chesterfield, former Lord-Lieutenant of Ireland, is listed, who had secured for Du Bois' mother the pension that supported the family until Simpson's death in 1765. Also listed is the Archbishop of Dublin, Charles Cobbe, whose presence would have reminded readers that Simpson won several cases against the earl in the ecclesiastical courts in defence of her marriage. John Annesley, the main Irish rival to her half brother Arthur's claim for her father's title, appears styled as the "Right Hon. Lord Annesley." Many aristocratic subscribers, in a show of largesse, are noted to have purchased multiple copies. Recorded as buying two is the Irish belle Elizabeth, Duchess of Hamilton (née Gunning), sister of Maria Gunning, who was perhaps the most celebrated beauty of the age until her early death in 1760. In *Theodora*, Du Bois implies that she was once an intimate acquaintance of the Gunning sisters through her depiction of Theodora's short-lived but intense friendship with two beautiful sisters named Garden while she frequents balls among the fashionable set at Dublin Castle as a young woman. Du Bois is thus eager to signal that she does not simply have the backing of the establishment, but that, despite her reduced circumstances, she is truly one of them.

The poem "A True Tale" ends with the declaration that only the law could right the wrongs Du Bois' mother had suffered: "To Law! voracious Law, fair Anna now/Must have Recourse, it cannot disallow/Her Right" (300). It is impossible, knowing the outcome, not to hear a plaintive tone in the double negative of "cannot disallow" in this apparent statement of confidence. The decisive blow for Du Bois' campaign came in September 1765 when the Irish Attorney General, Philip Tisdall, recognised her half brother as the late earl's rightful heir without even bothering to refer the case to the Irish House of Lords, though countless suits regarding the competing claims were still pending in Ireland and Britain. There may have been a political motivation for his abrupt decision, since, as Viscount Valentia, Arthur proved a reliable vote for the government. In *The Case* Du Bois openly challenges the legal grounds of Tisdall's judgment for the partiality he had shown to her half brother throughout the proceedings and the dubious nature of some of the evidence he had accepted without question. Written in the vocabulary of the law, this text displays Du Bois' impressive command of legal concepts and terminology. Her arguments are legally sound and evince a keen understanding of the finer points on which her case rests. Intent on pursuing her argument to the fullest, Du Bois does not content herself with dissecting the behaviour of her enemies; she also criticises her ally, John Annesley, for not pursuing the matter of her parents' marriage more forcefully. Indeed, she laments that throughout the whole process barely a cursory mention was made of the issue that was, for her, of such existential importance.

The Irish Attorney General's long-awaited judgment of 1765, by recognising the legitimacy of Du Bois' half brother Arthur, was in effect a declaration that she and her sisters were illegitimate. Yet there was one more card still to play – a direct appeal to King George III. In *The Case* Du Bois asserts her confidence that had the evidence been set before "his Majesty," there could be no doubt but that he would have ordered it to trial (209). It is in this context, with all her hopes pinned on the monarch's intervention, that Du Bois' most ostentatiously unionist poems, such as "On the Death of his late Majesty and on the Accession of his present Majesty to the Throne," which Sarah Prescott notes for its "congratulatory royalist-loyalist strain" (186), should be read. The dedicatory verses that open her *Poems* are an even more transparent effort to curry favour ahead of this important judgement, as Du Bois presents herself as a humble "female bard" submitting herself to the king's protection in the hopes that the "wish'd Reward" would be forthcoming (iv). At last, on 19 February 1767, the king's Attorney General referred Du Bois' petition requesting that the case of the Annesley inheritance be delayed until the outcome of her suit regarding her parents' marriage to the Committee of Rights and Privileges in the British House of Lords.[5] The committee took up the case in May of 1770 just as *Theodora* was making its way into public view.

By the time Du Bois came to publish *Theodora*, the Irish House of Lords had accepted her half brother's right to his father's titles in Ireland, but the question of his right to the earldom of Anglesey was still to be decided by the British House of Lords. *Theodora* thus must have seemed like Du Bois' last chance to affect the outcome of the great question of her life. The form of publication "for the author" concedes, however, that Du Bois' star had fallen somewhat since the publication of her *Poems* three years earlier. There is no starry list of subscribers to flaunt this time. It would appear her more distinguished supporters had deserted her just as the case ground toward its conclusion. In the event, in April of 1771 the British House of Lords rejected her half brother's claim (*Minutes of the Proceedings . . . Earl of Anglesey* 64), in a judgement that was widely read as a statement that the marriage certificate of 1741 produced by his mother was likely a forgery, and let the earldom of Anglesey go extinct. This left Arthur Annesley, absurdly, legitimate in Ireland and a bastard in Britain. Du Bois may have felt some satisfaction at seeing someone she regarded as a cuckoo in the nest humiliated in such a public manner, but the ruling does not seem to have held her half brother back – in 1793 he was made Earl Mountnorris – and it had a devastating sting for Du Bois herself. The committee did not even address the validity or non-validity of her own parents' marriage. Since the only issue of that marriage was female – Du Bois and her sisters – it did not warrant the committee's attention. Her legitimacy was, evidently, of no consequence to the law.

That *The Monthly Review* chose to hold Du Bois up as "not a very correct writer" (43: 66) when the case to which she had devoted her life was nearing its final judgement suggests a desire to shut down, publicly, a campaign that all but Du Bois must by then have recognised was hopeless.[6] There is the implication that in this context her perseverance with her quest had come to be seen as unseemly and unladylike. In the grovelling dedication to the Duchess of Hertfordshire which prefaces *Theodora,* Du Bois indirectly acknowledges that she had acquired a reputation as "troublesome and importunate" (3) by giving thanks to her patron for not viewing her, as others had done, in those terms. Du Bois was still not, however, ready to give up the fight. As various claimants renewed their attacks on Arthur Annesley's right to the Irish titles in the wake of the British judgement yet another trial ensued, this time in the Irish House of Lords. During the proceedings her half brother's legal representative referred to Du Bois as the "prime engineer" of the cases against his client (*Minutes of the Proceedings . . . Viscount Valentia* 167), and multiple witnesses disclosed under questioning that it was she who convinced them to step forward. It was all to no avail, however; Arthur's claim to the Irish titles was upheld yet again.

Let down by the law, Du Bois in her later works allows her female characters to give vent to their righteous anger. Her work of etiquette in letter-writing, *The Lady's Polite Secretary* (1771), features a model letter in which a girl protests at her father's highhanded treatment of her.[7] And in *The Magnet* (a short musical piece of 1771) Du Bois even gives a version of her poor, beleaguered mother a moment of power, brandishing a hatpin at her female rival and driving her off. Neither Du Bois nor her mother was to get such satisfaction in life – their many efforts to seek redress or even recognition had ultimately come to nothing. Du Bois' claim that she published *Theodora* from "necessity" was not merely a cover for the continuation of her quixotic campaign. She had six children to support, and upon her mother's death, her family's only regular form of income, her mother's pension, evaporated. A measure of her financial difficulties in this period can be judged from the fact that the "Decayed Musician's Fund" in London held two concert benefits, nominally for her husband but advertised in "Lady Dorothea's" name, in February 1769 and again in February 1770.[8] Whatever her motive in becoming an author, by this time she and her family were living by her pen. Alongside the *Lady's Polite Secretary*, published in 1771, she continued to contribute to periodicals such as *The Lady's Magazine* and *The Gentleman's*

Magazine and to collaborate in a number of "musical entertainments" and other small-scale projects through the early 1770s.

Du Bois' death notice appeared in the Leinster newspaper *The Freeman's Journal* on 27 January 1774. It read simply, "In Grafton Street, of an apoplectic fit, Lady Dorothea Du Bois" (3). She would surely have been pleased that the honorific was included without qualification. Over time, however, the assessments of her life and career became more dismissive. Mary Hays' short biography of Du Bois, published as part of her *Female Biography: Or, Memoirs of Illustrious and Celebrated Woman* in 1803, is more devastating in its own way than the disdainful assessment of the *Monthly Review*, referring to Du Bois as "the wife of a musician" who "passed her life in indigence, and in the ineffectual claims for the recovery of her birthright" (66). In the centuries since, she has often been written off as a deluded woman who could not accept her place and insisted, pathetically, that the world indulge her fantasy. Yet there is much more to Du Bois than this distorted caricature, as even the short discussion of *Theodora* that follows, demonstrates.

Theodora, a Novel

Theodora was published in London in 1770 in two volumes. The title, an anagram of "Dorothea," coyly advertises its claim to have a foundation in fact. With its depiction of well-known scandalous events in the form of thinly veiled fiction, *Theodora* can be thought of as a throwback to the *roman à clef* mode of the early eighteenth century popularised by writers such as Delarivier Manley and Eliza Haywood. The novel may also be grouped among a clutch of novels that appeared in the late 1760s and early 1770s exposing the bad behaviour of high society, such as *The Lovers; or The Memoirs of Sarah B* (1769) and *Harriet: or the Innocent Adulteress* (1771). Du Bois' work, however, has rather more claim to literary value than these contemporary texts, and, in its presentation of its young heroine's struggles to define herself, it may be compared to Charlotte Lennox's *The Life of Harriot Stuart, Written by Herself* (1750), rumoured to have been based on the author's early life. Indeed, the allusions generously sprinkled throughout *Theodora* to John Milton, Samuel Richardson, Cervantes, Epictetus, and more speak to the author's desire to establish the intellectual credentials of her writing. This extends to Du Bois' repeated warnings, in typical reactionary style for the era, against the brain-rotting effects of novels, in an apparent attempt to distance her work from the perception of women's popular writing as frivolous and morally corrupting. In some ways, Du Bois' representation of the injustice of women's position in society anticipates the works of later politically minded female writers of the Romantic era such as Mary Wollstonecraft, Mary Hays, and, in her representation of real personal suffering, Charlotte Smith. However, although Du Bois' depiction of the myriad abuses Theodora and her mother endure amounts to a clear indictment of her society, the radical implications of this critique generally go unarticulated, since the author's intent was to recover her place within the hierarchy rather than to challenge its value system outright.

Theodora can also be understood as part of the mid-eighteenth-century vogue for all things sensibility. In *A History of the Irish Novel* (2011) Derek Hand deems it one of the "more interesting sentimental novels" of the period, though he notes that sensibility is often used in the text primarily to sort those capable of refined sentiment from those who are not (54). On the numerous occasions in which the child Theodora is required to rehearse her mother's sad tale for others, the truly genteel react with appropriate demonstrations of pathetic feeling. These performances represent the deployment of pathos as an elite code that only those who are worthy (one of those who responds correctly is in fact named "Mrs. Worthy") can deploy, one that Theodora is still conversant in despite her apparent fall in status. Yet while Hand is right in recognising the classist and, indeed, sectarian overtones of Du Bois' invocations of sensibility,[9] it is also true that while the lower classes are incapable of performing the signs of sensibility themselves, they recognise in Theodora's refined politeness the marker of her rank. In fact, in the absence of official recognition of her position, Theodora's noble status is repeatedly defended by various members of the servant class, including a cook, a laundress, various maids, and a steward. At the moment in which Theodora is most endangered by the viciousness of her father's supporters – that madcap trip to see him on his deathbed – it is the people of the nearby town who rise up in her support and secure her release in a display of loyalty that reads as quasi-feudal in its connotations. These plebeian background figures function like a Greek chorus, affirming the rightful order of things even when those higher up the ladder, whose silence is ensured by bribery or fear, allow the disruptive effects of the earl's lust and greed to continue unchecked.

The sentimental inheritance of Du Bois' novel is further in evidence in her initial representation of her parents' courtship and marriage. The young "Angelica," as Du Bois renames her mother, at only fourteen or fifteen years old, is whisked away unbeknownst to her father by "Varilius," the representation of Richard Annesley, who forces her to marry him. This scenario would have immediately recalled for the contemporary reader the plots of Richardson's popular mid-century novels, with Varilius behaving more like a Lovelace than a Mr B. to put it in Richardsonian terms. However, given *Theodora*'s implicit claim to be founded on real events, the valence of Du Bois' text is rather different from works that portray purely fictional misconduct of this sort. What Du Bois describes is a clear-cut case of "heiress abduction" or ravishment – in her portrayal of her parents' marriage. She thereby implies that her father committed a serious crime against her mother for which the perpetrator, under Irish law, could face execution.[10] And, while the opening of *Theodora* has echoes of Richardson's works, particularly *Clarissa* (1748), Du Bois' narrative departs considerably from the conventions of sentimental fiction in how it unfolds from there. There is no long, teasing exploration of the psychological eddies and flows of consent – the courtship of Angelica and Varilius is dispensed with in a handful of pages. When Angelica objects to Varilius' plans, he swears a "horrid oath" and declares that she must either receive him as her "husband" or as her "bed-fellow, without that title." "Remember," he warns Angelica, "you are now in my power" (6). She has, in reality, no choice at all; she must comply or face ruin. The bulk of the narrative is then devoted to the unhappy marriage that is the consequence of this event, territory which sentimental fiction usually leaves unexplored. Angelica and Varilius' marriage, which would in a romance signal the securing of the rake within the regularising bonds of matrimony, in *Theodora* represents anything but the restoration of order. In the years they remain together Varilius becomes only more boorish, and Angelica must tirelessly devote herself to placating his volatile temper until, at last, he can be mollified no longer.

Although Du Bois in *Theodora* may traffic in the currency of sensibility, with characters frequently overcome by melting sighs, floods of tears, and fainting fits, the workings of the narrative insistently expose the conventional novelistic economy of sentiment to be bankrupt in this world. The demure feminine delicacy of Theodora's mother does not secure her from public vilification and only serves to make her easier prey for her enemies' many schemes. The pathos which Theodora's tales of her mother's pitiable plight inspires in the bosoms of the powerful may appear to enlist them in her cause, but these efforts repeatedly fail in the face of the ingenious malice of her father's cronies. As the years pass, the receptive audience for Theodora's stories of the countess's saintly suffering drifts away, and the chances of a miraculous reversal of fortune dwindle. Later in the novel Theodora's own suitors display the signs of sentimental sincerity again and again, but these exquisite performances do not translate into any kind of durable support or fidelity. Eventually, Theodora comes to realise that only wealth confers true power, and that since she is "moneyless," she must also be "friendless" (94). The harsh lesson she must learn and relearn is that she can rely on no one else but herself.

Theodora may sigh and cry with the liberality of a sentimental heroine, but she is in truth made of much sterner stuff, and as the work shifts its attention from the long-suffering countess to Theodora herself, it begins to take on the contours of a *bildungs roman*. It is Theodora's "masculine" spirit (149) that allows her to survive the relentless twists of fate she is subject to and, in time, to become her mother's protector. Indeed, the passionate Theodora's facility with firearms becomes the surprising hallmark of her character in the second volume. Armed with her pistols, she defends her honour and her interests in a manner that is more reminiscent of a young male hero than the blushing maiden of sentimental fiction. Though she shows as much gumption as her male counterparts, however, as a woman, Theodora can never claim for herself the agency of the autonomous masculine subject that the hero of a novel such as Henry Fielding's *Tom Jones* (1749) might aspire to. Indeed, if in the early stages of the second volume it seems as though the adversity Theodora faces might satisfy some larger narrative purpose – strengthening her faith in God, teaching her the realities of a world in which women are subject to men's whims – in the end the travails she and her mother endure come to appear almost Jobian in their relentlessness.

With its refusal to gloss over the grimmer aspects of reality for women without a male protector in this period, there is a sense in *Theodora* that Du Bois was increasingly unwilling to confine herself to the kinds of polite appeals to the public's sympathy that had characterised her previous efforts to publicise her struggles. The inescapable reality presented in the text is that even legal recourse exists only for those with the money to buy it for themselves, as solicitors, magistrates, and pillars of the community submit, sometimes brazenly, sometimes reluctantly, to the will of the powerful. The unflattering portrayal of various recognisable figures can also be read as a settling of scores on Du Bois' part with those who have wronged or disappointed her throughout her life, including her father's last wife, various aunts, governesses, and even her own sisters, who at times act as foils for the perpetually put-upon Theodora. It is the men in the text, however, that receive the brunt of Du Bois' uncompromising attitude. The inadequacy of Theodora's male admirers is a consistent feature of the work. Even Theodora's final suitor, "Mellidore," a musician who is quite clearly an evocation of Du Bois' actual husband Peter Du Bois, does nothing to shield her from harm. Indeed, he can be classed among the manipulative and untrustworthy men that litter the text, securing her unwilling hand in marriage in a thoroughly ungentlemanly manoeuvre when she is still grieving the betrayal of a previous false lover. Their courtship and marriage end the work on a surprisingly sour note. Acknowledging that her novel has concluded without a satisfying resolution, Du Bois promises further volumes (which never came) and defers to the example of Laurence Sterne's *Tristram Shandy* (1759) in defence of a work that resists the expectations of its readers. Whether or not Du Bois ever truly meant to pick up the story again, the disappointing outcome of the various court cases perhaps at last exhausted her drive to tell her story.

Du Bois' writings have, until now, received little sustained critical attention, and what there has been has focused largely on her poetry (see Carpenter; Schirmer) or her letter-writing manual, *The Lady's Polite Secretary*. I hope this edition of *Theodora* will be the start of a critical re-evaluation of her novel and of her work in general, as such a reappraisal is long overdue. The neglect and even scorn that has characterised her reception since the late eighteenth century is the legacy of the contemporary discomfort Du Bois' ever-so-public efforts to regain her position provoked among the establishment. Over time, the perception that her publications were the product of a failed and distasteful publicity campaign shaded into a complacent assumption that they must therefore be of little intrinsic value. A quick glance at her output proves this is simply not the case; Du Bois was an accomplished author who wrote in an engaging and direct style about matters that still have relevance today. For critics of her time who deemed themselves the gatekeepers of their culture, Du Bois' motivation in publishing *Theodora* may have had the effect of discrediting her novel as respectable literature from the start. Thanks to the work of recent decades to recover the voices of those marginalised by the mainstream in eighteenth-century society, however, we can now set aside this cultural baggage and appreciate the exciting and transgressive nature of Du Bois' writings on their own terms.

A BRIEF CHRONOLOGY OF DOROTHEA DU BOIS AND THE CONTESTED INHERITANCE OF 6TH EARL OF ANGLESEY'S ESTATE

c.1693	Richard Annesley is born.
1715	Richard Annesley marries Ann Prust of Monkleigh, Devonshire, and abandons her soon after.
1727	Richard Annesley marries Ann Simpson, mother of Dorothea Du Bois, in Dublin.
1727	Arthur Annesley, 4th Baron Altham, dies. His brother Richard Annesley inherits the title and styles himself 5th Lord Altham.
1728	Twelve-year-old James Annesley, the abandoned son of Arthur Annesley, is kidnapped and sold into indentured servitude in America, allegedly on the orders of his uncle, Richard Annesley.
1728	Birth of Dorothea Du Bois, née Annesley.
1737	Arthur Annesley, 5th Earl of Anglesey, uncle to Richard Annesley, dies. Richard Annesley becomes the 6th Earl of Anglesey.
1740–41	Richard Annesley separates from Ann Simpson.
1741	Richard Annesley and Juliana Donovan begin cohabiting.
Sept. 1741	According to Juliana Donovan, Richard Annesley marries her in Camolin Park, Wexford, in a secret ceremony.
May 1742	Richard Annesley marries Anne Salkeld in London.
Nov. 1743	James Annesley brings a suit against his uncle Richard Annesley in order to have his rights and privileges restored. His suit is successful, but the verdict is not enforced.
1744	Arthur Annesley is born to Richard Annesley and Juliana Donovan.
1752	Dorothea Annesley marries Peter Du Bois, a French musician.
Oct. 1752	Richard Annesley marries Juliana Donovan in front of witnesses in Camolin Park, Wexford.
1760	James Annesley dies penniless in London.
Nov. 1760	Dorothea Du Bois attempts to visit her dying father and becomes involved in an altercation with her half brother, Arthur, and her father's attendants.
Feb. 1761	Richard Annesley dies. Arthur Annesley (Richard Annesley's son by Juliana Donovan), John Annesley, and Constantine Phipps (both cousins of Richard Annesley's) all assert their claims to his British and Irish titles.

D. DU BOIS AND EARL OF ANGLESEY'S ESTATE

1764	Du Bois publishes *Poems on Several Occasions, by a Lady of Quality* by subscription.
Aug. 1765	Ann Simpson dies in Dublin.
Sept. 1765	The Irish Attorney General, Philip Tisdall, rules that Arthur Annesley is the rightful heir to Richard Annesley's Irish titles. When he comes of age Arthur Annesley takes up his seat in the Irish House of Lords as Viscount Valentia.
1766	Du Bois publishes *The Case of Ann Countess of Anglesey*.
Feb. 1767	King George III's attorney general takes up Du Bois' petition to delay the hearing regarding Arthur Annesley's assumption of the Rights and Privileges of the earldom of Anglesey until the decision of the ecclesiastical court regarding the legitimacy of the marriage between Ann Simpson and Richard Annesley.
1770	Du Bois publishes *Theodora* in London.
1770–1	The Committee for Rights and Privileges in the British House of Lords reviews and rejects Arthur Annesley's right to the earldom of Anglesey. The earldom of Anglesey is declared extinct.
1772	John Annesley (cousin of the late earl) and Richard Annesley (son of the late earl and Ann Salkeld) sue Arthur Annesley for the late Richard Annesley's Irish titles.
Jan. 1774	Dorothea Du Bois dies "of an apoplexy" in Dublin.
1776	Juliana Donovan dies.
1793	Arthur Annesley is made 1st Earl Mountnorris.
1816	Arthur Annesley dies.

A NOTE ON THE TEXT

This text is produced from the British Library copy of the first and only edition of Dorothea Du Bois' *Theodora* (1770) printed for the author by C. Kiernan of Holborn, London, and sold by the bookseller William Nicol. The work was produced in the duodecimo format favoured for popular novels and listed at the price of six shillings, which was reasonable for a two-volume novel in the period. The text of the novel is imperfect and includes many errata such as repeated words (beyond catch words) and obvious typos – these have been silently corrected. Apart from the replacement of the long "s," all variant spellings and grammatical idiosyncrasies have been preserved.

The copy held by the British Library entered the library's collection via a bequest from William Musgrave (1735–1800), a private and reserved man whose keen interest in contemporary biographies drove him to assemble a pioneering collection of British examples of the genre from the latter half of the eighteenth century.[11] The copy is signed by Musgrave on the back of the title page and is particularly notable for his inscription and the annotations he included throughout the text. Musgrave's inscription to *Theodora* is written on the blank page after the title page and continues on the following page beneath the epistolary dedication. The note, which may be taken to reflect the consensus view of the case in the wake of the various judgements in the courts regarding the Anglesey case of 1765–72, reads in full:

> This Book contains the Story of the Authoress and of her Mother, who asserted herself to be the Wife of Rich.d Annesley E. of Anglesea though disowned by him.
>
> It is said that Rich.d L.d Altham & E. of Anglesea the hero of this Memoire never scrupled to marry any woman whom he pursued but who wo.d not surrender on less honourable terms & when these deluded Ladies attempted to claim the benefit of their Marriages he alwaies set up some of his prior m.[arriages?] in Barr of it – His first Wife was Ann daut. of Jn.o Prust of Monkton[12] in Devonshire who died in 1740.
>
> Consequently as Miss Simpson's Marriage was contracted and the Authoress of this work was born subsequent to the marriage of L.d

Anglesea with Miss Prust and during her life – both the Marriage & the issue of it be illegitimate.

Musgrave's characterisation of Simpson as one of Annesley's "deluded" ladies reflects the generally dismissive attitude that greeted Du Bois' public efforts to have the legality of her parents' marriage recognised after the initial judgement of 1765 by the Irish Attorney General that her half brother Arthur Annesley was the rightful heir to her father's estate. Musgrave's annotations identify various characters with their real-life counterparts and, in some instances, the legal cases in which they were involved related to the inheritance of the 6th Earl of Anglesey's estate. Some of Musgrave's identifications are obvious, but others seem to be gleaned either from his own personal research or popular knowledge of the various lawsuits. I have therefore included Musgrave's notes for the interest of the reader in such instances.

Alongside the text of *Theodora* I have also included two appendices which shed further light on Du Bois' campaign to have her title and rank recognised by the public and the law, which intersect with some of the events depicted in the novel. Appendix A consists of the poem entitled "A True Tale" included among Du Bois' *Poems on Several Occasions* published by subscription in 1764. This publication, which came the year before the decision of the Irish Attorney General to recognise Arthur Annesley's claim to the late Earl of Anglesey's Irish titles in 1765, seems to have marked the high point in Du Bois' efforts. The list of subscribers demonstrates that much of the Irish establishment was at least somewhat sympathetic to her claim. "A True Tale" recounts her parents' courtship and separation along with an episode, also related in *Theodora* volume II, in which "Dorinda" (as she is styled in the poem) attempts to visit her father on his deathbed and is assaulted by her half brother and his attendants. The introduction to Appendix B, *The Case of Ann Countess of Anglesey* of 1766, relates the same tale, though in much more stark terms than either "A True Tale" or *Theodora*. The allegations made in that work against a person who was, by then, sitting in the Irish House of Lords as Viscount Valentia are serious and disturbing, though nothing seems to have come of them. The rest of *The Case* outlines the legal arguments in favour of the legitimacy of the marriage between Richard Annesley and Ann Simpson, Du Bois' parents, and displays a familiarity with both the language of the law and its application that is impressive for a woman with little formal education.

Notes

1 While a review in *The Critical Review* of June 1770 is less critical than that of *The Monthly Review*, it similarly asserts that since *Theodora* retells the well-known events of Anglesey inheritance, Du Bois cannot truly be taken for a "mere novellist" (29: 474).
2 For more on Ascendancy Ireland in this period, see Ian McBride; Toby Barnard, *A New Anatomy of Ireland*; and James Kelly, *That Damn'd Thing Called Honour*. It is also useful to read Du Bois' representation of the Ascendancy class alongside the chapter in

A NOTE ON THE TEXT

volume two of Arthur Young's *A Tour in Ireland* (1780) on "Manners and Customs," in which he claims that such bad behaviour was by then a relic of the past.

3 James Annesley, nephew of Richard Earl of Anglesey, resurfaced in London in the 1740s. He then attempted various legal measures to have his inheritance restored (see, for example, *The Trial in Ejectment Between Campbell Craig, Lessee of James Annesley Esq. . .*) but was unsuccessful. For more on the tumultuous life of the unfortunate James Annesley, see Roger Ekirch.

4 In a sign that *The Case* enjoyed some success as part of Du Bois' campaign, the introduction of the work was printed as a footnote in the "Earl of Anglesey" entry in the 1766 edition of *The Complete English Peerage* and was published in full in serialised form in the Irish newspaper *The Freeman's Journal* to coincide with the final legal challenge to Arthur Annesley's right to the late earl's titles in May of 1772.

5 The record of the petition reads: "Copy of petition of Lady Dorothea Du Bois, eldest lawful daughter of Richard Annesley, late Earl of Anglesey, by Ann Simpson, late Countess of Anglesey, his wife, in behalf of herself and her two sisters, Lady Caroline White and Lady Elizabeth Hyde, against the issue of a writ of summons to the claimant of the title of Earl of Anglesey and Baron of Newport Pagnell, pending a suit touching the validity of their mother's marriage, and also praying a reference of their petition to the Attorney General at the same time as that of the claimant. The petition enters into particulars as to the marriage, &c. Referred to the Attorney General, Feb. 19" (*Calendar of Home Office Papers of the Reign of George III* 161).

6 The shift in the representation of her husband, Peter Du Bois – from "A True Tale" (Appendix A) in which he appears in the guise of a loving spouse who supports "Dorinda" in her struggles, albeit somewhat ineffectually, to *Theodora* in which "Mellidore" is largely irrelevant to the protagonist's emotional life – can be read, in part, as an oblique commentary on the ways in which Du Bois' singlemindedness with regard to the matter of her legitimacy had isolated her from those around her.

7 For a deeper analysis of *The Lady's Polite Secretary*, see Lyda Fens-de Zeeuw, Linda C. Mitchell, and Taylor Walle.

8 See Simon McVeigh.

9 While Du Bois treats the lower classes in general with the haughty attitude typical of those of her class, she reserves a special contempt for "papists," implying a particular tendency towards coarseness and mendacity.

10 For more on the significance of the crime of heiress abduction in Irish culture in the period, see Kelly, "The Abduction of Women of Fortune in Eighteenth-Century Ireland"; Barnard, *The Abduction of a Limerick Heiress*; Maria Luddy and Mary O'Dowd 181–216; Thomas P. Power.

11 For more on Musgrave, see Anthony Griffiths.

12 Properly, John Prust of Monkleigh, Devonshire.

THEODORA, A NOVEL

In two volumes.

Vol. I.

By the Right Honourable
Lady Dorothea Du Bois

Adversity's a school, – wherein we're taught,
To form and regulate, the growing thought.
The AUTHOR.

LONDON:

Printed for the AUTHOR, by C. KIERNAN, in Fullwood's-Rents, HOLBORN.

M.DCC.LXX.

TO

THE RIGHT HONOURABLE

The Countess of Hertford[1]

MADAM,

AT the same time that I have the honour to commit my THEODORA to your Ladyship's protection (perfectly satisfied that *your Name* is sufficient to recommend it to all who have the happiness to be acquainted with the many virtues of which its PATRONESS is possessed) I cannot resign the favourable opportunity it gives me, thus publickly to testify some part of that gratitude with which my soul is actuated towards my noble BENEFACTRESS.

YOUR Ladyship, contrary to the generality of the world, seems to delight in deeds of CHARITY; nor does the repeated solicitations of the distressed appear to offend you. Your heart is ever found susceptible of pity, and the hand of liberality still open to the relief of the wretched; without bestowing on them the harsh epithets of *troublesome* or *importunate*. But this is not so much to be wondered at, when we consider your Ladyship is, in every respect, a PATTERN worthy the imitation of all your SEX.

IN an age like this, to be a fond wife, tender mother, kind friend, and generous benefactress, are characters so rare, that we cannot but look with veneration and esteem on one possessed of such uncommon, yet shining qualifications; in all which your Ladyship is too conspicuously known to excel, to doubt that you are the admiration of them who know you; but of none more particularly than,

MADAM,
   Your Ladyship's,
      Most gratefully obliged,
         obedient, and devoted,
           Servant,
               DOROTHEA DU BOIS

ADVERTISEMENT

AS I am impelled, *by more pressing motives* than a vain desire of applause, to subject these volumes to public inspection, I trust I shall meet with that indulgence, to which my sex, and unhappy circumstances may *unambitiously intitle me*.

I have had the warmest wish to render this work *useful*, as well as *entertaining*; anxious to place VIRTUE in her loveliest dress, and mark VICE with her every feature of deformity; for notwithstanding my distresses, and the partiality I might naturally be allowed to have for my THEODORA, I would much rather consign it to oblivion, than be the means (as some female authors have been) of flushing the *cheek of innocence*, or contaminating *the mind of youth*.

The AUTHOR.

THEODORA,

A

NOVEL

VARILIUS,[2] the father of *Theodora*, was the younger brother of an ancient and illustrious family, in Great Britain. He was endowed with a sprightly wit, and fertile genius; together with a taste for polite literature. Nevertheless, he was extremely credulous, and easily led astray by evil counsel; which, he never failed to find in the low company, with whom he chose to associate; from the desire he had of exhibiting, and maintaining, his own superiority, which, he cou'd not do with those on a level with him, in point of understanding, or rank. In fine, he was haughty with his inferiors, and cringing to a degree of meanness, with his equals, or superiors. And from this unaccountable compound of contradictions, sprang the many evils, that accrued to his family.

He lived in a state, but a few degrees removed from absolute want, until his fortieth year, when he was introduced by Baron *Altamont*,[3] his elder brother, to *Probus*;[4] between whom and the baron a strict friendship had long subsisted. *Probus* was an eminent merchant of the city of *Dublin*, whose character for justice and integrity was so universally known, that it became proverbial. He had been a widower for some years, and had by his deceased wife three children, two sons, and a daughter. He determined, on account of his children, not to enter into a second engagement; and had refused several very advantageous offers on that head.

His daughter, who was called *Angelica*,[5] had not as yet attained her fourteenth year; but the charms of her person, and mind, so far exceeded her years, that she was the admiration of all who knew her.

Varilius saw, and admired her; but was particularly enamoured of that part of her qualifications, which, by men of his cast, is accounted the most attractive, viz. a large portion; which, it was supposed, her father would give her, as she was an only daughter, and his favourite. This was a circumstance, that invigorated the pursuits of *Varilius*. He left nothing unessayed which he thought could render him agreeable. Flattery, protestations, sighs, and tears, were made use of, but without effect. She paid more attention to the innocent amusements, with which the minds of those at her years are generally occupied, than to his most passionate sollicitations; to which the disparity of their years did not a little contribute.

Finding that all his attempts had hitherto proved unsuccessful, he determined to possess by fraud, or force, what he could not attain by the gentler method of persuasion. In order to accomplish his laudable design, he concerted a scheme with her governante, (whom he had by a few presents, and large promises, attached, to his interest) which he soon after found means to put in execution.

Having one evening received intelligence from his worthy agent the governante, that *Probus* was gone out upon business, and *Angelica* alone, he immediately waited upon the object of his wishes, and intreated the favour of her company to the play. She excused herself, by saying, that she never went abroad but with her father, or entrusted by him to the care of some lady of his acquaintance. But, he still persisting to sollicit her with all the rhetorick he was master of, and her governante joining in the request, she at length consented.

A coach was called, into which *Varilius*, Angelica, and her governante went; but instead of going to the play-house, the coachman drove directly to a place called the castle, the usual residence of the vice-roys.

When the coach stop'd, *Angelica* perceiveing where she was, refused to alight, and strugled until her strength was entirely exhausted; when unable longer to resist, *Varilius*, having stopp'd her mouth with a handkerchief, carried her in his arms to his apartment, where a parson, and two or three of *Varilius*'s acquaintances, waited his arrival. Terror had deprived *Angelica* of the use of her senses; and she remained a long time in this state, notwithstanding their united efforts to revive her.

On her recovery, *Varilius* desired the clergyman to perform the ceremony. – What ceremony? exclaimed *Angelica*. What is your intention? *Varilius*, I desire that you will permit me to return to my father – If you can obtain his consent, I shall be satisfied, without which, I will never give my hand to any man. No, said he swearing an horrid oath, perhaps my little dear, you had rather live with me, without the sanction of the holy shackles. You have your choice, either to receive me as your husband, or as your bed-fellow, without that title. Remember, that you are now in my power.

Angelica, struck silent with amazement, answered only with her tears; whose dumb eloquence would have softened any heart, but that of the obdurate *Varilius*. The parson, surprized at the sorrow that was visible on the countenance of *Angelica*, turning to *Varilius*, said, Sir you informed me that the lady had given her consent. She has, replied *Varilius*; but the artful little gipsey, like most of her sex, would be forced to that which she most ardently desires. While he spoke with the clergyman, his worthy friend the governante did not fail to exert herself with *Angelica*.

My dear, said the perfidious woman, do not expose yourself by an obstinate resistance. *Varilius* is of a noble family, and loves you to distraction. With respect to your father, his affection for you is so great, that you cannot doubt of obtaining a speedy reconciliation; besides – Ah! cried *Angelica*, what proportion is there between his age and mine? That consideration, replied her governante, is at present but of little moment. You should reflect that you are now in his power; and it is better to – Ah! replied *Angelica*, interrupting her, I understand you. Good heavens! to what streights am I reduced! I must comply, tho, I foresee my ruin. Is it possible that I can ever love a man, who has thus basely deceived me!

The governante, perceiving she had gained her point, called out to *Varilius*, and informed him, that *Angelica* was ready to give him her hand. Provided, said *Angelica*, with a voice interrupted by sighs, that he will permit me to return home, immediately after we are married. Yes, my dearest, cried *Varilius* in a transport of joy, I shall not only acquiesce to this, but to every other request you shall make, when I can call you mine. Then eagerly seizing her hand he led her to the clergyman, who united them in those bands, which nought but death can loose. The ceremony being ended, he conveyed her to her father's door, which he saw her enter with her governante, and then departed. *Angelica* flew to her apartment, threw herself upon her bed, and gave way to the most immoderate grief. Her governante made use of all the arguments she could think of to comfort her; as she feared her despair might prompt her to discover the affair to her father.

She at length prevailed upon *Angelica* to go to bed. *Probus* returning soon after, enquired for his daughter. Her governante informed him, that she had got a violent head-ach, and was gone to bed. Alarmed at this, he would have gone directly to her apartment; but the governante prevented him, by saying, that she had left her asleep; and as rest was the most salutary remedy for such disorders, it would be improper to disturb her.

The next morning *Angelica* ventured down to breakfast; but so little was she skilled in the art of dissimulation, that her father could not fail of observing her confusion, and consequently of discovering the cause of it, had not some people just come in upon business engaged his attention.

In the interim Lord *Altamont* arrived, who, drawing his chair close to *Angelica*, says in a whisper, My pretty little sister-in-law, I come as an humble suitor in behalf of my brother, who hopes you will not treat him with as much severity tonight, as you did last night. My Lord, replied *Angelica*, I do not understand you. Come, my dear, said he, do not endeavour to conceal what I am well acquainted with. Well, my lord, said she, with some emotion, you are acquainted with more than I could wish: I knew myself, and immediately left the room. His lordship soon after took his leave, and went to inform his brother of the ill success of his embassy.

Varilius was frantic with rage, on hearing the manner in which *Angelica* had received his message. He went immediately to her governante and declared, that if she did not procure him admittance to his wife in private, he would demand her of her father. The governante, whose interest it was to conceal the affair as long as possible, desired him to come the next night about nine to the back door of *Probus*'s house, where she would wait his arrival. *Varilius* did not fail to attend at the place appointed, and was conducted by the governante to *Angelica*'s chamber, where she concealed him in a cloaths press.

Angelica at her usual hour retired to her chamber. Having performed her accustomed devotions, she undressed, and was just going into bed, when *Varilius* stealing softly from his covert, caught her in his arms. She would have cried out, but was prevented, more thro' fear of being heard by her father, than by the intreaties of *Varilius*, who on his knees beg'd her to be silent.

He took care to be gone in the morning, before any of the family were up. He continued his visits to *Probus* as usual, and at night was concealed in the house. This legal intrigue, however, was soon discovered. *Angelica*'s younger brother met *Varilius* one morning, coming out of his sister's apartment. *Varilius* dreading the consequence of this rencounter, as soon as he arrived at his lodgings, sent a billet to *Angelica*, desiring her to meet him at a place, which he appointed, on business of the last importance to them both. *Angelica*, alarmed at this unexpected summons, hastened to the place appointed; but the perturbations of her mind was so great, that she tottered at every step.

When *Varilius* had informed her of his suspicions, she burst into tears. Alas! said she, *Varilius*, you have made me compleatly miserable! How shall I behold the face of my injured father? Would to heaven that I had never been born! What a requital for the tender care and love of a parent, who even prevented my wishes?

Varilius, clasping her in his arms, in the most affectionate manner, endeavoured to calm her grief. My dear *Angelica*, said he, you will never have occasion from my future conduct to repent of what is done. Our marriage could not be concealed long! and I look upon the discovery that your brother made this morning as a fortunate circumstance, by which the affair may be brought (thro' the mediation of my brother) to a speedy conclusion. But until this can be done, it will be advisable for you to remain with me. The apprehension of her father's resentment, made her readily acquiesce to his proposal. She went home with him to his lodgings; where we shall leave them, in that suspence and anxiety, which persons, in their circumstances, must naturally feel; and view the effect her elopement had on *Probus*.

Angelica's brother (as *Varilius* had suspected) as soon as his father was risen, informed him, that he met *Varilius* coming out of his sister's room; that, soon after she received a note, which having read, she immediately dressed and went out. *Probus* made his son repeat his intelligence several times before he could credit it; and then, as if still unconvinced, rang the bell for the governante. As she entered the room, he cried out in a frantic manner, Where is my daughter? And gripping her fast by the shoulder, before she had time to answer, he repeated, Speak quickly, tell me, where is my child, my dear *Angelica?* The guilty wretch quite disconcerted, at being thus suddenly interrogated on a matter, which she was not prepared to answer, turned pale, and strove to speak, but could not utter one word. Perceiving her consternation, he quitted his hold, and striking his breast, cried out, I read my fate in thy silence; my child – the darling of my heart – is ruined – lost for ever – that villain *Varilius* – oh! – and fainted. As he had never before been attacked in that manner; his servants feared he had breathed his last; but alas! he never till then experienced what parents feel, when frustrated in their most sanguine expectations, of a favourite child.

Many advantageous, offers had been made him upon her account, far beyond his highest ambition, which he would not have refused, but that he thought her too young, and inexperienced to enter into the cares attendant on the marriage state. She might have had a coronet,[6] were he a man that could be allured by sound rather than substance. But that not being the case, *Probus* notwithstanding the noble birth of *Varilius*, looked upon his daughter as inevitably lost, on falling into the hands of a man, the greatness of whose family could by no means compensate with him, for the indifferent character he bore.

Nature, however, still predominant over every other consideration, made him anxious to know the truth: and being assured by the wretch, to whom he had injudiciously entrusted the care of his child, that they had been married some little time before; he endeavoured to compose himself, and said, she had made an unfortunate choice, and therefore would consign her, to her fate.

As for you, said he to the governante, who have blasted my hopes by your treachery, I leave the punishment of your crimes to the Almighty, who will avenge me; but I desire, that you will immediately leave my house, with whatever belongs to you. He ordered his servants to deny admittance to *Varilius*, or his wife, should they attempt to see him; but desired that her cloaths might be sent her, of which, through his indulgence, she had a great quantity.

Matters were now in a melancholy situation, with the new married couple. Love was a diet too slender for *Varilius* to subsist on. Her pocket money indeed served them for a few days; but that being exhausted, he was put to his wits end. He dispatched a letter to his brother (who had gone to his country seat, a day or two before *Angelica* had left her father) informing him of the necessity there was for his presence. The Baron, on the receipt of this epistle, set out for town, with the utmost expedition; and having concerted with *Varilius* the part he was to act in the affair, went directly to the house of *Probus* with a numerous retinue of attendants.

When he sent in his name, *Probus* hesitated for some moments, whether or no he should see him; but some deference being due to his rank, his lordship was admitted. The Baron, intimated his business in the most delicate manner; but notwithstanding this precaution, when he mentioned the name of *Varilius*, *Probus* could not conceal his resentment, which the Baron endeavoured to calm in the mildest terms. It is true, said he, addressing himself to *Probus*, there is a great disproportion between the age of my brother, and that of *Angelica*; and I must even confess, that there is no great prospect of happiness for her; but tho' there were, should you continue inflexible, you would prevent it. It is probable that the good humour, and good sense of *Angelica*, may chain his roving fancy, and prove the happy means of his reformation. And as I never had, or am likely to have; a child by my present lady, *Varilius* will in all probability succeed to my estate and honours; besides, he has a chance of succeeding to the earldom of *Volpont*. Therefore, I think it adviseable, in order to prevent future disputes, that you should have them lawfully married, which without your consent cannot be done, as Angelica is not of age.[7] I am certain, continued the Baron, that a little money will be very acceptable to *Varilius*, and as an encouragement to your giving a fortune with your daughter, I shall join with my brother in levying a fine, and suffering a recovery, to settle 1000*l*. per ann. upon my sister-in-law, in reversion of the *Volpont* estate.

The Baron perceiving that *Probus* listened to him with attention, enforced his argument with all the rhetorick he was master of, and again repeated the offer of settlement. *Probus* at length broke silence, and said, I must confess, my lord, that there is reason in what you have advanced; and although my daughter has disobliged me in a manner hardly to be forgiven, yet, paternal fondness pleads strongly in her behalf. I will, continued he after a moment's pause, see her married again; and will give her what I can spare, without hurting my sons. I am infinitely obliged to your lordship for your kind offer; but, as there is a possibility of your surviving your lady, you may have issue by another wife; in which case, the settlement you have proposed would be of no effect. There are many things which may intervene, to prevent *Varilius* from ever attaining to the title and estate of *Volpont*. But, as all things are in the hand of providence, should it so happen, (a circumstance which I neither expect nor wish for) my daughter will be entitled by her thirds,[8] to much more than the dower your lordship has stipulated.

The Baron asked whether it would be agreeable to him, that they should return home. No, said *Probus*, I will first see them married; and named the time, and place, for the celebration of their nuptials. Matters being thus adjusted, the Baron took his leave; and flew with the happy tidings to *Varilius* and *Angelica*, who waited the result of his negociation with the utmost impatience.

Angelica quite overcome at the unmerited condescension of her father, testified her gratitude by her tears. *Varilius* went immediately, and in the usual forms took out a licence.[9]

The happy day of reconciliation being arrived, *Varilius* and *Angelica* hastened to the place appointed. Words are too weak to describe *Angelica*'s distress on beholding her father. Pale and trembling, she threw herself on her knees before him, her eyes streaming with tears. She attempted to speak, but could not pronounce more than, Oh! my father! and fainted. This awakened all the parent in the breast of *Probus*. He clasped her in his arms, and bedewed her face with his tears. Imagination cannot form a more affecting scene, than that, which now presented itself to the eyes of *Varilius*. He felt for the first time, those tender sensations, to which he was naturally a stranger, and wept.

Probus having revived the drooping spirits of his daughter by his caresses, and assurances of his protection and favour, saw them married, and the ceremony being ended, took them home with him. He gave *Varilius* a fortune of some thousands with her, and equipp'd him in all respects suitable to his birth and family. Scarce a day passed, in which they did not receive some new favour from *Probus*.

They were not a twelvemonth married when Baron *Altamont* died,[10] which gave *Angelica* greater concern than the acquisition of a title had charms to attone, he having ever treated her with the highest respect and tenderness. They one night having been for some hours in bed, heard a loud rapping at the door and presently one of *Altamont*'s servants, to make good the old adage, Salute the rising sun, came rushing into their room without any ceremony and throwing the curtains aside, cried out with an unpardonable gust of joy, My lord and lady *Altamont*, I wish you both health, and long life to enjoy that title, that your brother about an hour ago has left you.

Angelica through surprise and sorrow, gave a shriek at this unexpected salute, when *Varilius* without any seeming concern, other than for her preservation, said with great composure, What, my dear, do you grieve at your husband's good fortune? Good heaven! replied she, do you call it good fortune to lose a kind brother? Do not think that I can be so elated with the sound of a title, as not to feel the most sincere concern at his sudden death.

Varilius drest himself immediately, and set off for his late brother's seat, which was a short way from town; and as soon as he had taken possession, drove back again in his deceased brother's chariot. The next day he went there again, accompanied by *Probus*, to give orders about the funeral; and to examine what cash there was to defray the expences. But not finding near so much as would answer the demand, he intimated his design of having him privately interr'd. To this *Probus* objected; and said, that tho' the Baron died many hundred pounds in his debt, he should be buried in a manner suitable to his rank, and that he himself would make up the deficiency, which he generously did.

Tho' *Varilius* had, by his brother's death, arrived to the honour of a peerage; yet he had not a foot of estate with the title, and some years had elapsed, before he could even get a pension. During which time he was entirely dependent on the bounty of *Probus*; who supported him, in all respects, equal to his new acquired dignity.

After the death of his brother, *Varilius*, whom we must now call Baron *Altamont*, left the house of his father-in-law, and went to reside at the late Baron's seat. Here he gave into an extravagant way of living, quite unmindful of his dependent state, and at whose expence he was to gratify his inclinations. He kept a pack of hounds, several carriages, race horses, &c. As his cellars were always well stored by his provident father-in-law, his boon companions were certain when they honoured him with their company, not to leave his house without being totally deprived of the little senses providence had allotted them.

At this period *Theodora* was born,[11] who even before her birth, was destined to suffer by the unaccountable jealousy of her father. The late earl of *Blanvil* was under many obligations to *Probus*, and a strict intimacy had subsisted between them for many years. As the Baroness had from her early infancy, been a great favourite with this nobleman, bespoke himself sponsor to the child she carried, and declared that he would make a settlement of five hundred pounds per ann. on it, from the day of its birth, whether male or female.

This was a pleasing circumstance to *Probus* and seemed not a little to flatter the ambition of the Baron; who received the congratulations of his friends on the occasion, with a satisfaction, that shewed in what light he viewed so great an obligation. About a week before the birth of *Theodora*, he invited, with several others, Earl *Blanvil* to dinner. When Lady *Altamont* appeared, after the usual compliments, the Earl with his wonted good humour, turning her round, cried out with jocular surprise, What! is this the little girl, I but the other day dandled on my knee? Fye Lord *Altamont*, how could you thus spoil the finest shape in the world? It is not long since my hands could more than span her waist.

This was but a trifling freedom from a person, who had always treated her as his child; but such was the effect that it had on *Altamont*, that he could scarce behave with common decency the remainder of the evening. This was unobserved by all but Lady *Altamont*, who perceived the storm gathering, which she was certain would be discharged on her; for she had before experienced the oddity of his temper, but carefully concealed it from her father.

When the company were gone, the Baron behaved in the most extravagant manner. He said that the Earl had a design on his wife, and only intended to serve the child, on account of the mother. However, added he, I will take care that he shall have no opportunity; nor shall he be sponsor to a child of mine, tho' he should settle his whole estate on it. In this he kept his word, for he made a proxy stand for his cousin Lord *Avremont*,[12] in the room of Earl *Blanvil*.

Tho' Lady Altamont was married very young, yet her knowledge, so far surpassed her years, that she was a perfect pattern of prudence and œconomy. She nursed her children; nay so indefatigable was she, in the duties of her household, that she has been known to spin very fine yarn, give suck to her child, and read at the same time. A thing which very few ladies would, or indeed could have done.

One day that she was thus employed, and Lord *Altamont* from home, a woman with a fine girl, of about a year and a half old, came to the house, and enquired for Lady *Altamont*. The Baroness was sitting in the parlour, when the woman entered (for she was never denied by her own orders to the poor,) but was so intent on what she was about, that she did not perceive her. The woman was amazed at the manner in which the Baroness was occupied; and could scarce believe her eyes. She gazed in silence for sometime, but at length awakened the attention of the Baroness, by crying out, Good God, is it possible! On which the Baroness started, and had like to have let fall her little daughter *Theodora*. The woman fell on her knees, and intreated her pardon for having disturbed her in so abrupt a manner; but declared, that she could not avoid crying out; for she had never before seen so fine a sight. Lady *Altamont* smiling, bid her rise, and assured her, that her pretty compliment more than compensated the surprize her exclamation had occasioned.

But what is your business, good woman? said the Baroness. I came, replied she, to make you my complaint, and to implore your Ladyship's pardon and protection, which I was encouraged to do, from hearing what a sweet good Lady you were. Good woman, said the Baroness, if you knew how little I am pleased with flattery, you would not be so very prodigal of it; if I can serve you, I will. Whose fine child is that? The poor woman blushed, and held down her head. I suppose it is your own, continued the Baroness; pray, are you married? No, my Lady replied the woman, Who is the father of the child? Said the Baroness, with some emotion. 'Tis – 'tis – replied she, faultering, 'tis – Speak, said the Baroness, if any of my servants is the father, I may, perhaps, by my authority cause him to marry you. Oh! said the woman, falling on her knees, and bursting into tears, forgive me, my good Lady; I am a poor wretched woman, that was ruined by your Lord before he was married to you. I have nursed his child such as you see; living ever since upon my father and mother, who are unable to support us longer. I cannot consent to put my baby into the poor-house. – Yet, I know not what else to do. I have got people to write several petitions to my Lord; but I cannot obtain the smallest relief from him. Indeed my good Lady, I am almost starved, and my little one is quite naked; for I borrowed the cloaths it has on, to make it fit to appear before you. The Baroness, touched with pity more than resentment, made the woman rise, and giving *Theodora* into her arms, took her child in her own, and kissing it said, she believed it was her husband's, for it resembled him. She held the child up close by *Theodora*, and asked the woman if she did not think it like her little darling.

She then ordered the woman some refreshment, and kept her child until she had finished her repast. She desired her to come the week following, and she would have some things ready for her child; and giving her a piece of money, with an assurance of a fresh supply, dismissed her unexpected visitant with a heart overcharged with gratitude.

The woman came at the time appointed, the Baroness dressed the child out very fine, and gave the mother several changes for it, together with the promised supply. This innocent intrigue was carried on for more than three months; the woman still taking care to come when the Baron was out. But unfortunately for her, the Baron's fondness for *Theodora*, who was then sick, made him return one day sooner than was expected: He met her coming out of the house, and immediately recollecting her, D——n you, said he, you w——e, what business have you and your bastard in my house? My lady, answered She, has been good to me, though you never have; and it is a pity that an angel such as she, should fall into the hands of a brute.

His lordship immediately set his dogs at her, and turned into the house. The huntsman, very luckily, for the poor wretch, happened to be in the court-yard, who, as soon as he saw the Baron gone, called off the dogs. They had already rent her cloaths, while her fondness for her infant made her hold it over her head, to preserve it as long as she could from their fury. The Baron's first salute to his Lady, for an act, which a grateful man would have admired, was, D——n you – you mean spirited little b——h, how dare you to notice or harbour my bastard? By G-d, if I ever find out, or hear, that you do the like again, I will make you repent it. Notwithstanding his menaces, she still found means to relieve the child, who did not long enjoy the fruits of her charity; for the poor babe died soon after this notable adventure.

The Baroness was now to feel the severest stroke of fate, she as yet had ever experienced. Her father, tho' still in the prime of life, was seized with a complication of disorders. She hoping that the country air might be of service, invited him to her house, where he lingered for some little time, with his darling child. But the melancholy prospect he then saw of her unhappiness, hastened his death.

Probus finding the time of his dissolution draw nigh, made his will; in which he bequeathed to the Baroness a small annuity, and a few hundreds to her husband to buy mourning. The residue of his fortune, he divided between his two sons. *Probus* had in his life-time, done so much for the Baron and his Lady, that he could not leave them any great matter at his death, without doing a manifest injury to his sons; which the goodness of his heart would not permit him to think of. He waited the stroke of death, with the greatest fortitude and resignation, comforting and encouraging the Baroness, who was scarcely ever from his bed-side during his illness. When the dreadful moment arrived, after having implored the protection of heaven for his children, and embracing the Baroness, who kneeled by him, dissolved in tears, he rendered up his soul into the hands of his Creator, without a groan. Thus died a man, who, in the strictest sense of the words, was universally beloved and esteemed.

I shall not attempt to describe the sorrow of the Baroness on this occasion: Let it suffice to say, that she felt all the grief, that a dutiful child must naturally experience on the loss of a parent such as *Probus*.

The Baron, who, at the time of his marriage, judged, and not without reason, that Probus might live as long as himself, paid off those of his creditors who were the most importunate, with the money he had received from him at that period. As he knew that *Probus* would not see his daughter want, he made no reserve; so that on the death of his benefactor, he found the source of plenty stopt. He was now convinced that he must endeavour to do something for himself. He immediately sold his legacy, being unable to wait the stated time, and prevailed on his wife to sell her annuity. The money arising from those sales, enabled him to go over to England to sollicit a pension, in which he opportunely succeeded.

Flush'd with this success, he returned to Ireland, to his wife and little family; for the Baroness had by this time, two or three daughters; and as if fortune meant to heap her favours on him, a near relation of the Baroness gave her a very pretty seat within a few miles of Dublin, to which a considerable portion of land was annexed. To this place the Baron, with his family removed, and lived there for some time very agreeably. But he soon grew tired of this delightful spot. He loved company, and preferred the noisy revels of the town to the calm delights of a rural life. He sold his concerns in this part, and removed to town. Here he retrenched part of his expences. He gave away his hounds, and sold all his horses, except those that were wanted for his carriage and servants.

Now the Baroness proved herself a perfect mistress of œconomy; for, notwithstanding the narrowness of her husband's circumstances, she kept an elegant table, at which she entertained the first nobility of the kingdom.

The Baron being one night at a tavern, with a noble Lord of his acquaintance, whom we shall call *Pulvillo*, came home about three in the morning greatly intoxicated. Being with some difficulty put in bed, he soon fell into a sound sleep. He had not been in bed an hour, when the Baroness hearing a loud rapping at the door, immediately got up to enquire who it was. She was scarcely half drest, when she heard *Pulvillo*'s voice very loud in the hall; fearing lest he should awake the Baron, she slipp'd on her wrapper, and opening her chamber door softly, leaned over the stairs, and bid his lordship good morrow: May I, without offence, my Lord, said the Baroness, enquire the important business that brings you here at this unseasonable hour? I am sorry, replied *Pulvillo*, for having disturbed your Ladyship, but my business is with your husband, whom I must speak with immediately. He is now incapable of transacting business, said the Baroness; it is not an hour since he went to bed. By heaven, cried *Pulvillo*, I must, and will see him.

The Baroness judging from this, that *Pulvillo* and her husband had quarrelled, went down in order to prevent his Lordship from disturbing him. Come, my Lord, said she, let us go into the parlour, where we may talk over this affair coolly. But how great was her surprise to behold, on her entrance into the parlour, a pair of pistols lying on table.[13] What, said she, my Lord, is the meaning of this? I imagined that you and my husband were on better terms. Is it possible that you, who professed so much friendship for him, could come to attack him in a hostile manner, in his own house? I disclaim, cried *Pulvillo* in a rage, all friendship with such a man. – He has affronted me, and is a *villain*, nor will I leave the house, until he has given me satisfaction.

So, said the Baroness, you are come with an intent to kill Lord *Altamont* in his own house. It is well for you, perhaps, that he does not hear you. But do not imagine that I will stand tamely by, and hear you bellow such epithets on my husband. Come *Pulvillo*, you are a very little man; the Baron is a good mark. I will not suffer him to engage on such unequal terms. You and I are better matched – There is *villain* back to you – and snatching up one of the pistols, she cocked it, and stood in a posture of defence. *Pulvillo* now made a very laughable appearance. – He stood aghast, his mouth wide open, not daring to speak, or move, while the sweat poured in large drops from his face to the floor.

The Baron, who had been awakened by the noise stole softly to the stairs, and listened until she came to this part of her address, when he cried out – That's right, *Angelica*, but I will save you the trouble. If he wants pistoling, he shall have enough of it immediately. So saying he ran into his room, drest himself in a few minutes, came down with a pair of pistols; and addressing, himself to his noble antagonist said, Come my Lord, to the Phoenix park, this is no place to decide matters of this nature.[14] Then embracing the Baroness with tenderness said, My dear *Angelica* God bless you, and went out directly with *Pulvillo*.

Here the Baroness's courage forsook her. She ordered the footman to call a chair, intending to inform the officer on duty at the Castle, of the affair, that he might order a guard to put these furious combatants under an arrest. She was just stepping into the chair – when the two Lords returned laughing immoderately. *Angelica* my dear, said the Baron, was there ever anything so comical, 'tis but a jest; *Pulvillo* only meant to make me a present of these silver-mounted pistols. Look my dear, are they not extremely handsome? Good heavens, cried the Baroness – a jest, – surely my eyes and ears deceive me – do I dream, or am I awake? and then humorously rubbed her eyes. Nothing but a jest, indeed; said *Pulvillo*, and now I hope you will give me a breakfast for the present I have made your husband. But tell me, Lady *Altamont*, continued he, would you indeed have fired? Undoubtedly, replied she, if you had attempted to take the other pistol. Then by Heavens! said he, I am glad I did not; – why *Altamont*, thy wife is a very *devil* of a little woman. This caused a second hearty laugh; Much was said by *Pulvillo* in praise of the Baroness's heroism, fidelity, and unprecedented affection to her husband. They breakfasted very friendly together, and thus terminated this memorable exploit.

This adventure however was the forerunner of eight or ten days diversion. For a lady calling on the Baroness to take an airing with her in her coach, and the Baron being in an extreme good humour, proposed to make one of the party, asking *Pulvillo* to accompany them. Which he readily consenting to, together they went to the Phoenix park, at the entrance of which, they met two or three coaches full of their acquaintance. Having stopt each other, one of them said there had been a wager lost, and they were going to have it paid in a dinner. The gentleman who lost the wager, immediately invited the Baron and his company to partake of the entertainment; and all agreeing, they went to the place of rendezvous, where they passed a very agreeable day, and had an extreme good dinner.

As this little excursion seemed to give general satisfaction, the Baron proposed that every gentleman present, should give an entertainment in their turn, at different outlets, while the weather would permit. This social scheme of the Baron's being put to the vote, passed nemine contradicente.[15]

They then balloted to determine, who should he second, third, &c. when the lot fell upon the most extravagant man in the company to give the next treat. He was an abandoned rake, who valued neither his cash, or health, in the gratification of his passions. His life was one continued round of debauchery and excess. The ladies now began to look at one another, as if they promised themselves great matters from the turn of this gentleman's mind. They gathered in a knot, and began to lay schemes in order to escape the drunken scene, they naturally concluded the next day would present them with.

The Baroness gave it as her opinion, that they should not go by any means; but others of them being willing to partake, at least of the solid part of the entertainment, prevailed on her to change her mind. They agreed to meet at the place appointed, before the gentlemen, in order to examine the bill of fare. Having formed the plot, they separated, and enjoyed in their way home, the pleasure of their next meeting by anticipation.

The next day, the ladies, having repaired to the place appointed, enquired if Mr. B— had been there, or, if he had sent any orders for the entertainment of a large company, that was to be there that day. Being answered in the affirmative, they called for the bill of fare, which having read, they were greatly surprised at the scanty dinner he had bespoke. They all agreed that the Baroness was the best caterer among them; and insisted that she should alter it to her own taste, as she was then great with child.

They beg'd that she would make it as extravagant, as the gentleman himself was reputed to be, as they knew he could afford it, and were certain that, if he had some of his favourite females, instead of them, he would not grudge the expence. The Baroness gave general satisfaction in her alterations, having ordered double the quantity of dishes, and those of the most costly sort.

They took a turn in the garden 'till the gentleman should arrive, and hug'd themselves on the success of their scheme, and the mirth it would occasion. On the arrival of the gentlemen, the master of the feast enquired when dinner would be ready, and being answered, Very soon, went in search of the ladies, whom having found, he informed them that dinner waited. They immediately obeyed the summons; but on entering the room, their frugal providore started back, thinking the entertainment of some other company was served up by mistake.

The ladies at this bursted into a loud laugh, and asked him if he did not know his own dinner? He replied, There was certainly some mistake, for that was not the dinner he had ordered. This reply caused a louder laugh among the ladies, who by this time had taken their places at table. And one of them, undertaking to speak for the rest, told him, that there was indeed a very great mistake, but it was in himself, who intended to treat them with the neglect he always did virtuous women; But we are determined, said she, to submit once in our lives, to be treated by you, as profusely as your more favourite part of the sex, and have therefore alter'd the bill of fare to our present humour.

This explanatory note threw the gentleman into the greatest confusion, and caused the rest of the men to join with the ladies, in the laugh against him. The first course was followed by a second, still more elegant, and that by a dessert. The ladies, who were resolved to rule for that day, asked what liquors there were in the house. The waiter informed them, that there was claret, rum punch, &c. These, said the ladies, might do at home, but not in a tavern; and ordered the above-mentioned for their servants. One said she liked arrack punch, another chose burgundy, a third champagne; in short, every one made a different choice of the dearest liquors. Their disconcerted providore could scarce speak during the whole time; and soon after dinner, saying he was engaged to be in town at such an hour, on business of great importance, beg'd their excuse, discharged the bill, and withdrew. He was chagrin'd no doubt, on being obliged to misapply so much money; which might have made him happy that night, in the company of those more suitable to his taste.

When he was gone, the gentlemen laughed immoderately at the malicious trick the women had put upon their companion. They concluded this evening very agreeably at their joint expence. The next day's entertainment fell upon one of the gentlemen, who was as remarkable for his avarice, as the other was for his prodigality. The ladies were now certain of having a wretched treat, when, as if to prove that they could not form a right judgment in any thing, the man, who was in fact a miser, in every other respect, said that he would keep his day at a little village near town, remarkable for its delightful situation, and the exorbitant prices that are charged for every thing that is sold there, on account of the numbers that crowd thither from the capital, during the summer season.

The females on hearing this, looked on each other with surprise; when he politely addressing them said, he would take the liberty to lay the groundwork of the feast; but must intreat them to take the trouble of making what additions they should think proper to it, as they were better acquainted with these matters, than he could possibly be.

This compliment was returned by the fair ones in a suitable manner, the agreeable party broke up, and each retired to their respective habitations. The next day they assembled at the place appointed, and in consequence of their promise over-night, desired to see Mr. M— 's bill of fare, which consisted of every delicacy the season afforded. They would have gladly struck off many of the articles, but the master of the house acquainted them, that they might make what additions they pleased, but he had strict orders not to retrench any part of it.

Never were people more amazed than our ladies. The gentlemen arrived soon after, and brought with them the person, who the day before had quitted them with such visible dissatisfaction. When he saw how much he was surpassed, he was much confused, but quite reconciled to the expence he had been at. A band of music play'd all the time they were at dinner. After they had drank a chearful glass, their providore presented each of them with a box ticket for the play; to which at the proper time they repaired. There he treated them with fruit and sweetmeats in abundance.

The play being over, they thought of parting, but he told them, that he had not done with them yet, for he had bespoke a supper at a tavern nigh the play-house, where they might, if they pleased, have a dance, as he had provided music for that purpose. Unable to withstand his solicitations, they went to the tavern, where they were met by a number of ladies and gentlemen, who were invited at the play by Mr. M— Nothing could be more elegant, or profuse, than this entertainment; from which they did not retire until five in the morning.

This obliged them to postpone this day's amusement to the day following. Having recovered their fatigue, each in their turn kept his day. None of their treats, however, equall'd that of Mr. M—.

The night before the Baron's treat, his lady, like a frugal wife, as if she meant to save her husband an expence, that his purse could not so well bear, as the rest of the company; was taken in labour, and delivered, two months before her time, of her fifth daughter. This put an entire stop to their innocent revels.

About a year after this, the Baroness being again pregnant, *Theodora* and her two sisters *Carina* and *Eliza*, were taken ill of the small-pox. As the Baroness had never had this disorder, she dreaded it extremely; nevertheless, she attended her children closely, so much superior was her maternal fondness, to the care of her own preservation. The children were now past danger, when it pleased God, that she was safely delivered of her sixth daughter, who was born with the disorder full upon her. The Baroness was never after so much afraid of the small-pox, concluding that she might have had it in her mother's womb, as the infant had, of which she was delivered.

A droll mistake happened at the birth of this child. The Primate having a great esteem for the Baroness, (whom, as he was an intimate acquaintance of her father he knew from her infancy,) bespoke himself sponsor to her first son. Being anxious for her safety at this critical juncture, he sent twice or thrice in the day, to enquire her health. The morning she was delivered, the Primate's servant came almost at the instant, and seeing the family in great joy at the happy event, concluded that a son and heir had been brought to the world. He posted back, without waiting to be undeceived, to inform his Lord of the news, who knew nothing of the matter. The Baron was then at the Castle. Thither the Primate went directly, when perceiving the Baron, went up to him, and in the midst of the crowd wished him joy, of a son and heir.

The Baron, who was always anxious on this head, and very much dissatisfied at having so many daughters, started, and asked his grace what he meant. The primate answered, that his servant had just brought him an account of Lady *Altamont*'s being delivered of a son. The Baron's joy was very visible during this recital. He received the congratulations of the viceroy, and all the nobility present, on the occasion. He immediately returned home almost beside himself with joy, and believing what he heard to be a fact, went, without asking a question, to his wife's bed-chamber. He wished her joy in a most affectionate manner, then asked with impatience to see his boy. What boy? said the Baroness. What boy? repeated he; why the child you have been delivered of – Indeed, my dear, said she, you have been misinformed, it is a girl.

Never was disappointment greater than his; he left the room without saying a word, shut himself up in his closet, and would not be seen for several days. His behaviour on this occasion, gave the Baroness great uneasiness. She could not conceive how the mistake had happened. But the Primate's wife, who soon after visited her, acquainted her with the whole affair; and perceiving the disagreeable effect that it had on the Baron, informed her husband of it. The Primate came the next day, and insisted on seeing the Baron; whom he endeavoured to convince of the absurdity of his chagrin. The Primate at length prevailed on him to visit his Lady, and be reconciled to her.

At this time the Baron had heard, that Earl *Volpont* was in a declining state of health. As there was none between him and the earldom of *Volpont* but this nobleman, he thought it prudent to reside near the place, where his expectations lay. For which purpose, he disposed of his house in town, and removed to that part of the country; where he had taken a very elegant house, delightfully situated in the midst of a polite neighbourhood. Here the Baroness tasted all the sweets of the conjugal state, without the bitters. But the true cause of her happiness in this retirement, was the restraint the Baron was obliged to lay on his temper, in order to ingratiate himself with the inhabitants of a place, wherein he was likely to have so great a property.

The time glided sweetly by, peace and tranquility reigned throughout the whole family. Every morning and evening, the servants were called together, and the Baron or his Lady read prayers. They were hospitable without prodigality, and frugal without meanness. The Baron had long been subject to the gout, but here he had some very severe fits of it. He was extremely impatient in sickness, the effects of which the Baroness often experienced; being frequently obliged to sit up for whole weeks together with him. Should she chance to doze, through the fatigue of rubbing his feet the whole night on her knees, he would never fail to awake her with a loud roar, crying out, *Angelica* my dear – rub – rub. This was her constant employment during his illness, from which she would never exempt herself, until her strength and spirits were entirely exhausted.

It was after one of these fatiguing nights (when great of her seventh child) that unable longer to support the want of rest, she sunk down at his feet, as he thought, to take a nap. He endeavoured to wake her after his usual manner; but finding he could not, rang the bell for the servants, who, when they came up, found their Lady in a swoon. They recovered her with great difficulty; and apprehensive of the fatal consequences that might ensue from such fatigue to a person in her condition, sent for a country midwife to attend her in case of necessity, until a better could be had.

The poor woman, who had never seen a stair-case before, when the servants desired her to come up, looked quite scared, and cried out, Is it I go up that high place to break my neck? not I, by my troth; I know better things than that, though so great a fool as you may think me. Finding that they could not persuade her by any means to venture up, two of the footmen were obliged to lay hold on her. The old midwife, frighted out of her senses, began to kick and scream in a horrible manner. However they at length got her up. She then seemed greatly concerned to know how she should get down again; but the men, assuring her that they would take her down as safe as they had brought her up, prevailed on her to commit herself to the care of the women-servants.

Having led her through the different rooms, in each of which she expressed her wonder at the fine things she saw, they brought her at length to that where their Lady was in bed. This room was hung with tapestry, the figures as large as life. At the first view of them, she started back, crying, By my own sweet soul, agrah,[16] I won't go into a place where there is so many fine gentry. This caused the Baroness to laugh, notwithstanding the pain she was in. The servants eased her scruples with regard to the fine gentry, by putting her hand upon the tapestry. This again excited her wonder. Faith, honey, says she, I did not think they wer dead people, I thought they were all alive. The woman hearing the Baroness laugh when near to the bed-side, says, *O honey*, my dear joy, if you can laugh so heartily, 'tis sign you are not after being so bad as they said you were: I don't believe but you sent for me to make your own game of me, honey. The Baroness now laughed so immoderately, that the poor midwife was quite enraged; she squatted herself down on her haunches by the fire-side, pulled out of her bosom a tobacco-pipe of about two inches in length, black as jet, which she set fire to, and began to smoke so furiously, that she almost suffocated the poor Baroness. It had, however, a good effect upon her; for from that moment she grew better. The poor woman was handsomely rewarded for the mirth she had created, and went away well satisfied.

Two or three days after this risible affair, as *Theodora* and her sisters were playing in the court-yard, they saw a man ride furiously down the avenue. He alighted at the house, scarce able to speak, and enquired for the Baron, who was then occupied in drawing off a cask of brandy in the cellar. One of the servants told the man, that he would call his Lord; but the stranger, who seemed, by his looks, to have something of importance to communicate, went into the house with the servant. Curiosity, which is ever predominant in the fair sex, urged *Theodora* to follow the stranger, who, having arrived at the cellar, cried out, before the footman could deliver his message, My Lord, I wish your Lordship joy, you are now Earl of *Volpont*; and shewed him an affidavit he had made of having seen the late Earl dead at his seat in *Wales*.[17]

At this sudden news, the Baron, whom we must now call Earl *Volpont*, fell back against the cask, and let the liquor run unheeded. Being a little recovered, he caught *Theodora* in his arms, kissed her several times, and told her she was now a Lady. The sound, we may imagine, was by no means disagreeable to a girl of *Theodora*'s age. He carried her in this manner to her mother's bed-chamber, where, setting her down, he flew to his Lady, clasped her in his arms, and bursting into tears, said, I wish you joy, my dearest, you are now Countess of *Volpont*. The little one you carry has waited to good purpose.

The Countess, to the surprize of all present, seemed in no-wise elated, but fetched a deep sigh. The Earl tenderly asked her, if she was not well? Thank Heaven, my dear, replied the Countess, I am pretty well; but I fear you will not so well support the weight of grandeur and opulence, as you have hitherto done a mediocrity. Wealth is the touch-stone of human inclinations, and proves us to be what we are. It seemed as if she spoke prophetically; but of this the reader shall judge hereafter.

The scene was now entirely changed with respect to *Theodora* and her sisters. Their young ears were not a little pleased with the adulations of those around them. The Countess was the only person who seemed the least to partake of the frenzy that infected the family.

The Earl, in order to lose no time, solicited, that evening, the interest of the neighbouring gentlemen; and saw himself, the next morning, at the head of a formidable party of his friends and other followers. They marched directly for *Volpont Grove* (for so the mansion-house on that part of the *Volpont* estate was called). On their approach, the doors were shut against them by the servants, who were in the interest of *Bouviere*, the next in succession to the earldom of *Volpont*.[18] It was thought by many that the late Earl would have left all that was in his own power to *Bouviere*, and, amongst the rest, the mansion-house, and the estate annexed to it.

However, the Earl and his friends soon found means to enter the house, notwithstanding the opposition made from within; and having left a sufficient number of men to keep possession, returned to congratulate the Countess on her new acquired dignity, and their late success.

The Countess was conducted to *Volpont Grove* by the Earl, attended by those who had been with him in his late expedition. Having settled his affairs in this part of the country, he set out for *England* to take possession of his estates there, and his seat in the *British* parliament.

The Countess had so conciliated the affections of all her acquaintance, by her polite and affable behaviour, that *Volpont Grove*, in a short time, became the receptacle of all the neighbouring gentry for many miles round. The abundance of an open house, which she then very judiciously kept, did not a little contribute to ingratiate the Earl with his tenants; the good effects of which she soon after experienced. She received an express from Dublin, which informed her, that *Bouviere* had hired a number of desperadoes, to come down and take possession of *Volpont Grove*. The Countess having communicated this intelligence to her visitants, saw, in about three hours, above six hundred men raised for her defence; consisting of her own tenants and the country militia.

Her first care was to settle a fixed rule of entertainment for her numerous guests, and dependents. A fat ox and a certain number of sheep, were killed every day, besides lamb, veal, fowls, &c. A proportionate quantity of strong beer was allowed, with wines and spirituous liquors. She appointed officers to receive her commands every morning, when she reviewed her little army. She caused port-holes to be made in different parts of the house and out-offices, and took every other necessary precaution for the defence of her garrison. A patrole was appointed to go round the house every night, and cry the hour. Scouts were placed at the different avenues leading to the house, to give the alarm in case of the enemy's approach. If any man was absent from his post, or officer neglective of his duty, he was tried the next morning by a court-martial, and some laughable sentence passed on him. If any gentleman or lady was absent at meal-times, he or she, so offending, was transported to one of the islands that stood in the midst of a lake before the house. There they remained for as many hours as it was thought the nature of their crimes deserved. In short, the Countess regulated every thing with an ease and propriety that astonished all who knew her. A deputy-governor was appointed to act in her stead, should she chance to lie-in during the siege. It fell out as they expected; her Ladyship being delivered of her seventh daughter.

Great rejoicings were made on the safe delivery of the Countess. A letter was dispatched to the Earl, informing him of the increase of his family; but he was so chagrined on finding that it was a daughter, that he would not answer the letter. The friends of the Countess had maintained their post for about a month; when *Bouviere*, dropping his design of forcing possession at *Volpont Grove*, set out for *England*, and soon after compromised the matter with the Earl. The Earl having settled his affairs, returned to *Ireland*, and brought with him a *French* governess for his daughters, with several handsome presents for the Countess. Among the rest a beautiful lap-dog, called *Fidelle*, sent her by Lady *Avremont*, the Earl's sister, who was then newly married. As this Lady has not been mentioned before, it is necessary to remark, that old Baron *Altamont*, the Earl's father, had four children, two sons and two daughters. The sons the reader is already acquainted with; the daughters were called *Dorinda* and *Althea*. They married two brothers of the name of *Vere*.[19] *Dorinda*, the elder sister, married the younger, and *Althea* the elder brother. It was, however, a very unhappy union with respect to these gentlemen, who were both ruined by it.

As the two ladies were excessive proud, a dispute arose between them about precedence. *Dorinda* insisted, that although she was the younger brother's wife, nevertheless, she had a right to take place of her sister, as eldest daughter of a peer. *Althea* maintained, that, being wife to the brother, who had the estate, she had a right to take place of the younger brother's wife.

This ridiculous contest was carried to such a length, that they instituted a suit to decide this important point. Both parties were obstinate, and continued to harrass each other so long, that the richest of the brothers found himself at last in the

Fleet,[20] where he remained 'till his death. In this time of distress, Lord *Avremont* being related to the family, took the haughty *Althea* into his house. She in return for this kindness, sowed discord between that Lord and his daughters; at length, causing him to turn them out of doors.

The ascendant she had over Lord *Avremont*, furnished abundant matter for the tea-tables of her acquaintance, who attributed it to a cause, that reflected no great honour on the character of Mrs. *Vere*. She did not, however, stop here; she resolved to throw off all restraint, and pass for a widow, it being very probable, that her husband would never hear this report, or if he did, would not, from his dislike of her, contradict it.

She had the address to bring to her lure, a very honest man, an apothecary; who married her. This affair was carried on so secretly, that Lord *Avremont* knew nothing of it, until he heard that she had gone home to her husband, the apothecary. She lived some time with this husband, but her temper was so diabolical, that the poor man often cursed the hour they were linked together. He had heard to his unspeakable satisfaction, about the expiration of the second, or according to his estimation, the two and twentieth year of his bondage, that his beloved spouse, *Althea*, was the property of a gentleman, who at that time, resided in the *Fleet*.

The apothecary was immediately seized with a qualm of conscience on this welcome information; of the truth of which, he resolved to be convinced. He went to the prison, enquired for Mr. *Vere*, and was introduced to him. Compliments being past, the apothecary enquired of Mr. *Vere*, if he was not married to the honourable *Althea Altamont*? Yes, replied *Vere*, to my sorrow. I am likewise married to her, said the apothecary. I care not, returned *Vere*, if a hundred besides you could say the same, for she is an infamous woman. However, I am sorry, Sir, for your misfortune, in meeting with such a devil. Thus ended this extraordinary conference. The apothecary returned home in haste, and gave the *virtuous Althea* her dismiss, telling her at the same time, to provide another lodging for herself, as he had an invincible repugnance to the cohabiting with another man's wife. Mrs. *Vere*, being obliged to decamp, was necessitated to make every possible submission to Lord *Avremont*, in order to reinstate herself in his favour. This she accomplished; and her husband dying soon after, she continued to live with his Lordship as usual, until her brother became an earl.

The Countess, who was well acquainted with the shameful conduct of her husband's sister, never mentioned her uneasiness to him on that head, while he was unable to remedy the evil, but as soon as he became possessed of a good estate, she seized the first opportunity to speak to him on this subject, and begged that he would endeavour to prevail on Lord *Avremont* to marry his sister, in order to wipe off the blot she had brought on the family; which, if it continued, would be a great disadvantage to his daughters, when they grew up to women's estate.

This was the first request she made him, on his change of circumstances. Having obtained his promise to comply with her intreaty, she remained better satisfied; but finding that he did not mention any thing about it, in his first letter from *England*, she reiterated her request. She was informed by him in his next, that he had, agreeable to her desire, taken his sister from Lord *Avremont*; and that he was then negotiating a match between them; but the demands of Lord *Avremont* were so exorbitant, that he did not know how to comply with them, in justice to his children.

The Countess, in her answer, beseeched him, not to let slip the opportunity, while Lord *Avremont* was in the mind to marry her, let the fortune he asked be what it would; as nothing could compensate to his daughters, for the dishonour her living in that way would bring on them. The Countess now looked on the affair as already done; when, to her great mortification she received another letter, in which, the Earl inveighed against his sister in the bitterest terms; and declared, he would never see her more, or do any thing for her. She had insulted him to the highest degree, to sum up all, had made an elopement, and was gone again to her old keeper. – He then acquaints her, that he intends to set off in a day or two for *Ireland*.

The Countess was so afflicted with this unhappy news, that she wet the letter with her tears; and declared to a friend of hers, who was present when she read it, that she had never met with a more cruel disappointment. The Earl, according to his promise, arrived in a few days after the Countess had received his letter; but how great was her surprise to see him, and all his attendants, with wedding favours on. After he had embraced her and his children, taking his infant daughter in his arms, he cried out, *Angelica*, my life, I have news to tell you, that I am sure will please you. I have given my sister in marriage to Lord *Avremont*. They have sent you and all my little girls gloves and favours, not forgetting even this little hussey.

The Countess said she was amazed at the account he gave her, after the letter she had so lately received, and testifying an unfeigned satisfaction on the joyful occasion; she begged that he would inform her, by what means he had brought the affair to so happy a conclusion. I was, said he, pretty far on my road home, when, to my great surprise, I was received at the door of an inn I stopt at, in order to dine, by my sister, and Lord *Avremont*. She threw herself on her knees, and beseeched me to see her married before I left *England*. Knowing that I could not do any thing more pleasing to you, I suffered myself to be overcome by her intreaties. Lord *Avremont* and I soon settled matters. He had brought a licence with him,[21] and I saw them fast tied before I left the inn. I have given seven thousand pounds with her, and three hundred a year during her life.

The Countess thought this a large fortune, but as it was done at her own request, she had no room to find fault. The Earl then presented the French governess to her, who told the Countess, that Lady *Avremont* begged that her Ladyship would be pleased to accept from her that little lap dog; that its name being *Fidelle*, it was an emblem of her good wishes for her sister. The Countess received the little creature, saying, she was obliged to her sister for this mark of her attention and regard. – Nothing could demonstrate the goodness of the Countess's heart, more than the pains she took to accelerate this Lady's marriage, notwithstanding the diminution of her childrens fortune.

The parliament being to meet this winter, which was now pretty far advanced, the Earl, with his whole family, removed from *Volpont Grove*, to *Dublin*. Now the Countess was visited by all her old acquaintances. She was introduced to the Viceroy as Countess of *Volpont* by the Earl, who at the same time presented his favorite *Theodora*. Her little heart was elated with the praises every one bestowed on her.

Early the next spring the Earl and his family set out from *Dublin*, for *Volpont Grove*, with a numerous retinue. They were met on the road by the gentlemen of the country, and the Earl's principal tenants on horseback, for whom a grand entertainment was provided. The sons and daughters of the lower Tenants waited their arrival, about five miles from *Volpont Grove*; the men dressed in their shirts, white drawers, and stockings, with bunches of ribbands tied about their elbows; the girls in white gowns, their heads and breasts decorated with ribbands. They danced (the foremost couple bearing a garland of flowers) before their coaches to the house. The inhabitants illuminated their houses, lighted bonfires, and shewed every other demonstration of joy.

If to be universally beloved and esteemed, could make the Countess happy, she would now most certainly be so; but alas! the Earl began to give a full indulgence to his inclinations. This the Countess one day remarked to him, when he was in one of his best humours, and said, that he was quite changed from the man he was some time before. You are mistaken, replied the Earl, I have been always the same, but different circumstances gave me different appearances. I was then unwilling to shew myself, but I am no longer necessitated to wear the mask; I had always the inclination, but not the ability, and as they both now coincide, I shall for the future cast off all restraint. This the reader may imagine was no very pleasing prospect for the Countess.

She was now rendered extremely miserable by the unjust suspicions of her husband. Should a gentleman chance to look on her, it wakened his jealousy; or should her eyes happen to meet those of the person who viewed her, he was certain she was ogling him, and had some private intelligence with him. He would retire to bed at eight in the evening, and cause her to go with him, though the house was full of company, under the pretext of being taken ill suddenly. When in bed, he would often pinch and beat her, being certain that shame would prevent her from crying out. One time he followed her from room to room, with a cocked pistol in his hand, and frightened her almost to death. Another time in his own closet, after consulting with her on business of consequence, he took her on his knee, and drew his chair close to his bureau. She perceived him searching in his pocket for the key, which having found, he strove to unlock the bureau. The Countess, reading a malignity in his looks that terrified her, asked him, with some emotion, what he was about? I only want a razor, said he, holding her still closer. Not to cut my throat, I hope? cried the Countess. No, no, my dear, he replied, I would only scarify your face, which *Jago* (who was the family surgeon)[22] will soon heal. I shall not then be so unhappy as I am; for by G-d you are now so handsome, that every fellow who looks on you, is in love with you.

The Countess on hearing this, and perceiving he had laid hold on a razor, gave a sudden spring and disengaged herself. She fled as fast as she was able, until she reached her dressing room, where her woman and some others of her attendants were. As soon as she entered the room, she dropt down in a fit.

The Earl hearing a great bustle in the house, and reading consternation in the looks of all the family, was ashamed of the unaccountable attempt he had made, called for *Theodora*, who generally mediated on those occasions, and told her he had vexed her mamma. He desired her to go, and endeavour to reconcile her to him, and to promise faithfully on his part, that he would never disoblige her for the future. *Theodora* succeeded in her embassy. The innocent caresses of the pleasing little flatterer, pleaded so strongly with the Countess, that she could not resist her.

The parliament being to meet this winter, the Earl and his family removed to *Dublin*. Here the Countess, notwithstanding the incessant fatigue of paying and receiving visits, regulated her family with the utmost exactness. She kept her drawing room on Sunday, to prevent gaming in her house, though she was obliged to play sometimes, out of complaisance to those, who liked it better than she did. She would play for a trifle to amuse herself, but did not chuse to run the hazard of losing a sum, that might be appropriated to a better purpose, in relieving the wants of some distressed families. Her charities were frequent, but private.

She inspected every morning the bill of fare for the day; and accounted every Saturday with the steward for the expences of the week past, of which she herself kept a regular account, nor did she ever run in debt with her tradesmen. Her servants were regulated in such a manner, that tho' the house were crowded with company, there was never any hurry or bustle, every servant had his own department, and never interfered with that of another.

As the Earl dined very late during the sitting of parliament, the Countess thought it a great hardship for the servants who rose and breakfasted early, to wait so long. She observed that hunger often obliged them to snatch the meat from off the dishes as they carried them out, and return'd with their mouths and hands greased. To prevent this disagreeable circumstance, she order'd that the lower servants should dine every day between one and two o'clock.

I would not have been so minute in the description of the Countess's management, but that I look upon it to be an example worthy of imitation, and what very few of our nobility take the least notice of. By this conduct, they give those, whom thro' indolence, they confide an opportunity of embezzelling the greater part of what they pretend has been expended; while the inactive beings at their head, are masters of their own wealth, only in name. They frequently have it not in their power to do a charitable act; by which self-created inability, they obtain the name of parsimonious, unfeeling, pityless, &c. For the censorious part of mankind, who ever judge by appearances, are never at a loss for epithets descriptive of the follies they discover, or at least think they discover, in their fellow creatures, but seem to take a pleasure in setting the actions of others in the worst point of view.

It is a duty incumbent on all masters, and mistresses of families to take upon themselves the superintendance of their own affairs. The faculties of the mind, like those of the body, are weakened and enervated, by being permitted to remain in a state of inaction. If every man of fortune would be his own steward; and every woman her own housekeeper, they would soon experience the salutary effects of daily employment. The world would be freed from many of those enormous vices, that are produced by a too great love of ease.

The mind of man, in this lethargic state is like a stagnate pool over-run with weeds; its corrupt waters breed only poisonous creatures, and its noxious vapours infect the air around. On the contrary, the mental powers, when properly exerted, may be compared to those streams, whose waters are purified by their continual motion. But to return.

In the midst of this winter, which was a very severe one, *Theodora*, and her two sisters, took the measles. *Theodora* and *Carina* in a short time recovered; but *Eliza* the youngest caught cold in taking physic. The consequence of which was a large white tumour on the side of her neck, together with a consumptive cough, that was expected would prove mortal. She at length grew so weak as to be unable to walk, and the doctors declared, that there were no hopes of her recovery. She was in this weak condition, when the Vice Roy left *Ireland*. On his departure, the Earl purposed to set out for *Volpont Grove*, with all his family. *Eliza* could not possibly undergo the fatigue of so long a journey; and the Countess could not think of leaving her behind. She was for a while undetermined between her duty to her husband, and love for her child. The Earl at length resolved to go to the country, and leave the Countess to wait the event of *Eliza*'s illness. Could the Countess have foreseen the consequence of this separation, she would undoubtedly have run all risks with respect to the child, rather than have permitted her husband to take this journey without her.

The Countess took lodgings near town, hoping that the air, and a simple regimen, which she had heard of, and was resolved to try, might be of service to the child. While the Countess was thus between hope and despair about her daughter's fate, the Earl wrote her a very pressing letter, intreating her to come down to the country. In her answer, she begg'd that he would excuse her not complying with his request, on account of the critical situation in which *Eliza* at that time was.

The Countess's simple regimen had the desired effect on her daughter. As soon as she had recovered strength sufficient to bear the journey, the Countess informed her husband, with a joy, that none but such a mother is capable of conceiving, that contrary to the opinion of all the physicians, her little girl was out of danger, and might live to make him a happy grandfather; adding, that she wished ardently to see him, and would obey his summons to the country when he pleased. To this he returned a very affectionate answer, but said, he would dispense with her coming down for some time longer. This she was well satisfied with.

Not long after, the Countess received a letter from an unknown person, acquainting her, that the reason the Earl excused her coming to the country, was on account of an amour he had with the daughter of one of his lowest tenants; of whom he was extremely fond. The anonymous writer advised her to hasten her departure, and not to wait for an invitation, which, they feared, he would never send.

The reader may imagine, how great the consternation of the Countess must be, on receiving this unexpected intelligence. She compared this anonymous account with the letter she had just received from the Earl, and could scarce believe her eyes, or imagine, that a man could write in so tender a manner, and at the same time act quite contrary. After a moment's reflection, on the part she should take in a situation so critical, she sat down, and wrote the Earl an epistle, in which she informed him, that she was determined to be with him on such a day. This she sent by post. The Earl on receipt of her letter, sent an answer immediately, by the running footman, as the most expeditious mode of conveyance, with orders, if he met the Countess on the road, to cause her to return to *Dublin*, and to assure her, that the Earl would be in town in a few days.

If in doubt before, as to the certainty of the Relation given her by her unknown friend, this extraordinary care to prevent her going to *Volpont Grove* but too clearly convinced her of its truth. As the Countess was universally beloved in the country, the inhabitants were highly irritated at the Earl's conduct, and wished for her arrival to put a stop to this low intrigue. This he was aware of, and in order to lessen her in their esteem, he said publickly that he expected her down on the day mentioned in her letter, which he shewed.

Accordingly the gentlemen of the country went on the day appointed, to meet her, with the greatest acclamations of joy and respect. But the Earl, (as the reader has been already informed) took care to prevent her arrival. The gentlemen were much dissatisfied at their disappointment. This scheme of the Earl's succeeded to his wish; and his innocent Countess again helped him to impose on the gentlemen; she sent him another letter by the running footman, telling him, she was determined to go down to him, and named another day; with which he acquainted the gentlemen of the country, and made an excuse for their first disappointment.

He had, previous to this, sent off *Jago* express to stop her, and again permitted the gentlemen to go to meet her, being certain they would be disappointed. *Jago* was a surgeon by profession, and one of the Earl's favourite companions in most of his debauches, before he knew the Countess. Whether he was the confidant of some illicit practices of the Earl's or not, we shall not pretend to determine. However, it is certain that he had a great ascendant over him, which he took care to improve to his own advantage. He was a master in the art of dissimulation. If he aimed at any particular object, his conversation led your attention a different way, and winded your imagination in a manner so artful to bring you to his point, that he seldom failed in his designs, tho' never so foreign to your intentions. He was a fawning sycophant, revengful, malicious, and ungrateful. In short, he was in all respects an accomplished villain. Such was *Jago*, the worthy confidant of the Earl of *Volpont*.

Jago having arrived at the Countess's, delivered verbally to her, the Earl's absolute commands, not to go to the country on any account whatever. The Countess was so much amazed at this news, that she sat for some time motionless, and unable to speak. At length she burst forth into tears; and with a tone of voice, and air of dejection, that would have pierced a heart of adamant, said, Alas! it is now too plain. – I am convinced. *Jago* hastily demanded of what she was convinced? Of my own unhappiness, replied the Countess. He begg'd that she would explain herself. She took the anonymous letter out of her pocket, and gave it to him. When he had perused it, he hung down his head, and with a sigh declared, that the contents of it were but too true. But why, said the Countess, should I make myself uneasy about this, more than other affairs of the like nature? He has often before been unfaithful to my bed; and has owned it to me with a contrition, that in some measure attoned for the crime. Why may he not do so again?

Jago smiled, and would insinuate, that she was more in danger of losing his affections now than ever, and represented his present mistress, as one of the most artful creatures living. He said that she had obtained an almost absolute dominion over him, which he feared she would not only maintain, but would likewise increase. Well, replied the Countess, I am resolved to set out immediately for *Volpont Grove*. I would by no means advise your ladyship to take this step, said the crafty *Jago*. The Earl assured me, that if you came down, he would take care to confine you in such a manner, that you should not be able to impede his pleasures. The Countess was extremely terrified on hearing this; which the artful *Jago* perceiving, inveighed bitterly against the Earl, for the base design he had formed, of depriving the Countess of her liberty. But being rather too bitter in his invectives, she stopt him short, and said, *Jago* you lose your respect for me, when you speak disrespectfully of my husband; for however ungrateful he may be to me, you ought not to forget that he is your friend and patron. Having said these words, she quitted the room, to the no small dissatisfaction and surprize of *Jago*.

While the Earl was indulging his criminal passion in the country, the Countess was overwhelmed with the bitterest anguish. Notwithstanding the just cause that detained her in town, she frequently condemned herself as the cause of her husband's inconstancy, whom she tenderly loved with all his foibles. She endeavoured to persuade herself that there was no truth in the information she had received, and looked upon those who gave it, as her enimies. She imagined they might have done it with a view of making a breach between them, by stirring her up to reproach him with her wrongs, which she well knew would but irritate and make him more eager in his criminal pursuits. At any rate she thought it the most eligible method to take no notice of it, but to endeavour rather by tenderness and affection to draw him from what the violence of his temper might cause him to plunge deeper in, if he met with any opposition.

Having formed this resolution, she sat down and wrote him a most affectionate letter; in which she expressed her earnest desire of seeing him, but hoped she stood acquitted in his mind, of having a wish to offend him in any thing. For which reason she had combated with her inclination of going to the country; and hoped he would soon indulge her with the pleasure of his company in town. This letter had, for that time, the desired effect, being answered in a stile equally tender, and obliging.

Shortly after this, the Earl came to town, and was received by the Countess with the most cordial affection, and sincerest satisfaction, which was too visibly pictured on her countenance for him to suspect that she knew any thing of his intrigue; insomuch that *Jago*, who was certain that she was acquainted with it, was amazed at her being able to act in so heroic a manner in an affair that had given her so much previous pain.

The Earl was indisposed when he came from the country, and soon after was seized with an inflammatory fever, which was rendered more dangerous by the impatience of his temper. The Countess, her woman, and the trusty *Jago* sat up with him; for the Earl refused every thing but what came from his hand. As the Earl was rich, the reader may imagine that he did not want a sufficient number of the faculty to attend him, as well as to prolong his disorder in a manner suitable to his rank.

The Countess saw with pleasure his disorder decrease, and in compliance with his request left him one day quite chearful, to dine in the parlour. Having dined, and finding the doctors had been with him, she went up; and going to the bed-side enquired his health. He answerd in a very feeble tone of voice, that the Doctors had pronounced him in great danger, and had ordered a vomit to be given him immediately, and a blister to be applied to his back. Never was person more amazed than the Countess on hearing this. She however took courage, and feeling his pulse, assured him that the opinion of the doctors was founded on ignorance, or interest, rather than any real, or even apparent danger he was in, so saying, she went into the next room, where the first thing that presented itself to her view, was the Apothecary armed with the awful apparatus of vomit, blister, &c. The Countess's patience now entirely forsook her; she cried out in a violent rage, He shall not take your prescriptions, you are all a pack of interested villains, and would destroy my husband. I know he has not patience to bear a blister, it will make him mad. So saying, she snatched the things out of the apothecary's hands, and threw them into the fire. But immediately recollecting herself, she intreated the gentleman's pardon, and brought him to the Earl, in order to judge himself of the truth of what she had advanced.

The apothecary, on feeling his pulse, declared that his lordship was not in the least danger, and was surprised that the doctors had ordered him such violent remedies. The Earl on hearing this, ordered the curtains to be drawn aside, sat up in the bed, and taking the Countess by the hand, said, my dear *Angelica* you are the best doctor, but I see you can be angry as well as other people. O! my Lord, said the apothecary, her Ladyship had good reason to be in a passion, and would have been justifiable had she beat the doctors. At this the Earl laughed heartily, and jested a good deal on his Lady's passion.

Jago, who had been out upon business, being now returned, the Earl told him what had happened; which he greatly approved of, and said, He thought the doctors were wrong, but it was not his part to contradict them. The Earl then asked him, if his agent would be with him that night, according to his desire; which *Jago* answering in the affirmative, the Countess said, She hoped he would not think of business until he was better, but telling her, It was a business he would not any longer neglect on any consideration, as he could not be at ease until it was done, she dropt the discourse. And on the arrival of the agent, she by the Earl's desire retired.

The next morning, when the agent arrived, the Countess was again desired to retire; which she did, very much at a loss to know what the business could be, to which she might not be privy.

In a day or two after, this secret was explained. *Jago* came into the room where she was at work, with a sheet of parchment in his hand, and asked her in what manner she would have the sum mentioned in the parchment, which he shewed her, divided between her three daughters. The Countess seemed much surprised at this request; and instead of answering his question, asked him, What they were about? He informed her, That his Lordship was about to execute a deed, by which he charged his estate with two thousand pounds per ann. to her, and the sum stipulated for his daughters, agreeable to the power vested in him, by the agreement between him and *Bouviere*.

The Countess seemed very much displeased at this information, and hinted, that she was entitled to more than two thousand pounds per annum, by her right of thirds. *Jago* informed her, that it was his Lordship's orders, and that the agent, with her Ladyship's brother, and another person, waited to see his Lordship execute the deed, to which they were to be witnesses. After a few minutes consideration, she told him the manner she would have the sum mentioned for her daughters divided, upon which he immediately filled up the blanks, and returned to the Earl.

About half an hour after, the Countess's presence was desired. As she entered the room, the Earl cried out, *Angelica* my dear, I am now easy, let me die when I will, you, and my children, are provided for; at the same time, he delivered the deed into her brother's hand, and desired him to take care of it for his sister.

The next day, a servant recommended to the Earl by *Jago*, came into the room where the Countess was, with a letter in his hand, which, on seeing her, he endeavoured to conceal; but did it in so awkward a manner, that she could not avoid perceiving it. She asked what letter he had there, and he hesitating to answer, she repeated the question. He said at length that it was for his Lord. She desired him to leave the letter on the table, and she would take it in herself. The servant not daring to refuse, did as he was commanded, and withdrew.

When she cast her eyes on the superscription, she perceived it was a woman's hand, and the words very ill spelt. This raised a curiosity in her, she till then had never experienced. She took the letter up with a trembling hand, and before she knew well what she was about, severed the seal. She found that its contents consisted of the lowest phrases of fulsome fondness, signed *Borana*.[23] She informed his Lordship "That Ranold (the servant who had brought up the letter), had told her, – That her deer Lord was in a very bad sickness, and that she could not sleep for thinking of him. – That she was come up to *Dublin* after her deer Lord, and hoped to see him so soon as he dared venture out, and not be-danger himself, and Ranold would tell him where to find her."

The breast of the Countess, on reading this delicate epistle, was fired with indignation and contempt; but summoning all her fortitude and patience, she folded the letter, and taking it in her hand, went into the Earl's bed-chamber, saying, My dear, here is a letter, I will open it for you; which pretending to do, she threw it unfolded on the bed to him, and went to stir the fire, in order to conceal her confusion. He read it, and calling to the Countess, asked if she could forgive the man who had so often given her cause of discontent, and who had now an affair to disclose to her, that rather merited her hatred than forgiveness? You know my dear, replied the Countess, your power too well to fear my anger; for, however great the provocation may be, a concession on your part would erase the remembrance of it.

The Earl gave her the letter, which she read in an accent suitable to the stile, and making some droll remarks on the diction and spelling, concluded with saying, that her rival was not much to be dreaded. But I think, said the Countess she should have made me some acknowledgment in her letter for the care I have taken of you. The Earl gazed on his wife with astonishment while she spoke, at length seizing her hand, and kissing it, he cried out in a transport, by heaven you are an incomparable woman. – No my life, you have no reason to be afraid of the impudent wretch, of the truth of which I will immediately convince you. Give me my dear said he that prayer book on the table. The Countess guessing his intention, said, that she could not permit him to take an oath on such an occasion, for being convinced of the return of his affection, his word was sufficient.

He then desired her to transport the hussy. To which, she also objected; and said, That such a procedure would prove that she feared her power, which, she repeatedly assured him she did not; adding that she could not entertain an opinion so injurious to his Lordship's understanding, as to imagine that a creature such as *Borana* could have any influence over him. A thorough reconciliation now took place. The Earl seemed to have a due sense of his Lady's merit, and she fully persuaded of his reformation. The Countess now experienced a tranquility, to which she had been long a stranger. But her happiness was to be but of a short duration.

The Countess had a particular regard for the wife of *Jago*. She had made her several valuable presents, and her purse was always at the service of her, and her family. One day that the Countess and she were alone her Ladyship perceiving an unusual gloom in her countenance kindly enquired the cause of it. Indeed, my Lady, replied *Jago*'s wife, I am extremely unhappy on account of my husband's ill state of health. He has for some time past been plunged in the deepest melancholy. He seldom sleeps, and often wakes me with his sighs. I have enquired the cause of his grief, in the most affectionate manner; but he still evades my questions, seems insensible to every thing, and tho his health declines visibly every day, he refuses the assistance of medicines. I beg that your Ladyship will condescend to speak to him on this subject; perhaps you may prevail on him to disclose this secret that so much afflicts him. For my part I cannot divine the cause of his sorrow; but I fear it will be his death. Here the poor woman burst into tears. The Countess, who was naturally humane and compassionate sympathized in her grief and promised that she would speak to *Jago*, and endeavour to penetrate the cause of his grief.

Accordingly the Countess took the first opportunity that offered to speak with *Jago*, she began by telling him, that she was extremely concerned at the account his wife had given her of his ill state of health. She apprehends, said the Countess, that you have some secret grief, which you would conceal from her. If her suspicions are justly grounded, continued the Countess, you have treated her unkindly. Who could you with more propriety confide in than her, who must naturally be attached to your interest by the strongest ties, her own preservation, and that of her children?

While the Countess was speaking, she observed a tear steal down his cheek, which greatly excited her compassion. As he seemed unable to reply, she continued her discourse, and encouraged him to open his heart to her, by making him a generous offer of her purse, if it was a pecuniary matter that caused his uneasiness.

How foreign was it from her thoughts, that the discovery she so ardently sought, would throw her into the utmost confusion, and supply the place of generous compassion, with resentment and contempt? He continued a few moments silent, when, on a sudden, seizing her hand, he pressed it with fervour to his lips; and falling on his knees, declared in a passionate and distracted tone, that she was the sole cause of his grief. I have long, said he, entertained the most violent passion for you, which I in vain have endeavoured to suppress. The frequent opportunities I have had of contemplating the many perfections that gave birth to my passion, has daily increased it.

Her astonishment had kept her silent, and suffered her hand to remain in his; which he construing to an approbation of his villainous address, pursued his discourse. Adorable countess, said the wretch, the earl has again, unmindful of your charms, like the dog returned to his vomit. He has renewed his intrigue with *Borana*, and is so infatuated with his love for her, that should you comply with my warm wishes, he will never be able to perceive our happiness. My influence joined to yours would keep him ever subjected to us; nay, I am able of myself to cause him to take any measures I please to adopt.

The countess permitted him to take off his mask thus far – when fired with indignation, she pulled her hand from him, and struck him so violently over the face, that his mouth and nose bled abundantly. Then in a tone of voice, expressive of the wrath with which his presumption had inspired her, she cried, "Villain, is it thus you would return the many obligations you and your family are under to my husband? is this the friend in whom he has, with so little prudence so long confided? slave, dare you think to aspire to the arms, your master, your patron, your benefactor, has filled for so many years? what have you ever beheld in any part of my conduct – monster of ingratitude – that could give encouragement to so presumptuous a hope? but you shall not escape unpunished. I shall let my husband know what a viper he has so long fostered in his bosom.

It was now *Jago*'s turn to be actuated by all the different passions that had fired the breast of the Countess; but with the addition of disappointment and revenge. He, for a time, remained on his knee, as one thunder-struck, his face and cloaths covered with blood; when, rising as if bereft of sense, he wiped himself, and traversed the room with hasty strides. Just as she had finished her speech, he had collected breath sufficient to stammer out these words: Well madam, – 'tis very well. – Don't imagine that this usage shall pass unrevenged. – No, cried he, with the most horrid imprecations, – I'll plunge to perdition, or be revenged. Do monster, said the Countess, do thy worst, and immediately flung out of the room.

As soon as he had composed himself sufficiently to make his appearance in the street, he quitted the house, vowing vengeance against the Countess, who had offended him by a strict adherence to that, which should be the fair foundation of respect and love, namely VIRTUE!

When the countess came to reflect cooly on what had happened, she felt an uneasiness which seemed to be a presage of the woful catastrophe. She was sorry she had given way to the violence of her resentment; and wished she had been more moderate in her anger, so as not to have drawn upon her the wrath of a man, who was in all respects so well qualified for the perpetration of every species of villainy. She considered, that if he really loved her, his love was now turned to a hatred the most violent and unsurmountable. After such an affront, to permit him to come to the house with his usual familiarity, was by no means prudent. To desire the Earl to forbid him the house, would raise a curiosity in him to know the cause of such a change. To suffer him still to be imposed on by so specious a villain, was acting, as she thought, ungenerously by her husband. Yet to give his attempt on her virtue as her reason, would perhaps lay her open to the censure of a man, who had not the most favourable opinion of her sex, from the debauched life he had formerly led; and who might conclude, that some part of her conduct had been defective, which had emboldened *Jago* to hope for success in his attempt.

Reflections crowded fast on her mind, and still left her undetermined in what manner to act. She had not concluded on any thing, when the Earl came in; and perceiving her discomposed, asked her, what had disturbed her? Before she could answer his first question, he asked her, had *Jago* been there that morning? On the mention of his name, the Countess's confusion was but too visible. She answered, he had, and involuntarily added, she wished never to see him there again.

The Earl seemed surprized, and impatiently demanded the reason, of her making so extraordinary a wish. Immediately she saw her error, and would have evaded his question; but this only served to increase his curiosity. So that at last, she was obliged to give him a full account of the whole affair. But he appearing willing to turn it into a jest, she indiscreetly vowed, if *Jago* was suffered to come into the house, she would that instant quit it; which it was apparent, his Lordship did not then wish she should, for he immediately rung the bell, and gave a general order that admittance should be refused *Jago*, or any of his family.

When the servant quitted the room, she said, it was uncharitable to withdraw his assistance from the wife and children on account of the husband. He replied with great warmth, He would have nothing to do with the pack, for he did not doubt in the least from what he heard but the wife would be a pander[24] for the husband, if she found her account in it. This the Countess said was an unchristian way of thinking; but when his Lordship had resolved on any thing, he would not be dissuaded. So the Countess, tho' unwilling, was obliged to acquiesce with his opinion.

A little after this, the Countess having for some time before had a letter of attorney from the Earl to let, fall, nonsuit and do every thing as himself; in examining matters, she found *Jago* had been intrusted by the Earl with several hundred pounds to lodge in the bank; and having then occasion for money, she ordered her coach, and went to take it up; but was there informed that he had not lodged, at that time, near the sum he was so intrusted with; and, that having put in the remainder in an I, O, U, he had taken it up a day or two before this inquiry. When the Earl was informed of this fresh instance of *Jago*'s knavery, he flew into a most outrageous passion, and taking up a bible, bound himself by a solemn oath, never to forgive him. The Countess did all in her power, to moderate his anger, represented it as perhaps the effect of poverty, more than any real design in him, to wrong his Lordship. D—n you, said the Earl, How can you speak in behalf of a villain, that would have debauched you?

This at once stopt the voice of compassion which, though she despised the man, pleaded for his misfortunes. The Earl, ever prone to revenge, and generally too sudden in his determinations, immediately had *Jago* arrested, and cast into prison. *Jago* wrote his lordship word, that he had ordered a bill in chancery against him, in order to compel his lordship to make good a promise he had formerly made him of an hundred pounds a year during his life, and fifty pounds a year during his wife's life, if she survived him. This being for secret services, his lordship might blame himself only for the consequences.

One day, during the confinement of *Jago*, an anonymous letter was flung into the Earl's coach. The writer informed him, with the cordiality of a friend, that the countess was carrying on an illicit intercourse with his professed friend *Bellario*; and that they had frequent private interviews, and secret places of assignation. The Countess, happily for her in this respect, never went abroad without her daughter *Theodora*, who was then about eleven years of age, and a young lady, the daughter of one of the Earl's most intimate friends.

The Earl, however, seemed at this time to be fully convinced of her innocence; insomuch, that instead of forming any schemes to detect her, he immediately communicated to her the contents of this letter. He even offered a reward in the public papers, for the discovery of the person who wrote the anonymous letter abovementioned. The next time *Bellario* visited him, he informed him of the letter he had received; and said, he was certain it was the base contrivance of some evil minded person, calculated to make a breach in their friendship. However, continued he, their intentions are frustrated, it will only serve to cement it the more; and to convince *Bellario* of the sincerity of his professions, immediately proposed a match between his eldest daughter *Theodora*, and *Bellario*'s son, when they arrived at a proper age.

The Countess by no means approved of her husband's having informed *Bellario* of the letter he had received. She frankly told him, that *Bellario* was the last man on earth that should have heard of it; and gave for her reason, that the generality of people were more inclined to believe an evil than a good report; that as *Bellario* was accounted a man of gallantry, were she as innocent as an angel, she might incur the censures of the ill-natured; and therefore requested he would not encourage that gentleman's visits. She proposed, in order to furnish the Earl with the means of declining the acquaintance of *Bellario*, to take a country villa, as the searching for it, and furnishing it in a proper manner, would cause them to be frequently out of town, and prevent his taking offence.

This advice happened to be relished by the Earl, and they immediately set about the execution of her project. They soon found a house, with handsome gardens, and a large quantity of land within a few miles of *Dublin*. This they took, and went often there, to order the manner of its being furnished and fitted up, for their reception the approaching summer.

In this interval the letter before mentioned came, at which the earl seemed greatly disturbed, and proposed to the Countess to have an accommodation with, and forgive *Jago*; but on her reminding him of the oath he had taken, he dropped this design. And comparing this with the anonymous letter, thought he found a great similitude between them, and from that, concluded him the author of it, in order to blacken the character of her, he had not the power to seduce. This was a conjecture natural enough.

The Earl's temper now grew insupportable; he was seldom at home; but when he was, the united efforts of his wife and family to please him were ineffectual. When he returned from his debauched companions, which was generally about four in the morning, he would not only act with the inconsistency which is the general effect of liquor, but so brutally, that on recollection, he used often to declare, "he believed the Devil possessed him." At other times, he seemed to glory in his brutality.

In one of these latter humours, the Countess summoning all her courage, said, she knew the reason of his treating her so cruelly; but that if his harlot was come-at-able, she would find her out, and make her suffer for it all. "Will you, by G-d! replied the Earl; I'll take care of that. By heavens! she is a fine girl of seventeen, and better than you." Oh! my Lord, said she, in the most pity moving tone of voice, "Can you say so to the mother of your children?" D—m you, replied he again, you are a she breeding bitch. "*Jago* said you had too cold a constitution to bring me a boy, and I believe he said right." And can you blame me for that, were it in reality so? "Yes by G-d I can, and do," said he.

She then argued, that he flew in the face of Providence by saying so; but that she was still young enough to have many children more; and that it might please God yet to bless them with a son; which she would gladly bear to retain his love, tho' she were sure to lose her life by it. – This speech quite overcame him: he threw himself at her feet, kissed off her tears, while he bathed her hands with his. She wept for joy at his reviving love, and he with contrition for having treated her so ill.

She now once more flattered herself, but vainly, that she had won him, and might happily keep him. But alas! he was too deeply plunged in a criminal passion. He was wearied of that virtue, whose delicacy and softness had chains too feeble to hold one of his complexion. He again relapsed into vice's violent fever, and lost all sense of prudence, nature and honor. *Borana* held dominion over him, and any thing of a gentler mold was not to his taste. And now we behold him insensible to all the Countess's virtues and full blown charms; infatuated, lost for ever to the world and to his family!

But notwithstanding all his faults, the Countess loved him with unabating passion, which was at last the completion of her ruin, and that of her family: for love caught her in the snare the enemy laid, which was as follows:

She went out one fatal morning to pay some considerable debts; among the rest, for the furniture of the country house: which having done, the following anonymous letter was thrown into her coach.

"My Lady,

"This is to let you know, that your lord has brought a hussey from the country, and has her on the quay with him every day. There is a trooper with her, this is common. She is a vile jade, and common to him every where; so that the town rings of them. *Draco* came into the bawdy-house where they were together, and would have the w— from him, and they quarrelled and challenged one another about her. I can't tell your ladyship half the vile things that are said of him; and I believe they are all true by the company he keeps, which he ought to be ashamed of. He is a scandal to nobility, and scorned by every one. I would not let you know this, but you may prevent the consequence that may attend it; and if you are acquainted, or can get acquainted with any one of *Draco*'s acquaintance, to be sure they will let you know more; but be advised and be very secret in this, until you find it out. You'll find friends to assist you, never fear."

The Countess, without perceiving the snare that was laid for her, considered nothing further than the preservation of her husband's life, which she apprehended in danger. Therefore after setting the young lady who accompanied her down at a place where she was engaged to dine, she, instead of returning home as she had intended, ordered the coach to drive to her brother's, in order to consult with him and his Lady, on this affair, and to advise with them how to act, or whom to address; her distraction at that time, not having allowed her to recollect who was most intimate with *Draco*.

On her communicating her distress to her brother and sister, they readily named *Bellario*, saying, he and *Draco* were as intimate as brothers. The Countess as readily objected to him, as she did not esteem it prudent to apply to him, after what had happened concerning the first anonymous letter; and added, that she would not on any account send for him to her house.

Her sister-in-law then named another gentleman to whom she immediately sent a note; but as fortune would have it, the note was returned unopened, the gentleman not being in town. On this, her sister proposed inviting *Bellario* to drink tea with her, and laughingly said, "Sure no one can think this a place of assignation for you; if you are not safe in your brother's house, I don't know where you would be so." – This the Countess could not possibly object to; whereupon her sister sent her compliments by her own servant to *Bellario*, requesting his company that evening to tea, on business of the greatest consequence, and the Countess staid for dinner to wait his arrival.

At the time appointed, that gentleman came, and being informed by the Countess, in the presence of her brother and sister, of the cause of their invitation, he promised to settle every thing to her satisfaction before he slept.

After tea, a game at quadrille was proposed by the Countess's sister. The cards were scarce dealt round, when they heard a loud rapping at the door; at which the Countess gave a sudden start, turn'd pale, and said, "'Tis Lord *Volpont*, I am undone. *Bellario*, save, save yourself," and then fainted. – *Bellario* in amaze, cried, "Why should I save myself? What have I done to offend the Earl?" I am afraid of no man. – What scheme is this? Was I invited here to be made a tool of? for – he was proceeding, when they heard the Earl loudly asking Was his wife there? A servant answering, she was, he cried out louder still; "By heavens, if she be, *Bellario* is here also: bring *Jago* to help me." *Bellario* hearing this, laid his hand on his sword, saying, "If that was the case, it was time indeed to provide for his safety;" and immediately drawing, stood ready to receive his Lordship; who, in a violent manner, demanded where they were.

The door instantly flew open, and presented to his view his Lady in a swoon. *Bellario* with his sword drawn, and the Countess's brother and sister, with the cards in their hands, almost petrified with surprize and astonishment. The Earl stopped short at his entrance. The scene before him would have justified a wife in the eye of any other husband; but that was not his aim; he came there determined not to be undeceived, nor to credit his own eyes.

Bellario was the first that spoke, who said with great spirit, "What, my Lord, is the meaning of all this? Is this the produce of your mean artifices? I have ever had too high an opinion of lady *Volpont* to think she would be your accomplice in a trick of this sort – but now am convinced to the contrary. If you have any thing to say to me, I am ready to answer you with the point of my sword."

At these words the Countess revived, and starting from her chair, ran, as she thought, to prevent the effusion of her husband's blood: for which, in return, his lordship gave her the last signal mark of his favour, by a violent stroke with a heavy cane, over her out-stretched arm, which every one present thought he had broken: but her ladyship might have saved herself the trouble; the Earl was not disposed to enter into that sort of conversation *Bellario* had proposed, though he had his sword by his side. – *Bellario*, who did not design to commence hostilities, but only to defend himself, if attacked, not finding his antagonist in a fighting humour, very deliberately put up his sword, took his hat, and wishing the Countess's sister a good night, walked off; giving his lordship a jostle in the way.

The Earl immediately followed him, saying, he was convinced, he had ocular demonstration of his wife's perfidy, and that was enough for his purpose.

Here the reader will perhaps say, that the Countess should have immediately returned to her own house. The Earl could but have ill treated her; and this he had so frequently done before, that one would think she might by that time have been well accustomed to it. But those in health can prescribe with ease; and it is admitted that persons of the greatest presence of mind have, at some certain times, been struck with a panic. Besides, it is probable, that pride and resentment were more concerned in her resolution of not going home, than terror. She saw herself abused and wrongfully suspected; and what she bore heroically, whilst her husband continued to think her what she was, a virtuous woman; she could not bear now he had traduced her character, which she still knew to be equally untainted.

It is true she seldom went to sleep by his side, that she did not expect to awake in eternity; but never expected that he would part with her, or reflect on her character. And indeed, if the reader will candidly reflect, he will not hesitate a moment in crediting this assertion. For had she had a notion that matters would turn out in the manner they did, or had she been a woman of artifice and intrigue, she would have taken care to have provided for herself in several shapes. She had it in her power to have sold his whole estate for his life, and to have appropriated the money to her own use.

She might, contrary to his desire, have got the deed of settlement before mentioned, registered; and by that, have secured herself and children. In short, she might have prevented that deed, which she carelessly left in her drawers, being seized and destroyed by its maker. But it is plain, too plain, she never harboured a thought of what befell her. The greatest fault she could be said to have, was being too fond of a man, who undervalued himself, and therefore could not be expected to set a right estimate on any thing else.

The distraction the whole family was thrown into by this melancholly event, exceeds all description. One of the Countess's footmen came express with the dreadful tidings, and brought the Countess's keys, with orders to her nurse, to send her all the papers and other matters contained in a particular bureau, in which her jewels and other valuable articles were deposited. There lay the deed of settlement, the letter of attorney, the title-deeds of the estate and all, or at least most part of those long leases which were the growing part of the estate.

The most favourable opportunity then presented itself, to have put the Countess in possession of what would have made her formidable enough, to resist the black scene of iniquity practised against her; for the Earl did not return for three hours after the affair happened.

The nurse, however, as ill fate would have it, had been so often the witness of their quarrels and reconciliations, that she made light of this. And taking the keys, instead of hasting to send the things the Countess wanted, only replied, as they fall out, I will answer for it they will soon fall in again; and giving herself no further trouble, retired into the room where the children were in bed.

Theodora, who knew nothing of what happened, was surprized in the morning to find, that instead of her mother, the Earl had made *Jago* the partner of his bed the night before; notwithstanding the oath she had heard him take. She saw confusion in the countenances of all the servants. – But when she was informed of the Countess's unhappy situation, she seemed petrified with grief and amazement. A frantic despair succeeded. – She tore her hair, that flowed in ringlets on her neck, beat her face, whilst her shrieks resounded from every part of the house. Her little sisters, *Carina* and *Eliza* joined in her grief; tho' they poor innocents, were unconscious of the cause.

She ran wildly from one to the other, and clasping them to her breast, cried O! *Carina*; – *Eliza*, we have lost our mother. That dear, dear mother, who attended to all our wants, who nursed us, who loved us, and by her example, would have made us good and wise. The Earl was attracted to the children's apartment, by the outcries of *Theodora*. Instead of being awed by his presence, she ran up to him, with clasped hands, crying still louder, What have you done with my mother? Where is she? Oh! mother, mother, mother, shall I never, never see you more? And then she began to commit outrages on her face and hair, which she pulled out by handfuls, and even attempted to tear her flesh.

How this affected the Earl we know not. But apprehensive that she would alarm the neighbourhood, he commanded her to be silent; which she not regarding, he gave her a stroke, that fell'd her to the ground. When to his no small surprise, regardless of the blow, she instantly got up on her knees, and clinging round him, raised her streaming eyes to his, and said, Do strike, strike your *Theodora*, who loves you as well as she does her mother. – Dear papa, I would do as much for you, as for my mother. But never, never will I quit my hold, though you should kill me, until you promise to bring home my mamma. Oh! sisters, sisters, join me – help me. –

Here her spirits being quite exhausted, she sunk motionless on the ground, but still held fast by her father. While the servants endeavoured to loose her hold, and to recover her, the Earl seemed impregnated with paternal pity, and stood silently gazing on her, while a heaven-fraught tear stole softly down his cheek.

Jago perceiving, that the Earl was moved, and fearing the effects of powerful nature, which then visibly pleaded for her; and did not in the least correspond with his interests, persuaded him to quit the room, altho' he did not attempt to prevent his striking his daughter, saying, So dismal a scene, might hurt his Lordship. The poor well inclined, but ill advised Earl, with seeming, and perhaps real reluctance, followed his advice; being a prelude to that influence it ever after had over him.

The governess and the rest of the domestics that were spectators of this affecting scene, used every endeavour to bring *Theodora* to herself, which they could not effect, untill she had been blooded and put into bed. When recovered from her swoon she refused all sustenance, and determined to starve herself until her governess at last prevailed on her, by observing, that to destroy herself, would not only offend heaven, but would add to her mother's affliction; that if she loved her, the best way to shew that love, was in taking care of herself for her sake, and by improving her father's affection put it in her power to reconcile them to each other. This hope, and this only, mitigated her grief, and made her desirous of preserving a life that she was, even at that tender age, sick of.

She found that her father had taken every precaution to prevent her mother's coming to the sight of her and her sisters, or having access to the house they were in. He still kept his worthy friend *Jago* to sleep with him. One night when she had been in bed about two hours, but had not closed her eyes, she heard a cautious step, come towards her bed; and on the nearer approach hearing a voice, in a low tone, say, don't be afraid, my Lady, she soon perceived it was one of her mother's footmen, who told her that the Earl kept so strict watch in the day, that there was no possibility of coming at the Countess's bureau, but that he had the keys, and therefore begged that she would get up and go with him to take out the things his Lady wanted, as otherwise his Lord might accuse him of robbery.

She instantly obeyed the summons and went trembling with him to the dressing-room; he led the way with a dark lanthorn, he opened the drawers, but behold, all her jewels, and every thing of consequence, had before been taken out, by the means of a picklock; by which they had been again locked. Her diamond girdle buckle only was left, which the servant rightly judging to be left there for a bait, advised her to let it remain. All the papers that they found they took, but alas! none of those that were material were left for them.

They then returned as cautiously as they came, to their respective rooms, when, in their progress, hearing the Earl and *Jago*, and fearing they were heard, the poor fellow had scarce time to get, with his bundle, into a store-room, that luckily lay open, where there was a great quantity of feathers, in which he hid himself, when the Earl with a lighted candle in his hand, was up after him. He looked into the room, and not seeing any thing, he went from one, to the other, and finding all quiet in that part of the house, at last came into *Theodora*'s room. She pretended to be fast asleep; to be sure of which, he held the candle to her eyes. On which she gave a sudden start, dashed the candle out of his hand, and cried out *Thieves, Thieves*.

The light was extinguished, and it is not improbable but she frighted his Lordship more than he had done her on his approach. To stop her outcry, he said, *Theodora*, my dear, it is I; I thought I heard a noise, and was afraid you were ill. Oh! dear papa, replied she, how could you startle me so? I am sure any one in the world might have taken you for a *rogue* as well as I; thus stealing to my room in the dark. He then said he did not come in the dark, but that she had driven the candle from his hand, and put it out.

He then sat himself down on her bed-side, and taking her by the hand, which trembled extremely, he observed she was cold, and asked her what made her tremble so. She readily answered, he had frightened her terribly, which no doubt was true enough; but she did not tell him how she came to be so cold. He then began to speak of her mother; and asked her, Was she not a vile woman? Oh! papa, said she, how can you ask me such a question? when your own heart must tell you, she is one of the best women in the world. I am sure she always loved you dearly, and so sign, when you were ill the other day. Ay, Ay, she loved me dearly the other day to be sure, when she poisoned me. She poison you! replied *Theodora*, what my mamma poison you! whosoever says so, is the greatest liar that ever was; no no, my poor mamma loved you too well; and papa, if you recollect, no one had it in their power to hurt you but one – Who is that? replied he; but speak softly, for *Jago* is in the next room, and will hear you. I don't care, returned she, I would say it to his face; you may have been poisoned for aught I know, but I am sure if you were, no one could do it but him; for all the while you were ill you would take nothing but from his hand. But, continued he, you say she loves me; how can that be when she *w*— with *Bellario*? O! fye, papa, said she, how can you say so? I could say, if I was dying, my dear mamma never did any such thing in her life. You should not listen to the stories of bad people, my dear, dear papa, and threw her arms about his neck. Bring my poor mamma home to us again, and God will bless you. She had touched him, and would willingly have proceeded, but their evil genius was too near, and overheard their discourse. *Jago* called out to the Earl, and told him, his Lordship would take cold, as he had no stockings on. With this the poor deluded man left his daughter, and went to the serpent; who instilled sufficient poison into his ear, to stifle every good effect her simple argument might have had on his good nature, had he been left to himself. Their misfortune was, he was a credulous man, as we said before; being diffident of his own abilities, he depended too much on the opinion of others, and thereby became the dupe of *knaves* and *rogues*. By the pernicious advice he daily received, his talents, for want of action, every moment grew more and more relaxed; until at last, they were totally enervated, and he could not be said to have a will of his own; which the reader will be amply convinced of, in the course of this work.

The next morning, as a proof of his having edified by the advice he got after he left *Theodora*, he took her to task, insisting that she knew of her mother's intrigues. He endeavoured, by pompous promises, and terrifying menaces, to make her say things that he would have put in her mouth, derogatory to the character of that innocent parent. Finding that he could not get her, on any consideration, to deviate from the truth, he at last desisted to importune her, on that subject; but said, tho' she denied things so stoutly, he would find ways and means to get rid of her infamous mother, as he call'd her, and would procure a devorce, if it should cost him ten thousand pounds. The reader may judge of *Theodora*'s trouble, at hearing him make such a declaration; for young as she was, she knew the influence of money, and dreaded the power it might give him to ruin what, were he his own friend, he should have preserved as invaluable, namely, the good name of a wife, whose virtues would have lent him their radiance, and whose prudence wou'd have protected him from those to whom he afterwards became a property.

Theodora, who had now been a week without seeing her mother, was almost distracted. She concerted a scheme with the footman already mentioned for her escape, but was frustrated as she was about to put it in execution. He had placed himself in the window of an upper room in the adjoining house, into which *Theodora*, with his assistance, could have easily got, but her governess, who suspected that she would attempt to escape to the Countess, watched her narrowly. *Theodora* now flattered herself with the hopes of soon embracing her mother; and thinking the coast was clear, went up to the garret, opened the window, and was just steping out, when her vigilant governess, who had hid herself behind some lumber in a dark part of the room, laid hold on her.

The Earl being informed of the attempt *Theodora* had made, thought it adviseable to send her to the country. He wrote to *Benevolus* a relation of his own, who lived a few miles from town, and informed him he intended to commit his daughter *Theodora* to his care for a few weeks, but intimated his desire that *Benevolus* would himself invite her, as he did not chuse that she should know he had wrote to him on that subject.

Benevolus, in a few days after he had received the Earl's letter, came up to town. He informed *Theodora*, that he would ask her father's permission to take her with him to the country, where his wife, mother and sister would be glad of her company. *Theodora* was rejoiced at hearing this. She had been several times at his country seat with the Earl and Countess, and esteemed him more than any other of her father's relations. *Benevolus*, in a conversation he had with the Earl, at which *Theodora* was present, intreated him to permit her to pass a few weeks with him, at his house in the country; to which the Earl with seeming reluctance consented. *Theodora* set out the next day with *Benevolus* for his house, where she was received by all the family with the most cordial affection.

This gentleman was heir to some of the Earl's honours in failure of issue male in him, and his cousin *Bouviere*; he was very personable, and his wife a compleat beauty; join to this, he was a man of great understanding, undaunted spirit, facetious temper, and strict integrity and honour; in short, he was one from whom a title might have derived honor.[25] His lady had a temper, to which one of the finest faces in the world was a true index. The old lady his mother, was a truly valuable pious person, with whom no one could be acquainted, without reaping benefit from her conversation, which from her knowledge of the world, was rendered instructive and entertaining.

Ardelia his sister was a figure very capable of supporting so amiable a groupe; and from her care and attention to *Theodora*, became in a short time so dear to that young lady, that the love and respect she had for *Ardelia* fell little short of what she had for her mother.

'Tis not to be greatly wondered at, if in the society of such a family as this, one of *Theodora*'s age, and sprightly cast of temper, soon forgot the misfortunes of her own. They always talked with good nature and compassion of her mother, which the more strictly linked her affections to them. They saw a great deal of company, but those that she liked best, were the family of a reverend doctor, who was married to the sister of the old lady. Their daughters and she contracted a great intimacy, on being frequently together, and in a little time she found herself so happy, that she in a manner did not miss her mother.

She here got great insight into housewifery, in which all the female part of the family excelled; but not willing to be confined to this alone, she often solicited her cousin *Benevolus* to let her partake in his amusement of agriculture. The morning was entirely devoted to learning, and the study of books, from which her too early initiation into the gaieties of life, in some measure, withdrew her attention.

All the instruction she had ever had in writing, was one month she learned from her mother, and another from the same master who had taught the Countess. Here she had leisure and grew fond of her pen. But still an enemy to confinement, it was a sort of drudgery to read so long as her cousin *Ardelia* would have her; she had rather been out in the fields seeing ditching, fencing, cutting drains 'thro the land, or any thing in the farming way.

One thing she was, remarkably fond of, which was, when she could find an opportunity to steal out, and walk a mile or two by herself, and visit all the poor people in her way, who in a very short time knew her perfectly well, and seemed to feel an undissembled satisfaction at her approach; putting up their prayers to heaven with great fervency, to bless her, and grant she might live to be a good old woman.

A love of variety, (a philosophical turn it could not surely be at her tender age) made her often think she could with pleasure have exchanged her fine cloaths for their rustic weeds, to enjoy that content they seemed to do, with their *potatoes* and *milk*, of which she often partook. When she saw their children barefoot and bare legg'd, she was sure to supply them with her own shoes and stockings; and sometimes returned home with a peticoat less on her than when she went out. This naturally attracted their love to her, that in some time after, being seized with a most violent scarlet and purple spotted fever, wherein her life was despaired of, she was prayed for in all the churches and Roman catholick chapels throughout the country, and there was as great lamentations for her, as tho' she had been a crown'd head.

Ardelia never forsook her bedside all the time, tho' *Benevolus* and his Lady quitted the house on the account. Not a servant man or woman, but sat up night after night, in their turn; yet so fortunate was she, no one took it from her.

This fever was epidemic, of which vast numbers died. One very particular circumstance happened on her taking it. There was a man who lived near the house, who had ten or twelve children; he was taken off; and on the very day that she was taken ill, the eldest child, a lad about eighteen, was also seized with the same disorder. The distracted widow, and the rest of the family, depended on him for their future support, and there was no less than six of them down at the same time.

This melancholy story came to *Theodora*'s ear, before she was deprived of her senses; she therefore made it her earnest request that whatever medicines &c. were ordered for her, should be sent this young man, tho' she had never seen him. Her request was punctually observed. There was nothing that was thought proper for her that was not got; and as if Providence particularly ordered it so, for the preservation of both, she could take nothing but surfeit water. She relapsed twice, at the same instant of time, so did this young man, and the very day she first went out to take the air, he came to return her thanks.

At *Theodora*'s return from this airing, she found the doors crouded; when *Benevolus*, who was then returned, asking the reason, he was told, they came to make the good young Lady some little presents on her recovery. In short, every one brought as they could afford. Some chickens, some eggs, and others butter, &c. so that *Benevolus* said, *'Twas an ill wind truly, that blew no one good*; that *Theodora* should be ill once or twice a year, for the good of the house she was in. There were publick thanksgivings put up for her recovery, in every place that she was before prayed for in.

Every one was surprised at the Countess's not coming to her daughter in so perilous a situation, and concluded it was because she imagined the Earl would not permit her to see her. But we shall exculpate both, by acquainting the reader, that the Earl was in the greatest distraction imaginable on *Theodora*'s account, and had given *Jago* orders to make the Countess acquainted with her condition, which he never did, tho he made the Earl believe he had; and urged the little notice she took of the information, as an argument against the innocent Lady he had already so much injured. He represented to the Earl, that the Countess was unnatural; who was afterwards heard to say, he was more displeased at the indifference she shewed to *Theodora* than any thing else.

It was plain he, at that time, had the sincerest affection for *Theodora*; a physician had twenty guineas and the Earl's own chariot and six, to bring him down to see her, and give her all the assistance he could. When he came, he did not even write a prescription, but gave her over the first moment he saw her; so that he made a tolerable night of it, setting off from *Dublin* in the evening, and being back again before six in the morning.

When the Earl received this account, he shut himself up in a room and wept bitterly. Every other day after this, he sent down the running footman to know how she did, and gave him a white cambrick handkerchief to hold up as a signal of her recovery, when he came within sight of the house. The Earl, while the handkerchief remained undisplayed, was always seen to weep; but on her being past all danger, the footman coming down the avenue, with the signal expanded, over his head, his Lordship hastened out to meet him, and clasping the fellow in his arms, he cryed, My *Theodora*, my child lives. Yes my Lord, replied he, she lives, and is likely to do well. Thank God, thank God, said his Lordship; and gave the welcome messenger a handsome reward, for the intelligence.

When she was pretty well recovered, she was by the Earl's orders taken up to *Dublin*, and put to Mrs. *Ducelles*'s boarding school, where her two sisters and the governess, with a servant man and maid, already were. It is true, she had the pleasure of seeing her sisters again; but her concern was unfeigned at the leaving *Benevolus*'s family.

Mrs. *Ducelles* was an extreme good woman, she was cousin to their governess, kept a great school, and was vastly clever in the discharge of a trust, that, (however lowered in the opinion of the world, has ever been considered important in the eyes of the judicious.) She was particularly kind and civil to *Theodora*, and when they were put there, being desired not to let their mother have access to them, she answered, she would not take them upon such terms; her house was no gaol, nor had she any notion why she should deny a virtuous mother the liberty of seeing her children. If the Countess did her the honour of a visit, she should always be extremely welcome. Her frankness rather pleased than offended the agent in whose care they were put; for he smiled and said, I have done my duty, and have nothing further to say.

This was nobly generous in Mrs. *Ducelles*, to which the agent was not much inferior. Had their governess been as good, they had been much happier than they afterwards were, but being chamber boarders, they were intirely under her command. One day when the Countess came to see her children (of which their governess got private intelligence) she drove them, like a parcel of lambs to the fold, up to the very top of the house, where she put them into an inner room, under two locks, and then would neither see her lady, nor let her see her children. Mrs. *Ducelles* treated the Countess very respectfully; her tears, and strongly expressed love to her children, having excited her compassion, so as to make her shed tears also; and finding it impossible to see her children. The Countess got into her chair, and returned home, to indulge that grief her disappointment had heightened to a very great pitch. When the young ladies were released, Mrs. *Ducelles* informed *Theodora* what had happened; at which she was greatly troubled, and said she would take care how her governess locked her up again; which occasioned a great quarrel between the two cousins.

This good-natur'd woman then informed them that their mother was very big with child, and with a significant look, said, if it happened to be a boy, they would soon see great changes; and then fervently prayed to God it might, and live; to which we may suppose they heartily said *Amen*.

Upon the Countess's perceiving herself pregnant, which she did not know at their separation, she wrote a very affectionate letter to her Lord, acquainting him with her situation, wishing it to be a boy, that he might see his error, and repent, before it was too late, the cruel usage she had met with from his hand. This letter was carried by a gentleman, who was a mutual acquaintance of both; he watched the Earl's eye whilst he was reading it, and saw him change countenance several times. But when he came to the material part, he cried out, with an involuntary emotion, What! with child! By heaven, if it be a boy, I will cut *Jago*'s throat. The gentleman immediately caught up the word, and said, he thought he deserved it whether or not, if he was any way accessary to the unhappy breach between his Lordship and his innocent Lady. The Earl, as if he had recollected himself, and was sorry he had said so much, added, "as *Bellario* had got the cow, he might have the calf also." The gentleman having endeavoured to reason him out of this absurd way of thinking, but without effect, returned with a dejected countenance, and aching heart, to the Countess, and told her what had passed. All the answer she made to it was, "Well, God's will be done," and returned him suitable thanks for the friendliness of his intentions.

The reader may possibly be desirous to have a description of the lovely object that had, with the assistance of *Jago*, alienated the Earl's affections from his virtuous Lady. He must therefore know that at the time the Earl came to the *Volpont* title, her father was a poor tenant on the estate, had a miserable hut and potatoe garden; sold a despicable sort of unlicensed beer, which was brewed in small quantities, and sold to the peasants:[26] – but poverty is no reproach! – He was a very honest man, and descended, in an *illegitimate* line, from a respectable family. This *Ishmael* race[27] settled in the same county *Volpont* grove was in; and taking root there, throve tolerably. But this poor man was rather more unfortunate than the rest, and at last reduced to the circumstances before-mentioned. He fell ill, and was in great want, when the Countess, of *Volpont* hearing of his distress, sent him ten or twelve guineas at different times, by the rector of the parish, who often went to visit and pray by him. Her Ladyship being informed by this gentleman, that he lay on a clay floor on a little miserable straw, sent him immediately a bedstead, bed, and proper covering. – The poor man being removed from the wretched condition in which he lay, into the bed the Countess had sent, prayed fervently for his kind benefactress, and told the clergyman who attended him, that he would gladly commit his daughter to the care of the Countess; and hoped her Ladyship would take her into her family. – In a few days he died, and was buried at the expence of the Countess.

The clergyman neglected at that time to communicate the dying man's request to the Countess, who went to *Dublin* to pass the winter before-mentioned. On her return to the country, he remembered the charge the father of *Borana* had given him, and informed the Countess of it. – She immediately sent for *Borana*, who gladly obeyed the summons, and came dressed in a long camblet cap (or hood), and cloak. – She was what might vulgarly be called a clever strapping wench, with beauty sufficient to take the lead at an Irish fair, such as good black eyes and hair, high cheek-bones, wide mouth and nostrils, a swarthy complexion, and a number of moles on her face. – The Countess told her, She had not been made acquainted, until then, with her father's dying request, or she should before have endeavoured to provide for her, as she had a value for the honesty of his character.

Borana made an aukward curtsey. Her Ladyship then asked her, how she had employed her time since her father's death. She, with another reverence, said, "She had spun at the school her Ladyship (long life to her) had set up, and that she was to have a wheel and clock-reel so soon as the year was out." The Countess smiled at her ignorance, and continued to ask her many questions, until at length the Countess bid her put off her cloak; which *Borana* with some reluctance did; when the Countess perceiving she had no stays on, remarked to her, that all her female domestics wore stays; it was indecent, where there were so many men, to go without them, as it often encouraged them to take too great liberty. *Borana* told her Ladyship, "That she had none, and therefore could not wear what she had not." The Countess, with a benign smile, said, that should make no difference; for if she hired her, she would have a pair made for her.

So saying, she rung the bell, and ordered the governess to be called, and told her, she had heard her find fault with the children's maid, and therefore recommended that young woman to supply her place. The old governess opening her eyes, quite wide, cried, "O! my God! my Lady, Is it *dat awkward creature* you would have about my young Ladies? No, no, nought we know is better dan nought we do not know, I like my *Deligence Embourbé*[28] better dan dis." This was a nick-name she had given the children's maid, because she went slowly about everything; but notwithstanding, she was a very honest, sober girl. The Countess laughed heartily at this speech, and ordered the housekeeper to be called. She asked her if there was a vacancy for a woman servant, as she would gladly take that young woman into the house. The housekeeper answered, there was not. The Countess then said, she must make a place for her; but she answered rather roughly, that there were already too many. On this the Countess apologized to *Borana*, and dismissed her.

The Countess of *Volpont* thought she discovered something in the countenance of her housekeeper rather mysterious; that, denoting some personal dislike to the girl, which willing to know, she asked her what was the meaning of her answering her so rudely. The housekeeper asked her Ladyship pardon, if she had offended her; but said she had her reasons, which, on the Countess's expressing her desire to know, she told her, that *Borana* had a very bad character, and often occasioned the men servants to stay out whole nights together; that they frequented her mother's house, for the sake of her company, on the pretence of drinking beer, which the mother sold, who was herself no better than she should be. When the Countess heard this, she expressed her concern for the unfortunate creature, bid the housekeeper give the girl a piece of money from her, but said she would have no further concern with her.

Notwithstanding this, *Borana* often came by stealth to the house, to run up seams for an upholsterer, who worked for the family, and was said among the rest, to be one of her admirers. At the time the Earl went without the Countess to *Volpont-grove*, he called one day in a frolick at the house of *Borana*'s mother, and demanded the rent, which was about thirty or forty shillings. The old woman told him that she had it not. The Earl in order to divert himself, swore he would distrain her; she begged very hard to save her little goods, which she said, and with a good deal of truth, were not worth the sum. Well, said the Earl, if I have not the money, I must have your daughter. The old woman did not seem to dislike the alternative, and the Earl having as he thought, sufficiently terrified her, departed.

In a few days after, the Earl happening to be at a fair that was held near *Volpont-grove*, was accosted by a woman, who asked him, Would he have a pretty girl? Yes, replied he; where is she? The woman pointed to *Borana*, who stood by one of the stalls. His Lordship went directly to the place, bought a silk handkerchief, and putting it round her neck, asked her if she would be his bed-fellow that night. She curtsied, and said she would. – The agreement was made in a few words, and the woman who had introduced her, borrowed a shift for her of one of the Earl's servants, her own being somewhat too coarse and dirty to go to bed to a *Peer*.

Borana was then taken to the Lodge, where his Lordship had ordered a bed to be put up, on pretence of its being better air, because on a hill. To this rendezvous his Lordship departed in the evening. His black, on hearing of this intrigue, was seized with a fit of jealousy, and attempted to murder the Earl; who very narrowly escaped falling a victim to this negroe's rage. He would have sent him to gaol; but fearing the ridicule of the world, should the affair be made public, he wisely put the poor fellow away without any noise, and so the matter dropt.

One night, as his Lordship was going on his nocturnal expedition as usual, two of his servants, who had observed his haunts, and were convinced of the cause, determined to play him a trick. There was a plank laid across a deep foul dyke, over which his Lordship must pass. A rail was fastened to one side for the safety of the passenger. This rail they had fixed so as to give way on the least pressure; then hiding themselves in some furz-bushes, nigh the place, waited the desired event. His Lordship from the frequent attacks of the gout, was a little feeble in his feet, so on he came; the plank was narrow, he fearful, and when he came to the middle, leaning a little too hard, plump in went the noble Lord over head and ears.

He struggled so long that our arch sparks began to be frightened, lest he should be suffocated; yet they were unwilling to help him, being certain he would revenge himself on the first he met. So they left his Lordship to shift for himself, and made their escape from the place, as fast as they could. However he at last got out, and came back to the house; but in such a pickle, as quite took away his appetite for pleasure that night; to the no small mortification of his Dulcinea, who, no doubt, diverted herself stringing pearls, in the absence of her Don Quixot.[29]

She it was, by whose influence, together with that of honest *Jago*, the Earl was guided; and in the end, totally became their slave; seeing and judging only thro' them. He kept all the Countess's clothing, and jewels, not so much as a second gown had she, nor would she have had the second shift, had not the laundress supplied her with a few things she had of hers, in her possession at that juncture; for which good-natured act, his Lordship never payed her bill.

He had *Borana* to the country house he had lately taken, where he provided her one to teach her to dress, and behave herself. This person, so intrusted, had been tutoress to his daughters, before the French governess came over. She was a woman of a good family, and had, when at *Volpont Grove*, (being then made own woman to the Countess), greatly offended her Lady, by marrying the gamekeeper, but she was always esteemed a virtuous, sober woman: which makes it the more surprising, that she should undertake such an office, as that of *Duena*, or governess to *Borana*. But poverty, and her husband's dependance on the Earl, explained the matter.

Here *Borana* had the Countess's clothes made to fit her, but the finest were locked carefully up by the Earl. Some people when they saw *Borana* thus adorned in the Countess's clothes, loaded this intruder with curses and imprecations; while others laughed at the ridiculous awkward figure she made. But every one joined in blaming the Earl, for the cruel and ungrateful part he had acted, by the best of women, and of wives.

To give a true idea of the state of ignorance, in which this favourite female minion of the Earl's was, before she profited by his tuition; one day when he had company, she, her mother, and *Duena*, dining in a room together, the servant who brought the victuals to them, not having much regard to order, nor respect of the persons, brought up a salt leg of pork, with which, there was at his Lordship's table, a peas pudding; but unfortunately for *Borana*, there came with it some currant-jelly sauce for roast venison, which was that day at dinner. Miss and her mother immediately sated themselves, when the daughter, with filial respect, first helped herself, and then her mama, with a large slice of boil'd pork, and poured currant jelly in abundance over it. They began to eat heartily, miss saying, The great folks lived rarely; though for her part, she'd *as lief eat pork, as the poor people did, with green kale.*

The *Duena* did what she could to contain herself, tho' she was ready to burst with laughter. About the time they had eat plentifully of this new fashioned fare, the venison and peas pudding came. When she helped as she had done before, peas-pudding, mustard, and venison, which they eat together, while their companion waited until they had filled themselves. Then taking some venison with its proper sauce, they began to stare at each other, as she did to give vent to her *mirth*. It must be however remarked, to the credit of *Borana* and her mother on this occasion, that they were, perhaps, the first persons who introduced those heterogeneous dishes.

When *Borana* said to her mother, *Indeed and* I believe *mamma*, we eat the wrong things together *sure enough*, or else she would not laugh so. Plague take you, says she to the *Duena*, why wouldent you tell a body? *Arrah honey*, don't you tell the Lord now, for if you do, I shall never *be after hearing* the last of it. The other promised she would not tell his Lordship, but for a long time after, could not help laughing, whenever she thought of *Borana*'s nice distinction, as to the sauces proper to be eaten with salt pork, and roast venison.

While *Theodora* was at *Benevolus*'s, and her sisters at the boarding-school, the Earl would sometimes steal his charmer the back way, into his town-house, but she never dared to appear at the front windows, lest they should have been broken about her ears. The publick in general were enraged against her and her keeper, so that the lower class of people openly vowed vengeance against them. And one day, they having information that the coach waited at the back door for his Lordship and his Miss, they ran round to meet them, telling those they met the occasion. Whereupon they gathered a formidable croud; who, on the appearance of the coach, began to pelt it with brickbats, stones and dirt, crying, in an outrageous manner, they would tear his doll[30] to pieces, whenever they could lay hands on her, if he did not bring home the good Lady his wife. Their indignation against them was, in fact, sufficient to have made them put their threats in execution, had they not ever after that, taken the covert of the night to make their excursions in.

The Earl of *Volpont* was now very industrious to get a divorce from the Countess. To accomplish which, he offered large bribes to some of the lowest persons in and about his house, such as helpers in the stables, her chairmen, and even the porter who brought the victuals from the market. This denoted a weakness and folly in him, incompatible with the understanding, with which nature had endowed him.

She must surely have been a second *Semiramis*,[31] to give such people as these an opportunity of seeing, or knowing any thing of her intrigues; allowing even she had any. But *vice* is as destructive to reason, as aquafortis[32] is to metals; and makes as great a devastation in the mind, as the boiling bitumen, that is sometimes vomited from *Mount Vesuvius*, does on the fertile vallies beneath it.

This was then his Lordship's situation. He had embraced that enemy to virtue, and saw not the impropriety in any attempt, that wore an appearance of facilitating his wish; which was then, without doubt, to obtain a divorce from his unhappy, greatly injured Lady.

He now made several attacks on the integrity of his Lady's own footmen, who attended her wherever she went, and was indiscreet enough, to send one of them several messages by different hands, with the most pompous promises.

This honest man, tho' placed by Providence in an humble sphere, yet soared above many in principles, and scorned to better his condition, upon the villainous foundation of traducing the character of an innocent person.

When his Lordship sent to desire to speak with him, as the husband and head of the Lady he served, he acknowledged his authority, in obeying the mandate. He went to know his Lordship's commands, who received him with all the familiarity of an intimate friend, and shewed him a servile respect, unbecoming a master to his menial. Honesty there gave his Lordship reason to blush, had not his sensibility been rendered callous. The servant boldly declared the truth, and withstood the melodious chink, and irresistibly dazzling charms of two hundred guineas in an open net purse, which was displayed to the best advantage, to gain the wished for point. This glittering temptation was backed with a promise of a good farm on the estate, or the best places in his house, for him and his wife, being then newly married. But proof against all; he told his Lordship, He knew nothing but what was virtuous, honourable, and good of his Lady; and that he would not swear to an untruth, tho' his Lordship were willing to purchase it, at the expence of his whole estate. This, his tempter said, was saying nothing, and after giving him two or three hearty curses, tho' all along before, it was Dear Mr. Good Mr. &c. they parted for that time.

The touchstone, distress, soon proved the sincerity of the Countess's friends; which, indeed, is scarcely ever known to fail, when fortune makes the experiment. All the flashy part of her acquaintance, like the motes that are seen to play in the sun's golden ray, on the approach of a cloud disappear. The magnet had lost it's attractive quality, except to a few, who superior to vicissitudes, still remained inviolably attached to her interest.

One night, being to sup with one of her friends, she ordered her footmen and chairmen to call for her about eleven. The hour appointed drawing nigh, they set out to wait on their Lady, but were attacked in the way by several men armed and masked, who laid hold on the footman, with whom the Earl had been tampering, and gagged him. A coach was at hand, into which they forced him, and drove directly to the Earl's country seat; on the way he was informed, by those who guarded him, that what they did was by the Earl's orders, and that he would never return with his life, if he did not do as my Lord would have him.

When arrived at the house, he was closely confined, and all who spoke to him confirmed what his conductors had told him. The footman willing to know his fate, desired to speak with the Earl. He was immediately admitted; the fine promises were reiterated, with additions, the bribe again offered, and again refused, with a greatness of soul, worthy the highest encomiums. His lordship at length lost all patience, swore violently that he should never see his wife again, and laying hold on his ear, attempted to cut it off. The honest creature dreading the hands he was in, thought it necessary to use a little art, to extricate himself as easy as he could, and therefore entreated his Lordship to hear him. He then told him, that as he would have him take a false oath, it was necessary to give him time to recollect circumstances, that would give it an air of truth.

This seeming condescension his Lordship was highly pleased with, and said he now spoke like a reasonable man. That his evidence would have more force than that of twenty others, as he always attended his lady where-ever she went. But let us suppose, said his Lordship, it were impossible to prove her guilty of adultery; you are certain that no body can keep my wife from me. Very true, my Lord, replied he. Yes continues his Lordship, but do you see that monkey yonder? Yes, my Lord, answered the other. Then by heaven, that monkey shall have a better life than Lady *Volpont* shall have. The footman's blood ran cold on hearing this cruel declaration; but however, this was no time to make remonstrances. So, on giving a promise, which he never intended to perform, of returning in a day or two, to do as his Lordship directed him, he once more regained his liberty, and returned to his Lady.

The Countess was in the greatest trouble imaginable, on account of his absence, together with the account her chairmen had brought of his being forced into a coach, and carried off, they knew not whither; but particularly as there was good reason to think, there was a plot formed that night, to deprive her of her life or liberty. She however waited, tho' impatiently, the arrival of her chairmen, but they not appearing, one of the company offered her Ladyship their chair, which she readily accepted. Before she got into it, her own chairmen came with this intelligence; and one of them being observed to be in liquor, it was not judged proper to trust them to carry her. Wherefore she got into that offered her, and two of her friends footmen with flambeaux[33] were sent to wait on her home.

They had not gone far, before they observed several ill looking fellows, lurking near a dead wall, by which they were to pass; one of whom the servants heard say, 'Tis not her, 'tis the judge's daughter. This Lady and the Countess being much about the same size, caused the mistake; and the judge's liveries helped to save her, by deceiving these ruffians, who certainly meant her a mischief. For her chairmen coming by afterwards, they were still lurking in the same suspicious place; and one of them looking into the chair, perceiving it empty, asked them what was become of their Lady? To which the chairmen gave for answer, Go look! at this they seemed disappointed and enraged, and threatened the chairmen to beat them. This account they brought their Lady next morning; which perfectly agreeing with what the judge's servants had heard the night before, her Ladyship had reason to apprehend herself in danger. She was applying for an order from the government, to compel the Earl to deliver up her servant to her, when to her no small joy, she saw her faithful servant appear, who gave testimony of what had happened him.

But the Earl, tho' indefatigable himself in this praise-worthy affair, did not chuse to depend too much upon what he alone might do, therefore had many associates in the business, among whom was an attorney; nor could he fix upon one fitter for his purpose. This fellow was one of the Earl's boon companions, a sort of a sycophant, who could accommodate himself to any man's humour, provided he found his own account in it. He had been formerly a dependant on the bounty of *Bellario*, but was then his inveterate enemy.

There needs very little gall to give a description of so worthless a character, when it is told, that he married a very handsome woman, on the infamous principle of bartering her charms, for his own pecuniary advantage. With this view he gave *Bellario* frequent opportunities of being in her company. The Lady was tempting, the gentleman no Stoic; the consequences may be then easily supposed.

Cornuto (for so we may properly call this self-created monster) often, under pretence of business, would stay out whole evenings, when he was so fortunate as to prevail on his worthy friend *Bellario*, to bear his wife company. Sometimes he would, out of his extreme love, no doubt, cause the fair one to keep her bed, and then would introduce the lover; saying, "It is only *Bellario*, my dear." When out at any friend's house, he used to say, "Well, I can stay contentedly with you to-night, as I have left my friend *Bellario* with my wife, who, poor thing, is ill, and keeps her bed." This frequently occasioning people to say, Egad, I should not chuse to leave such a man as *Bellario*, night after night, with my wife; his answer was, No matter, I know what I am about; he may dance – but I know who shall pay the piper.

While *Bellario* continued to make him and his wife genteel presents, all was well. But when, from the natural inconstancy of that gentleman's disposition, to whom variety was alone the attractive charm, his fervour began to abate; and that *Cornuto* perceived his golden harvest was at an end; he pretended to discover what he knew from its commencement. It was then time to bring the matter to an issue. Accordingly he caught the lovers in tender dalliance; took out an action of damage in several thousand pounds against *Bellario*; brought it to a trial, and acquired the duplicated character of *pander* and *cuckhold*, with six-pence costs; being all the jury pronounced him intitled to. His wife likewise immediately quitted him, nor did she ever after this memorable transaction, cohabit with him.

With all the above-mentioned perfections, who so proper an engine to be played off against the Countess as *Cornuto*? He searched every receptacle of vice, in order to find out some one ignorant or wicked enough, to make an affidavit such as should be dictated to them: this he at last found, in a poor creature imprisoned by *Bellario*, to whom she had been a servant, on suspicion of having robbed the house, or some of his visitants, of linen and other articles. The first step *Cornuto* took to bring her to his lure, was to terrify her, by telling her *Bellario* had sworn he would hang or transport her.

After this sweet preparation, he asked her, Did she not once live with a person who had kept a public garden? She answered in the affirmative; he then asked her, Had she ever seen the Countess of *Volpont* there? The girl amazed at these questions, replied, Yes, to be sure, and little lady *Theodora* with her. That was no matter, he said; but was *Bellario* ever there at any time when her Ladyship was there? "O dear, ay, says the girl, several times." He next asked, Did she ever see him speak to the Countess? "Yes, yes, I have," said she. And can you swear that? continued he. For what? replied she. Why, to save your life, my girl, said he, and to be taken over to England by the Earl of *Volpont*, and made his housekeeper.

We need not doubt but this was readily agreed to by one in her circumstances. *Cornuto*, who knew perfectly well to dress a proof of this nature, drew up an affidavit, such as none but an infernal could invent. This he read in terms quite different from those it contained, and the poor wretch being totally illiterate, swore to it. Thus was this great acquisition of a false oath made; *Cornuto* hugging himself, no doubt, for his invention made no small merit of the affair with his employer, who, it is to be presumed, amply rewarded him.

His Lordship exhibited this villainous affidavit against his lady; but found her character was too well established to let it, or any thing of the sort have the least weight.

> If on the polish'd marble, dirt you throw,
> Rub it but off, and twill the brighter grow.

This wicked scheme therefore proving abortive, the next step the Earl had to take, was to deny her being his wife; which was very little regarded, on account of the notoriety of their marriage, and public cohabitation. He then said, that he had another wife when he married her, and that, at that period, she knew of it.[34] But this was so absurd an assertion, that no one gave it the least credit. Every one, to the Earl's no small mortification, agreeing, if it really was so, he should not be suffered to set up a dead wife against a living one, nor yet criminate himself, in order to injure others.

When the Earl *Volpont* found that every scheme against his Lady was unsuccessful, he went every where abusing and calumniating her; but to very little purpose, for it seemed only to serve to raise her still higher in estimation. One morning he went to the Primate,[35] and was running on at a great rate, when the worthy Prelate told him, it was shameful for a man to abuse his wife after the manner he did Lady *Volpont*. On this he swore very violently that she was none of his wife, for that he never was married to her. No! says Lord Primate, that is surprising, when you have all along acknowledged her as such, to the Lord Lieutenants of the kingdom; to me; nay, to every one. He replied, He was sorry he had done so, but that indeed he never was married to her. Notwithstanding which, he would take good care of his children, and that he had already settled large fortunes on them. "Upon my word, said his Grace, that is kind, considering they are bastards." "Bastards! said the Earl, my Lord, they are no bastards." I thought they were, replied the Primate; did you not say, you were never married to their mother?

This quite disconcerted the Earl; which the Primate perceiving, he said, Come, come, Lord *Volpont*, I am the last person in the world that you should attempt to impose upon, in regard to the Countess of *Volpont*; I knew her, before she had the misfortune of being your wife, and have known her ever since. I have always found her a virtuous, valuable woman; I have the licence by which you were married to her in my custody, and you may depend upon it, while I live, she shall never want a friend to see her righted. Upon this, his Lordship rose from his chair, and said, If that were the case, he had best withdraw, as it was to no purpose to speak to his Grace on that head. The Prelate replied, he could not do him a greater pleasure, than by removing from before his eyes, a man that he could not view with any degree of satisfaction, after the villainies he had practised against the best of women. So saying, without offering to quit his chair, or ring the bell; he suffered the Earl of *Volpont* to find his way down stairs by himself. A disrespect with which that good man would not have treated the meanest man, who added *honesty* to his character.

He went from him to another Archbishop. Here he began in the same manner he had done at the Primate's; but this Prelate had not the patience to listen to his discourse that the Primate had; for rising from his seat, with a virtuous warmth and honest bluntness, he said, "Get out of my house my Lord, fye upon you; fye upon you; you are a scandal to nobility; no honest man should keep you company. I think there must be a curse hanging over the place, where-ever you are, therefore, pray get out of my house, I'll have nothing to say to you." And, finding his Lordship willing to make a reply, he opened the door of the room they were in, and in some measure pushing him out, shut it in his face. Would that every one united thus in discountenancing *vice*, we should find the world forced to reform, and *shame* establish a conduct, which propriety could not.

His Lordship finding there was no good to be had from Episcopacy, he repaired from thence to the coffee-house, where meeting with those less scrupulous of associating with him, he told them that Lady *Volpont* had prepossessed all the Bishops against him; and as for the Lord Primate he added by G-d, he kept her himself.

Whether the pretensions of a young man,[36] who laid claim to the *Volpont* estate and title, had infected the minds of some of this family; or whether it was a prophetic view they then had, of what was afterwards to happen, in having another pretender of the phoenix kind, to rise out of his ashes, is unknown; but certain it is, there was a report industriously propagated that the Countess was with child of another daughter; her sister in-law (who was also pregnant, and much about the same time gone) carried a son; that on their delivery they were to exchange children, in order to furnish the family with another impostor.

This was sure a supernatural knowledge of futurity, that well entitled them to the epithets of wizards. But ridiculous as it was, it nevertheless gave the Countess some uneasiness, which was not much to be wondered at, in the condition she was then in, abstracted from her misfortunes, as it generally is the cause of a dejection of spirits, tho' the circumstances are ever so good. But she had sufficient trouble at that time, that needed no heightening. However, contrary to all their expectations, nay, we may add wishes, she carried her burden to its full time, and, a week before her sister-in-law, she was delivered of a still-born son, to her great misfortune, and the universal regret of all her friends, particularly as the poor Lady was not expected to survive her infant.

The child was laid in state, in order to suffice public curiosity. Her sister had also a son which lived, so that the world was convinced to a demonstration that she had no intention of imposing on the family. How much had the Earl of *Volpont* now to answer for? And how sensible should he have been, that the correcting hand of Providence was here seen? O! presumptuous man! who thus darest think to cut and carve to thy liking, those occurrences that are in the womb of *time*, and which that alone, under the direction of Providence, can discover.

As if the friends of the Countess of *Volpont* waited the foregoing event as a thing that would make her fate decisive; trusting, no doubt, that if she should bring forth a son to live, her Lord would as eagerly solicit a reconciliation with her, as he had before done a divorce; or if a daughter, it would put an entire end to every expectation of the sort. Soon after she was past all danger, and began to return those visits that had been made her, by her openly avowed friends, during her illness. One night she was told by her servant, that there was a person disguised in a great coat wrapped closely about him, that wanted to see her. But they, fearful of any villainous design against her life, did not care to admit him.

Innocence ever unsuspecting, made her ridicule them for their idle fears, and desire to see this *incognito*. Accordingly they shewed him into the room, where her Ladyship was, when he immediately discovered himself to be one of her Lord's attornies. She expressed her surprize at seeing him, together with a desire to know to what she was indebted for this unexpected visit. He told her, that he saw with concern the unmerited ill treatment of her Lord; who he feared was now too closely linked with her enemies, to permit him ever to see his error. But that he thought it a duty incumbent on him as a christian, to put that into her possession, which might hereafter be serviceable to her and hers. That he wished from his soul she had happened to have her settlement registered, or that he had the original to present her instead of the copy, which he had taken from the original draft as filled up by council. That he was of the opinion a copy, proved by the witnesses, or any two of the three, would be sufficient to force his Lordship to fulfil its conditions, at least with regard to her daughters. He concluded by observing, he paid this visit by stealth, of which if the Earl knew, he would never forgive him; and that he might likewise prove a sufferer, as his Lordship owed him money.

The Countess promised secrecy in the affair, returned him thanks suitable to the friendly office he had done her, and he took his leave, carefully concealing his face from her domestics; her Ladyship considering it, as it really was, a mark of the protection of Divine Providence.

Soon after this, the Countess received another proof of the peculiar guardianship of heaven. Her Lord's having set up another wife against her, was so mortal a stab to her peace, as equally to bereave her of appetite and sleep; in short, she was tired of a life so full of vicissitudes; and had, in a manner, devoted herself to her woes; when she received an unexpected visit from a near relation of the Earl's, who came with the compliments of *Bouviere*, requesting she would not make herself uneasy on that head, for if her Lord proved his marriage with the wife he set up against her Ladyship, he could, and would prove one between him and a milliner in London, prior to the other; which wife was living when he married her, and dead long before he married her Ladyship.

The Countess resting satisfied, that neither he that sent the message, or him that brought, it, would impose upon her in this matter, as they could have no view in deceiving her, she soon conquered the trouble it had given her, and once more smiling peace sat on her placid brow; again the modest rose blushed in her cheek, and her eyes re-assumed the language of internal peace.

But let us now return to the boarding-school, where we left our Heroine and her sisters; whereby we shall learn somewhat about the Earl. His Lordship it seems had made an excursion in his own yacht to England, accompanied by his dear and faithful *Jago*, together with an infamous *reprobate Parson*, who had been silenced for several years, and obliged to go to the colonies, on account of the repeated irregularities he had been guilty of. These two, and some others of the same cast, the Earl took along with him, leaving his *Dulcinea* under the direction of her *Duena*, and mother.

This excursion over, he arrived in Dublin, and sent immediately to Mrs. *Ducelles*'s to enquire after his daughters; with a particular invitation to *Theodora* to dine with him the next day, and desired she might be drest, as he was to have company.

Theodora went accordingly, and was received by her father, with the greatest tenderness and affection; even shedding tears of joy, at seeing her again, after the severe fit of illness she had had. He left her for a little time, but presently returned, bringing with him all her mother's jewels, and put most of them on her with his own hands. The girdle buckle being last, he asked her where he should fix that? she answered that if he would give her leave, she would fix that properly herself: and seeing his hat on the table, she took it up and placed the buckle with a gold girdle round the crown of it; then turning to her father, presented it him, saying, I shall be obliged to you, Sir, if you will do me the honour to wear it, until I am able to do so myself, which I shan't be, for these some years to come.

Never man seemed more delighted or pleased than the Earl did, at the behaviour of his, daughter; he looked with surprize and affection at her, and launched out warmly in her praise, while she returned his kindness with the most endearing expressions, and innocent caresses. When the company came in, he placed her at the head of the table, paying her all the respect imaginable, shewed every one his hat, and told in what a pretty manner she had done it.

After dinner, the cloth being taken away, he gave her as the first toast, saying the separation between him and his wife, made her of great consequence, as it was not probable he should ever have a lawful son; that *Bouviere* never had a child, nor was likely to have one; so that in consequence of the agreement between them, the *Volpont* estate was settled upon his three Daughters, after the death of him and his cousin. He added, that the fortune he had already settled upon *Theodora*, made her a match for the greatest man in the kingdom; and then told the company, that he intended shortly to propose her to the Earl of *Belmour* for his son.

The reader will not wonder, I presume, if *Theodora* felt her vanity a little flattered, on her father's declaration; vanity being for the generality inseparable from the sex, in their younger years; we may venture to say, at any period of time in the female career.

The Earl of *Volpont* was, in this, as good as his word; for in a few days after, he sent a gentleman with the above proposal, to that truly great man, the Earl of *Belmour*, who received it with a politeness inseparable from his every action. His answer, however, gave a convincing proof, that he esteemed men more for their real virtues, than the paltry acquisitions of titles and fortunes; that he considered the connection of *virtue*, superior to that of *rank*; the latter being often inherent to those who are totally deficient in the former; he wisely thought, that the higher a man was born, it only served to place his *virtues* or *vices*, in the more conspicuous light; therefore, when good, it was an advantage both to himself, and the world; but if the contrary, it might be esteemed a public misfortune; example being more prevalent than precept. But let the worthy Earl's own words speak for him.

" – There was a time, Sir, said he, and that not long since, that I should have esteemed my[self] honoured by the now proffered alliance of Lord *Volpont*, but his conduct of late has, so deservedly drawn on him the censure of the world in general, that I am obliged to decline his offer, tho' ever so advantageous in a pecuniary view. But tell his Lordship, nothing would give me a greater pleasure, than to be the happy means to make him look into himself, so as to atone for his past errors; that if he will, by a speedy reconciliation with his Lady, take off the odiums he has unjustly, and ungenerously, cast on her character, his daughter, and my son being both young enough to wait a few years, I may, on seeing him, continue to act like an honest man, in my turn, sollicit, what I now, thro' his own fault must reject."

Nothing sure could be nobler than the foregoing sentiments. Every thing that is good and great was contained there. How any one endowed with the Earl of *Volpont*'s sense could withstand their force is surprizing. But it was obvious, they had no effect, tho' faithfully recounted to him, by the gentleman he had entrusted with this negotiation; who afterwards told it to many, as the highest panegyric he could bestow on the Earl of *Belmour*, for whom he had a very sincere, and well founded veneration. This is a proof, amongst many other examples, that when once vice gets an establishment in the heart, the best understandings become dupes to its irregularities.

Not long after this affair, the Earl of *Volpont* went to *England*. *Borana* repaired to *Volpont* Grove; and his three daughters, in a few months afterwards, were taken from Mrs. *Ducelles*'s to his house near town, where they had a sufficient number of servants to wait upon them. Among the number of the men, was one of the brothers of *Borana*, who could not but see his near affinity to the bane of their happiness was not of the very greatest advantage to him, in their eyes, particularly *Theodora*, who being older than the rest, was more sensible, of the injury his sister had done them. This prejudice the young man seemed desirous to remove, by his general attention to all her commands.

Here they lived quite retired, saw no company but such as were approved, by the agent and their old governess, who allowed them the liberty to range in a large garden contiguous to the house, whence she used to summon them, like a swarm of bees to the hive, by the tinkling of a little bell.

Theodora however was of a too volatile and sprightly humour, to be confined to such narrow limits; there was a pallisade gate in it, which opened into a fine meadow, that led to the sea. Over this gate, (for it was kept constantly locked) would she frequently clamber, tho' the spikes were stuck with tenterhooks, and of a very considerable height; but she was young, unacquainted with fear, and thought that life not worth the preservation that she must lead in a prison. Under such restrictions, this appeared no better, when the objects about her were grown familiar to her eyes. She panted after sweet variety, and when past her boundaries, like a bird that had made its escape from a cage, she winged her flight towards the sea side.

That element afforded her a melancholy satisfaction, in contemplating its varieties. The smooth and tranquil part, reflected on by the effulgent beams of the sun, she compares to that period of her life, when the radiance of prosperity gilded every part of it; the tempestuous, to those inconveniencies which adversity produces. The meditation disturbs her, and dwelling on this last picture, she exclaims, – My golden dreams alas! are over, and I am doom'd perhaps, to live in tempest, the wretched remainder of my days.

A flood of tears attended this melancholy reflection, while the heavens seem to sympathize with her woes, in a sudden shower of hail and rain. She stands the storm's tempestuous rage, nor seems to heed the inclemency of the weather. Behold! the clouds disperse, the sun breaks forth with doubled lustre, the sea grows still and calm, the winds are lulled, into a gentle breeze, and nature all around seems thankful and refreshed.

More struck with gratitude, than just before with grief, our moralizer falling prostrate on her knees, the big tears of joy rolling down her cheeks, breaks forth in fond ejaculation: Yes, my God (she cries,) I feel this mild reproof, for my desponding folly; I shall for the future, alike adore thy *power*, thy *goodness*, and thy *mercy* – The face of nature, I see thou hast instantaneously changed; why not the less arduous task my afflicted situation? To thee then will I apply for protection, on this hope shall I rest, and hence shall defy every gloom adversity can bring.

Thus fortified by natural reason, afflicted by example, every ambitious care subsides in the breast of *Theodora*. She repairs to the house, where she finds them all in confusion at her absence.

Her governess having warned them to retire, on seeing the gathering clouds portend a storm; *Carina* and *Eliza* returning without *Theodora*, she asks impatiently for their sister. They inform her, that she had gone over the gate. She frets, and sends different messengers out to seek her. They not imagining she could get down the deep descent to the sea-side, she returns without their meeting with her. On seeing her again, all fears subside, and anger takes their place. Her governess scolds; *Theodora* makes an apology for the uneasiness she had caused; but the old harpy, not suddenly to be appeased, tho' very prone to passion, will hear no reason; on which *Theodora* repairs to the spinnet, and by harmony strives to elude the effects which giving an answer might produce.

To this passive state of mind the young *Theodora* was brought, by mere chance, some two years before. A violent temper was hereditary to her; she was impatient, fiery, and vindictive, could not brook controul, nor bear disappointment; which latter meeting one day in some favourite diversion, she cried, roared, stamped, and behaved in such a manner, that she terrified all about her. In this frantic fit she passed by a glass, into which she accidentally looked, and seeing the deformity of her own features, she stopped aghast. She saw, with disgust, the ravages of passion; and reason began to hold a parley with her. "Is this, she cried then, the effect of passion? How deformed I look: if it causes me to dislike myself, sure I cannot be agreeable to any one else; I'll instantly discard this guest, which, under the mask of an indulgent friend, constantly turns out an avowed enemy."

She kept her word, and from that moment became mild, passive, and obedient; to the no small surprize of every one who knew her. Her mother the Countess of *Volpont* observing this, put her philosophy often to the test; by ordering her to be drest to go to some pleasing amusement; and when thinking just to step into the coach, her Ladyship has said, she was drest to great advantage, and looked very well, but that she had changed her mind, and did not chuse to take her; then desired her to go to her apartment, undress, and have her sister got ready to go with her. *Theodora* has made her reverence to her mother, with a smile, and done as ordered; seemingly as happy with her grammar, and music, as if she had gone with her mother.

Of all conquests, certainly that over ourselves is the greatest, but few can boast they obtained that conquest at the age our *Theodora* did. Let no one argue that it is a task too hard; why has Providence endowed us with reason, but to subdue our passions, and hold them in subjection to it? We are not born wicked; it is the indulgence of our passions that renders us so. Then how earnest should we be, in our endeavours to keep them within due bounds, is obvious to every rational being, who will allow himself time to think.

In this retired state the children of the Earl of *Volpont* lived for near two years. *Theodora* in this time became greatly enamoured with reading, and greedily devoured every book that came in her way; but this place afforded none by which she could profit much. Novels and romances were, for the generality, the only sort that she could borrow of those that came to see her; and there by no means satisfied her thirst of knowledge.

Sometimes she would amuse herself in the garden for hours together, in pruning the trees, fastening some to the wall, grafting on others, setting down flowers, transplanting them, and making experiments on them, variegating, doubling and adding to their magnitude. She took great delight in spreading the carnation over a card; forming little ornamental lures for the vermin, to divert their attention from the flowers. Often when she found in the cool shade, the lilly of the valley, or the violet, who bashful hangs its head, she would say to those nigh her, See, after all my care and fond attention to the garden flower, how much superior nature is to art. Which, of all my nursery, think you, dare vie with these in odoriferous sweetness, or in beauty? They seem to me, like some sequestered philosopher, who knowing the world and all its follies, prudently avoids it, and seeks the lonely forests to dwell in. The minuteness of the flower, is the poverty of the *sage*, and its matchless sweetness, that wisdom with which his mind is stored. Both alike can captivate the senses of those who happily can meet with them; but with this difference to wisdom, it leaves its sweet traces in the mind, on which to feast as long as memory can retain it; the other ravishes the senses for the time you smell it, but is lost on the approach of a different scent.

Methinks, I can discern almost every part of human life in the garden. The gawdy tulips are the giddy part of the creation, who place all their happiness in external show. The rose defended by the thorns upon its stem, is beauty and virtue. The carnation are those, by fortune, raised to vie with the greatest, but who are unable to stand, thro' their own merit, if she withdraws her prop. The sweet pea is the courtier, that bends, and twists, and twines, but with intent to out-top, in time, the patron that supports it. Its overcoming scent, is their fulsome flattery; which, though to most people, pleasing on its first aproach, occasions a meagrim[37] in the brain, by smelling it too frequently; as when pride grows intoxicated with flattery, the senses are thereby overcome, lose their faculties, and so become the dupe of adulation.

Thus would *Theodora* moralize. By which she would often engage the attention of her companions to such a degree, that the astonished look they wore, would sometimes actuate her risibility, and cause them to blush at the absurd figure their unmeaning stare presented her with, to occasion mirth in the midst of a subject whose emblematic stile was beyond the compass of their understanding.

Her turn of mind was masculine, tho' her form quite effeminate; for if she could but lay hold on fire arms of any sort, she would practise for hours together, at firing at a mark; at which she in a little time became very expert. But this was always at the further end of the garden, and unknown to her governess. However, one day hearing repeated shots, she went to seek whence it came. At the end of a long walk she beheld, to her great surprise, her young Lady, at this Amazonian exercise, who firing at the instant, she at once saw the flash, and *Theodora* enveloped in a cloud of smoke. This so frightened her old governess, that she fell down, and shrieking violently, called all the people about her, the agent among the rest, having just then arived from *Dublin*.

She immediately made a great complaint of this terrible affair, to that gentleman, who laughed very heartily at the manner in which she told the story, and to her no small mortification, instead of taking the pistol from *Theodora*, as she had requested he would do, he said he was glad to find she had so good a spirit, and that she should not want powder and shot enough to amuse herself that way. So saying, he challenged the young Lady to fire again, at a mark; which she readily complying with, lodged a ball at a considerable distance in the center of a bit of white paper the breadth of half a crown. In this she beat him; he allowed her superiority, saying it was ten thousand pities she was not a *man*. Never mind that, replied *Theodora*; my papa always told me, I should *turn* to one: of which I make not the least doubt, replied he. So ever after she had free liberty to use fire arms.

One day, when her sisters and she were innocently amusing themselves in the garden, a private door into it opened; when, who should appear to their astonished view, but that dear, long absent mother, who so tenderly loved them, and was so deserving of their best affections. Nature, here, worked powerfully, and presented a scene of tender distress, that drew tears from every one present. They all three at once gave a loud cry, and flew to the extended arms of that beloved parent, who willing to embrace all, knew not which to give the preference to; till the conflict too great, and her joy too abundant, it had like to have proved fatal. She was deprived of sense and motion for a while, but when recovered from her faint, O! mamma, mamma, and my poor, dear children, was re-ecchoed a thousand times; she folding them alternately to her maternal breast, they falling on their knees, imploring her blessing, at the same time, beseeching God to bless and spare her to them, and to grant a reconciliation between their papa and her, that they might again enjoy the blessing of a mother's protecting love.

Theodora unfortunately had let her governess lock up the jewels that her father had given her, or she undoubtedly would, now, have presented them to their right owner. But to prevent a possibility of this, the governess shut herself up in the house, nor would she let any one come into it, till her lady was gone; a trouble she need not have been at, for the Countess would not have put her foot into it, had it lain wide open for her reception. All the token poor *Theodora* could give her mother of her affection, was to cull her choicest flowers, of which she formed a fine nosegay. In return, the tender mother gave her daughter some salutary advice, which *Theodora* thankfully received, and stored in her mind, as a valuable acquisition.

Night coming on, it was found necessary that her Ladyship should leave them; sure parting was never more moving. They all caught hold on their mother, while her affections divided between them, caused her streaming eyes to turn from right to left, and left to right, a thousand times, before she could consent to quit them. They (in their turn) hung about her, unwilling to resign that happiness they but for a moment had enjoyed. At last the friends that came with the Countess, and the servants that waited on her daughters, were obliged to interfere, and lend their assistance in parting this fond mother, and her hapless children. They at length effected the separation, but not without having the air rent with their cries.

When the Countess of *Volpont* was gone, the doors were opened to receive her daughters, whose governess saluted them with the most abusive language, with the tack, every now and then, of, O! my *money*, my *money*, my Lord will never pay me my *money*, now I have let your mamma see you. In this frenzy she continued all night. The next day the agent was sent for, and acquainted by her with this dreadful disaster, which she did not fail to conclude with her usual lamentations. Damn you, and your *money* too, replied that gentleman, where's the crime, that a mother has seen her children? I should think it a much greater, had she not attempted it; and so would my Lord too, if he was let to think for himself. But now I think on't, you are excusable; being an old maid, you can have no conception of the force of maternal love. Take care, my dears, said he, turning to *Theodora* and her sisters, not to be old maids; for they are always cross. This was all the satisfaction she got; who, in order to exculpate herself from future blame, wrote a full account of what had past to *Jago*, who she knew would not fail to communicate it to the Earl.

Soon after this affair, at the earnest request of a gentleman and his wife who lived in *Dublin*, the young Ladies were permited to go with their governess to pass some time at their house; where they were received, and treated with the utmost humanity and respect. This Lady had been acquainted with the Countess in her grandeur, and retained for her a very sincere regard; which gave *Theodora* frequent opportunities of dwelling on the favourite subject of her mother's goodness, and unmerited misfortunes, never failing to draw the tear of compassion from the eyes of her friends.

The Countess heard where her children were, and that the two youngest were indisposed. Alarmed at this, she came to the house of her friend, and sending in her name, intreated admittance; this was immediately granted, tho' contrary to the will of their governess. Her Ladyship, for a few days, enjoyed the pleasure of seeing and being almost constantly with her children. Their governess was so disturbed at this indulgence, that she insisted upon taking them back to the country; though it was judged dangerous to remove the two youngest, who were then very ill of an ague.

A physician, who was brought to them by their mother, declared it was hazarding their lives to take them away at that time. But all remonstrances were to no purpose, with that mercenary woman, who would sooner have run any risque, than that of losing her darling *money*. So to the country she took them, tho' the young ladies had like to have died on the road. Of this she made a merit, and took care, ever after to prevent their holding any correspondence with, or seeing their mother again, not allowing them even to go nigh a window that looked to the road.

The agent being one day to dine with them, took *Theodora* into the garden with him, signifying that he had something to say to her in private. When there looking carefully about, least there should be any listener near, he said, Lady *Theodora*, I have the pleasure to inform you, that your mother has obtained a decree against your father, notwithstanding all the illegal steps he took to destroy her.[38] She came into court herself, drest all in white, emblematic of her innocence, and there pleaded like an angel.

The reader may imagine how pleasurable this account was to *Theodora*. She expressed her joy in such lively terms, that the agent was obliged to request she would in some measure restrain her transports, for her own sake; as she might otherwise put it out of his power to be serviceable to her. Their governess she knew might represent matters in such a manner as to have the care of them put into hands, less willing to oblige her than he was, which would give him great trouble. *Theodora* was not quite so simple as not to perceive the necessity of this precaution, and so returned with him, as if she had not heard any thing about it; though the concealment of her pleasure was a task somewhat difficult, and laid her under much constraint.

The Earl of *Volpont* soon after returned to *Ireland*, with some sparks of paternal love, for his daughters, were as yet unextinguished in his breast; which led him to the place of their abode, only attended by his own gentleman, before any one had warning of his arrival. They rode down the avenue; *Theodora* on the first glimpse of her father, from the window where she stood, knew him, and eagerly ran down stairs to meet him. But what was her surprize and concern, when he rudely put her from him, to embrace her sisters? who in reality were not half so glad to see him, or loved him so well as she did. Here what little pride she had was piqued;

conscious to herself that she merited his attention as much, if not more, than those he seemed fonder of. She therefore would not solicit his blessing a second time, but retired, immediately, to her apartment, bursting into tears as she turned from him. Struck with her unfeigned concern, and the tender joyous manner in which she flew to meet him, the Earl sent up one of her sisters to desire she would come down. *Theodora* was too much hurt by the rough salute she had met, not to shew some resentment. She therefore with her duty, returned for answer, "That till his Lordship could view her with the same eyes he used to do, she would not offend him by her presence; that all she asked, was, that he might continue to love her, but the half as well as she had ever loved him." Upon this message all the father burst forth, and coming to the foot of the stairs, he called out in a tone of voice expressive of reviving love, *Theodora*, my dear *Theodora*, Will you refuse to gratify the request of your too fond father? The effect these words had on the feeling heart of *Theodora* was demonstrated in her actions, for she flew rather than ran down, and was in an instant at his Lordship's feet, bedewing his hands with her tears, and imploring his blessing, while he bid Heaven bless her, with a fervour, that shewed he said it from his soul. Striving to raise his prostrate child from her knees, to his arms, he involuntarily fell upon his own, and strained her to his breast, while he bathed her face with his tears, saying, My child, my child, Who could have the heart to be angry with thee? How cruel are they, that would, and did try to set me against thee? But my *Theodora*, little as you deserve it, you have your enemies. However they shall miss their aim; I shall only love you the better for it. May Heaven be praised for that! replied *Theodora*, and you may depend on it, Sir, while I live, I never will willingly do any thing to forfeit your protection and love. I do believe you, said his Lordship.

All this time her governess seemed self-condemned by her visible confusion, and at last, unable to stand it, she retired out of sight, while the father and his children enjoyed a short lived scene of happiness, in the conversation of each other. He asked them about the coming of their mother to that house, of which *Theodora* gave him a circumstantial, and ingenious account, with which he was often affected, even to the dropping some tears. A sure sign that the part he acted, and continued to act towards her, was more owing to others than to himself, whose natural good-nature could have no hand in it, other than through the influence of his wicked, villainous advisers.

In the afternoon (for it was morning when he arrived) he walked into the garden with *Theodora*, and leading her into a walk, the most distant from the house, he began to ask her many questions concerning her governess's behaviour towards her, or whether the agent had provided plentifully for them? To each of these questions, *Theodora* who did not love to give a character behind the back of any person that did not reflect honour to them, made satisfactory answers, such as could not do them an injury in his Lordship's opinion.

The Earl, with some confusion, then asked her, had she heard any thing concerning *Volpont grove*. She answered in the affirmative, and that she was told it was in a very ruinous situation, all unslated, the furniture, most of it stolen away, and that it looked like a wilderness. Whilst she was speaking, she perceived his countenance change, as his mind was differently actuated, until at length taking courage, she said, How different is every thing now, my dear papa, to what it was, when you and my mamma were together! What order, what regularity was then, but now every thing wears the face of desolation and destruction!

That is true, *Theodora*, said he, after a moment's pause, but I will turn over a new leaf, and send the crew a packing: And bring my mamma home again, papa, said *Theodora*, with impatience: I do not know that, said he: Do you think, *Theodora*, after what is past, that she would be friends with me? I do, papa, indeed, replied she, for I am sure, by her manner of mentioning you, she loves you as well as ever. Go, go, said his Lordship, you tell fibs, she cannot love me now. Here he heaved a sigh. Upon my word, my dear, dear papa, said *Theodora*, mamma loves you still.

Here they were interupted by *Jago*, who had been advertised by the old governess of their Lord's arrival. He seemed much dissatisfied at seeing his Lordship and his daughter together in the garden; such *tête a têtes* were no ways agreeable to him, who dreaded more than death a reconciliation between him and his Lady, which these conversations might bring about in a little time. He therefore found it expedient, for the future, to prevent them as much as possible; whereby *Theodora*, from that moment, could never get to speak a word in private with her father, which greatly grieved her, having conceived great hopes of bringing about a re-union between him and her mother.

Theodora did every thing she could, to ingratiate herself with her father, who seemed sensible of her attachment and love to him, and willing, but unable, to answer her intentions. Thus they continued for near a fortnight; when to the great surprize of this young Lady, his Lordship informed her, That *Jago* and her governess, who were both then present, thought it adviseable to send her and her sisters to *England*, but that their governess should go with them.

Theodora, like one thunder-struck, could not speak a word for some moments; but when she had recovered her speech, asked him, What she had done, to deserve being banished from his sight? That could he but know the trouble she felt at his long absence, he would not think so soon to deprive her the pleasure, of being under one roof with a father she so dearly loved. Her words made an impression to her wish, and he seemed willing to comply with her desires which *Jago* and the old governess perceiving, they urged, how improper it was to let them stay in *Ireland*, where they were liable to the seeing their mother, and receiving bad advice from her.

Poor *Theodora* could scarce suppress her indignation at this impudent false insinuation; when looking earnestly at her father, she said, O! Sir, can you bear this? *Jago* not permitting him to make a reply, cried! You see, my Lord, the effect her seeing her mother has already had; and judge from that, what you may in time expect. I think there should be no time lost in sending them off immediately. And I think, said *Theodora*, putting on a lofty air, my papa has great patience to suffer such a man as *Jago* to dictate to him, what is proper to be done with his children; were I a man, I would shew *Jago* he should not dare take such liberty, with impunity.

Very spirited upon my word, retorted he with a sneer, you have not profited a little by your mother's advice. Nor you a little by my father's bounty? replied *Theodora*. Come, come, said his Lordship, interfering, *Theodora*, you go too far. This was mild but *Jago* took care to blow up the Earl's anger against the unfortunate *Theodora*, whose power he saw he had reason to fear. In short, he never rested until he had every thing got ready to pack her off to *England*; which his Lordship encouraged her to submit to, by telling her that he had a very good House within nine miles of London, where she should be entirely her own mistress; that there was a coach, and horses at her command; but that he had a house-keeper, by whom he had a fine boy, of which he hoped *Theodora* would be fond for his sake. This, she answered him she would, but hoped the mother would take no airs upon her. His Lordship assured her, she would not, but would obey her orders, as any other servant in the house.

With this assurance, *Theodora* was quite satisfied, and began to feel her pride flattered, in becoming the mistress of one of her father's houses, where she should no longer be subject to the authority of her old, ill-natured governess who had, on pretence that *Theodora* intended giving them to her mother, returned all the jewels to the Earl, together with those he had bought purposely for her, and her sister *Carina*; but his Lordship was kind enough to give *Theodora* a pair of diamond sleeping earrings, and a repeating watch, telling her, he would take care of the rest for her; which in fact he did, she never having seen them afterwards.

Every thing being in readiness for their departure, *Theodora* took a melancholy leave of all those who appeared her friends; but her dear mother was not permitted to see them, before they left the kingdom, though there was a possibility, from the season of the year, and the uncertainty of the seas, she might never see her children again. The Earl accompanied his daughters himself on board the vessel that was to bring them over to *England*; but soon as they came on deck, unfortunately for them, either his Lordship, *Jago*, or the governess, perceived among the passengers, two or three that were declared friends to the Countess of *Volpont*; upon which they were immediately taken back to *Dublin*, and, in a day or two afterwards, put on board an old, dirty, crazy coal vessel, and committed to the mercy of the waves, in very tempestuous weather, with the wind contrary.

Theodora viewed the dangers they were cruelly exposed to, with a serenity of mind, and composure of countenance, that surprized all that saw her. The other two young Ladies, and their governess, expressed the greatest terror and dismay; at which she smiled, and said, At what are you affrighted? Is there not the same God to protect us by sea, as by land? It is very true, replied her governess, but there is no occasion to tempt Providence. I will allow that, continued *Theodora*, but as I am not accessary to the crime, only submitting to the authority of a father, I look upon it, that whilst I act in conformity with my duty, I am under the particular direction, and care of that Providence, who having all things in his power, can bring me safely out of the most perilous situation. Her governess had nothing to say, in opposition to what *Theodora* had advanced, and therefore dropt an argument, that she was not able to support, though she took upon her to instruct youth.

How careful should people be, in the choice of such, as they intrust with the morals of their children! How often do we consign them to a person, who abstracted from the knowledge of the French, and a few fashionable institutes, are incapable, either by example, or precept, to form their minds to virtue, which is of far more material consequence to them, in their success through life, and the estimation of the good. Not that I mean to discountenance the ornaments of a polite education, which not only render us agreeable to others, but are in reality, a satisfaction to ourselves. I only would recommend it to every one, to let virtue and a thorough knowledge of religion, be the fair foundation, whereon to raise the superstructure of a brilliant and superficial education. If this hint was properly attended to, we should soon feel its good effects, and exchange the froth of conversation, for a solidity, that would add to the glory of the commonwealth of reason, and make an acquisition of many worthy members to society, which it now loses, through this neglect.

A dreadful hurricane ensued, three days and three nights, they laboured to pass the *Head*, but all to no purpose, the wind being full in their teeth; and had they passed it by dint of tacking, they ran the chance then of being dashed to pieces against it; their provision began to grow scant, and they to think it were best to put into the *Isle of Man*; on which *Theodora* insisted, the master of the vessel would return to *Dublin*; well knowing, the money their governess had to defray the expence of travelling, would not hold out, were their course diverted from the destined port; the captain said he would comply with her request, but at the same time, was far from thinking to do so. For in two hours after, observing the ship was still under a struggle, (that would not have been, had she sat full before the wind, which blew fair for *Dublin*,) *Theodora*, suspicious of his intention, went and examined the compass.

This the captain was far from thinking she understood, when, to his great surprize, she said, How could you say, captain, that we were sailing to *Dublin*, when it lies contrary to the point to which you are directing your course? He said, she was mistaken; but she knowing herself in the right, persisted, and told him, if he attempted to take them any where but to *Dublin*, her father, she was sure, would punish him for so doing. On this he complied, and a very few hours brought them to anchor at the Quay in *Dublin*. Happy for them, as the vessel had sprung a leak, and shipped water faster than the pump could discharge it.

They landed about five in the morning, and went to the house of their friend; who, with his family, were thrown into the greatest consternation at seeing them return, after being so long out at sea: they got them proper refreshments, and put them to bed, being greatly fatigued with their disagreeable expedition.

The Earl of *Volpont* naturally felt some concern on seeing the weather so extremely bad, and often repented having sent them, in some measure giving them up for lost. But, the very day they left the country, *Borana* came to the Earl, and, no doubt, used every possible method to reconcile him to a loss she secretly wished he might sustain, having presented him with a daughter herself in a few months after he went to *England* as before-mentioned; but notwithstanding all her endeavours to eradicate the love of his daughters from his heart, he appeared very happy in their having escaped the danger they had been in, and approved very much of their returning to *Dublin* where he determined they should stay till the weather was more settled. In a little time they again sailed, and arrived, in two days and one night, at *Parkgate*.

We now behold *Theodora* arrived at an age wherein she begins to commence actor on the stage of life, and though in fact too young, yet full of the thoughts of becoming her own mistress, (agreeable to the fine promises of her father.)

When they landed on the *British* Soil, they found a coach and six, which, by the Earl of *Volpont*'s order, had been waiting their arrival a fortnight. Their retinue consisted only of their old French governess, and one woman servant which they acquired by their returning to *Ireland*. This servant was an honest, faithful creature, and proved a steady friend to the interests of *Theodora*. She was an elderly, sensible widow, and had lived well in the world; but meeting with a bad husband, was reduced to the necessity of servitude, and having a brother in *London* was glad of the opportunity of seeing him.

When they arrived at *Chester*, they met with several well-wishers to their unfortunate mother, who paid them great respect. They prevailed on the governess to let the young ladies stay there two days; during which they were taken to the play, and a ball given purposely on their account; which was far from being disagreeable to them, particularly *Theodora*, who had not been at a public place since the separation of her father and mother. Several made her presents, and amongst the rest one Lady gave her half a dozen yards of remarkably handsome French ribbon, being just then arrived from that country; and attended by a thousand blessings, and prayers for safety, and happiness, they set out for their father's house near *London*.

They had not travelled far, when *Garven*, (which was their maid's name,) speaking to *Theodora*, addressed her in the usual stile of My Lady; at which their governess took her up short, and said, the word Lady must drop; that the Earl had ordered they should all be stiled *Misses* for the future, – *Theodora*, all amazement, cried out, Good God! what do I hear? My father could never order any such thing: he himself gave me my title, the last word he said to me. Her governess replied, Let that be as it would, she had received such orders from him, and would obey them; and that she, or others, had authority to turn away any one that called them otherwise than *Miss*.

Don't imagine, madam, said *Theodora*, that I pride myself in an empty title; no, I despise it, and should be sorry to find my consequence derived from sound alone; all that hurts me, is, that you, my father, or any one else, should have treated me with so much hypocrisy, and deceit; but, at my journey's end, I shall write to his Lordship an account of your proceedings, and have hopes I shall find it a mere invention of your own, or your tutor, that villain *Jago*. – The governess immediately let her know she must curb her high spirit, for she was not now in *Ireland*. It is but too true, replied *Theodora*; and here, like the most villainous enemy, you level a stroke to undermine the *rights* of my virtuous mother, by representing her children as *bastards*; but this is a country of Liberty, and while I have a tongue, I will justify her character, and assert my own right.

The governess made no answer, but sneered, as if conscious that the hapless *Theodora* should have no opportunity to do what she threatened. – All the remainder of her journey *Theodora* scarce spoke a word, but by her sighs and tears plainly discovered the perturbation of her mind to be very great.

In three days, they arrived at their journey's end, in a pretty rural village. The house was decent, but not large, and only separated by a little parterre from the road; at the left side was the kitchen, as were the stables and other out offices; close by which was a small pond with a gravel walk round it, divided from the road only by wooden pales breast-high.

They were received by the domestics in a manner that indicated they were expected; and shewn into a handsome parlour, that looked into a neat flower garden; but judge of *Theodora*'s surprize, when on a rich flowered silk settee she saw, lying at her length, in a most affected languishing attitude, a beautiful young woman, of about eighteen years old, drest in a straw-coloured and silver-sack, with every other part of her dress answerable; and an elderly gentlewoman, in a white sattin night-gown, flowered with silver, gold and colours, with a large black patch in the middle of her forehead.

Both arose, on the entrance of the young travellers, and the younger of the two welcomed them with an air, and in a manner, that left no room to doubt but that she esteemed herself the mistress of the habitation. Poor *Theodora*, tho' naturally polite, could make no return to their compliments, otherwise than by bursting into tears and falling insensibly into a chair that stood by the door; where she continued for a long time, wholly resigned to a grief, that seemed to strike every one who saw her, with pity, save her wicked governess, who appeared rather pleased with the agony of mind she was in.

Dinner was presently served, and *Lucinda*[39] who was represented by the Earl to his daughter, as no other than a house-keeper, that was to be subject to her command, took, without any ceremony, the head of the table; every one seated themselves, except the disappointed, wretched *Theodora*, who excused herself on account of her fatigue.

Lucinda had a very pretty little lap-dog, with which the sisters of *Theodora* were greatly taken, and paid much court to the mistress, thro' her favourite, while the governess left nothing unessayed, to render herself agreeable to the Lady of the ceremony; whom her tall, elderly, gaudy companion always addressed with "My Lady, and your Ladyship", as did every servant that attended at table; all which seemed an enigma to *Theodora*, much superior to her comprehension.

Tho' prepossessed against *Lucinda* from the splendid appearance she made, and the state she so unlawfully assumed, *Theodora* could not behold her, without a degree of admiration – her youth, her beauty, the elegance of her form, her genteel behaviour, which shewed she had the advantage of a good education, made a very favourable impression on the mind of *Theodora*, who looked at her in a short time with pity, rather than resentment.

To compleat the conquest, a child richly drest, of about nine months old, was brought in by his nurse, who carried it to his mother; but she attempting to take it in her arms, he shrunk back, as if afraid: on which she said, Is it not strange the boy will never come to me. The old Lady said, he ought to be whipped for not going to his mamma. The governess, and her two youngest ladies, each strove to allure him to them, but all to no purpose; he squalled when they went near him. The nurse seeing *Theodora* looked melancholy, and feeling herself prepossessed in favour of the young Lady, brought the child up to her; on which the pretty little innocent stretched out his dear arms towards her, and seemed eager to get to her.

Unable to resist this attack of nature, she fondly took him in her arms, while he wrapt his about her neck and sunk his head upon her bosom. Never was astonishment greater than theirs. Good God! said *Lucinda* to her nurse, did you ever see the like? No, replied she, but I'll answer for it, this young Lady has more good nature, and good humour than any one in the room; which makes the child give her the preference.

Do you think, Miss, said the old Lady (addressing *Theodora*) that my Lord *Altamont* is like your father? To this *Theodora* made no answer, but finding herself grow faint, she asked for a glass of water; which one of her sisters officiously bringing, told her, after she had drank, she had taken the dog's leaving, he having before drank of the same. This, from a sister, was like a dagger to the heart of *Theodora*, who was obliged to quit the room, overwhelmed with grief and discontent.

When *Theodora* was retired from their sight, *Garven* came to her and whisper'd, that there was a person in a meadow behind the garden, who desired to see her. She asked her maid, if she knew him; who answered, she did not as yet know his name, but it was one who wished her Ladyship, and the Countess her mother well; and she would, if *Theodora* pleas'd, attend her to the place he had appointed to meet her at.

The young Lady consenting, the faithful *Garven* conducted her to the place of rendez-vous, where they were met by a young man, who, on *Theodora*'s approach, pulled off his hat, and with much respect, held it in his hand. She, with a gentle but melancholy air, accosted him, saying, You have told my maid, Sir, that you are my friend; if you are sincere or not, I am unable to determine. But alas! to meet a friend in this place, I thought, was of too much consequence to be neglected, which caused me to step a little out of the path of prudence, in complying with your request.

All this time the stranger stood with his eyes fixed on *Theodora* seemingly unable to speak, until a deluge of tears gave vent to his words, by relieving his oppressed mind. At last he spoke. – Oh my Lady! he said, Little did I ever think to see the day, my Lord would send his children to a place where he keeps a mistress; those children, whom I remember him to have so much loved and regarded, that he did not think any thing good, or fine enough for them. It seems you know me then, said *Theodora*; and yet I cannot call your face to my remembrance, nor recollect where I have seen you. That's not to be wondered at, replied the young man, though a domestic in the family; my station as under-cook not giving your Ladyship many opportunities of seeing me. My name is *Cross*.

Jemmy Cross! cried *Theodora*, I now recollect you perfectly; but you are greatly grown since I saw you last. I know you respect my mother. Oh *Cross*! Did she but know where we are, it would break her heart. – What shall I do? – What will become of me? To whom shall I complain? With whom advise? Cruel, cruel father! thus to betray my innocence into the hands of those, who having lost their *own*, will perhaps try to bring me on a level with themselves. The unfortunate *Theodora* then wrung her hands, walked distractedly about, and gave a full indulgence to the most lively grief, in which the honest cook, and tender-hearted *Garven* sincerely joined. –

Come, my good young lady, said *Cross*, moderate your concern, which if you give way to, may possibly destroy your health, and deprive you of life. – Happy, happy, were it for me, said *Theodora*, if it could: No, my dear child, replied *Garven*, you must not talk so; we must live as long as God pleases: You see I am alive, and yet I have gone through more than, I trust, you will ever experience. *Theodora* struck with this sensible and gentle rebuke, gratefully thanked her for it, and said she would endeavour to resign herself to the will of heaven.

Cross then told her, that he thought his Lord had used him ill, by leaving him behind, which he would not have consented to, had he not assured him, that he was to be cook only to himself, and that he would shortly return to *England*, and bring his daughters with him; which *Cross* believing, he rested satisfied that he would fulfill his promise; but finding how much he was deceived, had determined to leave the house, only that he hoped now to be of service to *Theodora*.

He then informed her that there lived near a relation of the Earl's, who had been particularly kind to him, that he had thereby an opportunity of acquainting him with the melancholy situation of their family, and the injustice done to *Theodora*'s mother, which had highly prepossessed that gentleman in their favour. That he would, that night, let him know they were arrived, and he was sure, he was so good a man, that he would do every thing to serve them; as would some others that he knew. Also that he had made her party stronger in that family than she imagined; that as for himself, now *Theodora* was there, he would submit to the authority of no other, and he was pretty sure, all the servants would follow his example.

None but such as are endowed with the same grateful spirit as *Theodora*, can be sensible how much her gratitude was actuated by this nobly generous declaration. She fell upon her knees, and with uplifted hands, for a few minutes, silently adored the goodness of Providence, in thus raising up friends for her in her distress. Then springing up with spirit to her feet, she shewed, with a becoming dignity, the sense she had of the obligation conferred on her by her inferior, and assuring him if it should ever lie in her power, he should amply reap the fruits of his humanity; she wished him a good night, and immediately repairing to the apartment appropriated for her, which was the best in the house, she sent down *Garven* to order something to be got ready for her supper, and brought up to her apartment, determined to begin as she intended to go on.

Every one in the house commended her spirit, and with alacrity obeyed her; she therefore supped like a little queen alone, whilst her sisters and governess, not quite so delicate in sentiment as herself, found vast entertainment in the company below stairs.

At the hour of bed time, *Carina* the second sister of *Theodora*, came up to take share of her bed; *Garven* having told the rest of the family that her Lady's indisposition and fatigue prevented her seeing any one else. Her sister soon falling asleep, the unhappy *Theodora* being left alone, gave herself up to thoughts so perplexing and disagreeable, that she passed great part of the night, before she could persuade herself to submit to nature, which at last growing weary, acquiesced with the repeated solicitations of fatigue: notwithstanding this, the perturbation of her waking mind, transferred itself to her fancy, and busily employed it in the following dream.

"She imagined that she stood on the summit of an high hill, while gaping crouds seemed to pay vast homage to her exaltation, that a creature, in the figure of a woman fantastically dressed, whom she understood to be VANITY, came up to her, and breathing on her, she felt her heart exult at her own superiority; when a parcel of spectres arose, whom she knew to be DISSENTION, SCANDAL, ENVY, HATRED, HYPOCRISY and DECEIT, who taking hands, ran violently against her, and tumbled her down a dreadful precipice into a troubled ocean that rolled beneath; in her fall she thought DESPAIR tried to catch hold of her, and pursued her down, but that HUMILITY, in modest attire, and with gentle aspect, caught her in her arms, and broke the fall, which FAITH, HOPE, and CHARITY seeing, they all assisted to buoy her up, and pointed to a land at some distance where they promised her she should arrive, and find peace, and rest for evermore."

Here *Garven* drawing the curtains of her bed aside, informed *Theodora* it was time to rise for all the family had breakfasted an hour ago; that she had been before to call her, but finding her in a sound sleep, she did not care to awake her; then asked, would she breakfast below or above? Signifying the latter, it was brought to her apartment, where she breakfasted with her sister, who soon after leaving the room, *Lucinda* came, with much civility, to inquire after her health, hoped she slept well, and was quite recovered from her fatigue.

Theodora answer'd with equal politeness, but visible coldness; on which that Lady observed to her, that she appeared very grave: *Theodora* replied, That she had no reason to be otherwise now, though her temper was naturally quite the reverse, but she of late met with what was sufficient to alter it. The other answered, She saw no reason for that; for, she would herself do all in her power to render *England* agreeable to her. That I don't in the least doubt, return'd *Theodora*, and perhaps had I met you any where else but here, assuming a privilege in my father's house, that I cannot think belongs to you, I should prove grateful for your kindness. But – A privilege that don't belong to me, said *Lucinda!* Pray, my dear, what do you mean by that? I mean, madam, replied *Theodora*, the privilege you, or any one else, may assume in his house, only belongs to my mother, who is his lawful wife; then judge in what light I must hold any one who usurps her right.

Your mother his wife! cry'd *Lucinda*; that cannot be: I am his wife: your mother was never married to him; and besides, she is since dead. Whoever told you so, answered *Theodora*, deceived you; the Countess of *Volpont*, my mother, has proved her marriage; and has obtained a decree in the ecclesiastical court, against my father.

Good God! said the unhappy *Lucinda*, you don't tell me so. I certainly tell you true, said *Theodora*, and feel myself inclined to condole with, rather than condemn you, if you can shew me you are ignorant of the crime you have committed, in living with another woman's husband. O God! said she, it cannot be; he swore to me your mother was dead, and that he was never married to her. He also told me, that he had a son by his housekeeper, and that she was to be subject to my command; make his word true in that, and believe the other if you will.

Lucinda now began to give way to a most violent agitation, and walked disorderly about the room, exclaiming loudly against the perfidy of man. She looked so lovely in her distress, that *Theodora* began to relent she had caused her so much uneasiness, and kindly conjured her to bear with patience the misery she had brought inconsiderately on herself. O! said she, if you knew my story, you would not say, I had brought my misery on myself. I was noways accessary to my own ruin. No, no, I am only the unhappy victim to the wickedness of others. I am innocent of any crime.

Theodora endeavoured to comfort her, by saying, it was so much the better for herself, if she was. That I am so, said the other, you yourself shall be judge; and promising that she would give *Theodora* a full account of it all after dinner; she prevailed on her to go down with her, the servant having brought word that dinner was ready: Whereupon she composed herself, and they went down together, to the no small surprize of the rest of the family.

Theodora's anger being now quite subsided, and her pity, as well as curiosity, awakened, she took the earliest opportunity, after dinner, to remind *Lucinda* of her promise. The unfortunate fair-one complied, and retiring to *Theodora*'s chamber (after premising her story with a sigh) began as follows:

The story of L U C I N D A.

I AM the daughter of an eminent and wealthy merchant in the city; there are three sisters of us; my father had some cause to disapprove of my mother's conduct, and has not lived with her for some years; I was, from my infancy, brought up with my grandmother in the country, who spared no pains, nor cost in my education; and, at a proper age, put me to a genteel boarding school; where I made a tolerable progress in my learning. My grandmother having inculcated the love of virtue early in my mind, I knew not what it was to entertain a vicious thought; and was virtuous, as much through habit, as inclination. Hence, I was the darling of that venerable parent, who unable to bear my absence any longer, took me from school when I was about fifteen years old.

I was tall of my age, and my figure, and face such as you see; which, with my being the declared heiress to my grandmother, and the expectancy of a good fortune from my father, naturally engaged the notice of many. I found myself soon surrounded by a great number of suitors: few, however, were approved of by my grandmother, who entertaining high notions, hoped to settle me in a conspicuous light in life: But alas! youth and inexperience do not always listen to the voice of prudence.

There was a gentleman of good fortune, who was held in preference to all the rest by my grandmother; but my young heart had previously made its choice, in a young officer of good family, yet small expectations; which was amply made up in comeliness of person, and delicacy of sentiment. Our love was innocent, sincere and reciprocal; which my dear grandmother discovering, and being a woman of excellent sense, considered with herself, that a mutual agreement of temper, and inclination, might insure my happiness, whilst her higher views in aggrandizing me, might make me wretched; she therefore wisely concluding that a competency of either side would be sufficient, she kindly sounded my inclinations; and I, unacquainted with dissimulation, readily made a confession of my love; to which she generously gave the sanction of her approbation.

Never was gratitude more lively than mine, for her thus gratifying the impulse of my soul; I threw myself at her feet, and testified the high sense I had of her goodness, in words that plainly demonstrated, the excess of rapture my heart felt.

In my lover's next visit, that venerable parent shewed him the great height of her fondness and indulgence to me, by taking him apart, and examining the state of his heart; which finding entirely to correspond with mine, she would not delay any longer his happiness, by keeping him in suspence; but informed him instantly, that she freely gave her consent to our union, which she would communicate to her son, and endeavour to obtain his consent also; which she fancied, as her's was already given, he would not refuse.

After making a proper acknowledgment, for such an unexpected, and unmerited condescension, the dear youth flew to me, in a rapture of joy, not to be described. – He clasped me to his faithful breast, where his fond heart, big with the expected bliss, seem'd as though it would break its prison, to unite more closely with its partner; whilst on my part, I sought not to conceal the share I took in an ecstacy, which promised a succession of delight for the remainder of our lives.

In this happy state, we continued for two, or three days almost constantly together, unless when decency separated us, to enjoy the sweets of soft repose; when my grandmother received a letter from my father, testifying his desire of having me up to town, to pass a few days with him and my sisters; one of whom, the eldest, he informed us, had made a match for herself, with one Captain *Hales*, and both had teazed him, to let them be introduced to their sister, whom they had not seen since she was a child.

I don't know how it was, but I felt a something of repugnance, to comply with my father's wishes, and did not shew the least desire to see my sisters, which I condemn'd myself for, as they were so desirous of seeing me, and accused myself of ingratitude on this account: But alas! I have since wofully experienced, that it was a sure presage of the ill that was to befall me, through the wickedness of these unnatural sisters; who, it seems, had made a sordid bargain, to sacrifice me to their interests.

Never was trouble so great, nor at that time more apparently unaccountable, than that of my grandmother, my lover, and mine; he could not leave his regiment without permission, or else he certainly would have come with me, and then I had been safe, but it was not so decreed.

My grandmother thinking it a favourable opportunity, wrote by me to my father, on the subject of my marriage, and gave me a handsome purse, to purchase my wedding cloaths to my own taste; flattering herself, that my father would make an addition. A week was the time limited for our separation, which to us all appeared an age; and then, O God! we parted, – never more to meet with the unallayed joy that innocence ever produces. – My lover saw me into the voiture, and yielded unwillingly his darling to the lions.

Here a flood of tears, (in which the tender hearted *Theodora* shared) interrupted the discourse of *Lucinda*; and it was so long before she could get the better of it, that *Theodora* begged she would not fatigue herself too much; and added, that greatly as her curiosity was excited, she would postpone the gratification of it till the next morning, to give her time to recover herself; the remainder of the evening, they passed away tolerably agreeable, and the next morning *Lucinda* came again to *Theodora*'s chamber, and continued her story in the following manner:

I left off at the commencement of my unfortunate journey to *London*; where on my arrival, I was received with an unfeigned affection by my poor father, and an assumed one, by my sisters; who I observed with some pain, not to behave with a proper respect to that worthy parent; who in his turn, appeared not perfectly satisfied with them, which redoubled his fondness for me. I gave him my grandmother's letter, which he read with seeming pleasure; and presently communicated its contents to my sisters, who, methought, eyed me with some degree of envy and disgust, which they however strove to conceal, and frequently gave a sneer at each other by stealth; which wore an air of mystery in it, that a good deal alarmed me, though I knew not for what; for I was far from penetrating into the true cause, and only thought it the mere effect of envy, at my grandmother's and father's too apparent partiality to me.

My father being called out upon business, my sisters proposed to me, with an affected desire of pleasing, to go to the play that evening; which I, after much entreaty, consented to. – Would it had been to my grave! – We went to the play, but I must tell you, before we went, I having informed them that I had a sum of money to buy clothes; they said it was best to leave that and my watch behind me; lest they might be stole from me, in coming out of the house. I readily followed their advice, and they took them, to put them in a place of safety, which they did, I presume for themselves; as I never saw them since.

The gallery was the place they chose to go to; where we were not long, before an elderly well looking man, in a brown great coat, by appearance a common grazier, came and seated himself by me; at which my deceitful sisters seemed much dissatisfied, and wished the boorish clown (as they called him,) an hundred times hanged, for taking up a place, that might be filled by some pretty young fellow. My heart, however, was too much wrapped up in the object of my fond desires, to make any distinction of persons of his sex, when he was absent, and was therefore the more reconciled to the rusticity in appearance of my neighbour, who, to my no small surprize, behaved with vast politeness; treating me with sweatmeats, oranges, and such things as the place afforded.

This unexpected behaviour a little surprized me, and occasioned my whispering to my sisters, You see we should not always judge by appearances. In short, my old grazier became quite warm, and whispered such a quantity of agreeable nonsense in my ear, as would be palatable enough, did not the idea of the deserving youth, who was shortly to be mine for ever, engross every atom of my attention.

When the play was over, my sisters, whilst I was returning thanks to my enamorato,[40] disappeared; on which expressing my uneasiness, he offered to protect me, till I found them; this offer I readily accepted, and he took my hand. On coming into the street, he cried out, There they are, I see them getting into that coach, make haste, and we shall get quickly up to them; which (I little suspecting the villainous plot against me) believing, went as fast as I could. Perceiving the door of a nobleman's coach open, to which he was going to lead me, I stepped back, and would have fled; when I found myself violently seized upon, gagged, a handkerchief tied over my eyes, and forced into it. I would have shrieked, but could not; I struggled, but it was in vain to resist the superior force of many.

The coach drove very fast, and went a good way before it stopped. When, quite ignorant of the place to which I was taken, they carried me up two pair of stairs; where I was no sooner arrived, than I was charged by an unknown voice, not to attempt making a noise, lest worse should befall me than what was intended. They removed the gagg from my mouth, and permitted me to see, by the light of two wax candles, that I was in a very handsomely furnished room, with a bed in it.

I found myself attended by two female servants, who told me, they had orders if I committed the least outrage, to keep me in proper subjection; but they might have saved themselves this trouble, for grief, despair, rage, and vexation, instead of driving me into any extravagance, had in a manner stupified my senses, and deprived me of speech. I stared wildly, without knowing at what I looked. I heard them speak, yet seemed to know nothing that they said; and at last fell my whole length upon the floor in a swoon, where I lost all sense and recollection. Happy had it been for me, I had never recovered from it; for with the return of reason, came the sense of my own misery.

I now found a gentleman busied about me, drest sumptuously in scarlet, almost covered over with silver-point d'espagne;[41] he seemed extremely anxious for my recovery, and whenever he spoke, his servants answered him by the title of my Lord. At the unexpected sound of dignity, curiosity made me raise up my head, to examine this unknown more attentively; but judge what was my astonishment, when I beheld my old grazier metamorphosed into a Lord. When he found there were certain signs of my perfect recovery, and that I began to bewail my unhappy situation, he gave the signal, and his servants disappeared; he then seated himself by me on the bed, and taking my hand, he said,

You see my charming girl, the trouble I have been at to obtain you; I laid aside my dignity, and assumed a character far beneath me; for which don't let me be lowered in your lovely eyes. No, said I, I don't think you demeaned by the dress you wore, but that demeaned by you; for tho' you were the greatest personage in the land, the title only serves as a cloak to conceal the basest of villainy. You ought to blush at thus degrading your rank by your actions, rather than make it your boast. As for me, I belong to another; my heart and hand are the promised right of one, who is possessed of the greatest honour, and integrity; and who, tho' no Lord, I prefer to the greatest that ever was; then know that sooner than submit to do any thing that may render me unworthy his love, I'd die a thousand deaths.

A very heroic speech, truly, says his Lordship, tauntingly; but pray my dear, don't be deaf to your own interest? Would you not like better to be a Countess, than live in obscurity all your life? By my soul I would not, replied I. Well, well, said he, if your love is so very much fixed, I have no objection to your becoming his wife. Then said I, with warmth, may heaven bless you, send me to my father back again. Don't mistake me child, said he, I mean hereafter, you will then be wife good enough for any rascally plebeian in *England*. If you think proper to give your heart, I'll make you a Countess, child; if not, why, when I have enjoyed your *person*, you may give your *heart* to the fellow that prevented you from making your fortune. Good God, exclaimed I, is it possible, there can be such wickedness in the world? What you call wickedness, my dear, replied his Lordship, I will assure you, does not bear the appellation among the knowing part of mankind.

We had a great deal more of this sort of conversation; 'till at last he grew quite angry, and swore a dreadful oath, that if I did not by good will, he would compel me by force, to comply with his wishes. Upon this, I threw myself upon my knees, and implored him to pity me; but this humiliating posture only seemed to inflame him the more. He had recourse to force; I struggled with all my strength; at length exhausted, I fell a hapless sacrifice to his passion.

I continued for a long time without sign of life, or motion; so long indeed, that he began to fear I was in reality dead; that the punishment due to his crime, would overtake him; and was actually, as he afterwards told me, thinking to provide for his safety by flight; when I discovered some signs of life; at which he was quite overjoyed, and expressed it by the most tender and endearing expressions imaginable. But Oh! just God! What tongue can tell the distraction, the horror, that seized me, when I found myself ruined beyond redemption: my tears and lamentations might have moved the most flinty heart.

For three days I denied all manner of sustenance; a fever ensued, which seemed to baffle all the skill of *Jago*, his Lordship's surgeon, which was all the assistance the nature of the circumstances would allow, he being your father's bosom friend. – At the mention of this hateful name, *Theodora* shook her head, and *Lucinda* asked, Did she know him? She answered with a sigh, But too well; it is that gangrene worm that hath gnawed through the peace of our poor family; but of that hereafter: Pray, Ma'm, conclude your melancholy story: which she reassumed in the following manner.

Let *Jago* be bad or good, I believe he has skill in his profession; for, contrary to expectation, and even my own will, he, under Heaven, preserved my life. Shame now forbad my return home, as innocence before incited me to wish to be under the protection of my friends. I was polluted, and rendered unworthy the acceptance of the man I loved; so suffered ambition to smother, or rather lull to sleep, the purest and most tender affection.

In the course of conversation with my undoer, I found he wanted money; I had learned from every one that came nigh me, that he was the person he had represented himself to me to be. He had told me that he was a widower, and I formed notions of soldering up my honour, by becoming his wife: I brought him about to my lure, by telling him what expectances I had from my grandmother, and the flourishing circumstances my father was in; all which advantages I had lost through him. The bait took, and shortly after finding I was pregnant, it hastened him to swallow it, and he married me. He soon notified it to my father, as I, by his desire, did to my grandmother but all to no purpose, both making answer, that I was ruined, and they had done with me.

I could not then divine the reason of this, and wondered they were not dazzled by my unexpected aggrandation, but now fear they had too good foundation for what they said; I suppose they knew of his being the husband of your mother, and that she was still living; though both he, and *Jago* assured me to the contrary, and said he had none but illegitimate children, for whom he had made ample provision.

One day when your father, *Jago*, and I were at dinner together in the dining-room, the door flew open; a very genteel well dress'd woman, big with child, made her appearance, and asked his Lordship how he could find in his heart to act so cruelly by her, as not to provide for her in the unhappy situation to which he had reduced her. Tho' added she, I should not wonder at your barbarity to me, when you have treated your wife, one of the best of women, and your daughters by her, so ill, that all the world cries shame upon you. I see you have got a new mistress; to make room for whom, you turned me off; and to get another, you will soon serve her in the same way.

Never was fright equal to mine, at this terrifying salutation. His Lordship repeatedly bid his servants kick the b——h down stairs, which they not daring to do, to a woman in her condition, he himself arose, and in a passion (greater than I ever saw mortal in before that moment) turned the poor creature out of the room, cruelly striking her, and kicked her from the top to the bottom, down the stairs. Her shrieks rent the air, and brought a mob before the door; as soon as she was able, she got into a chair, and went directly to the next magistrate, who sent two of his officers to bring the offender before him.

His Lordship thought to avail himself of his dignity, which he imagined would protect him against an assault of this kind; but he found himself mistaken, for they told him the higher he was, it only served to enhance his crime the more; that the woman he had abused was in danger, and that if she died, or the infant she carried, his being a peer would not exempt him from standing his trial for his life.

When he saw he must submit, he desired a chair might be called; but this they also objected to, saying, they had orders to bring him before the justice, like any other common man; as his actions had demeaned him below the lowest. Away they took his Lordship, one of each side, and made him walk all the way with a rabble at his heels, who hooted at him as he went. This was certainly a very mortifying circumstance, though no doubt what he richly deserved. The magistrate bound him over to appear, in case of death, and to maintain the child, if it survived the ill usage its mother had received. The poor woman was delivered of a daughter in a short time after; he sent the infant to the poor-house; paid ten pounds to the parish, and so got rid of the unhappy Mrs. *Coles*, who by all accounts was a very valuable woman, all to the unfortunate connection she had with the Earl of *Volpont* your father.

He still continued, seemingly, fond of me, and on bringing him a son, expressed the greatest joy imaginable; but I soon found out, to my cost, that he had other mistresses; the ill consequences of which still attend me. Since he left me, I have been told he has a criminal conversation[42] with a poor, mean wretch in *Ireland*, by whom he has had a daughter: (In that, replied *Theodora*, your information is very right.)

My friends, continued she, quite abandoned me. My dear grandmother died of a broken heart, in a few months after the completion of my ruin; being informed by my goodly sisters, that I went off voluntarily with a strange man from the play, with whom I readily struck a bargain, and that they were quite scandalized at my behaviour while there.

I took all this greatly to heart; and to heighten my misery, I found one day a letter that your father had dropped, which taking up, and knowing to be the handwriting of my eldest sister, I opened it: but, O God! what was my distraction, when I found it contained the whole plan of operation practised against me; that his coming to the playhouse, in the dress he did, was the result of their wicked advice and contrivance: but what more grieved me, than all the rest, was, it fully proved to me, that he had possessed us all three in rotation; and that incest filled up the sum of my unwilling transgression; a weight upon reflection too heavy to bear.

I wished myself a thousand times dead, and felt the most extreme anguish of heart, that visibly impaired my health; which my undoer seemed to behold with concern. I sighed incessantly, and grief having exhausted all my tears, a settled melancholy sat on my brow. To do him justice, he strove all he could for a time to raise my spirits, until finding his endeavours vain, he began to grow cool, and to slight me: but now resentment drew the secret from me, that I had, until then, carefully concealed my having the least knowledge of. I reproached him for his perfidy to me, and the villainous conspiracy between him, and my unworthy sisters; but he only laughed at my squeemishness, as he termed it, and said, they were hearty girls, and more desirous to please him than I was; for which reason he had got the eldest a good husband, and would try to do the same for the youngest; but he fancied she had too much good sense to resign her liberty while she had the power to please, and could taste the sweets of variety.

When he found that their wickedness was no longer a secret to me, he had them frequently to his house, and my mother with them; when I had an opportunity of seeing that my father had just cause of complaint against his wife; and reason for viewing my sisters with less love than he did me, when I first came to town. My mother seemed greatly satisfied with the affluent sphere I was in, and argued me into a sort of liking for it; as what will not example do! But the true cause of my acquiescence with my fate, was, that they assured me, my Lord had no wife but me; and bid me not believe any thing to the contrary.

In this disposition of mind was I, when your father left *England*; and continued in it ever since, though I will confess your account has in some measure, raised doubts in my mind.

Here *Lucinda* left off speaking, and *Theodora* perceiving her story was at an end, gave her thanks for the trouble she has been at; and with real good nature told her, she greatly pitied her situation, and was grieved to her soul, to hear the part her father had in her misery. That notwithstanding all, he was her father still; as such, she could not but respect him, and feel the tenderest concern, when ever she heard him spoken lightly of: let it be ever so justly. That her mother was indubitably his lawful wife, let *Lucinda* be ever so prepossessed with an opinion to the contrary; and that time, the rectifier of all things, would convince her of its certainty. But, added *Theodora*, methinks I am interested to know, what became of the young gentleman your lover.

Upon this *Lucinda* blushed, and said he had been to see her, and offered to marry her, notwithstanding she had a child. He told her the engagement she had with the Earl of *Volpont* was not in the least binding; but she thinking otherwise, absolutely refused him; tho' she was sure he loved her as well as ever, and was convinced of her innocence. – But, continued she, there is no depending on man; and tho' now seemingly satisfied that my ruin was not of my own seeking, there might come a time, when he might reproach me with [it.]

I must differ with you in opinion, said *Theodora*, the man whose love could surmount the obstacles his did, must be endowed with too much honour, and generosity, ever to reproach you with a fault, that you were no way accessary to, unless, by your conduct, he perceived your principles were vitiated; and that you had contracted a liking for the way of life you were innocently, and unfortunately drawn into at first. I am sure, were I in your place, I should instantly have accepted his offer, and made it the study of my life, to prove the height of my gratitude; by making him one of the best of wives, and sincerest of friends.

O you are quite refined, said *Lucinda*, in your notions; I dare say, I satisfied him as well, if not better, than if I had complied with his ill-judged, request. This speech discovered too much of levity in it, to be agreeable to *Theodora*, who, in her own mind, concluded the request was indeed ill judged, and that the infatuated lover had a very happy escape by her refusal. For she had reconciled herself to vice; and as she herself said in the beginning of her story, her virtue being but a habit, she with ease exchanged it for another.

She presently discerned the change in *Theodora*'s countenance, which from bearing the most visible marks of compassionate softness, became cool and reserved. Her behaviour, which before wore the air of freedom, and confidence, was now supplied by that of constrained civility; and from that moment, *Lucinda* envious of the superiority that young lady had over her, in the possession of that virtue she had lost, formed notions of bringing her on a level with herself, and conceived an implacable hatred for the innocent *Theodora*, over whom she assumed the most intolerable authority.

Her envy was, not a little aggravated by the respect paid the daughter of the Earl of *Volpont*, by the servants, and by some of the Earl's nigh relations; who whenever they came, which was often, enquired for her, and her sisters by their proper titles, and particularly if they were alone; at which times *Lucinda* was obliged to retire, perfectly convinced that this precaution was on her account.

Lucinda's great imperiousness was soon hardly bearable; they had news that a great law-suit in Ireland was likely to go hard against the Earl;[43] whereupon the husband of *Lucinda*'s companion, on pretence of serving the Earl, prevailed upon *Theodora*, to lodge what plate was in the house, in the hands of a friend of his, who would return it to her, or her father, when the danger was over. This she at first objected to, saying she had no authority in the house, and therefore wondered at their asking her to do any such thing; but he, his wife, and *Lucinda*, in this particular, yielding up the power to her, and at the same time saying, that if the execution of this design was delayed, the plate would all be seized upon, whereby the Earl would be a loser, she at last complied; and went with it, accompanied by that gentleman, to a friend of his in London, where she deposited the plate; for the receipt of which, there was an acknowledgement given under his hand, to whose care he intrusted it, with a promise to return the same when called for.

This promise and acknowledgement her conductor took care afterwards to get from her; nor is it improbable but this affair was made use of to hurt *Theodora*, with her father, and represented to him as an act of her own; tho' she, in reality, was only the instrument, in their hands, to answer their own purposes; while she thought she was acting for the interest of her father, and preserving for him, what they said he otherwise run the risque of losing.

When this was accomplishe'd, *Lucinda* treated her with an indignity no longer to be brooked. One of the footmen calling *Theodora* always by her title, whenever he mentioned her, or answered her, was to leave the house; he suffered her to pay him his wages, but would give no receipt but to *Theodora*, whom he requested, before *Lucinda*'s face, to give him a discharge, as having lived with her father, saying he would not degrade himself so far as to own he ever served such a creature as *Lucinda*.

Now dissention grew to a great height; no little republic being ever more divided by party than this family. *Theodora*'s party however, was vastly the stronger, she having the good fortune to ingratiate herself with all the domestics. *Cross* the cook sent up whatever was for dinner, or supper to her appartments first; and when she had helped herself as she liked, it was taken to the table of *Lucinda* in the parlour. *Theodora* had won her sisters over to her way of thinking; and their governess willing to keep in with both sides, sometimes took share of the first of the victuals, and at other times eat, in the more humble way, with the parlour gentry, after her young ladies had done. Every one was amazed at the uncommon spirit displayed in *Theodora*; but she felt great uneasiness at her being obliged to have recourse to extremities, and heartily wished herself out of such a disagreeable situation.

END OF VOL. I

Notes

1. The Countess of Hertford, Isabella Seymour-Conway (1726–1782).
2. Richard Annesley, later 6th Earl of Anglesey, Du Bois' father.
3. Arthur Annesley, 4th Baron Altham, older brother of Richard.
4. John Simpson, father of Ann Simpson, Du Bois' mother.
5. Ann Simpson, Du Bois' mother.
6. i.e. she might have married a titled peer.
7. The 1707 Marriage Act (passed in response to the abduction of a thirteen-year-old Protestant heiress, Margaret MacNamara) made it illegal in Ireland for women under eighteen to marry without their parents' consent. If convicted, the man who married her could be punished with three years in prison while those responsible for abducting her could be executed (Power 56).
8. The custom in inheritance was to leave a third of an estate to the widow, a third to the children, and a third to whatever the dead person wished. After early-eighteenth-century changes to inheritance law, this custom had no legal force but was still widely observed.
9. Given the controversy regarding her parents' marriage, Du Bois is at pains to spell out to the reader the legal basis of "Angelica" and "Varilius's" marriage.
10. Arthur Annesley died in 1727.
11. Dorothea Du Bois, née Annesley, was born in 1728.
12. In his annotations, Musgrave identifies this "cousin" as Maurice (Green), Lord Haversham, the son of Richard Annesley's aunt, Frances Annesley.
13. During the eighteenth century the Irish nobility were notorious internationally for their enthusiasm for duelling. For more on the peculiarly Irish culture around duelling, see Kelly, *That Damn'd Thing Called Honour*.
14. The Phoenix Park in Dublin was a common venue for such encounters, especially in the later decades of the eighteenth century, because its large size afforded many secluded spots in which duelling could take place.
15. *Latin*. With no one speaking against.
16. A phonetic rendering of the Irish language expression "a ghrá" meaning "my love."
17. Arthur Annesley, 5th Earl of Anglesey, died in 1737.
18. Charles Annesley, a cousin of Richard Annesley and rival claimant for the earldom.
19. Richard Annesley's sisters, Dorothy and Elizabeth, married a pair of brothers named Green.
20. Fleet prison, London, commonly used in this period to house debtors and bankrupts.
21. Musgrave notes that Richard Annesley's sister Elizabeth married Maurice Green, Lord Haversham, in 1737.
22. Mr Ians, a Catholic surgeon and close friend of Richard Annesley.
23. Juliana Donovan, later Annesley.
24. A procuress.
25. The character Benevolus may be a flattering portrait of John Annesley, one of the claimants for Richard Annesley's titles upon his death, and an ally of Du Bois'.

26 Du Bois uses the fact that Juliana Donovan's father kept a "shebeen," an illegal drinking establishment that sold unlicensed ale, as evidence of her low birth. However, Juliana was a member of the ancient and noble lineage of O'Donovan, descended from Donal Oge na Cartan, and her uncle, Richard Donovan, was a wealthy landowner near Camolin.
27 According to the Bible, Ishmael was the first of Abraham's sons born to his wife's handmaiden Hagar.
28 *French*. A colloquial expression (literally, a stagecoach that has becomes stuck in the mud) that suggests someone who gets hopelessly bogged down when completing tasks.
29 Dulcinea is Don Quixote's invented lady in Cervantes' novel, who embodies an idealised womanhood.
30 *Slang*. A mistress or prostitute.
31 An ancient Assyrian queen who ruled Babylon and who was represented in Christian legend as lustful and incestuous. In Dante's *Inferno*, she appears in the second circle of hell within the Temple of Lustful Shades.
32 A corrosive liquid made of saltpetre that dissolves metal.
33 A type of lantern.
34 This is presumably a veiled reference to Ann Prust, the woman Richard Annesley had married in 1715.
35 Musgrave's note on the identity of the Primate is illegible, but this is almost certainly Hugh Boulter, Primate of All Ireland from 1724 until his death in 1742, who was a supporter and confidant of Ann Simpson according to Du Bois in *The Case of Ann Countess of Anglesey* (see Appendix B).
36 James Annesley (1715–60), son of Arthur Annesley, Lord Altham, and nephew of Richard Annesley. In 1728 he was kidnapped and forced into indentured servitude in America, allegedly on the orders of his uncle Richard in order to clear the line of succession. In 1741, James reappeared in London and began a years-long effort to regain what he believed was his rightful title from his uncle. Though he became something of a cause célèbre, inspiring a biography by Eliza Haywood, *Memoirs of an Unfortunate Young Nobleman*, and a chapter of Tobias Smollett's *Peregrine Pickle*, he died disappointed and destitute.
37 Migraine.
38 This is likely a reference to the 1741 suit Ann Simpson took in the ecclesiastical courts against Richard Annesley for Cruelty and Adultery, which Du Bois refers to in *The Case of Ann Countess of Anglesey* (see Appendix B).
39 Likely Du Bois' representation of Ann Salkeld or Saulkeld, another woman who claimed to have been married to Richard Annesley. In the Dublin trial of 1772 to determine the rightful successor to the earl's titles her sister, Catherine Buntin, testified that the marriage occurred in August 1742, that a son Richard was born in 1743, and that Ann died in 1749 of consumption (*Minutes of the Proceedings . . . Viscount Valentia* 3–4).
40 *Italian*. Correctly, "innamorato," meaning lover or sweetheart.
41 A luxurious form of Spanish needlepoint lace made with silver thread. Notoriously, Richard Annesley appeared at a London trial against James Annesley in 1742 (for accidentally killing a man while hunting) dressed in "a birth-day suit of scarlet and silver point d'espagne" in order to intimidate witnesses into a conviction (*An Abstract of the Case. . .* 43).
42 I.e. adultery. Criminal conversation referred to a form of civil action a husband could take against a man for monetary damages who committed adultery with his wife.
43 This is likely a reference to the lawsuit brought by James Annesley against Richard Annesley challenging his right to his title, which was tried in London from 11–25 November in 1743.

THEODORA, A NOVEL

In two volumes.

Vol. II.

By the Right Honourable
Lady Dorothea Du Bois

Adversity's a school, – wherein we're taught,
To form and regulate, the growing thought.
The AUTHOR.

LONDON:

Printed for the AUTHOR, by C. KIERNAN, in Fullwood's-Rents, HOLBORN.

M.DCC.LXX.

THEODORA,

A

NOVEL

AT the conclusion of our first Volume, we left *Theodora* in the midst of party and dissention, raised in the family on her account. The servants were all inclined to serve her before *Lucinda*, which naturally heightened Madam's jealousy, and piqued her pride, in so much, that, every day, her enmity to *Theodora* gathered new force; and gave that unfortunate young Lady fresh cause of dissatisfaction. But to proceed with our story:

Theodora frequently wrote to her father on this head, and made the most piteous complaints to him; but he, either never got her letters, or else was deaf to their contents, until the unhappy young lady was almost reduced to a state of despondency; when one day there rode up to the door a gentleman attended by one servant, both extremely well mounted, and dressed accordingly. He enquired for the three daughters of the Earl of *Volpont*, by their titles, requested he might see them, and as an inducement to make them comply, sent word that his name was *Brutus*; that he was an old school-fellow of their father's, who had heard of their situation, and came purposely to make them a tender of his service.

A drowning person, they say, will catch at a straw; *Theodora* thought that Providence, no doubt, had sent her a friend in this gentleman; who, though a stranger to her, she immediately admitted, and received with a grateful transport; saying, thank heaven! she had now found a new friend! This gentleman's appearance and figure fully answering his assertions, she could have no reason to doubt the sincerity of his professions. He was tall, lusty, and well looked, seemingly above fifty.

He accosted *Theodora* with great respect, and politeness; expressed with warmth his concern at seeing her in such a place as that; wondered much that his old friend *Varilius* would let such a charming young creature live one moment under a roof with a wretch that had been subject to his brutal will; and who, no doubt, would leave no scheme unpractised, to withdraw her from the paths of virtue. He therefore advised her, with the cordiality of a father, not to listen to the evil council of an abandoned woman, but to be strictly on her guard, not to make acquaintance with any one that was on a footing of friendship with *Lucinda*; (whose name he had enquired, as not knowing it) particularly of the male sex, as it might prove of the most fatal consequence to her honour.

These salutary instructions were so pleasing to the unsuspecting *Theodora*, that she (never considering that the devil can *preach*, though he cannot *practise*) readily believed all he said, to be the mere dictates of the ripened understanding of a worthy man, attained to by long experience. She thanked her monitor, with becoming grace; and as dinner was just ready, prayed him to take share of it. This he readily agreeing to, they dined; their governess bearing them company from the first, by *Theodora*'s desire; who never chose to receive any gentleman, without such present as might prevent any insult being offered her.

After dinner, *Brutus* declared, he was so attached to their interests, that he would, if he could find one, take a lodging in the village where they lived, on purpose to be nigh them, on any emergency: he therefore proposed to take a walk in search of one. This *Theodora* not readily assenting to, her governess told her, she and one of her sisters might go, and that there was not the least impropriety in so doing. So with the sanction of her old directress's approbation; she, with her sister *Eliza*, went with the gentleman, through the garden the back way into the town, that they might not be seen by that *whited wall*, as he called *Lucinda*; whom he saw by chance, he said, as he came in.

The way lay through a meadow, and as they went, the little *Eliza* diverted herself, with picking up daisies and butterflowers. *Brutus* took this favourable opportunity to launch forth into *Theodora*'s praise; but she, ever a foe to flattery, told him, she always suspected the sincerity of those, who too highly praised her self as generally partial; but that her glass, more honest than he, had never presented her with any thing in her own face, or form, that seemed to merit the smallest admiration, or in the least, served to inspire her thoughts with vanity; which she as much despised, as she did its abettor flattery. This sentiment so pleased *Brutus*, that it put him quite off his guard; and catching her in his arm, he pressed her, in a manner new to *Theodora*, with rapture to his breast, and swore she was the loveliest creature in the world. But to his no small surprise, extricating herself from his disagreeable grip, she gave him, in return for his fine compliment, a pretty smart slap on the face; saying, no man should dare to treat her with such freedom, with impunity; that she imagined him a friend, and that the disproportion of their years, she thought, exempted her from any assaults of that nature; but she was glad she had in time found out her error.

More amazed now than ever; he begged a thousand pardons; said, that her youth, her innocence, her wit, and personal accomplishments, were sufficient to warm the breast of an anchoret;[1] but that he would, for the future, lay such restraint on his wishes, as never more to offend her. He swore he was glad he had made this experiment, as it fixed him in the opinion, that her virtues and her prudence as much surpassed her years, as did her sense; which, he foresaw, would, one time or other, gain her the admiration of the whole world. In short, he made so many handsome apologies, and seemed so concerned, for the offence he had given, that *Theodora* promised, on his never attempting the like again, to think no more of what was passed. No lodging being to be had, they returned home and drank tea;

after which, he took his leave with profound respect, leaving *Theodora* perfectly satisfied, that he was a very worthy, honest man.

This *Brutus* made them frequent visits, until at last, he ventured to request, they would fix a day to dine with him at *Hampstead*. (They were now grown quite familiar with him; that is to say, the two youngest Ladies and their governess; but *Theodora* always kept him at a very great distance; and though the rest refused not some trifling presents from him, he never could prevail on her to accept of any thing.) His invitation was accepted by the governess, whom he promised to treat with claret, of which she was extremely fond. The day was fixed. *Theodora* being always fond of riding, chose to go in that way; and proposed that the rest should go in a one horse chaise, to be led by a servant, while the steward attended herself. Every thing being got ready, and the day arrived, they set off.

Theodora being a good horsewoman, she and her attendant arrived at *Brutus*'s a quarter of an hour before the rest; he received her with vast civility; and an elderly woman appearing, she told the young Lady, that it was best to walk upstairs, to adjust her head dress. This she acquiescing with, the woman helped her off with her riding coat, and went to hang it up behind the bed; on which *Theodora* said, there was no occasion to hang it up there, as she would want it in the evening. In the evening, replied the woman? Why I understood from the Captain, you were to stay here all night. What Captain? cried *Theodora*. Why, Captain *Brutus*, said the woman. It is the first I heard of it, answered the other; but pray, madam, be so good as to give me my Joseph;[2] and tell me how long he has been in your house. About a fortnight, or three weeks, replied the woman: *Theodora* thanked her for the trouble she had given her; and taking her coat in her hand, went down stairs, hearing her sisters come to the door.

While *Brutus* was complimenting them, she took the opportunity, without being observed, to speak to the steward, charged him not to drink, to keep within hearing, and to have the horses ready at a moment's warning. All which he promised faithfully to observe; and she returned into the room where *Brutus* and the rest were; but in a situation of mind easier to be imagined than described. Her fears were alarmed, her suspicions roused, she dreaded she had inconsiderately plunged herself into a difficulty she hardly knew how to extricate herself from, and was uncertain of the event.

All these quick revolving in her mind, and yet obliged to conceal them, for fear the discovery might prevent her putting her desires into execution, she appeared as composed as she could; and soon after, an elegant dinner was served; she strove to eat, but could not; the agitation of her mind was too great, to suffer her to eat or drink with any degree of appetite.

During the time of dinner, she observed *Brutus* took care to ply her governess well with claret, and that she began to be intoxicated; at which she was greatly troubled. He endeavoured to make this young Lady drink, but besides her natural aversion to liquor, she was now on her guard; and all he could do, she would not take more than one glass.

But now, gentle reader, judge the terror and dismay that struck the heart of *Theodora*; on seeing three tall, ill-looking fellows enter the room they were in, who saluted *Brutus* with great familiarity, by the title of Captain. – Oh! thinks *Theodora*, if such are your intimates, surely you are all highway-men; she thought it now high time to decamp; for which reason she got up, and walked about the room, during which time she heard one of them give the following play-house whisper: Egad captain, she's a delicate bit, a delicious morsel! The other bid him hush. – At this instant, *Theodora* being near the door, laid her hand on the lock, on which *Brutus* started, and asked where she was going? Only a little way, said she, with a forced smile, and a significant free nod of her head; I'll be back again presently. – Interpreting her meaning to be quite different to what, in truth, it was, she was suffered to withdraw, without difficulty.

She put on her riding-coat, and hat, the instant she left the room, and looking for the steward, found him in readiness with the two horses. She clapped her foot in his hand, and mounted, before any one had taken the alarm; when the capering of her Rosinante[3] brought *Macheath*[4] to the windows, who, immediately with his gang, rushed out of the house, each attempting to lay hold on her; but she avoided them as well as she could; and her guard being by this time mounted, she put her beast to its full speed, and her attendant drawing a pistol from his holster, bid them touch his lady if they dared, and so saying, followed her. They were presently out of sight, and kept the same pace till they got home, which was better than four miles, inclusive of a disagreeable heath.

When *Theodora* alighted, she was unable to stand, it was then when the danger was past, that she felt the effects of her fright. As soon as she got into her own room, she fainted; and when recovered, she wept bitterly, which eased her a little; next she fell on her knees, and gave God the glory of her preservation, beseeching him evermore to bless, protect, and keep her in his faith and fear. Her trusty maid had by this time learned the cause of her agitation of spirit, and said she had a good mind that morning to put a stop to their visit; but she had no notion there could be any danger as they were all together.

Theodora hearing her say this, asked what reason she had for it; she replied that the day before, the servant of *Brutus* being in the kitchen, he asked her how old her eldest young lady was; that she answering, between fourteen and fifteen, he replied with a smile, oh! that that will do well enough; my master loves a tit bit. She asked him his reason for saying so; but he answered he did not know; and on her asking him a second time, he said his master seemed to like her, and he did not know but it might be a match; only he feared she would think him too old for her. Her servant agreeing with that, said, she hoped her young lady would get a better husband; on which the discourse dropt; but she declared it raised some distrust in her, particularly as she had hints given her, from whom she would not tell, that he did not go by his right name: moreover, that he had formerly been a member of the *hell-fire* club;[5] which was the wickedest society that was ever instituted, and consisted of the most profligate men in the kingdom. *Theodora*, upon hearing this terrifying account, ordered herself to be denied whenever he came; which her servant promised to do, and also to give it to him *tightly*, as she termed it, the first time she saw him.

While they were thus discoursing, the governess, and the two other young Ladies arrived; the latter extremely frightened on *Theodora*'s account, and the former totally deprived of sense through liquor, which *Theodora* beheld with concern; and when every other person, laughed at the ridiculous figure she made, could have wept at the scandal it reflected on her sex.

Nothing certainly can be more odious, than the sin of drunkenness; nor a greater insult to humanity, than to deprive it of that reason, that distinguishes it more than form, from the brute creation. It is degrading in men, but abominable in women, thus to swallow an enemy, that robs them of every guard to virtue, and renders them liable to the insults of tasteless lust. In my opinion, the woman that grows enamoured of this vice, is a bane to society; and should be held in a greater degree of detestation, than the common prostitute, who is free from it. For she who seeks not to stifle reason by the fumes of liquor, has a chance of one time or other seeing her errors, and reforming. But drunkenness is seldom or never to be conquered; and leaves its votaries a hapless prey, to the brutal desires of every villain.

Theodora's sisters informed her, that when she was gone, *Brutus* stormed like a madman; and so soon as his horse could be got ready, with his companions, went in pursuit of her; that as they did not meet them in the road, they were afraid the ruffians had overtaken her, and carried her to some other place, but were quite overjoyed to find that she had escaped.

The next day he came again to see them, when the faithful *Garven* went open mouthed, to give him his promised salute. She told him her Lady was not at home to such a villain as he; and that she had given orders to be denied, whenever he came. She reproached him with his wicked intentions, gave him to understand she knew who he was, and mentioned the honourable club, of which he had formerly been a worthy member. He cursed, swore, damned, and called the poor woman, by the most opprobrious names. As soon as he had sufficiently vented his spleen upon her, and found there was no further chance of success, in the villainous scheme, that was laid against the innocent *Theodora*, he boldly took off the mask, and dismounting, without any ceremony, went into the house; where he was received as an intimate acquaintance, by *Lucinda* and her mother, who was then with her.

The black conspiracy was then explained, and viewed with horror by all; As for *Theodora*, she would not after that, walk even in the garden alone. *Lucinda* now sent orders to the kitchen, at the peril of the cook, and servants, not to let the victuals go up to *Theodora*, until she had first dined; but they not heeding her threats, were carrying dinner up to *Theodora*, as usual, when she intercepted, and forced it to be brought into the parlour. After she, and her friends had dined, it was sent up all cold and disfigured. The young Lady's spirit, however, could not brook to eat after such persons; and her sisters following her example, put up for that time with a dinner of dry bread. The next day, *Cross* having sent word when dinner was ready, *Theodora* and her sisters went into the kitchen, had the cloth laid, dined there, and then sent in the meat to madam.

The landlord of the house, hearing how they were treated, having been before to see them, came again, and brought with him plenty of provision from *London*, which he ordered to be put into the best larder, and the key given to *Theodora*; who was now a strong housekeeper, and had her dinner every day an hour sooner than *Lucinda*.

The worthy landlord, sent them fresh provisions twice every week, at which, they were quite happy for some time. But this transient felicity was of short duration; for one Sunday being at church, and having left a quarter of lamb to be roasted for their dinner, they returned at the hour they expected it would be ready. But how great was their surprise, and resentment, when they found their meat was seized by the parlour gentry, who it seems liked it better than their own. To perfect this larceny, they had broke open her larder; and left them not so much as a bit of bread to eat, but what they had swept away.

When they found the young Ladies were returned, *Lucinda* and her companions, by way of apology, set upon *Theodora*, and gave her such abusive language as she was little acquainted with, and quite incapable of returning; on which, she attempted to retire to her apartment: But behold, all the doors were locked; and she was made to understand, that if she did not keep them company, she must sit for the future in the kitchen with the servants.

Carina and *Eliza*, cried bitterly at this usage; *Theodora* did all she could, to persuade her sisters to comply with their desires, and not to mind her; but this they would by no means consent to; whereupon she proposed, to take a walk into the village. This they readily agreed to; the three unfortunate sisters went out together; and passing by their laundress's house, the good woman perceiving their eyes red with crying, demanded, with concern, what the matter was. *Theodora* informed her, at which she was so much touched, that she invited them into her cottage, and made them a tender of what it afforded, which was bread, and butter, she having already dined upon short commons herself. *Theodora*'s heart was too full, to suffer her to eat; but believing her sisters might be hungry, she said she should be obliged to her, if she would give them something; and she had the pleasure, to see them eat very hearty; which shewed the proverb true, Hunger is the best sauce.

While *Theodora* sat revolving in her mind, what she should do, a sudden thought struck her; on which she entreated the good woman, to give the young Ladies her sisters house room, until she returned, which would be soon. She had heard a very great character of a gentleman in the village, one of the people called quakers; and though she had never seen him, but in his carriage, when he passed, and repassed the house, she dwelt in, she determined to go, and make her complaint to him; and to implore his protection and assistance, in the desperate situation to which she was reduced. So, with a courage seemingly supernatural, she went boldly up to his house, and demanded to see its master; sending up word, that she was eldest daughter of the earl of *Volpont*, who would be obliged to him for his advice, in a matter of some importance to her. The worthy, humane man readily admitted her, and when she appeared, eyed her with some attention; then addressing her in a manner that shewed the goodness of his heart, he said, It seemeth thou art the daughter of that wrong-headed man, the Earl of *Volpont*. I have often grieved, that thy youth, and innocence should be exposed to the temptations of vice, that dwelleth under his roof; I shall therefore gladly do any thing in my power to serve thee, on thy shewing me, how I may assist thee. *Theodora* thanked him for his condescension, in words that proved, he would not serve an ingrate; at the same time discovering a modesty, which powerfully attached the good man to her interest, and prepossessed him in her favour.

She gave him a brief account of all her unhappiness, from the separation of her father and mother, to that moment. When she had concluded her narrative, he said, My poor child, thou art hardly treated in truth; but thou shalt not lose thy dinner to day, if thou wilt take share of mine, with my wife, my son, and daughter. This *Theodora* begged he would excuse her doing, as she could not think of feasting, while her sisters were fasting. The hospitable Quaker now seemed still more to admire her, for her sisterly affection; and ringing the bell, begged she would inform his servant where to find them, that he might bring them to her; saying, that he could not part with her, until he had considered, how he might serve her effectually.

Carina and *Eliza* were soon brought; and did not a little wonder, how their sister came acquainted at such a fine house. They had an extreme good dinner with, to *Theodora*, the most grateful sauce, that of a hearty welcome. All the family seemed possessed of goodness itself, condoling in the most friendly manner, the miserable state the suffering innocents were in; and each starting methods how to relieve them. At last their generous host concluded to represent the affair to the Lord Chancellor, through his secretary, who lived almost opposite to his house, and with whom he was very intimate; saying, that he thought it was best, to apply to the fountain-head; that the Chancellor was the father of the orphan, and though the father, and mother of these were living, they might be considered in the light of orphans. Also that he made no doubt, he would force the Earl of *Volpont* to make good the settlement he had made on his daughters, and then take care they were properly provided for.

Their persecutors at home, soon heard to whom Providence had directed their steps, and began to dread the consequence of their making friends; which it were impossible to avoid, if *Theodora* had an opportunity of communicating, in her own artless way, the miseries she endured. They were certain, from the general character of that gentleman, that she had not been kept to dine there, had he not perceived something in her that was worthy his notice. He was good, he was charitable, he therefore had the inclination to serve them; and he was in the possession of a fortune, that furnished him with respect; and gave his representations a weight, that insured success, to whatever he engaged in.

Such was the person, to whom the good genius of *Theodora* led her; to the no small astonishment, and dismay of her enemies. She returned home after tea in the evening, first making the due acknowledgment, for the favour conferred; and receiving a general invitation from that family of peace, unanimity and concord, with whom they passed the most agreeable day they had in a great while.

It seems that *Garven* had, in the absence of her young ladies, exerted herself in their behalf, as did the steward, cook, and others of the domestics, declaring she would join, in representing the melancholy case of these poor young Ladies, to their Lord, and let him know, how basely they were used. They reproached *Lucinda* and her mother, with being accomplices with the villain *Brutus*, in forming a scheme for the ruin of the innocent *Theodora*; to which she must inevitably have fallen a sacrifice, were she not under the particular guardianship of a GOD, to whom they, through their wickedness, had renounced all claim.

Guilt, ever timid, and dastardly, made them quietly resign to *Garven* the keys of *Theodora*'s apartments, which she had in readiness for their reception; with an account of what had happened in her absence; and also, informed her, that the steward begged leave to speak with her. To this chearfully consenting, the honest man was admitted. This man had been servant to the landlord, and entered the Earl's service on his taking that house. When he appeared, *Theodora* said, My maid has acquainted me with the obligations your humanity lays me under, in taking part with the wretched and forlorn; but I should be sorry, if the least disadvantage should accrue to yourself, from your attachment to my interest. Therefore, pray inform me, Is it in the power of the people below to hurt you? No, my Lady, replied he, it is not; if it were, I am sure they would; I could wish your Ladyship were as little in their power as I am; which I cannot think you are, while they are under one roof with you. But, where is the remedy, my good friend? said *Theodora*. You know, I am moneyless, and of consequence friendless. That you shall not, said this honest man, while I can supply you: I have a little, saved through frugality, which is at your service, while it lasts.

This uncommon instance of generosity, said *Theodora*, is too, too much for me to bear. O! God! why is it not found where abundance is? Why does not ability and inclination go hand in hand? I am as much obliged by the offer, Sir, as though I accepted it – a thing I can never do, because uncertain when, or if ever, it may be in my power to return the obligation. I have my days before me. – *Adversity* and I may become reconciled to each other; but you are entering into the vale of years, and I should look upon it worse than robbery, to make use of those little savings, that may be of use to you, if the infirmities, attendant on age, should overtake you. The steward was a sensible man, and for some moments could scarce credit his ears, that such sentiments, as he said, should proceed out of the mouth of inexperienced youth. This compliment not being intentional or studied, gave *Theodora* a secret satisfaction; but at the same time occasioned a confusion inherent to modesty, which caused her to turn aside her head, to hide the crimson blush of diffident merit; that chose not to betray a love of praise, even when most tolerated; which certainly that, founded on the conviction of our senses, must be. But *Theodora* was an avowed foe to flattery, and did not greatly like praise, notwithstanding the vast distinction between them; the foundation of flattery being *insincerity*, *hypocrisy*, and *deceit*, offering up incense to *pride* and *vanity*, while that of PRAISE is raised on TRUTH and REASON, and tributary alone to MERIT.

The steward continued his discourse, saying, that there was now a good deal of rent due, which not being paid with that exactitude promised on taking the house, it was in his master's power to re-enter the premises, and clear it of its present nuisances; which he had hinted he would do, if they continued to ill-treat *Theodora*. This good man therefore advised her to go the next morning to that gentleman's house in town, and acquaint him with their late insult, which he was certain he would soon find means to rectify. He then said he would have the chaise ready for her at eight o'clock in the morning, and wait upon her there himself. *Theodora* seeing reason in his advice, she did not long hesitate in following it; and this matter being settled, he respectfully bid her a good night, and retired.

The night being passed rather disagreeably, by the intrusion of melancholy reflections, *Theodora* rose earlier than usual, and before the rest of the family could prevail on themselves to resign the soft ligatures of the pillow, she drove herself to *London*, attended by the trusty steward. The landlord, and his lady were greatly surprized at seeing her so early in the morning, and judging all was not right, impatiently enquired the cause. On hearing which, agreeable to the steward's conjecture, he said he would soon remedy these evils. So saying, he prepared to set off with *Theodora*, for the country, where they arrived a little after breakfast-time. They were all in confusion at hearing that *Theodora* was gone to town; but much more so, when they saw her return in company with that gentleman, who, on entering the house, took possession of it, seized all that belonged to the Earl of *Volpont*, in, and about it, for the arrears of rent due, and then desired madam, and her retinue to decamp immediately.

This was a very unexpected turn in their affairs, who before looked upon themselves absolute monarchs of this little domain; *Theodora* begged hard that the little child and his nurse might be left there, as she grew to love him extremely; and was fond of the woman for her honesty and good nature; she never having joined with them in the ill treatment they gave her. But this they would, by no means, agree to; so off they went, bag and baggage, in a few hours time. The good land-lord put *Theodora* in the peaceable possession of every thing, leaving her the entire mistress of the house, and afterwards supplying her with provision for her family.

Now *Theodora*, like one released from a heavy burden, began to breathe; and to look upon herself in some degree happy. Youth soon loses the impressions of grief; it seems but as a summer shower, that dries away, as instantaneously as it wets, by the beams of the sun, and drought of the earth; the former by its intense heat exaling, and the latter greedily soaking up every particle of the refreshing moisture. She communicated her happiness, which she was short-sighted enough to imagine durable, to her hospitable neighbour, the worthy Quaker; but he more experienced in the casualties of life, and capriciousness of fortune, said, that notwithstanding the flattering appearances, with which the young *Theodora* seemed so much elated, he would pursue his first plan, and endeavour to get them out of the hands of a father, that was so little attentive to their well doing. That he looked upon it, that the settlement he had made on them, removed all the natural dependency of children on their father; which was a happiness for them, since he inclined not to take better care of them than he at present did.

He thereupon consulted with a relation of theirs, upon this affair, both jointly addressed the Lord Chancellor's secretary; and acquainted him with all the particulars of their insecure situation. The latter soon made it known to the Chancellor, but the intention began to take air; at which the friends of the Earl of *Volpont* were alarmed, and instantly determined to prevent the execution of a project, that would expose the irregularities of the father, and establish the rights of the daughters. Whereupon, about nine o'clock at night, there came a coach and six, into which the unfortunate young Ladies, with their maid and *governess* were hurried; without being acquainted why or wherefore. To prevent the servants from penetrating into the secret, of the place of their future abode, one was told, they were going to another of the Earl's seats; a second was made to believe, they were going to live with their aunt in the country; and a third told, as a mighty secret, that they were to be sent back to *Ireland*. But they were otherwise to be disposed of; for they arrived at ten o'clock at night, at their father's house in *London*; where they had been some months before, at the desire of their aunt, Lady *Avremont*.

The door was opened in the dark, by the maid servant, who was left to take care of the house; and who had been kitchen-maid to the Earl when in *London*. When this poor creature found who her unexpected guests were, for she could not see them, the coach driving away, so soon as they had alighted; she cried out, with great distraction, Good God! What do they mean, by bringing the Ladies here, where there is neither coals, candles, bread, or even salt to be found? As for my part, I am next to starving, my board-wages are so ill paid; nor have I a single farthing, to bless myself with.

On this, all but *Theodora* set up the most dismal lamentation, that added not a little to the horror of total darkness. On which she said with great composure, to her *governess*, I should have expected, madam, that you, to whom the care of our youth was entrusted, would rather, by your example, strengthen us, to bear up under such trifling trials as these, than thus increase the terror of those, whose small experience cannot be expected to have attained to a perfect resignation to the divine will. Crying will not remedy the evil, but increase it the more; we should rather think about administering a cure.

Ay, replied her *governess*; you are always preaching. It is certain, madam, returned *Theodora*, I, in that, incroach upon your prerogative; for it is from you, advice should come; and I should endeavour to follow it. Had you done your duty, I should not have spoke, but listened with attention. This reproof had no other effect on her old tyrant, than to cause her giving a very rude answer, not at all to the purpose. This so displeased *Hannah*, the servant that received them, that she bid the young Lady not mind her; and said, she found herself, so inclined to love and serve her, that if she thought, she could take a long walk, at that hour of the night, she would take her to the honestest person, with whom her Lord had dealings; and she was sure he would point out some method for their present relief. This being absolutely necessary, as not one of the whole family had the burthen of one penny about them, *Theodora* chearfully consented to go any where, that there was a probability of finding one willing to administer to their relief.

She therefore went directly out with the young woman, beyond *Lincoln's-Inn Fields*; who brought her to one of the Earl of *Volpont*'s attornies, whom she had before seen, when with her aunt. This gentleman was greatly surprised, at the cruel treatment they received, and very much affected with their necessitous situation; to mollify which, he gave *Theodora* a guinea, which she thankfully received; and flew rather than walked home; so impatient was she, to share her riches with her fellow sufferers.

In their way, they purchased candles, bread and butter, together with a pint of wine, to comfort her old *governess*'s heart. In short, they returned laden with their spoil. They were likewise fortunate enough, to find those still up, who could furnish them with coals. Then in a rapture of joy, she rapped at the door; which was opened to her, by the disconsolate *Garven*; whom embracing, she said, Come, chear up your spirits, my dear *Garven*, God Almighty has sent us a friend in our necessities. She then flew to her sisters, and did not even exempt her ill natured *governess*, from a participation in her caresses; as joyous and thankful to her Creator, as though she were the possessor of millions. To put the old Lady into good humour, she likewise gave her all that remained of this wonderful *guinea*; never having received one before, that was half so welcome, or seemed to possess so many properties.

From this night, they all subsisted, with very great œconomy it must be allowed, upon a *guinea* a week, paid every Saturday, by the master of an inn, in *Piccadilly*: a very proper person, no doubt, to be guardian to young Ladies of their quality! But *Theodora* was soon reconciled, to this manner of living, and her two sisters were still too young, to be sensible of their misfortunes; so that time glided on agreeably enough. *Theodora* was too fond of reading, to feel retirement disagreeable, or time hang heavy on her hands. Her favourite amusement, was walking; but that in places, the most abstracted from company. She admired *St. James's-Park* greatly; but the throng that were continually there, made her hold the *Green Park* in preference to it; where, about the basons,[6] or down by the Queen's library, she and her sisters, walked almost every day.

One of these days, being *St. Patrick*'s, (her ingenuity having furnished them with crosses, composed of artificial treffoil, so near nature, that it could not be distinguished from the real, unless upon a near examination,) they all went to take their morning's walk, with these badges of patriotism on their left sides, which they took care to display to the best advantage. The singularity of three young creatures, two in white frocks, with no attendants, attracted the eyes of every one who met them, but more particularly, drew the attention of two Ladies; of whom *Theodora*, being deeply engaged with *Milton*'s paradise lost, took no notice. However her sisters, begging they might go down by the Queen's library, withdrew her eyes for a moment from the book, when she saw an officer pass by these two Ladies, with *chapeau bas*,[7] to open the gate through which they were to pass; at which instant, the three sisters coming up, he politely held it open for them also; which made the respect paid to the other Ladies the less observable.

Theodora dropping a step or two behind her sisters, renewed the superlative pleasure she took in her beloved book; in which her every wish seemed concentered, to such a degree, that she did not at first perceive that the tallest of the two Ladies before mentioned, addressed her; until the gentleman seeing her inattention, came up, and gently tapped her on the shoulder to awaken her from her rêverie. Finding the incivility she had been guilty of, she made a proper apology. The Lady then asked her, whose daughters those two fine young Ladies were? At which *Theodora* found herself hurt, and imagining they took her for a domestic, she raised her head with a haughty air, and said, They are my sisters madam. I beg pardon, returned the Lady; then pray, if it is no offence, whose daughter are you? That of one of the first Earls of *Great Britain*, replied she. On which the Lady smiled, and turning to her companion, said in French, She is very smart in her answers. This *Theodora* understanding to the full, as well as she did her own language, answered her in the same tongue, Certainly, and so should we all be, to live in a world like this; and so saying, walked past her.

A croud now coming from *St. James's-Park*, they all stopped with great respect, and stood out of the path, until the Lady who followed *Theodora* went by. At this being greatly surprised, she ventured to ask who the Lady was? But judge of poor *Theodora*'s confusion and shame, when she was informed, that it was the Princess,[8] whom she had answered in so laconic a stile. It was too late, to make an apology, her Royal Highness being gone too far to overtake her; and then she considered with herself, that to make one, when she discovered who she was, were taking a greater liberty, and perhaps might offend more, than what was said, through ignorance of her rank.

The Sunday following, their *governess* took them to the chapel royal, which being very full, they were obliged to stand at the rails of the communion table; whereby they were the more conspicuously seen by every one, and particularly the royal family. The Princess soon distinguished them from the croud, and seemed to know them to be three sisters she had seen in the park; of which she had no doubt told, on her return to court; for she first whispered a Lady behind her, and then leaning towards her royal father, she seemed to particularize the spot where they stood. His Majesty[9] smiled; and then communicated the news to another of the Princesses; and presently the eyes of all the royal family were entirely fixed on them, but more particularly on *Theodora*; who perceiving it, was ready to sink with confusion; and would rather than all the world she was out of the chapel.

When the service was over, she made her way out as expeditiously as she could; which her *governess* encouraged her to do, having observed the particular notice taken of her, and fearing that enquiry might be made into their situation, which might possibly tend to their advantage. *Theodora*'s fear of having given offence to the Princess, did not a little assist to make her, for once, act in conjunction with her enemies, against her own interests; for else she would have esteemed the royal notice, the greatest happiness that could have befallen her, let it be engaged in what manner it would. Of this she was, when too late, convinced; being afterwards informed, by mere chance, that there was a person sent immediately after they were gone, to make enquiry who they were. Their governess took the hint, and was careful never after to let them have the like favourable opportunity; where we shall leave them awhile, to look into the melancholy situation of their father and mother.

The Countess of *Volpont* had prosecuted her cause against her Lord, with the utmost vigour and success; in which she was powerfully supported by the church. The Earl, as though Providence meant it as a punishment for his breach of faith, and cruelty to his Lady, was cast in his great law-suit; to which his character and treatment of her, in no small degree, assisted. By this we may observe, that propriety in our actions, and the acquisition of a good name, not only reflects the highest satisfaction to ourselves, but in a great measure secures to us our property.

Possession may truly be adjudged eleven points of the law; it was in reality the only friend the Earl now had. So prepossessed was the world against him, it seemed ready to believe the very worst that malice, or even falsehood could invent to his disadvantage; wishing to see him despoiled of that affluent grandeur, of which he appeared in its eye, unworthy. Never was man more hampered than he was, on every side; cheated, imposed upon by every individual, with whom he had the least dealings. But all was insufficient to bring him to a right way of thinking; or incline him, by a change of conduct, to change the ill opinion mankind had conceived of him. In short, he chose rather to lie under the odiums cast upon him, than resign one of his darling vices, tho' to the restoration of his fame, and the peace of his unhappy, injured family.

The unfortunate Countess, notwithstanding the wrongs she had sustained by her Lord, felt the most poignant concern at the injuries offered him, and took his part with as much warmth as tho' she had received none herself. This occasioned a Lady of great consequence, with a private present, to send her a hint, that she had better not interest herself in the cause of an unworthy husband; but wisely, with the generality of the world, SALUTE the rising SUN. This, the Laws of nature, truth and honour forbidding, she generously adhered to her first principle, and loudly exclaimed against the enemies of her Lord; which added a double lustre to a noble act done by the *supporter* of their common adversary. Who, hearing that her Ladyship had been insulted by the person with whom she then lodged, for the non-payment of a trifle of rent; in consequence of the trial going against the Earl of *Volpont*, inclosed her a bank-note in a blank letter; which extricated her from her difficulty, and enabled her to quit a place where she had been so ill treated, without letting her know from whence proceeded the obligation.

There could not possibly be a more striking instance of the delicacy of this gentleman's sentiments, than the manner in which he then relieved this lady; his own nobleness of disposition making him judge, that if she knew from whence the benefaction came, she would, tho' starving, have refused it, and he had missed his aim; which was to serve her rather than fix in her mind an idea of his disinterested generosity. The offer would no doubt have made her admire the man, but her spirit would have made her reject his favours; which she had not stood in need of, had her *friend*, her *benefactor*, we may say, her *father*, the PRIMATE been then living.

This great and memorable man was advised by his physicians to try if his native air would not restore his health, and relieve him from a lethargic disorder, that for some time had attended him. Accordingly he went to *England*; but held a constant correspondence with the Countess of *Volpont*, and assisted her as long as he lived. A short time before his death, he informed her that he was quite recovered, and had sat for his picture, which he had before promised her; that he hoped he had rendered her some service at court, and then referred her for particulars to his meeting her in *Ireland*, which he said would be very soon.

The poor Countess, who reverenced this good man as a father, and in fact had found him one, was greatly rejoyced at the news of his recovery, and was every day expecting and praying for his safe arrival; when to her unspeakable grief, and eternal loss, she was informed of his death; together with the aggravation of her being, in some measure, the innocent cause that the world was too soon robbed of one of its most shining characters. He was alas! her friend, and therefore was his sudden, unexpected end. His protection was too great an advantage for her long to enjoy, and his power too evident not to be dreaded.

He had a servant, who had long lived with him, and by his experienced fidelity, and known integrity, was become dear to him. He was treated by the *Primate* as an humble friend, rather than a servant. This worthy creature always went, thro' excess of love, and care for his medicines, and constantly administered them to his Lord. But one day, unfortunate we may call it for the world in general, but for the Countess of *Volpont* in particular, having been for a composing cordial, of which his *Grace* was to take only a single spoonful, at going to rest, he was met by some of the Earl's servants; who expressed great joy at seeing him, and intreated he would go into a *Tavern* just by, to take a glass of *wine*. The poor man was not quite willing to accept the invitation; but imagining they might give him some inteligence of their Lord with which to entertain his own Lord at his return, he complied. They told him a world of news, which he eagerly swallowed, with a too potent dose of the elevating grape, until his brain became unawares intoxicated. His state of acquired insanity prevented his perceiving that his joyous companions had examined the bottle of cordial, and slipped away the label, perhaps by accident, no matter, but so it was.

Tho' not very perceivably drunk, yet was he rendered incapable of knowing well what he did; in which situation he returned home, his head full of the accounts he had of Lord *Volpont*. There he communicated to his *Grace* while putting him to bed; when the deluded servant taking the cordial, and not finding it labeled, poured it all out into a vessel, and brought it to his beloved master; who, on seeing the quantity, said, he thought he had been ordered to take but a spoonful; the other answered he was surely to take it all, or else there would have been directions to the contrary. Thus over-persuaded, this excellent good man, drank his death; and was wafted to these regions of bliss, where joys unutterable awaited him.

With returning day, came the collected senses of his faithful domestic; alas! to make him but the more acutely feel for the dreadful consequences of his late mistake, which he was as yet a stranger to. Seeing his dear Lord in a fine sleep, as he thought, he would not disturb him; but finding his nap uncommonly long, and awfully still, his error shoots thro' his mind like a ray of lightening. He calls his Lord, but no answer; that angelic voice tuned to christian mildness, was gone to sing the praises of a loved CREATOR. He louder calls, and louder still, then in a gust of wild despair, that frantic sorrow soaring beyond the boundaries of reason, he raises in his arms the lifeless corpse, and by rude shaking, thinks to recall the heavenly spirit from its blest retreat. Now finding every effort fruitless, he motionless sinks upon his master's breast, to all appearance dead himself. But that was a mercy he was not as yet suffered to partake; his senses again returned, and he launches into bitter accusation against himself; he beats his venerable head, he smites his breast, and calls a thousand times on death to snap in sunder his knotty thread of life. After the rage of sorrows past, behold he resigns himself up, a prey to settled melancholy, refusing any sort of comfort.

Tho' not equally outrageous, yet not less afflicted was the Countess of *Volpont*, for the death of this great man; whose goodness she ever after held in the most grateful remembrance, paying a tributary tear to his memory, whenever she heard his name mentioned. Had he imagined himself so nigh his summons to eternity, he would no doubt have left her, what would at least, have defended this unhappy Lady, from absolute want; to which she was frequently reduced, without creating pity in the breast of him to whom she had once proved a useful support. She was refused all communication with her children, not so much as allowed to hear from them, nor knew she where to direct to them; a perfect stranger to their fate, and in perpetual terror lest they should, particularly *Theodora*, be drawn astray. She thought they were with their aunt; but that Lady was not, in her judgment, a proper person to guide their youth; or one, by whose example they might profit much.

In this shocking situation, this poor Lady remained until the government took her case into consideration, and granted her a pension on that establishment;[10] seeing that her Lord continued obstinate in the obvious, and elegible design of starving the woman he once so loved, and to whom he had been so much obliged. So soon as she found herself mistress of this trifling pittance, with an eagerness that did honour to the maternal name, she tried all she could, to discover how her children were disposed of; determined, if they were in need of her assistance, to share her scanty provision with them. In this laudable pursuit, we must therefore leave the Countess of *Volpont*, and return to the hapless objects of her fond attention.

They had been frequently, at that Lady's request, to pay their respects to their aunt *Avremont*, the sole indulgence they had. Her increasing fondness for them, greatly engaged the affections, and actuated the gratitude of her three nieces; but more particularly that of *Theodora*, who grew to love her sincerely, as well from inclination as duty. It is true, they were secluded from the world; but retirement was now grown habitual to them; which plainly appeared by *Theodora*'s dislike of a croud, and her haunting the then unfrequented walks about the bason, or in the wilderness in the Green Park, as was mentioned before. She was in her father's house, it was genteely furnished, they had two good female servants, their allowance was scant, but their food wholesome, and *Theodora* was no epicure. In the midst of abounding delicacies, the Countess of *Volpont* had always accustomed her to make her dinner of one dish, and that the most plain drest. This at first appeared hard, but by degrees became her choice; being so impolite as to hold to her old custom at tables, where there were vast varieties, and where it was the usual method, to eat, or at least, taste, of every thing upon them. High sauces vitiate the palate, many mixtures nauseate it, and from indigestion spring innumerable complaints of head, and stomach, which furnish abundant business for the learned faculty; whose greatest enemy is temperance. *Voluptuousness* begat *lust*, *lust* begat *rapine, rapine murder*, and so on; 'till we by woful experience find "of *sin*, the wages is *death*."

Here, as I was saying, resided peace and tranquility Virtue their Protector, and œconomy their Providore, companions suitable to the innocency of these three sisters. When, to prove that no happiness is durable this side the grave; they were informed, by ten o'clock at night, that the goods of the house they were in, would be immediately seized, that they must instantly leave it, and go to a lodging that was provided for them nigh hand.

This unexpected change was severely felt by *Theodora*; who, for some moments could not speak, or scarce believe what she heard could be true. At last she lifted up her hands to heaven, and with eyes brimful of tears, which grief's clear fountain fast supplying, rolled plenteously down her cheeks, she cries, Oh my God! to what will they at last reduce us? poor unhappy creatures as we are, thus to be tossed from place to place, the tennisballs of fortune, in the hand of wanton Fancy. When, Oh! when shall I find a place of rest and safety? This however was but a prelude to her distress, when she understood that her trusty, faithful, honest *Garven* was to leave her, as they were now to have but one maid, and that *Hannah*, no choice being left to the wretched *Theodora*. The steadiness of her friendship was now put to the test; submitting to make the most humble requests, that she might continue with them whatever was their fate. She even condescended to go upon her knees, in order to obtain this one favour. But she sued in vain, she and her beloved servant must part, being too much attached to the interest of her young ladies, to be found a proper person to stay longer with them; and whatever became of that valuable woman, they never saw her after they left their father's house.

If *Theodora* was dissatisfied at her being driven from her father's house, what must she have been, on finding the place they had provided for them to lodge in, was, where they sold *Ramsbury*, and *Dorchester* beer, wholesale and retail? The people of the house were honest, but the man had been a butler to a colonel, and his wife the cook, where they married, and remained until such time as they were able to set up for themselves. What a situation for the daughters of an Earl! But that was not all; if they were only to lodge, it were well; for then they could have kept to themselves, and had no connection with improper company, than which none was vastly preferable. But it was plain they were lowered, not only in their own eyes, but in those of the world also; and for that purpose were put to board with persons whose vulgar conversation, by instilling adequate notions into their young minds, might probably take off all the traces of a polite education; and in the end, prove the wished-for means of inducing them to throw themselves into the arms of their inferiors, when they found no hopes of resuming their former sphere in life. In which notion it is to be presumed, the sensible reader will readily join.

From step to step, behold, our unfortunates sunk, now at the lowest ebb, and on a par with commonality. But *Theodora* still retained her spirit, notwithstanding the care taken to suppress it, and as usual, made her party good with these honest folks. She took her opportunity to make her rank known to them, which secured her their respect; she pictured to them, in such lively colourings, the misfortunes of her family, as drew their pity; and behaved with an affability that engaged their love; without in the least derogating from her dignity. Here she wished to conceal her title, it being inconsistent with her situation to bear it, and contented herself with remembering who she was, so as that she should not, by any action of hers, forfeit the privilege of reaffirming it, whenever it pleased heaven to restore her to her proper sphere. She often chose rather to sit without fire in her own room, when the weather was extreme cold, than be obliged to associate with the mixed company that were frequently drawn thither to drink beer; while her governess and sisters submitted chearfully to this inconveniency, and seemed extremely happy, in the variety of faces this vocation gave them an opportunity of seeing every day.

This manner of living, voluntarily secluded from all the world, greatly increased *Theodora*'s thirst after knowledge; she soon devoured her landlord's little stock of books, and then prevailed on him to borrow for her from all his friends. Those could not furnish her with the quantity, or quality she most admired; so that she had many an hour that lay heavy on her hands. But that even proved of advantage to her, for it gave her a relish for devotion, that a too close application to study often destroys. This is evident from the atheistical principles that we daily see spring from a head too much incumbered with learning, and a desire of exploring hidden mysteries. Being too severely attached to any one point, biasses the judgment, and gives the deformity of obstinacy to conversation; besides which, it prevents the mind often from looking to objects vastly more deserving our attention, than the goal we fondly have in view. To enlighten our understanding within the precincts of christian prudence, is undoubtedly our duty; when to overleap its boundaries, in attempting to know more than we should, becomes sinful. The man who in the exultation of pride, vainly imagines his knowledge infinite, will, I am much afraid, in the end, find it only finite, and to his loss be convinced that he is a perfect stranger to the one thing needful, namely, the true knowledge of God.

The young *Theodora* found immense comfort in the word of God; to hear which she seldom failed once or twice every day in going to church; not to see or be seen, which too commonly is the inducement that brings most young persons there; her eyes and ears were only open to the truths of the gospel, and her whole attention fixed on the Deity, to whom she sent up her warm petitions.

In this disposition of mind, being at evening service, the clerk not there, and no one attempting to make the responses; she stood up, and in a voice modestly audible, took upon her that office. This attracted the notice of all present, particularly the clergyman, who after prayers were over, came up to her pew, and gave her thanks for the assistance she had given; telling her, he had not a little pleasure in seeing her so constant a follower; which was rather uncommon in one of her years, therefore merited the highest praise.

    She answered, that she could not think it deserving of any praise, that was to her the greatest gratification imaginable. So saying, a confusion that prepossessed him still more in her favour, was visibly seen in the face of *Theodora*, who immediately went out of church; she had not reached her home before she was overtaken by the clergyman, who felt a curiosity to know who she was, and, as he afterwards acknowledged, was not a little surprized at seeing where she took up her quarters: But thinking that she perhaps only went in to avoid him, he determined to enquire of her landlord who she was; when being informed by him that she was the eldest daughter of the Earl of *Volpont*, he exclaimed in great astonishment: What, and live here! the other assuring him of it, he begged he might be admitted to speak to them. He said, he was a father himself, and his heart bled for these poor young creatures. On this their landlord reported the clergyman's request, and this worthy man was received by *Theodora*, with a civility that shewed how much she was obliged by his kind notice: She, in fact, had reason to thank heaven for the acquisition of such a friend as this gentleman; as she thro' him got a supply of good books, and a great deal of profitable instructions.

    In about half a year after the Earl of *Volpont*'s daughters went to the *Ramsbury* Beer-house, its master, their landlord, failed, and the person who had them in care, on the arrival of this misfortune to the poor man, wanted to take them away directly, to put them to lodge in some other place. Here *Theodora* interfered, and begged they might stay now rather than ever; as their board might happily be a means of support to him, his wife and three small children, one of whom was but newly born, and help to extricate him out of the difficulties into which he was unfortunately plunged, by unforeseen accidents.

    Her request was granted, the poor people scarce knew how to express their grateful sense of her good nature, while the person who had placed them there, knowing well how disagreeable her situation was to her, stood amazed to see her put such a force upon her inclinations, merely to assist the wretched.

    Her guardian observing this to her, she says, it is true, had I my choice, I would not have thought of fixing in such a place as this; but if I submitted to it, while they were in a prosperous way, would it not be cruel to forsake them in adversity? What they get by us, will maintain us all, until such time as the poor man can settle with his creditors; and then I cannot say, but I should be glad to go to a more eligible place for us to be in; but while they stand in need of what we bring them, I could not leave them without experiencing much dissatisfaction.

    This affair turned out to her wish, matters were soon accommodated, and her landlord's credit once more established; but then she found there was no thoughts of removing, with which she acquiesced, because she could not help it.

    Tho' their board and lodging was as yet punctually paid, there was no care taken to replenish their clothes, which were by this time very much reduced. *Theodora*'s watch, by her own desire, was long since sold to supply her sisters, governess and self, with the common necessaries, such as shoes, stockings &c. But they were worn entirely out, and they saw no possibility of obtaining a single guinea for that purpose, from their guardian.

Poor *Theodora* could not know herself the possessor of a pair of diamond earings, and behold her sisters bare-footed and bare-legged, with scarce a petticoat to put on them: She therefore takes them out, views them for the last time, bursts into a flood of tears, kisses them, saying "Adieu thou last remains of former grandeur, I would not part with thee, but in compliance with sisterly affection: It were brutish to retain you and see them in want."

Then presenting them to her governess, she said, Here madam, you disposed of my watch already, please to do the same by these, to the most advantage you can: get what is needful, for my poor sisters; and if you think proper, I should be obliged to you, for the overplus of the money. The old termigant[11] took them, and gave *Theodora* about the fourth part of what they cost; declaring it was all she could get for them. Though *Theodora* was sensible, that the sum was more than the diamonds could have decreased in value; and of consequence, that she should have had, treble as much for them as she got; she thought it to no purpose to mention her doubts of the fidelity of the vender; and therefore tried to appear satisfied, with what she could not remedy.

She appropriated the best part of the money to her sisters use; and when she saw them equipped to their satisfaction, she ventured to purchase herself a brown camblet night gown, a light brown stuff petticoat, a scarlet cloak, and a straw hat; in which, when drest, she said, Methinks I like this disguise, sure no one can divine, that a title lurks beneath this gear. It was of a Sunday she first put on this fine dress; in which she went to church, in the morning with her sisters, and in the evening, by herself.

When service was over, and that she was opening the pew door to go out; behold, an elderly gentleman, dressed in dark brown clothes, trimmed with gold, came up to her, and saluting her, said, Would you venture yourself, young Lady, with an old man? It is what I never yet did, Sir, replied she, with young or old of your sex; and what I should not willingly do, without very well knowing with whom. Upon the word of a gentleman, returned he, I mean you no harm; I do not want to take you out of your own neighbourhood, being so nigh this, that you can walk it; therefore shall not attempt to put you into coach, or chair: come child, you may venture, you need not fear any thing; and I dare say, you will not repent the confidence I ask you to place in me.

He said this, with such an open, undesigning air, that after pausing for a moment, *Theodora* said, You seem sincere, Sir, I think I will venture. So saying, they went out of church together, walked past her lodgings, eight or ten doors beyond where they had formerly lived. When near the house, *Lucinda*'s affair coming into her head, she was determined to turn back; but a footman at the instant opening the door, the unknown gentleman took her by the hand, to lead her into the house. He now observing her to tremble, said, Do not be afraid, my dear, there is no one here will hurt you; and at the same instant, threw open the back parlour door, which presented to her view, a room full of gentlemen and ladies, most of whom were dressed in laced coats, and gold and silver silks.

Struck at such a pompous glare, *Theodora* shrunk into that nothingness, she had so long been used to; and recoiling a step or two back, begged the gentleman would excuse her going into so much company, to which her dress was not in the least suitable. At last, he insisting on it, she was obliged to comply; when he said, Mother, I here present you with a diamond in the rough; on which an old Lady, one of the finest women of her age in the world, with the most cordial affection, embraced the astonished *Theodora*; telling her she had long wished for the pleasure she now received in seeing her. He then presented her to another Lady, which was his wife, and daughter to the old Lady, then to her maiden sister, and next to his own son and daughter.

After which, *Theodora* being still in the middle of the room, he turned her about, saying, look here gentlemen and ladies, Is not this a pretty attire for an English Earl's lawful daughter? this is Lady *Theodora Altamont* the Earl of *Volpont*'s eldest daughter. Then turning to our heroine, he continued, you see my dear, I know you, tho' you don't know me; however, you shall not any longer remain a stranger to my name, it is *Palimon*; my mother in law, to whom I but now presented you, is Mrs. *Worthy*, and that her youngest Daughter Mrs. Anne *Worthy*. Then leading *Theodora* to the head of the room, he placed her above all the company.

After tea, being a little recovered from her surprise, Mrs. *Worthy* begged she would favour the company with the unhappy story of her family; which *Theodora* could not refuse to a Lady, for whom she had on the instant conceived the highest veneration. She therefore repeated most of what has been the subject matter of the foregoing sheets. The whole company seemed greatly affected, at the sufferings of the Countess of *Volpont*, pathetically described by her daughter. They launched into the highest praises, and approbation of this young Lady, on which the old Lady, with the gaiety of sixteen, said, you told me, son, that you presented me with a diamond in the rough, but I think it is as well polished a diamond as I ever saw, and one that might ornament a crown! I dare say, said he, Madam she will prove a crown to a *good* husband; and I hope, none else will get her, said young *Palimon*. Well said my boy, replied the father, I wish, she would think, you could make her one.

This gave rise to a great deal of mirth and good humour, in which the evening glided swift away, and *Theodora* seeing the company begin to retire, found herself unhappy in quitting them so soon. They kept her to supper, after which desiring her to favour them with her company the next day, they sent her home, attended by one of their footmen.

Now, I presume, my young and love-sick reader, will naturally conclude, from the subject of the last foregoing lines, that we are beginning to enter upon a scene of action suited to the languishing state of his, or her mind. But I must entreat their patience a little longer, the hour is not yet come, in which *Theodora* is to experience the force of that tender passion. Her heart continues still shielded with indifference to the sex, other than that respectful friendship which is inherent to a grateful spirit.

In this charming family she enjoyed vast satisfaction, and reaped great improvement, not only in their conversation, but also in literature. *Palimon* was very polite and sensible, well versant in men and books. He had a very good collection of these valuable conveyancers of knowledge, with which he furnished the young *Theodora*, making her set down her remarks on those passages, that pleased her most; and then support her opinion by argument. This manner of proceeding, brightened her understanding, and quickened her discernment.

He lent her a *Latin* grammar, with which, by the help of the *French*, and a little of his assistance; she soon became pretty well acquainted. The old Lady, when she was to have much company, would give her purse to *Theodora*, and make her sit down to cards, to give her an air of consequence; telling her, that what she lost, her purse would defray; and what she won, would be no burthen to her own pocket.

To this good Lady and family, *Theodora* presented her two sisters; unwilling to taste of any happiness, in which they did not participate. Mrs. *Worthy* was so prepossessed against their *governess*, that she would not admit her into her company; and she in her turn, experienced much uneasiness, at their having atchieved so creditable an acquaintance, though in the midst of their distress, and as she thought buried in oblivion. It is plain, the Almighty had not forgotten these young sufferers; each day, raised them up new friends, to protect, instruct, and assist them.

Theodora had now acquired another agreeable acquaintance, in the widow of a clergyman, whose name was *Arminda*. This lady was a most worthy, valuable woman; and one, by whose example and conversation, she could not avoid being edified. Between Mrs. *Worthy*'s family, the good Parson, and *Arminda*, this young Lady began to pass the time agreeably, and to think herself happy. Indeed all earthly happiness, consisting chiefly in idea, I do not know, but she really was so.

Such evenings as she did not pass with the above company, would *Theodora* sit in her own chamber, in the cold, contemplating the wisdom of the ancients; an amusement to her, preferable to any other. Often has she gone to the chandler's shop, when dark, bought a peck of coals, and some farthing candles, which she has dextrously concealed under her garments, then made her fire, and sat down to her book, as contentedly as though she were in the possession of millions; perhaps more so; for on abundant riches, wait innumerable troubles. When she had the appearance of a fire in the grate, which seldom rose above the second bar, she thought herself particularly well off; and preferred it vastly, to the sitting at the receipt of custom below *stairs*, where she was subjected to hear conversations no ways agreeable to her.

What rendered this last situation still more disagreeable, was, that she had unwillingly attracted the notice of the Captain of an *East-India* ship, who began to pay the most violent court to her, in which he was favoured by *Theodora*'s governess, and the good man of the house; the latter wishing her well, no doubt thought it might be a good settlement for the young Lady, as he was extremely rich. This *Tar*[12] had not the charms requisite to make a conquest of a heart, like to that of *Theodora*'s. His attacks were rude, and unpolished; and his temper seemed to have imbibed the roughness of the boisterous element, to which he was by nature adapted. Come my little snow, would he say, Sit thee down, and let me give thee a broadside; Ah! but Captain, would she reply, I will not come too nigh, lest you should grapple. Grapple, ay! That I will, and board thee too, if I can, returns he; come my dear, strike, and let me be thy captor, and I will make thee as rich as a Nabob.[13]

Such was the manner of this gentleman's address; which together with a fierce look, robust figure, and the loss of two, or three fingers, and upwards of fifty years already over his head, were no great inducements to *Theodora*, to become his wife. Love was yet a stranger to her breast; but fancy assumed so much the appearance of that passion, that she almost had persuaded herself, that she felt it, for a young *North Briton*, that was in the army; who seeing her in the *Green-Park*, reading, was at first, attracted by her manner of walking; and next, unnoticed by her, coming up close to her, was struck, at finding the subject of her meditation, to be one of the classics; which made him conceive no small opinion of her understanding.

Determined in his own mind, to find out who she was; with that intent, he followed her at a distance, that took off all apprehension of what he was about. He saw her enter the beer-house, where he, after she was gone up stairs, also went to bargain for a butt of beer; then carelessly asked, who the young lady was that just then went up stairs? The landlord, unwilling it seems, to gratify the curiosity of such a gay spark, gave an evasive answer to his question, at which, he was greatly vexed; but finding it was to no purpose, to ask him any thing further, our young *Mars* took his leave; For two or three days he never failed going to the *Park*, in hopes, again to meet *Theodora*, and boldly to address her; which she, from the account given her by the landlord, carefully avoided, having observed him follow her, when near her lodging, and recollecting she had seen him in the *Park*. A few evenings after, being desirous to see her friend *Arminda*, the clergyman's widow, she went to her lodging, and when a little time with her, she told her the story about the inquisitive *Mars*. Good God! cried the good lady, how odd this is; your *Mars* under the name of *Mercutio*, is this moment over your head, he lodges in this house; he is a most sensible, charming young man, and is desperately in love with you; he has entertained me ever since, with a sweet girl that he saw in the Park, but told me no further particulars; had he, I could soon have informed him how well founded his liking was.

While she was speaking, her maid brought her this young gentleman's compliments, and if disengaged, he would do himself the honour to drink a dish of tea with her. When *Arminda* answered, by all means, she would be glad of his company: on hearing this, *Theodora* got up and was for going, when her friend insisted on her staying; this she absolutely refused, and would have gone that instant, had he not entered and joined his entreaty to that of her friend, with such bewitching sweetness, and so much politeness, that it was impossible to withstand it.

Dear *Arminda*, said he, you know, I told you about a Lady I saw in the Park; you did, replied she; then judge, continued he, What must be my happiness in finding that Lady in your youthful friend now present; I trust, I shall no longer be ignorant of the name of one, who has my heart in keeping, and who has my happiness in her disposal; a crimson blush instantly overspread the cheeks of *Theodora*, who kept her eyes fixed on the ground, nor dared to raise them, lest she should encounter those of this declared enemy to her indifference: his tone of voice did not, in the least, displease; his figure was unexceptionable; then what had she not to dread from his eyes? She remained silent, while her new conquest was in the highest perplexity, lest an answer should be given that might put an end to his hopes.

Arminda, in pity to their situation (which she was no stranger to) took upon herself to be the interpreter, and therefore adressing the gentleman, told him that if he could make himself agreeable in the eyes of *Theodora*, she could not but say his lot had fallen in a fair ground.

Oh! madam, returned he, 'tis not fortune, it is not birth, I regard; say, is her heart unprejudiced in favour of any other, and I'm happy? Upon my word, replied she, I know of no dangerous rival you can have, unless it be those old musty philosophers, in whose company she passes too much of her time, to spare a thought to anything else; her name is *Theodora Altamont*, she is the eldest daughter of the Earl of *Volpont*, there has for some years past, been an unhappy separation between her father and mother. As to fortune, Oh madam say nothing of that, said he, lest you place the charmer quite beyond my hopes: Say she has none, none in expecancy, to remove some part of that distance the knowledge of her high birth, has placed between us.

My dear *Theodora*, said he, throwing himself at her feet, pardon me, my angel, if I lay by the title which I could wish you had no claim to, (as I fear that will prove the bar to my wishes) can you, dearest creature, condescend to a passionate lover, in the station I am? The choice my heart has made, is my highest recommendation; it is true, I am of a good family, and have friends to facilitate my rise in the army, but my fortune at present is not great. However such as it is, if you will share it with me, I shall, in possessing you, esteem it an abundance; speak my life, Oh! speak, suffer, me at least to hope, by saying you do not hate me.

With that *Theodora* raised her eyes, in token of her gratitude, for such noble declarations in her favour, and looking on him with complacency said, "I don't hate any one" Sir, not even my enemies; how then was it possible that I should hate one, who views me in such a partial light as your unmerited compliments would make believe you do? Thou heavenly innocence! said he, you will suffer me then to live and hope, that I may call thee mine. You are at liberty, Sir, returned she, to interpret my meaning to your wish. A tolerable beginning, I will be sworn, said *Arminda*, come, now ye are both arrived at a proper understanding, suppose we should have a dish of tea? With all my heart said the agreeable *Mercutio* and then imprinting a passionate kiss on the unresisting hand of his mistress, he took his seat close by her side.

This little triumvirate of love and friendship, passed the evening away very pleasantly together, and at the proper time for parting, *Mercutio* saw his adored *Theodora* to her lodging, where he was determined she should not long remain: nor would he quit her, until she had promised to meet him the next morning, in the Park.

Now *Theodora* began seriously to consider with herself, whether or no she could be happy for life with her new spark. She had imbibed a little of the romantick turn, by having, for want of better books, for a time conversed with this pernicious sort of writing. This adventure pleased her, the rapturous speeches of her lover flattered her vanity, from which none of her sex (let them say what they will) are thoroughly exempt. She weighed her *Neptune* in one scale, and her *Mars* in the other; with the former she put his riches and ill breeding, with the other his warmth of passion for her, and his polite behaviour; and found the odds greatly in favour of the latter. To assist which, after passing a night that was entirely given up to the contemplation of his generosity, the next morning, she understood that the landlord not being paid for some time for their board and lodging, had told his paymaster, that if it remained much longer in arrears, he should be obliged to turn his lodgers on the parish; being unable to support them, unless their pension was regularly paid. Their guardian to this replied, that he knew not what to do, that he had already advanced a great deal of money, which the Earl of *Volpont*, tho' he had frequently addressed him on the subject, did not think fit to reimburse him, and he would not give any more on such hazardous conditions.

This news greatly terrified *Theodora*, who dreaded much the disgrace of being turned upon the parish; and with a heart ready to burst thro' grief and vexation, she went to the Park to fulfil her engagement with *Mercutio*. He was there a long time before her, and began to fear she would disappoint him; but when he saw the object of his fond wishes appear, the sight of her soon chased away his fears, and he flew to meet the beloved maid, with an impatient joy that shewed how sincerely he loved her: "Now my angel, said he, I have got you to myself, and have liberty to speak the feelings of my heart, without fear of incurring the ridicule of a by-stander: do not infer from this, my love, that I wish for any clandestine dealings with you, or harbour the shadow of a thought to your disadvantage; No, by heaven! I don't. Nay, if this heart was capable of forming so black a design, I would tear it out of my breast, and offer it up, a bleeding sacrifice, at the shrine of that virtue, I am now convinced, you possess. Had you not met me here, I know not, if I might not have strove to undermine that prudence that might have cautioned you against taking this step; true innocence is never distrustful, and that conducted you hither, to make me its protector as well as admirer.

This noble sentiment (at the same time that it convinced *Theodora* of the honour and worth of her lover) nevertheless gave her a view of her own imprudence, in meeting a person in such a private place, whom she knew so little of; add to this, the impression the word *protector* of her *innocence*, had on one that was so depressed by her morning's intelligence, of standing soon in need of some kind protector or other, to save her from utter ruin, and shame.

She strove all she could, to suppress the high swoln sorrow struggling in her breast, which denied utterance to that gratitude with which her heart was impregnated, towards this second *Bevil* junior.[14] He perceives the agitation of her spirits, and fears she is going to swoon, he seizes her hand between his own, and pressing it with fervour to his lips, he cries, my angel, my soul, my *Theodora*, what is the matter? unbosom thyself to me, my love, let me share in thy dissatisfactions; you have not a friend in the world you may safer trust than me, my affection for thee makes thy interest mine; then why should you keep me from partaking of thy pain, as well as pleasure.

After a deluge of tears, fast flowing from the eyes of the wretched *Theodora*, she begins to find herself a little easier, and yielding to the entreaty of her fond adorer, she tells him the recent cause of her uneasiness; she then said, "You see, Sir, how little worthy I am of your notice, since so of that of a father." That you are forsaken by a father, is his eternal shame, but my glory, returned he, as it gives me an opportunity of proving to you the sincerity of my passion, and hastens the fruition of my hopes. I here open the arms of a husband to receive you, and happily for me, you may now look on my offer as an advantage, which, were you in your proper sphere, I dare not presume to aspire to, tho' a gentleman. Fortune was then my enemy, as much as adversity is now my friend. Why hesitates my love? has your heart any repugnance to become the wife of an honest man? a man that adores you.

Theodora replied, that his generosity was far beyond her deserts; that she had no objection in the least to his offer; but feared it was too precipitately entering into that awful state; that he might perhaps hereafter, on a closer connection, repent his choice; that she thought it prudent to be a little better acquainted with each other's temper, before they united for life. What, cried he; and in the trial suffer yourself to meet with those insults, and disgrace, that you, my dearest life, but this moment dreaded. Yes, said she, but you don't consider that you have removed that dread yourself; what have I to fear, with such an asylum as your arms, to fly into, on the first approaches of such a disaster? If I find it my landlord's real design, and that he persists in accomplishing it, do not imagine, too generous youth, that I will let disgrace lay hold upon me, to render me unworthy your acceptance. No, I will directly go to my friend *Arminda*, and throw myself under her protection, until you think proper to take me under yours; that is to say, if you continue in the mind you are in; after which, I shall make it the study of my life, to make my *friend*, my *benefactor* happy.

Friend and benefactor! What cold epithets are these, my *Theodora*? returned the tender lover. Will my dear *Mercutio*, said she, think I gave you those you wish me to do, but suffer time and a better acquaintance, to bring your *Theodora* to that freedom of speech. But indeed, I cannot so soon adopt it. Dear excellence, said he, I have done, you are right, but tell me, my angel, is that heart of thine entirely free. It was, replied she, till yesterday evening; and then, in the greatest confusion, she fixed her eyes on the ground; which the happy lover interpreting with reason to his advantage, appeared transported to the highest degree, saying, he looked on her from that moment as his own. They left the Park, first promising to meet at *Arminda*'s lodgings that evening.

When *Theodora* returned to her lodgings, she found a lady waiting, to see her; having refused to tell her business to any other but this young lady. On her entrance, the gentlewoman got up with much respect, and said, I believe your Ladyship don't know who I am, but this letter will inform you; on which she put a letter in to *Theodora*'s hand, to which she gave a gentle squeeze, as if to impose secrecy of the contents. But, O GOD! what was her transport at finding it from her mother; however, she strove as well as she could, to conceal her joy, and told the bearer, giving her a wink at the same time, that she was extremely sorry it was not in her power to relieve her distress. Then with an air of consequence, she put the letter in her pocket; and on the gentlewoman's retiring, took it out again, at a distance from every one, lest they should discover the truth. She read a piteous detail of distress, that only existed in her own imagination, of the bearer's name, her being a widow, having six children, being burnt out, and begging the charity of all well disposed Christians.

She put up the letter a second time, every one perfectly satisfied, that she read its full contents, and making their comments on the appearance of the petitioner, which did not in fact, betray the least want, being very genteely drest.

Close beset all the remainder of the day, *Theodora* could not get an opportunity to read this epistle with any satisfaction; her landlord took his opportunity to assure her what he had said to the person who had them in care was far from his thoughts, that he did it, in order to get his money, of which he stood greatly in need. This was a pleasurable circumstance; as an alloy to which, in comes her grim *Neptune*, and was for making her surrender up upon the spot. Out of his grapplers she extricated herself as quickly as she could, and flew to her friends, where her impatient lover, on her entrance, caught her in his arms: but oh! how different from the rude monster, from whom she fled but the moment before; she made no resistance here, nor sought she to conceal the pleasure she felt, at seeing the man she thought it her duty to love.

On the coming of the candles, entreating his excuse, and that of *Arminda*, she took out the countess's letter, and began to read it, during which time her lover fearing it might be from a rival, rivetted his eyes on her face. He found she wept; at which the manly tear started to his eye; he then saw a smile dispel the cloud of grief, at which his brow also cleared. *Arminda* observing all these changes, and thinking she discovered some uneasiness in his looks, pitied him, and told *Theodora* of the sympathy of soul she saw between them; entreating she would communicate to the worthy *Mercutio*, the contents of the letter she was reading, let it be what it would; this *Theodora* readily consented to do, putting it in his hand, saying, it was from one she loved best in the world; when behold it fell from his hand, and fetching a deep sigh, he said, he would not read it, if it was.

Now by my faith but you shall, said their friend, reaching it to him again; when looking tenderly at *Theodora*, May I venture, my angel? said he: With pleasure, replied his beloved. He then read it; and at those parts, that had before affected her, he discovered an emotion; he wept where she had wept, and smil'd where she had smil'd: –

> "The Lucky have whole days, in which to chuse.
> The Unlucky have but moments; those they lose."

And this was one of *Theodora*'s moments; if ever woman had happiness in view, she now had, in an union with this gentleman, there was that semblance of temper, that sympathy of soul between them, which is the true foundation of hymeneal happiness, that little *heaven* upon earth, while its reverse is *hell*.

When he had finished the letter, he changed colour several times; and looking, as though he meant to convey, through that look, his very soul into the bosom of her he loved; he says, I must acknowledge my weakness, my love, though I revere your mother, because she bore my *Theodora*; yet am I jealous of her power, and your vast attachment to her. I read my own misfortune in the design of her coming over; if that should happen before our union, she will prevent it; and then, farewell happiness; I am doom'd to be miserable the remainder of my life; for without thee, I never can be otherwise. Oh! my *Theodora*, if you have pity in your breast (I will not say love, lest that should offend thee) for a man that adores you, consent to be directly mine. You know, said he, you said this morning, you would regard these arms as an asylum, into which to fly to escape from ruin; by taking shelter in them, but a little sooner than you intended; you may, perchance, save me from death, by securing to me the only happiness this world can afford me.

Here, unable any longer to conceal the agony of spirit, that his own too well suggested surmise had occasioned; he turned away his head, to hide a starting tear, at which his manhood blushed; the hypocrisy of her sex not having affected the mind of *Theodora*, she sought not to conceal the effect, this pity-moving speech had on her; she melted into tears, and sank upon his bosom, attempting to speak, but could not.

This tender scene, not to be beheld without participation, the worthy friend shared in their distress, and interfered her friendly offices; she said, that a by-stander, could generally see more into the game, than those that played it; that she could not but think their acquaintance with each other, was rather too short, to enter immediately into that state. "Too short! said the passionate lover, Of what duration was that of the first pair, when they united? our souls were cast in the same mold; they were formed for each other, and held a tender intercourse, from their first creation. They need not length of time, to make them understand each other, better than they now do." If that is the case, replied *Arminda*, What room is there to fear you will not come together? Because, added he, the devil is industrious to disappoint those unions, in order to make mankind wretched; who would otherwise enjoy an envied share of fellicity, in these terrestrial regions.

Very prettily accounted for, upon my word, returned that lady; Come, make yourselves easy; if you were born for each other, no power on earth, can keep you asunder; if not, all your endeavours to meet, will avail nothing. Then I presume, said he, you are a predestinarian. That I am, answered she, in matrimony, and hanging at least.

This causing a laugh, *Theodora* plucked up courage to speak, and said, that had her parents remained unmindful of her, she certainly had a good right to commit herself to the protection of a worthy husband, such as she made no doubt, to find in her dear *Mercutio*; but as her mother promised to come over to her, it was her duty, she apprehended, to have her consent; which she made no doubt, she would readily grant, if she once knew how deserving, was the object of her choice; which she should take care to make her acquainted with, as soon as possible. She then told him, that the surest proof she could give him, of hereafter making a good wife, was, her being now a dutiful daughter; which she could not possibly be, if she attempted to marry, without the consent of either father, or mother.

Though unwillingly, the amiable *Mercutio*, was obliged to agree with her opinion, and submit to have their nuptials delayed, until the arrival of the Countess, which was not for some time after this; during which, the faithful lover expressed the utmost impatience; and the time drawing nigh that he was ordered abroad, he repeatedly urged his *Theodora*, to consent to his happiness, and her own. But so blind are we for the generality to our own interest, or else so potent was the influence of her malign stars, that she still refuted his arguments; and held out in her obstinate desire, of waiting the Countess's arrival.

Several letters had now passed between *Theodora* and her mother, thro' the hands of *Arminda*; in some of which, this Lady conveyed money to her daughter; but no notice was taken of these unfortunates, by their father; nor was the money due to their landlord paid, until it was absolutely out of his power to keep them any longer. Now the crisis arrived, that *Theodora*'s lover so ardently wished for. She must now seek the promised asylum of his arms; she informs him of her resolution, she imagines he don't receive the intelligence with that rapture she expected: In the interim, who should arrive but the Countess? her hapless children, fly to the shelter of the maternal wing; never was meeting more tender. Now the river, that was divided into three parts, by two joining, it will hereafter run in two distinct channels, and not divide the reader's attention as heretofore.

Never was joy equal to that of the mother and her three daughters; but she was determined, not to take them from out of their father's hands, while the people he had intrusted them with, were willing to provide for them: They therefore only[15] stayed the night about with their mother, but were all there in the day time; sending them home early in the evening, with her footman to attend them.

One evening, being *Theodora*'s turn to stay with her mother, the two youngest were sent home rather earlier than usual; when they were turned out of doors, and came back crying; but they might thank God, they had a mother to receive them, tho' the engines of their father had set them adrift.

The Countess had elegant lodgings, and was soon visited by many very genteel persons; among others, a Baronet's Lady in *Kent*, and her sisters: There was soon a very great intimacy contracted between them. *Theodora*, for a time, was totally devoted to filial duty, and affection; insomuch, that the joy she experienced, on seeing a beloved mother again, had almost suppressed every other concern. But now her regard for the generous *Mercutio* awakened, and like one out of a dream, she wondered that she could have lost him so long; she was piqued at the seeming slight he shewed her; she was too high to remind him of her, and yet unwilling to resign him. She at last grew quite uneasy, at not hearing from him, or seeing him, but strove to conceal it, with all her might; which occasioned her to go to the dear spot, where they had first met, and where, he had made her so many fond professions of a never-dying passion; there, she mused and indulged a pleasing melancholy.

She had a little *Epictetus* in her hand, and now and then looked into it, as if she thought his wise sayings would drive the tormentor from her mind, namely, that *female* pride, that could not bear to be slighted by a lover, that she had once held in chains.

She walked down the dark walk in the wilderness, and thinking no one in hearing, she involuntarily cried out, I will banish him from my mind, I will think of him no more; when looking to see what occasioned a little rustling among the leaves, who should she behold with arms across and pensive, but the object of her reveries? She started, and appeared ready to fall to the ground! This his friendly arm prevents; he catches her to his breast, and calls her, by the voice of love, to life and new alighted simple resentment.

Ah! my *Theodora*, said he, What have I done, that you should determine so cruelly to banish me from your mind? 'Tis plain, we are apt to flatter ourselves, said she, or you would not have so readily adapted my words to your own meaning. There was a time, my Love, said he, when you gave me permission so to do; and that time might have still subsisted, she said, had you not set the example of diversifying the scene. That was the most foreign from my thoughts, said he, though you give that unkind interpretation to my words and actions. Nay, I mean not to make any complaint, says she, I wish you a great deal of happiness. What! said he, Do you then determine to abandon me? You began to grow cool first, said she; and you, to be the cruellest of creatures, returned he. Oh my dear unkind *Theodora!* Think of the encouragement you gave me, think of the promises you made me, and next think you are mine, and can be no other's: I call the heavens to witness to the truth of what I say. Very fine indeed, said *Theodora*, I am sure, I never in my life said any thing to you, that amounted to a promise. But adieu, I fear my mother may want me. Don't my angel, said he, don't refuse me your hand before I leave *England*; on which she affects a gaiety, to which her heart was a stranger.

He then implores her to promise she will not marry until his return; but this she also refuses, saying, she makes no doubt but she may have two or three children by that time. With that she turns off, in a false heroism, that had like to have cost her her life; the last words she heard the deserving *Mercutio* say were, Oh God! then I am undone; cruel, cruel *Theodora!* Ten times was she tempted to turn back, and atone for that cruelty with which he charged her; this her pride would not permit, and when she returned home, a fever seized her, which had like to have revenged his cause. While delirious, she had discovered the cause to her mother, by every moment calling on his name, and begging her to send for him, that she might see the man once before she died, to whom she was so much obliged. Little did the unhappy *Mercutio* think how much he engrossed her thoughts, the first use she made of her reason, was to paint his character in all its highest colourings; to her mamma, and beg her consent to marry him, provided he would have her, for which she would chearfully become an humble suitor.

The Countess would by no means hear of the match, and took her opportunity to send *Theodora* down to the country, with the Baronet's lady, who had requested the favour of her company, and that of her three daughters; not being able to go so soon herself, she was glad to get *Theodora* out of the way, and so, with an aching heart for her *Mercutio*, the poor, unhappy *Theodora* set out in a coach and six for the country. In the little time *Theodora* had been with the Countess her mother, another *North-Briton* much older than her *Mercutio*, had fallen into the rank of her admirers. This gentleman was extremely handsome, and possessed of the most refined understanding, which he had not failed to improve to a very high degree; but having resided for some years as Consul in *Spain*, he had contracted an austere gravity, that might command respect, rather than create love. Having found out *Theodora*'s turn, he rather courted her in a constant supply of books, than soft speeches, and appeared more captivated with her sense than with her person. In fact, the most flattering adulation he could pay her, had her mind not been too deeply engaged with her languishing lover, to admit of a reasoning one. She liked the conversation by which she might improve her mind; but her youth made her rather lean to him that had attacked her heart; certain it is she would at that time have given *Mercutio* the preference to all that she had seen.

Her heart notwithstanding all this, had not yet experienced what love, in reality was; she must wait a little longer for that knowledge. Gratitude and self-love were the only springs that actuated her heart for the present, and these she fondly imagined to be all potent love. But presently the arch god[16] shall give the slighted lover ample revenge; though to do *Theodora* common justice, she would with pleasure, had it been in her power, have bestowed her hand on the deserving youth; and her heart would of course, through duty and inclination, have become his property alone.

After she had left the town, he wrote her the most pity moving letter imaginable, which he sent by an uncle of his, who was in a very high station in the army. The Countess of *Volpont* received him with great civility, and the General made proposals in form for *Theodora*, saying, the happiness, nay he much feared the life, of his nephew depended upon her answer. To this the Countess replied, that the disposal of her daughter was a privilege she could by no means assume, while she had a father living; that had she bestowed herself on the young gentleman, before her arrival, the love she bore her, would soon have reconciled her to the match, but while she remained under her protection, she must take care she took no step which could merit the blame of a husband, that would not scruple to throw all the odium he possibly could on her; that from the high character *Theodora* had given her of *Mercutio* she made not the least question of his being very deserving, but that to put it out of her daughter's power to throw herself into his arms, which she apprehended she intended to do, she had sent her a great distance from town, into the country, that she would send her *Mercutio*'s letter, and hoped she would have the prudence to answer it as she should direct her.

The General used all the intreaties he could, to dissuade the Countess from this resolution, and begged she would suffer the young lady to answer it, at least as her inclinations dictated; he then argued how ill judged it was of parents to counteract the inclinations of their children, when their choice was so well founded, as that of his nephew and *Theodora*, upon the lasting basis of equal merit; her ladyship promised she would comply with his request, and the General took his leave.

The Countess of *Volpont* kept her promise; she inclosed the letter to her, first having opened and read it herself. *Theodora* on the receipt of it, first read her mother's letter, and well knowing the effect it would have on her, retired directly to her own chamber, where, impatient to know the contents, with a fluttering at her heart, that she had never experienced before, she opened it. While dissolved in tears, with greedy eye, she traced the tender page, every line called to her memory afresh the pleasing moments they had past together, and the unparalleled generosity with which he had acted by her, she wetted it with her tears, and then she kissed the paper dry again.

Composing herself, as fast as she could, she sat down to answer it. Gratitude supplied the place of love, and had *Mercutio* received what she then wrote, he could not surely have complained; but, by the previous desire of the Countess, the Baronet's lady intercepted and sent it to her ladyship. She thought proper not to send it to the Captain, who, no doubt, concluded *Theodora*'s silence proceeded from indifference, when, to have been so to him must have proved her the most ungrateful of beings. She told him, in her letter, that if he thought it worth the trouble of coming down to the place where she was, she would not hesitate to throw herself into his arms, and share his fate wheresoever he went, for that all parts of the world would prove equal to her, if with him. She waited the necessary time for his answer; no answer came – she wrote again and again, but these meeting the fate of the former, she began to think, that her lover had changed his mind, that he was disgusted at her ready compliance with his desires, and chose not to hold any further correspondence with her. Nothing could be more grating to the mind of *Theodora*, than this notion, which his continued silence hourly increasing, she was determined to get the better of her prepossession in his favour, let the conquest cost her ever so dear.

In this disposition of mind was *Theodora*, when the Countess, her two sisters, and her new adorer came down to the country together. This gentleman laid himself out to please her; he banished great part of the severity of his temper, and assumed a gaiety more suited to her youth; he promoted all sorts of amusements, mingled in the dance with her, read to her, sang for her, and seized the advantage of the Sylvan scenes to inspire her with a tenderness that she was still a stranger to. The Countess in order totally to eradicate all thoughts of the abused *Mercutio* from the mind of *Theodora*, seemed to authorise this gentleman's courtship.

The young lady conceived a high veneration for his understanding, and found him very agreeable, for what would have made many of her sex hate him, namely, the liberty he took in correcting her fault, and pointing out the errors in her judgment. But in this she was certainly right, for there cannot be a more convincing proof of the sincerity of a friend, than his endeavouring to make you excel, which seemed to be this gentleman's design; at the same time, it gave him the best opportunity imaginable to judge of *Theodora*'s temper, who was always well pleased to be told when in the wrong, that she might for the future avoid it. She, from this mode of behaviour in her admirer, contracted a habit of calling him Monny from Monitor.

The archbishop of *Canterbury* being at this time in the country, and notifying that there was to be a confirmation in that cathedral, the Countess understanding that her two eldest daughters were not yet confirmed, expressed her desire of having them take that duty on themselves, for which their sponsors had hitherto been answerable. Accordingly *Theodora* and *Carina* prepared for the awful ceremony; the day arrived, the prelate was apprised of their intention, and they repaired to the church.

There was a very crouded congregation at this solemnity, whose eyes were instantaneously fixed on *Theodora*, her mother, and sisters; who were attended by the Baronet, his Lady, and several others; elegantly dressed, making all together a splendid appearance. At the proper time, *Theodora* and *Carina* were handed by two clergymen in full canonicals, from the pew to the communion table; at which, when arrived, they were by the Primate of all *England*'s order, admitted particularly within the rails, where there were cushions laid for the young Ladies to kneel upon.

This being a compliment, rarely or ever paid to any but the Royal Family, it occasioned a good deal of speculation. The Countess of *Volpont*, was overwhelmed with gratitude, at the signal respect shewn to her daughters, by so great, and good a man as the Archbishop of *Canterbury*. *Theodora* was differently actuated to what her mother was on this occasion; she felt herself hurt, at the great honour done her; and had rather been undistinguished from the rest of her brethren and sisters, who partook of the sacred ceremony, at which she imagined there should be no distinction of persons; but no doubt, this respect was shewn to their distresses, rather than to their rank.

They here passed most of the summer, vastly agreeable, and would not be permitted, to seperate company so soon, were it not, that they had an account, of the Earl's being in *London*; which determined the poor Countess, who had always a reconciliation between her Lord and her in idea, to return to *London*, taking only *Theodora* with her, and leaving *Carina* and *Eliza* behind, with the Baronet's Lady. But behold, the very day they arrived, the Earl set off in his return to *Ireland*, with his little son by *Lucinda*; attended by the very *Hannah*, who had before waited on the young Ladies his daughters, when they lodged at the beer-house, but who was in a short time afterwards taken from them, leaving them to tend upon themselves. Soon after this, the Countess got her pension doubled, and petitioned the senate against her Lord; to oblige him to a specific performance of the decree she had obtained in the ecclesiastical court against him; notwithstanding all his endeavours to prevent it. The Lords seemed unanimous, that she should have justice done her. There was accordingly a day fixed for the hearing, and every thing preparing for it, as fast as possible on the Countess's side; cases were printed, and as her circumstances were low, she was admitted *in forma pauperis*;[17] sending for her other two daughters up to town, to attend her on the trial.

Theodora's monitor, or lover, which you please, seeing the distressed situation of her mother the Countess, took now an opportunity of giving a striking instance of delicate generosity; for coming one evening, he took a book out of his pocket, and presenting it to *Theodora*, he said, I have taken the liberty, madam, to bring you a book, which I hope, you will find worthy your perusal; you must promise me, however, you won't look into it, while I am here, as it would prevent me the pleasure of your conversation, by engaging your attention; she promising she would not, received it at his hand, and laid it down by her on the table. He made his visit short that evening, and *Theodora*; who was longing to see the subject he thought proper to furnish her with, caught up the book, when at her first opening it, there lay on the title page of it, a letter directed to her; opening it, she found a bank note inclosed, of which he entreated her acceptance; saying, he was sure she was too good a daughter, not to know what was the best use to apply it to. He next begged, she would not let the Countess know whence it came, or ever mortify him with any acknowledgement of the receipt of such a trifle; that he would esteem it a happiness, if she could bring herself to believe she had a right to every service that was in his power to render her, without thinking herself, under the smallest obligation.

Theodora, upon reading the epistle, examined whether the note was *gospel*, and finding it as truly worth thirty pounds; as any of the same sum in *England*, she carried it with the greatest excess of rapture to her mother, and presenting it to her, said, you see madam, the Almighty has it always in his power, to relieve the necessities of such as place their trust in him; as a proof of which, here is a token of his bounty; so saying, she put the bank note in her hand. The Countess earnestly enquired whence the benefaction came. *Theodora* answered that it came from heaven, and begged her ladyship would ask no further questions; but she persisting to know how her daughter came by it, with some austerity, she was under a necessity, tho' contrary to her intention, to give her the conveyancer to read, at the same time feeling the most poignant concern that she should be so closely questioned about it, by a mother who ought to have known that to gain more thousands than there were pounds in the note, *Theodora* would not have stooped to a mean, or inglorious action.

The Countess blushed when she had read the letter, and condescended to ask her daughter's pardon. *Theodora* who was touched to the quick, said, the sole cause of her acceptance of such a favour from that gentleman, was to have an opportunity of serving her mother; otherwise she would return it, which it was not yet too late to do, if there was any impropriety in keeping it, until they had it in their power to repay it, which was her resolution one time or other. In this, coinciding with *Theodora*, she concludes to keep it, to relieve her present necessities, and so the affair dropped.

Before the tremendous day of hearing came, the Earl, in a pannic, employs persons to propose a compromise between his Lady, and him, on advantageous terms for her; she too credulous, is prevailed upon to let his solicitor and her's appear at the House of Lords,[18] to beg the day of hearing may be put off, on account of the fallacious compromise which was never intended to be put into execution. The scheme succeeded; the day was put off; the articles of agreement were never performed; the unfortunate Countess of *Volpont* saw her error when too late; she repented her credulity, became a prey to the most poignant grief, which terminated in an inflammatory fever. She now experienced the tender care and affectionate attention of her daughter *Theodora*, to her preservation; all the assistance that two eminent physicians could give, she had; and that without fee or reward. They visited the Countess twice or thrice every day, they consulted together with all the warmth of friendship, and tender feelings of humanity on her case; you might read the different symptoms they found in their patient, eligibly written in their faces. When, favourable, they looked happy, when the reverse, they would walk hastily to, and fro in the room, clap their hands to their foreheads, and say, she must not die; then, turning to *Theodora*, and her sisters drowned in tears, see there, they would say, look at these pleading, innocents, their tears bid us preserve their mother for their sakes. In short they succeeded, but before the Countess recovered, the parliament broke up; and rendered all her endeavours abortive.

Was there ever any thing more unfortunate? but one would imagine the Countess might have known better than it appears she did by the above, what little dependance there was to be placed on such overtures as those, from a man who had so frequently deceived her. But alas, love, it is most certain, overlooks every defect, and often glosses even crimes; she loved the Earl, and still believed him, what she wished him to be, SINCERE.

Theodora, who had all along given the most convincing proofs of filial duty and affection to both her parents, but particularly to her mother, met with a severe trial at this time; it seems that the enemies of this unfortunate young lady, in order to lessen her in her mother's affections, had found means to have her represented to the Countess as the chief cause of separation between her and her husband, than which nothing could be falser.

Tho' the Countess at the time that she first heard it, gave not the least credit to so villainous an assertion, yet now her temper being soured by her late disappointment, she reproached the innocent *Theodora* with a crime that she would sooner have submitted to be torn to pieces by wild horses, than have committed. Now, she began to reflect on the happiness she had missed, when she refused to give her hand to the worthy *Mercutio*, without that mother's consent, who harboured so base an opinion of her.

On her arrival in town, she had made enquiry after the dear youth, and was informed that he left the kingdom, soon after he had wrote to *Theodora*. This was death to her hopes; it was some time before she could get the better of the concern it occasioned her: but this unkind treatment from a mother she so dearly loved, naturally awakened every wish she might have had for her lover, and aggravated the loss she had sustained in him.

The Countess now having some business, that called her to *Ireland*, took her second daughter *Carina* with her; leaving *Theodora* and *Eliza*, in the care of a female friend, where *Theodora*'s monitor, frequently visited them. There they remained four or five weeks, when their mother wrote for them, to be sent immediately over to her, it being, as she said, absolutely necessary, on account of a villainous lie, to which, the Earl seemed to give credit, in regard to *Theodora*. That he had seen *Carina* by the means of a little stratagem; had wept over her, and seemed to be extremely fond of her; but on hearing *Theodora* was not come over with them, he seemed quite dissatisfied. That on her second, or third visit to her father, he had said, that he was now acquainted with the cause of *Theodora*'s staying in *London*; as he heard she was big with child of a bastard, by a colonel.

Carina told her papa, that whoever said so, was a great liar, that her sister *Theodora* was no more with child than she was; and more than that, she was never even acquainted, with any colonel whatever; that she might indeed have been married if she would, to a captain in the army, but her mamma would not give her consent, and the gentleman was gone abroad; that there was another gentleman even then, who would be glad to get her for his wife, if he could. To all this, his Lordship, who was prepossessed with another story, would not give the least ear; but said, *Carina* had got her story very pat; which having told to her mother, her Ladyship thought it quite proper, that *Theodora* by her immediate appearance, should give the lie to such a wicked aspersion cast on her character.

Never was astonishment equal to *Theodora*'s, at hearing this news; she read it three, or four times over, before she could persuade herself, that she had not made some mistake; thinking it impossible, that any thing in nature could be so wicked, as to invent such calumny against her. O my God, she cried, How severe my fate, not only to see my family separated by the villainous contrivances of wicked people, myself stripped of all those advantages to which my birth intitles me, but they even strike at my innocence, which sooner than I would resign, I would die ten thousand deaths. O! *Mercutio*, why did I not throw myself under thy protection? Thou, who knewest how to value that innocence; it had not now been in the power of my cruel enemies thus to stab my good name, had I yielded to the voice of reason, and of love, in being thine: But it is plain, I was born to be wretched, or I had not missed the happiness you so generously proffered me.

By this we perceive how natural it is for our misfortunes to enhance the value of such, as we imagine would have screened us from them; it was now near two years, since this gentlemen went abroad; *Theodora*'s lively disposition; and a succession of new admirers, had well nigh banished him from her thoughts; only at such times, as she met with disagreeable occurrences that occasioned her to look back; then she remembered him in the most favourable light, and exaggerated his every perfection; but yet this was not love all the while.

So soon as her monitor found that she was remanded back to *Ireland*, he spoke his concern in words, expressive of the most tender regard, offering to make her mistress of his fortune, who had long possessed his heart. *Theodora*, in fact, had no great propensity to marriage; or she might have thought herself happy, in accepting the offer of this excellent man, who was every way deserving of her.

She had bespoke a plain riding dress in which to travel, together with one for her sister *Eliza*, at which time this gentleman was present, and asked the taylor, in a cursory manner, where he lived, of which *Theodora* made no manner of account, thinking it no more than just to satisfy his curiosity. But behold, when her habit came home, she discovered the cause, on finding her sisters as bespoke, but her own richly trimmed with silver. She would fain have persuaded the taylor, that he had made some mistake, but he assured her he had put on every bit of the lace he had sent him; she was presently convinced, that this was a generous trick put upon her by her monitor, and could not but admire the delicate manner in which he bestowed his favours; nevertheless, she felt herself uneasy, at being under such obligations to one, who made a bankrupt of her gratitude, being unable to make an adequate return for them.

But at length the eve of her departure arrives, in which she is more convinced than ever, of the sincerity of his intentions towards her. The trouble pictured in his benign countenance, betrays, notwithstanding all his endeavours to conceal it, the situation of his heart; he holds her hand between his, he deeply sighs; he gazes on her face, as though he means to look his last, and shall I, must I resign thee then, my lovely *Theodora*, said he, perhaps never to see thee more; or what is worse, behold thee the property of another? Maddening thought! O! my *Theodora*, promise me, swear you will be mine; you know my dear Monny, she replies, I am not yet of an age to chuse for myself; Were I, I could not make a more worthy choice than yourself; If my father and mother agrees to it, you shall not find me refractory to their will. But suppose they should not consent, said he, must I then for ever relinquish all thoughts of having you? Why, what can I do in that case, she replies; sure, your good sense would not advise my turning apostate to my duty? Well said he, I have one more proposal to make you, as my dernier retort. What's that? said she. It is, he replies, that you will promise me if matters don't turn out to your satisfaction in *Ireland*, you will write me word, and consent to make me happy; on the pleasing summons, I will meet you, at your landing in *England*, and hold myself prepared to make you my wife the moment you arrive; nay, if you approve it better, I will go all the way, and bring you thence myself.

This, *Theodora* could by no means refuse; on which he put a paper in her hand, which he intreated she would not open, until she arrived in *Ireland*; he told her he must beg leave also to trouble her with a small parcel, of several thousand pounds value, to be delivered to a principal merchant in *Dublin*. This she chearfully promising to take charge of, and he agreeing to meet her at the inn, to which his brother should conduct her, he retired to fetch the parcel. They met at the inn, where he stayed until he put her into the stage coach. She and her sister were entered by the name of *Young*; here the lover's parting with his mistress became very affecting. She wept – he looked half dead with grief, when off drove the coach.

Now, for the first time, *Theodora* found herself in a stage coach, in which there was an elderly man, habited in all points like a country grazier, a young woman dressed in a lightish brown, common yard wide, stuff, cuffed, and robed with pink Persian, with every thing equivalent, quite in the stile of a housemaid, whom *Theodora* presently discovered to be daughter to the old man, who often called her *Charlotte*. There was also a woman and an infant at her breast; but one above the rest, soon attracted the notice of *Theodora*, because drest in a rich laced habit, a hat and feather, who by appearance must undoubtedly be something above the common, at least she thought so. But how great was her mortification, when at the inn they dined, she saw this fine tasty lady received as one of the family, and quickly transformed into the daughter of the inn-keeper, with a coloured apron attending them at dinner; she, with whom she had breakfasted in the greatest familiarity in the morning, and who took not a little state upon herself.

The old gentleman perceiving *Theodora*'s surprise, said, You see, miss, we must not always believe our eyes, they sometimes deceive us. I cannot but allow, Sir, said she, appearances are very deceitful. Yes, said he, and the longer you live, the more you will be convinced of the truth of that remark.

Theodora observed, where they breakfasted, that there was an elderly well looking man, in the basket; as she had no attendants with her, she thought it not amiss, to try and engage his attention to her service; wherefore she went up to him, and asked him, Would it be any offence to him, if she requested him to officiate as her servant, during the journey; for which favour she would gladly answer his reckoning all the road. The honest man replied, instead of an offence, he should esteem it an honour, to be thought her servant, without any view of reward: However, she insisted, to be at the charge of his maintenance, if she had his service; so this matter being settled, he from that moment, became as attentive to her commands, as though he were her hired servant; and by all her fellow travellers, was in reality, thought to be her domestick. The remainder of their day's journey began to discover a great deal of good sense, and what was still more wonderful, good breeding, in her old fellow traveller, and his daughter. Without feeling the least fatigue from the journey, they arrived at the inn, where they were to sleep. When as *Theodora* was stepping out of the coach, what was her surprize, to see her monitor run to take her out, who catching her in his arms, said, You see my angel, I could not part with you all at once. Good God! said she, *Dorimont!* how could you be so cruel to give yourself and me the renewed pain of parting again? Why, said he, my thoughts were so ingrossed by thee, that I quite forgot to give you those papers; to tell you the truth, my love, I was not sorry for a mistake, which gave me an excuse for coming hither time enough to order supper for you. When *Theodora* alighted her new engaged attendant brought her baggage in, and asked whether she would have a room with two beds, or but one? two, she replied, if that Gentleman will do me the favour to let Miss *Charlotte* sleep in the same room with my sister, and me; that I will, returned he, with all my heart, my little angel, and admire your prudence in making the request.

The generous *Dorimont* now expressed his passion in such tender terms, advanced so many arguments to persuade *Theodora* to return back with him, and relinquish all thoughts of prosecuting her journey any further; that finding her resolution began to stagger, she called in, as auxiliaries, to strengthen the obedience she owed to a mother's command, the tacit acknowledgement her stay might prove of the scandal propagated against her. Next came unasked a glimmering hope of reassuming her pristine grandeur, by being the long wished-for instrument to bring about a reconciliation between her father and mother, which had ever been of all her wishes the ultimate. These considerations gained the conquest over all the rhetoric of her lover; which was, we may imagine, pretty potent. She therefore took leave of him over night, and set off early the next morning before he was stirring.

They, at this stage, dropping the woman, and her infant, prosecuted their journey very agreeably, the old gentleman priding himself much all the way, in passing his three female companions as his daughters. They got a pack of cards on the road, and diverted themselves at playing whist, which it seems was his favourite game. Every inn they came to, his first care was to write, with a diamond pencil; on the windows, his own name, and those of his three daughters. In short, both he and Miss *Charlotte* brightned up amazingly; and he would often say, Miss *Youngs* you perhaps may be, but I am sure, my daughter *Theodora* betrays a great superiority over the character she now assumes.

At the journey's end, the coach stopping by his direction, at a genteel private House in the city of Chester, there came out to meet them an elegant dressed lady, followed by a fine slip of a girl, who, to the no small surprize of *Theodora*, and her sister, saluted their fellow travellers, as if they were his wife, and daughter; they invited him with the rest of his company, to come in, and take a glass of wine, and bit of cake, telling him they had just arrived there before him, as he might see, the coach being obliged to drive out of the way for the stage. What should the farmer, or grazier, no better at the first view in the eyes of *Theodora* at least, turn out to be? why no less than a man of five thousand pounds a year, who kept his coach and six.

Now *Theodora*'s wonder being vastly excited at a change so little expected, she pleased herself with the thought of repaying him in kind, when she arrived at the inn where she was known. She had the night before given a distant hint, that she should change her name when she came to Chester. Alas! her fellow travellers's change was more material; it was not in name, but in circumstances, while *Theodora*'s acquisition was a mere bubble, an empty title: However it pleased her, and it was not without some foundation that she hoped to surprize him, as much as he had done her; many being ridiculous enough to pay a vast difference to sound, while the SUBSTANCE is often disregarded, tho' at that time people were not quite so music-mad as they have been of a later date; witness the immoderate growth of *Peer-less* musicians &c.

This hint of *Theodora*'s, together with this gentleman's own favourable conjectures of her, had raised a curiosity in him, that he was determined to satisfy; wherefore he went with her and her sister in the stage coach to her inn, when calling for the mistress, she no sooner espied *Theodora* (of whose coming she had been apprized by the Countess) than she cried out, good God! Lady *Theodora*, how do you do? Lady *Eliza*, how do you, my little dear? the Countess your mother, waits impatiently for your arrival in *Ireland*; then knowing their companion, she enquired after his health with great respect, saying she was glad the young ladies had been so fortunate as to travel in such good company. 'Tis I, said he, Kitty, that you should congratulate, on being so happy as to meet with them: But though I knew not who they were, I could have sworn from the behaviour of Lady *Theodora*, I must not dare now to call her daughter, that she was at least equal to what I find her. But we must not part, until I know whose daughter she is. On which *Theodora* invited him to take a glass of wine with them; she gave him an account of her family, with a slight description of the misfortunes intailed upon it, by the wicked contrivance of her enemies; at which he was still more prejudiced in her favour, and took his leave of them with the warmest professions of a lasting friendship.

From hence they went to *Parkgate*, where they were wind-bound for some time; when, to prove the sincerity of his promised amity, who should come there, but their fellow traveller, and his lady from *Wales*? with intent to prevail on *Theodora*, and her sister, if possible, to go and pass some time at his Seat, for which reason they had left *Charlotte* at home; who longed to see them, on purpose to accommodate them with their coach; (though with reluctance) *Theodora* was obliged to refuse their generous invitation, for which she made the best apology she could, and testified the high sense she had of such unmerited favours. At last they set sail on board the *Yacht*, with some other noble passengers; had a tedious but very agreeable passage, and landed safe in Dublin, where they were received by their dear mother, with the greatest affection, and joy.

It seems that *Carina* had received a handsome present from her father, who had spoken to her of her mother very kindly, saying she should make it her study to please her, as she was one of the best of mothers; it had been very happy for the family, had he treated her like what she really was; one of the best of wives also. This circumstance was magnified, by the poor Lady's own regard for him, into the greatest mark of his favour, and certain she was in her own mind, that he was veering about, towards a re-union with her; which expectation had such an effect, that her daughters found her in the highest spirits imaginable.

What a trifle, at times, will depress or raise us? An imaginary blessing, or a fancied ill, frequently answers, equally, with reality. Fancy is certainly very fertile, and often produces effects in the mind, on which, in a great measure, depend the happiness or misery of the multitude; no where surely exemplified to a greater degree, than in these kingdoms: Wherefore, it is somewhat strange, that we do not abound more in philosophers than we do. The misfortune is, that we view matters in a different way to other people; the French, for example, take the illumined side of the state portrait; by which means, the shade only serves to enliven the colourings, and they are all joy and mirth, from the pleasing prospect. But we look at ours from the shade only, whereby the light is diminished, and leaves the idea clouded, gloomy, and discontented: merely from the want of discernment. There cannot be perfection here; the finest pictures have defects, if we look too nearly into them; but if we contract the sight with our hand, to throw it at a little distance, those defects disappear; our senses remain delighted with the excellency of the artist, and the beauty of the perspective.

Unfortunately for *Theodora*, the Earl was made acquainted with her being expected every day, and her enemies took care he should leave town before her arrival; lest the conviction of his senses, should prove the fallaciousness of the villainous story they had invented to her injury. But the Countess, to remedy this evil as much as possible, took them all down to a friend's house, within a few miles of the Earl. Here they were received with a hospitality, and good nature that was natural to the gentleman, his lady, and family. In a few days after their arrival there, Mrs. *Dumont* took the three young Ladies with her, in her coach to *Volpont-grove*.

There was a fair that day, at a town through which they were to pass, where there were gathered together a great number of the gentlemen of the county; which Mrs. *Dumont* well knowing, made them alight, and walk through the town; her servants apprising the crowd who they were, they were followed with peals of acclamations, and showers of blessings, from the mouths of all who saw them. The gentlemen entreated their acceptance of a dinner, at the best house in the town; which their protectress promised for them they should accept, if not received at their father's, to whom they were going to pay their duty; at which, many shook their heads, saying they were afraid he would not be permitted to see them.

But notwithstanding the screech-owl prophecy,[19] on they went. When arrived at the park-gate, they were denied admittance, and the gate refused to be opened to them; but determined to try their fortune to the utmost, they alighted out of their coach, got over the wall, and contrary to the expectation of their enemies, went towards the house, of which they were no sooner in sight, but there was a messenger dispatched, to stop their progress any further; but not to be intimidated at this, they marched still forwards, when another was sent to forbid them on their peril, to come any nearer; on which, Mrs. *Dumont* returned her compliments to Lord *Volpont*, and to acquaint his Lordship, that she did not expect such disrespectful treatment from him, as to forbid her approach to his house, when he had always found himself well received at her's. On the delivery of this message, another express was sent off, to acquaint Mrs. *Dumont*, he should be glad to see her, only for the company she had with her.

By this time, still advancing, they were pretty near the house, when two, or three were sent together, with orders to use them ill, if they attempted to come any nearer; at hearing this, they thought proper to halt; when they saw a one horse chair for a single person, led to the door, and his Lordship came hobbling down the steps, supported by a stick; *Theodora* presently knew her father, and falling on her knees, in the middle of the road, regardless of her clothes, which was a green silk suit, she cried out as loud as she could, Oh! father, father, My dear father, can you refuse your blessing to your poor *Theodora*? *Eliza* followed her sister's example, and joined as well as she was able, in her pathetic words; but *Carina* who had before seen him, thought there was no occasion for such humiliation then, and therefore stood with vast dignity; while the wretched *Theodora* almost doubled her body to the earth, she prostrated herself so low. But his heart was hardened, and he drove away without giving the least heed to the calls of nature, and of pity; while the eldest and third daughter rent the air, with their bitter cries.

Being unable to follow him, they were obliged to return back again; and in their road, were entertained by the gentlemen, by whom they were before invited. Every one pitied the disappointment the young Ladies had met with, and did what they could, to chase away the dejection of spirits, it had occasioned in *Theodora*;

who was a good while, before she could get the better of the concern this affair had occasioned; which was not a little encreased, by the Earl's sending a message to Mrs. *Dumont*, that he would see the two youngest Ladies, but absolutely refused seeing the eldest. They obeyed the pleasing summons, while the innocent *Theodora* was rejected; though as deserving to the full, of his regard, as her sisters; and if their claim was to be decided by the strength, and purity of their affection for him, vastly better intitled to his notice than they were. But it was dangerous to give one of her disposition admittance, lest she might counteract the malice of her enemies, and obtain too great an ascendancy over her easily infatuated father; they therefore found it necessary to exert all their influence, to prevent her getting a footing, where nature might have insured its duration; to the rooting out the weed of rancour, springing from the seed of credulity, which they had carefully cultivated in his breast.

It was very extraordinary, that *Theodora*'s dutiful humiliation should tend to her own disadvantage, and serve to the establishing *Carina*'s credit with her father. He had taken it in his head, or in other words, it was put into his head, that *Theodora* was too high spirited, to bend her knee to her father, and that she haughtily stood, without uttering a word, while *Carina*, and *Eliza* knelt, and cried for his blessing. Mentioning this surmise to Mrs. *Dumont*, she assured him, that it was *Theodora* knelt, and *Carina* that stood; but this he would not believe, particularly, as *Carina* said nothing in support of the truth. Perhaps fearful of acknowledging herself the aggressor, or what was natural, glad at the continuance of a mistake, that not only exculpated her from blame, but reflected honour to her, and endeared her to her father. Thus were *Theodora*'s virtues attributed to others, or construed into crimes, to serve the black purposes of her artful designing, foes. What was still worse, it was credited by a father, who, one might have expected, would be rather partial for, than inveterate against a daughter that so sincerely loved him as she did.

Nothing could be more agreeable to them than this excursion was; the sprightly family they were with, seemed to study nothing but how to entertain them. They rode out airing almost every morning; they fished, hunted, danced, walked; in short, every diversion that could be thought of, or devised, was had to please them. The two favoured sisters went frequently to see their father, who twice or thrice, while the Countess was there, sent them some of the park venison, with his compliments to Mr. *Dumont* and his lady, that as they had a large family, his lordship lent them some venison, which some of his guests might possibly have a desire to taste. Every one looked upon this as a happy omen, and we may be assured the good Countess thought their reconciliation half brought about already, though in truth as far from it as ever.

Having made their visit full long, in the Countess of *Volpont*'s opinion, at Mr. *Dumont*'s, she now began to think of returning to *Dublin* with her daughters; but was advised by her friends to leave the two youngest behind, as his lordship seemed so fond of them, always calling them by their titles, and treating them in every respect as his legitimate children. Though one day he set them in tears; for

Carina observing two boys hats hang up in the room they were in, asked her papa whose they were? Why, the owners of those hats are my two sons, said he, and shall share my estate between them, please God! This was such a damper to the young ladies, who at that time, entertained some degree of laudable ambition, that they could not well brook his Lordship's declaration, and their tears gave proof of the concern it occasioned them.

Agreeable to the advice of her friends, the Countess therefore left them at Mr. *Dumont*'s, and returned to her house in *Dublin* with *Theodora*, who had left some aching hearts behind her, having the good fortune to please where-ever she went. Her two sisters were indeed the least affected at parting with her, at least in appearance, for the daughters of Mr. *Dumont* seemed vastly more to lament their losing her, than they did, and one of the sons would perhaps have been more unhappy at it, but that he expected soon to follow her.

Now the Countess of *Volpont*'s burden being lightened, she entered a little into the gaieties of the town, for *Theodora*'s sake; a thing she had never done, since the separation of her, and her Lord till now. Her Ladyship on the King's birth-day, appeared at the ode,[20] did the honours of the castle as first Lady there, and was complimented, as was *Theodora*, by the Lords *Justices*, for it was not parliament winter.[21] The young Lady was of a lively turn of mind, and though she had so long been buried in oblivion, she had not contracted the least rusticity, or disrelish for amusements. They were visited by many, and renewed their old acquaintance; which is vastly preferable to the making new. *Theodora*, though far from handsome, was not without her admirers, and often had the pleasure to withdraw the attention of the fluttering fops from some of the most celebrated beauties; with whom, contrary to the policy of her sex, she made it her choice to associate; particularly two sisters, who were handsome as angels, and at that time, engrossed the admiration of the public in general. With these phœnomena for beauty, *Theodora* contracted so great an intimacy, that they were like sisters, and by every one called, the three *sofias*, or inseparables: Their circumstances were rather indifferent; but Providence to make up for the deficiency of fortune, had given them faces, and forms that has since placed them in a most exalted situation.

The acquaintance between their mothers, was of a long standing, which the friendship between their daughters greatly strengthened; and made them form a scheme, of passing the ensuing summer together, in the romantic strain of sheperdesses, all to be habited in a uniform. The three young friends pleasing themselves greatly with the thought of attracting to the sylvan scenes, most of the young beaux about town, and making the young clowns in the country turn poets for their sakes, and chaunt forth their praise in doggrel verse. The Countess of *Volpont* was to make choice of some rural retreat, where they might put their project into execution; which she was at a good deal of pains to find out; but now there was an advantageous proposal made to the Countess for *Theodora*, by a young gentleman of noble family, and great fortune, whose qualifications and perfections rendered him unexceptionable. This match had so many advantages in it, that the Countess rejoiced, at having a happy settlement in view for her daughter.

Matters were pretty far advanced, when they received news from the country, that *Carina*, with the Earl's consent, was married, to his agent's son. This was a fatal stroke to the promotion of *Theodora*; for if he provided, they said, no better for his favourite daughter, what might be expected from him by marrying her that he had abandoned? The match broke off; Mrs. *Garden* changed her mind, as to the rural scheme; the Countess was quite distracted, and retired to a distant part of the country, where she grieved immensely, at the step her second daughter had taken; she condemned herself, in some measure, as the cause, for having left her behind her; and to mend the matter, an old crafty widow in whose house she was, had near succeeded, in seducing *Theodora*, to marry her son, an ignorant looby 'squire; notwithstanding which, he had some hundreds a year; and his mother's art, glossing over his stupidity, as being the effect of a most violent passion for the young Lady, she had almost brought her to her lure, when the Countess discovered the conspiracy, fled with her daughter, and so saved her from the ruin intended for her.

This affair coming immediately on the head of *Carina*'s marriage, had such an effect on the Countess's health, that she was advised to bathe in the salt water; for which purpose, she took a small lodging, a little distance from *Dublin*, near the seaside; where she determined to be quite private, and unknown. For this purpose, she discharged all her domestics, and hired a woman servant, that had not the least knowledge of her. Here she indulged her melancholy; while her daughter's love of books, by solitude again reviving, fully compensated for the loss of company, and less beneficial amusements.

Theodora had her harpsichord, and sometimes entertained herself with music; which the silence of a village giving frequent opportunities to the inhabitants to hear, together with a tolerably pleasing voice; all the young men in the place, used to gather in crouds about the house. Her christian name was soon known, and on every tree, and spot in or about the town, you might read some rapturous verse, in praise of *Theodora*. It was not a little diverting, of a Sabbath day, when she went to church, to see the languishing youths follow her at a distance, joining in adulation of this their fancy-created goddess; or if she passed one by, to see the doughty bow and aukward scrape the *rustic* made, while down-cast eyes, and sudden blushings, declared what his tongue dared not reveal; and deep fetched sighs, did waft his anguish to her.

Love-letters she had in abundance from every quarter, yet knew not who the authors were, although they signed their names at full length; one made a merit of his love, another of his riches, to authorise their pretensions; *Jeremiah Wealthy*, said sure he had a better right to speak to her, than *Paddy Truelove*, for he could keep her as fine as a Lady, and take her to all the fairs, and patterns about the country. *Patrick Truelove* insisted, that he was better entitled to her, than any *Jerry Wealthy*, for he seed her first, loved her longest; and what matter of that, if he was not so rich, mayhap she might like him better for all that: Frequently these disputes terminated in handy-cuffs, and *Theodora* was the prize fought for by many, who had not the smallest probability of ever even speaking to her, while they lived; but if she happened to look near the place where any of them were, it was enough to boast of, until one of his rivals had met with the like favour.

They were in this retreat a few months, when *Theodora* begged leave of her mama to go to *Dublin*, to see Mrs. *Garden,* and stay a few days with her. This the Countess consenting to, she went; was kindly received, by that lady, and her daughters almost devoured her with their caresses. The winter was come round again, and a widower Earl being now Lord Lieutenant of *Ireland,*[22] the town was very gay. Mrs. *Garden* would have had *Theodora* make her appearance at Court, this she could not, as she was not prepared for the purpose; but as a play was her favourite amusement, she said she would go to one or two *incog.*[23] before she returned to her mother. The next morning, the gentleman-usher of the castle, (the very person that had first presented *Theodora* at court in all her splendor) came to pay a visit to Mrs. *Garden*, and her daughters; she had outgrown his knowledge, but soon understanding who *Theodora* was, he paid her the respect due, and told her he hoped she would come to the castle; for it was a pity she should bury herself alive, at her juvenile time of life. She told him, nothing would give her greater pleasure, if it suited her conveniency; but she could not think of taking diversion, while her mother was alone. Here the discourse dropped, and he, as she imagined, appeared satisfied with her apology.

However, the morning after, there came a most thundering rap at the door, and Mrs. *Garden* running to the window, to see what it was, cried out, that it was the gentleman-usher, coming in form, to pay his respects to *Theodora*, in one of the Lord Lieutenant's state chariots, with three footmen behind it. Never was a creature so surprised as *Theodora*, she said, surely Mrs. *Garden* must mistake, the visit could not be intended to her; but she was presently convinced Mrs. *Garden* was right; for the gentleman usher entering the room, came directly up to her, telling her, that he having informed the Lord Lieutenant, of her being in town, his Excellency had commissioned him to wait of her Ladyship, with his compliments, and to request the favour of her company at the castle.

Now, said he, I hope your ladyship will not refuse my Lord, though you refused me. This speech quite confounding *Theodora*, she knew not what answer to give: and he continued to say, that his excellency wished much to see her, as he had heard his son, and daughter often mention her, and many had assured him she danced to perfection. In short, there was no refusing, therefore she had no great merit in complying with his excellency's request; all that remained was his fixing the day, or rather night, for her introduction: on which he named one. Mrs. *Garden* immediately objected to this, saying, no one was ever presented on those days; and sure he would not have *Theodora* go, without being presented. He said for answer, he had his reason for desiring her to go that night; and therefore begged she would not fail being there in time, and named the room in which she was to meet him. This matter being settled he took his leave.

Theodora went directly and purchased herself a brocaded stuff, the manufacture of the country, put it into her mantua-maker's hands, and then set her milliner to work, to make her an entire suit of plain Cypress gauze.[24] Every thing she wore was elegantly neat, but as plain as possible. In this dress went *Theodora* to the Castle, where she had once shone in all the glare of gold, silver, and diamonds.

The gentleman usher, according to promise, met them. Mrs. *Garden* went into the ball-room to secure places for her daughters, and left *Theodora* in charge with him; when presently the door at the lower end of the room opened, and in came his excellency, attended by a vast number of Lords; he was subjected to the gout, which made his feet feeble, and rendered his march slow and solemn: There was immediately a mighty whispering who the lady was at the head of the room to whom his excellency bent his course; but when advanced near enough to her, the mystery was soon unravelled, by the usher's saying, my Lord, this is Lady *Theodora Altamont*; the eldest lawful daughter of the Earl of *Volpont*; on which his Excellency saluted her, and said, he was extremely obliged by her honouring the Castle with her presence, and hoped Lady *Volpont* was well. To this *Theodora* answering in the negative, he continued to say, he wished her ladyship found it convenient to make her appearance a little more in public than she did, as he imagined she would find it to her advantage. Then observing her dress, he told her, he admired her patriotic choice, of appearing in her own country manufacture;[25] that he thought she merited the thanks of parliament, for setting so bright an example, which he sincerely wished the rest of the Ladies might follow, for the good of their country.

Theodora blushed exceedingly at so unexpected a complement, of which she told his excellency she esteemed herself extremely unworthy. He then told her, he believed they were impatient to begin the dance, and offering *Theodora* his hand, he led her into the ball-room, where he resigned her to the care of the gentleman usher to place her properly. *Theodora* was taken out to open the ball; each lady then dancing two French dances, an earl danced the second minuet with her, so much to the satisfaction of the vice-roy, that he rose at her return to her seat, and made her a very low bow; a respect he paid to none but herself, answering all other salutes only with an inclination of the head.

So soon as the French dances were at an end, after paying his compliments round the room, he came up in turn to *Theodora*, and seated himself by her side on the bench, where he held a conversation with her in French, for above half an hour, to the no small mortification of many of the young ladies then present, who did not understand the language; and died almost with envy, at her engrossing so much of his excellency's attention. For the reader may remember, the vice-roy was a widower, and some of the young beauties, particularly the charming *Maria Garden*,[26] did not a little flatter themselves with the notion of making him change his condition, and place them among the rank of Countesses.

Not less buoyed up with this hope was Mr. and Mrs. *Garden*, than their beautiful daughter, at which *Theodora* was not a little surprised, because no stranger to an extreme liking, indeed what the vulgar might call love, that at that time subsisted between that young lady and a deserving young gentleman of pretty considerable fortune. They corresponded together under the titles, and in the strain of *Henry* and *Emma*,[27] in which this friend was very useful to the fair *Maria*, by aranging her thoughts in proper order, and putting them in a dress, that gave some small degree of merit to these tender epistles, and did not a little tend to the raising her in the opinion of her lover, who admired her good sense equal with her beauty, as he, in an extasy of rapture, frequently declared.

Theodora had contracted a sort of antedeluvian way of thinking, that looked upon it criminal to profess love for one person, and entertain thoughts of marrying another; which having declared to *Maria*, all she got for her pains, was to be most heartily laughed at for her false delicacy. So predominant is ambition over every other passion, when once it gets admittance into the human mind; which we see every day exemplified, in the breaches between lovers, and the disproportionate matches made between dotage and youth.

A man of fourscore with a great fortune, behold, rivals an accomplished youth of twenty, by prevailing on a blooming girl of fifteen, whom he truly loves, to wither away in his frozen arms, false to the dictates of reason and inclination; just to have it in her power to appear greater, and dress finer than her equals, which her lovers smaller fortune would not have afforded. But now the languishing youth seeks ample revenge, he misses no opportunity to render himself agreeable in her eyes. She begins to make comparison between her lover and her husband. The latter, wrapt up in flannels, and groaning under the infirmities incident to his years, appears loathsome to her; his essays to shew her his fondness disgust her, his caresses are death to her. In short, she curses her fate, hates the man, and yields up her assertions to him to whom nature had given the best right.

On the other hand, behold a sprightly young man, (who has won the heart of some deserving lovely maid, with whom he may be happy), led by ambition, break through the tender bands of fond affection, and unite with haggard age, to possess himself of her riches; which she had not the heart to part with, for those acts of charity, that would have smoothed the short remainder of her way to eternity. Lo! she reserves them for the meritorious end, of answering the profligacy of a man young enough to be her grandson; by which means, she becomes, in her last months, the encourager of that vice, she perhaps once railed at; and renders herself unable to support that virtue, that should have merited her best attention. Thus the sacrifice to another's ambition, her grey hairs are brought down with sorrow to the grave; the forsaken maid pines and languishes away a miserable existence, thinking all men false for the sake of him, who running the race of debauchery, spends his all merrily while it lasts, after which he ends his miserable being in a prison, or which is worse, turns pander for those whose extravagance he had before supported or shared in.

These are a few out of the many bad effects derived from ambition, which was the fall of angels, and is now the grave of love, of friendship, nay even of patriotism, though we may call the latter a sinking fund, to which no man contributes now a days, without a *view* of doubling or trebling his capital.

This same ambition being now dictator to this little republic of Venus, *Theodora*'s primitive notions did not weigh much with the infatuated fair-one, who had nothing running in her head, but coronets, stars, and garters, &c. so that poor

Henry had nothing now to do, but to tye himself up in his own garters, if so much enamoured as to be unable to live without his *Emma*.

Theodora went several times to the castle, and was still paid great deference to by the worthy Vice-roy, to whom she afterwards presented a very fine watch-paper[28] of her own cutting; having a taste for all the sister arts, 'tis more than probable, had she been instructed in them, she would have made some proficiency. But her genius, like a wild flower in the field, was indebted to nought but nature for any perfection it might boast.

Surfeited soon with the noise and hurry of the town, and sick of its diversions, before another would have thought they had well began to partake of them, *Theodora* gladly returned to her mother, who by the pain she felt at her absence, seemed doubly to rejoice at her return, and to take a particular happiness in her company, to which she declared she was, 'till then, a stranger, and knew not how much she loved her daughter. This condescension in the Countess, gave our *Theodora* a secret pleasure, which she enjoyed but for a short space of time, when they were informed that the Earl of *Volpont* was given over, and lay at the point of death.[29]

At this melancholy news, the poor Countess, who was far from being well herself, expressed the greatest anxiety of mind imaginable; *Theodora* was perpetually in tears, and lamenting that her father should die without giving her his blessing. Her mother seeing her distress, had pity on her, which made her speak as follows: I cannot blame you, my dear *Theodora*, for giving the proofs you do of a natural attachment to your father. I wish he were sensible, as I am, of your worth, he would then make a suitable return for your invaluable affections, and we might again be happily reunited; but I can read your thoughts, I know you wish to see your father. In the name of God, go, and try if you can obtain a sight of him before he dies; perhaps you may yet make him see his error, and bring him to repentance before it is too late. It is your duty, my dear, at least to try what you can do, to save the dear, ungrateful man.

Here the big swoln tears would no longer be confined, but poured down her beauteous cheeks, from which the rose, notwithstanding all her troubles, was not yet chased away, Duty, as well as inclination prompting *Theodora* to obey her commands, she is not long in preparing for her expedition: Two days suffices, in which time we see her set off, riding behind a man, the whole of her retinue, and the chief of her riches, the blessing of a fond mother; who, though she bids her go, can scarce part with her.

The horse she rides, being a hired one, is not endowed with the gift of celerity; and being as heavily burdened as *Sancho Pancho*'s[30] ass, on he goes, a good bone setting trot, as regular in his motions, save when he stumbles, as ever *Harris's time-piece*[31] was. This gives *Theodora* an opportunity of observing a beautiful spaniel, going so very lamely on the road, that she is pained at its misery, and would persuade her foreman to alight and lift up the poor animal to her lap. This he is unwilling to venture, not knowing what a good horse-woman she is, but reiterating her entreaties, he at last consents, and places the creature in her lap, which is scarce able to contain it; after which he with great difficulty remounts, and in this plight they arrive at the inn where they are to dine.

Theodora's first care is to find out the complaint of her quadrupede patient, which proving to be a thorn in one of its feet, she draws it out, applies burnt butter, and bandages it up very nicely. After dinner, not thinking more of it, they proceed on their journey, but find, that more grateful than the generality of the human species, shame to man, the creature follows them with its bandaged leg. When arrived at their journey's end for that day, with the over fatigue, *Theodora* faints at being taken from the horse; on which her new found dog comes up to her, licks her hands, and to the amaze of all present, moans and whines as though it were sensible of her illness; but on her recovery, frisks and leaps about her, as if it would congratulate her return to life. This so ingratiates the creature with its new mistress, that she again dresses its foot; in return it lies at her feet, and won't let any one near her, lest they should hurt her, we may suppose. After, this *Juno* proves the watchful protectress of *Theodora*, who is extremely pleased at the acquisition of such a faithful friend and servant, which adds one more to her pompous retinue.

The next day early they arrive at a place within four miles of *Theodora*'s father, but she is now so very ill, the honest man who attends her begins to be alarmed. The Countess her mother had furnished her with a letter to a worthy clergyman, then the rector of her father's parish, to whose protection she begged leave, though a stranger, to commit her only comfort, her *Theodora*. This letter her attendant, leaving her at the inn, undertakes to carry; here she was obliged to be put to bed immediately, with all the symptoms of a violent fever; but the next morning, somewhat, though but very little better, she rises, and writes a most pathetic letter to her father, and another to her sister *Carina*; the former she is told is quite recovered, and the latter, her sister, ready to lay in of her first child.

Just as she has done writing, in comes the reverend and truly respectable Mr. *Mawrice*, the gentleman to whose care she was recommended, attended by a lovely youth his son, named *Clytandre*. Compliments being passed on both sides, Mr. *Mawrice* says, that he esteems the confidence the Countess of *Volpont* has reposed in him, as the highest honour, and that there is nothing in his power but *Theodora* may freely command; she thereupon consults him in what manner was best to proceed, to obtain a sight of her father. Many methods being proposed, but none fixed upon, she shews him the letter she had wrote to her father, and tells him, as she is unable to ride, and no other carriage to be had, she intends to go on a feather bed, on a low backed car,* which would be almost as easy as a litter, and to send the letter by her servant express, the moment they had got footing in the park, but not before. All this being approved of, he begged his son might be permitted to wait on her; her equipage being soon got in readiness, they set off in solemn procession; at sight of which, all that knew her in happier days, could scarce refrain from tears, nay, some indeed wept, while every one joined in hearty prayer for her success.

---

* A carriage common in that country.

They got into the park without the least opposition, when her messenger rode on; the letter was received and read, but not by a father sure, or it must have had better success. The messenger was examined, and threatened, but on pleading total ignorance of the contents of the letter, he escaped, being ill used. By this time *Theodora* and her little party, consisting of the fellow who led the car, and young *Clytandre*, then about sixteen years old, came within a small distance of the house, when a party of two or three were dispatched to stop our unfortunate's progress; one of whom laying hold of the horse, in order to turn it about, her young champion with the but end of his whip, levelled the fellow to the ground; seeing some others ready to return this rough salute, *Theodora* exerting all her strength, and summoning all her resolution, leaped from off the car, saying, Villain desist, know that I am the daughter of thy Lord, and though thou mayest think to please him by ill treating me and my friends, you will find, that let my father like the treason ever so well, he will hate the traitor, and amply revenge my cause by thy ruin. This animated manner of speaking had the desired effect, and totally disarm'd their threatened vengeance; which taking the advantage of, she made towards the house; but this party being reinforced by a stronger detachment, they vigorously disputed the pass with her, she having begged her hero not to interfere; several times broke their ranks, visibly gained ground on them, and with a courage and fury not her own, distributed her favours liberally on such as attempted to lay hands on her, until, alas! closing upon her, two or three seized her at once; these she sprang from with an amazing agility, and ran so near the house, that they feared within, even to the barricading the doors against her. Her *Juno* was left tied at the inn behind her, or no doubt she would, have now played her part among them, had she seen her mistress so ill used.

Now they seized her a second time, her breath was almost spent with crying, Oh father! father! if you expect mercy from heaven, have mercy on me. What have I done? Oh! what have I done? thou cruel father, thus in thy sight to suffer thy child to be murdered by those ruffians? They still laid fast hold of her by both the arms, when screaming so loud that the woods echoed back her shrieks – she sinks down motionless between them, and they regardless of her rank, or sex, inhumanly trail her body on the ground.

Is this the spot, the very spot, whereon the may-pole was erected in honour of the unfortunate *Theodora*'s birth-day, but some few years before? Are there not now among the number of her present assailants, some who saw her in her former grandeur? Where is pity flown? Behold her pale, and languid features! View her silken tresses, all dishevelled, and sweeping the ground she was once thought too good to walk upon! Behold, the youth who never saw her 'till this morning, weep! See, he rushes through the cruel wretches, undeserving the names of men, and clasping her body, lifeless to all appearance, in his arms, he kindly bears her to the humble car, whereon he lays her, and calls, but calls in vain to them, to get something, if possible, to bring her back to life. They bring a dirty wooden vessel, which they fill with water from the pond by which they stand, and bring it to the generous boy; who fired with indignation, says, "Is this a proper vessel to bring to the daughter of your Lord? There, take it for your pains;" and so saying, he dashes it in the face of him that brought it. Now he proposes to take the dead *Theodora*, as he thinks her, to his father's house, the short way through the wood; but no, he must go three miles round through the town, near *Volpont grove*, to give the less chance for the preservation of her life, if there should be any.

While they are thus disputing, an old servant, who had been out that day, returns home, and enquiring the cause of this unexpected tumult, he no sooner finds it out, than breaking out into the most bitter lamentations, he fills the air with his cries. Oh! my dear, young lady, says he, Have I lived to see the dismal day, that thou wert murdered thus before a father's eyes; my poor lamb! that I have so often dandled in those ancient arms: Art thou gone then? You parcel of murdering villains, I'll have you all tried for your lives, not only you, but my Lord himself, for exercising such barbarity on his child.

Young *Mawrice* ordering the car to proceed, the old man moves on with it, and says, I will not part with my poor child, 'till I know she is dead or alive; so on they go, while before them flies an express to the town, to forbid any one, on pain of displeasure, to be seen at their doors or to administer the smallest relief towards the recovery of *Theodora*; but one who had more humanity than the rest, notwithstanding these orders, ventured to stand at her door with a bottle of hartshorn[32] in her hand which, when they came by, she threw into the car, and immediately shut the door, to prevent their knowing from whence the succour came, it being by this time quite dark.

They applied the hartshorn, in vain, to her nose, and chased her temples with it; she still discovered not the least sign of life. In this hopeless condition they brought her to the hospitable parson's house, where his sister-in-law was, by his direction, ready to receive her; but hearing how she was used, and that they believed her dead, she refused letting the corpse into the house; but the poor old man beseeching her, only, to let him try if there was any life left in her, before a good fire as the weather was very cold, and if she was in reality dead, he would stab her cruel father to the heart, with the sight of his murdered child, and bring the corpse directly back to the house to him.

On these terms Mrs. *Bingley* admitted him to bring her in. She had neither breath nor pulse for a long time, and was almost frozen to death with the cold, but they use every method that can be thought of, to restore her, in which at length they succeed; she gives a deep groan, and from being insensible, falls into strong convulsions, in which they every moment expect she will go off. But heaven, reserving her to go through many more exemplary trials, ordains she shall recover; at which her kind assistants seem sincerely to rejoice, and do all they can to revive her spirits, which are quite faint, and in a manner totally exhausted, with the force she had put upon them at *Volpont Grove*, together with the violent agitation the convulsions had occasioned in the œconomy of the whole animal system. A violent fever, however, was the least evil that could be expected, but terminates in a pleuresy, the pain very acute this her kind protector Mr. *Mawrice* endeavours to abate, by bleeding her frequently, which he performed with his own hand, having learned that art, merely to render himself of service, in cases of necessity, to his fellow-creatures.

The Earl terrified at the account brought him of her desperate situation, by his old servant, sent the next day to know how she was; as he continued every day to do, until he heard she was out of danger; but then fear subsiding, love seemingly having no part in the enquiry, several days past, without hearing any thing further from him; on which the unhappy *Theodora* expressed the greatest concern imaginable, and determined, if possible, to see her father, let it cost her ever so dear.

She used to sit with Mr. *Mawrice*, and form a thousand schemes, to attain her wish. One time, she would disguise herself, and go to the *Grove*, and offer herself as a maid servant; another time, she would personate a person who sold toys, and go vend them at the *Grove*; nay, sometimes, she determined to assume another sex, and go with Mr. *Mawrice*, as an assistant, to her father's. At all these contrivances, Mr. *Mawrice* would look with wonder at her, and say, Well, if I did not hear this from yourself, child, I could not have believed my own ears; I have often heard, of young women having run the greatest risks, and done the most extravagant things, for the sake of a lover; but never until now, did I hear of one, who so eagerly and madly pursued a father, as you do. In short, I am so much your friend, that if we can get clothes to fit you, I don't know, but I am fool enough, to forward your wishes, in bringing you to this same father; and presenting him with a jewel, that if he knew its real value, he would esteem himself the richest man in the kingdom. Had my eldest daughter been like thee, she would not have given me the uneasiness she did, by marrying the man she has imprudently thrown herself away upon: I wish to God, my *Clytandre* was old enough, and rich enough for you.

In this manner would the good old gentleman talk to *Theodora*, who often told him, she had not the least notion of any man; that if she could but see her father, and reconcile her mother and him, it was the only earthly blessing she desired; to which his answer would be, Well then, surely thou art the most extraordinary girl living.

However *Theodora*'s miniature size, no affront to little people, for they say, "That in the little boxes, is the precious ointment," could not be accomodated with mens apparel to fit her, wherefore she was obliged to drop this project, though most approved of by her protector. Several of the tenants on the estate now paid their respect to her, and invited her to their houses, even before she was thoroughly recovered from the pleuretic fever; and loth to disoblige, by making an excuse, she went on horseback, all round the country, Mr. *Mawrice* having furnished her with an excellent horse, and side-saddle, on which, drest in a sumptuous habit, and hat and feather, she made no trifling figure, among the rustics; But her complaisance cost her dearly, for her disorder, by not giving it due attendance, flew up into her head, and fixed very stubbornly there; insomuch, that she was almost distracted, and frequently rode, when the sight left her eyes through pain, and then she was obliged to commit her safety entirely to the guidance of her horse, while her hands were engaged, in holding her head.

Health! thou inestimable blessing, when possessed of thee, what little regard we pay thee! But when pain, and sickness usurp thy place, what wretched beings do we straight become, and how greatly do we lament thy loss, which millions cannot compensate! What has the ploughman, who enjoys a good constitution with peace and tranquility of mind, in the arms of his rustic fair one, to envy in a star and garter; oppressed with pain, labouring perhaps under hereditary disorders, and in the midst of delicacies, unable to make a comfortable meal. Behold! the rosy Goddess, flies the voluptuousness of courts; the intemperance of taverns, the debauchery of brothels; and takes shelter, with temperance and frugality in the cottage, where she lavishly bestows her favours, on the unadulterated progeny of love and innocence.

Theodora, now more wretched than ever, by the addition of excruciating pain, thought she would, whilst it yet remained in her power, which she had cause to think might not be long, make one more attempt, to see her father,[33] but spoke not of her intention to any one but her young hero *Clytandre*, who generally accompanied her wherever she went. Accordingly, having concerted with him every thing concerning the affair, they went out, as if to take the air in the morning; the young gentleman having, by her desire provided her with a case of pistols, and himself with another, determined to defend themselves, if attacked as before. Thus equipped, they directed their course the short way to *Volpont Grove* close by the wall of which, they found several men busily employed, in felling of timber, at sight of whom our young warriors were at first a little intimidated; when, *Theodora* for once, appropriating the motto of a well-wisher of her's to herself, said, Come on *Clytandre*, "*Do or die*" is the word; and so whipping her horse, she came up in a hand-gallop,[34] to the men; some of whom having seen her before, she was presently known; and said to them, pulling her handful of small silver from her pocket, and throwing it among them, My honest friends, you will please not to know me, or own that you have seen me, unless you find there is any mischief done me; they with one voice, declared they would observe her commands, but lamented that all the gates were kept constantly locked. As for that, said she, I do not value it, friends, pray for me; and so saying, she took a short career, and before them, to their no small surprize, leaped the gate fairly over; which the horse of her companion refusing to do, some of the men ran directly, and flung down a part of the wall, to facilitate his joining her. This he had scarce done, when he observed the elder brother of *Borana*, his Lordship's mistress, walking at some distance, with a gun on his shoulder, being then park-keeper.

They stopped a moment to consult what was best to be done; *Clytandre* advises to go on and take no notice of him; but this not agreeing with her opinion, they rode directly up to him; and *Theodora*, in a manner, and tone of voice that amazed even her young champion, said, You see Sir, I have got into the park, notwithstanding the care you take to keep the gates locked. But, were they as high again, my spirit is able to surmount them, determined as I am to see my father. I assure your Ladyship, he replies, did it depend on me, I should be readier to open the gates to you, than shut them against you. To prove the sincerity of your words then, said she, let me see you don't go near the house to give information of my approach, as it may prevent mischief: on saying which, she shews him a pistol, and he with a low bow says, he'll do as she would have him, and take no notice of having seen her; straitway directing his course into the wood; he kept his word in not coming nigh the house for a considerable time.

Thus far successful, they put their horses to their full speed, and pass by the window, where the Earl is with *Carina*'s husband, and two or three others, one of whom is the friendly *Jago*, that dissembling villain. On seeing this amazon fly past them, the Earl calls out to his son in law, *Belmont* is not that your wife? He runs to the window to look, but *Theodora* swiftly dismounting at the private door, is in the large hall before they can satisfy their curiosity; on which, judging from the celerity, of the action that it could not be *Carina*, who was not then in a condition to do such feats in chivalry, they concluded it must be *Theodora*; the parlour door on this is locked before she comes up to it, and she hears her father blasting at a great rate, to have her turned out, if she should get admittance by their being off their guard.

She hears these words distinctly, when stamping her foot, with a force that makes the house ring, and exerting her voice to the highest pitch, she clearly and distinctly, says, I come here for nothing but a father's blessing, I ask no more; and surely that is what can't impoverish mine; were I undeserving of it, I would not presume to sollicit it; but my father is deceived, imposed upon by villains, and I would willingly render him a service in disabusing him. I therefore must and will see him, or die in the attempt; and whoever dares offer me the least insult, save himself, I am a tolerable marks-woman, and shan't hesitate one moment in lodging a brace of bullets in his heart: therefore come on ye mighty valiant crew, who treated a defenceless sick creature as you did me the other day; know that now I am not afraid of thee, nay, I dare thee to the combat, though a poor, weak, injured damsel.

These words wrought a wondrous change; all was hush and still, as though there was not a creature in the house; and every order that the Earl gave, was hardly louder than a whisper; Zounds says he, who knows but she may be as good as her word? Let no violence be offered her, lest there should be murder committed. You had better see her, my Lord, says his son in law, who was longing himself to see a person whose words betrayed such spirit; Zounds, says his Lordship, who knows but she may shoot me too: now she is in such a damned passion? No, no, my Lord, says his faithful bosom-snake *Jago*, I would not advise your Lordship to see her, till her wrath subsides. That's true Jack, 'till her wrath subsides, says his Lordship, it would be dangerous; for to tell the truth, she was used very ill by the servants, and she might revenge all upon me: To prevent which, replies the friend, I will expose myself to the threatened danger first, and go and speak to her; if I find your Lordship may venture, I think you had best see her, give her your blessing, and get rid of her. "O! thou mighty judge, a second *Daniel*."[35] But this was the furthest from his thoughts; *Theodora*'s seeing her father, might prove his destruction, therefore it was to be avoided.

All this while she is trying to get entrance, first at one door, and then at the other, but all are fast locked, and refuse admittance; when *Jago* comes round by the vaults underground, and so through the same door she had come in at; on seeing this scorpion, she recoils a step or two, and bids him keep his distance, for she would let no one come within arms length of her. He says he don't come with a view of hurting her, only to advise her as a friend. That is out of thy power, said she, who have long been the declared foe of my poor mother and, by thee, undone family. He is sorry she should entertain so bad an opinion of him, who had ever done to the utmost in his power to reconcile my Lord to my Lady, but he was so obstinate, and unforgiving a man, that all his endeavours hitherto had proved ineffectual; but notwithstanding his past ill success, he would still persist, and he had some hopes now that, with her assistance, matters might be happily brought about.

Theodora is gulled by his fair speech; she listens, she believes, and is deceived. If I could believe you sincere, she says, and pauses – he entreats she will not doubt him, and with the most dreadful execration on himself, if he deceives her, swears he is her stedfast friend. Then says she, shew me you are so, by letting me instantly see my father. I am afraid, replies he, that is a thing impracticable at present, as he is in the greatest rage imaginable, has called for his pistols, and swore he would shoot you, which is the reason I undertook to speak, to warn you of the risk you run, in forcing yourself into his presence, without his approbation and consent. I would advise your ladyship to let him cool a little, and leave me to work the rest; but would not have you by any means quit the country, until you hear from me. The moment I get him in humour I will send for you, and make not the least doubt but you will be soon able to manage him as you please; for between ourselves, but you must not say I said so, his doatage is approaching fast: Pray how does the Countess do? I am not a little troubled that she should esteem me her enemy, who have ever been her steady friend, though she has used me very ill; but no matter, that is past, and we must forgive and forget; God orders us to do so. But what a change a few years has wrought! There's Lady *Carina* your sister ready to lie in, and you are grown so handsome, Lady *Theodora*, I should scarce know you, but for the extreme likeness you bear to the Earl your father. Well, when I can get him a little in temper, I shall make him long to see you. Shall I see is your ladyship's horse ready? By no means, Sir, returns she, I won't give you that trouble. Nay, but I am determined, continues he, to have the honour of helping you up.

Poor *Theodora*, can'st thou blame thy father for being imposed upon by this subtle knave? he who has ever believed him his friend, when thou, who came prepared with the notion of his being what he in reality is, art thyself deceived, by the specious mask of friendship he puts on?

She gives her hand with confidence to her bitterest enemy; who, with vast respect, leads her down the steps, and one of the servants awed into it by her glittering appearance, runs with a chair to raise her to the saddle; but the over officious *Jago* puts him away, saying that is an honour be must entirely reserve for himself, then clinching his hands together, he lays them almost on the ground to receive her foot, and by his assistance up she flies. She makes a low bow, and is just setting off, when laying hold on her bridle, he begs she will condescend to wait a moment or two until he tries whether his lordship will receive her or not.

Excellent hypocrisy! a thing that he is determined in his own mind the Earl shall not do; this no doubt she readily consents to, and while he is absent, the women servants all stand rank and file, blessing and praying for her, and even the men who had before ill-treated her, apprehensive of her future power, beg a thousand pardons of her for the crime they had committed, contrary to their inclination, against humanity.

Nothing could wear a more benign aspect than all this; *Theodora* forgot her pain, the remembrancer of that tragic scene, and freely forgave those, whose consciences by sin were accused. *Jago* returns and tells her aloud before them all, that his lordship is at present too much ruffled to see her with the pleasure he could wish, and hoped she would be contented with his sending his blessing by him, which he intended soon to give her in person, and that she had every thing to hope for from his affection, which he now found, by her ready compliance with his will, she was perfectly well entitled to.

Quite delighted with this message from her father, *Theodora* makes her grateful acknowledgments to the generous mediator between them, and sets off in a triumphant gallop, in which she arrives at the town of *Camolin*, in the middle of which, she takes out one of her pistols, and lets it off in the air, as a signal of her late victory. This draws every one to their doors; among the rest the mother of *Borana*, who on seeing *Theodora*, and believing her daughter's power at an end, and that spell broken, (which they said, she took some pains to compose by the help of her own familiar, and the infernal spirits of some other old witches of her own profession) she gave a diabolical shriek, and fell into violent fits, out of which it was with great difficulty she was recovered. Such are the mental and bodily disquietude that affect a breast conscious of guilt; it construes every thing to its own disadvantage, see imaginary evils; and as beautifully expresses it, "The thief doth fear each bush an officer."[36]

When *Theodora* returned home, her worthy host could scarce give credit to the account brought him by her and his son of this extraordinary event; he said he could not find words expressive of his wonder of the undaunted maid; and gave the Almighty thanks for this prelude to a reconciliation in the family. But alas! they were none of them fortune-tellers, 'tis plain, or they would have seen that such a thing was never to be; but undoubtedly it is a happiness that we are too short-sighted, to see into futurity. For if we could, by anticipating blessings, their value would be diminished, and by seeing evils at a distance, our dread of them would give them so great an increase that we should be unable to endure them. However they were in part happy, for they flattered themselves, that that would be, which they wished should be; in which belief they were the next day more strengthened by the Earl's sending a person to *Theodora*, with proposals to make over five hundred pounds a year immediately to her, together with a coach, six of the best black mares, a third part of his plate, which was worth ten thousand pounds, and all her mother's jewels, to live where she pleased, either in *England* or *Ireland*: Provided she would solemnly swear, never to see her mother more, or share any part of it with her.

At the beginning of this proposal every one stood amazed, praising the Earl's goodness in their own minds, but when the proviso was mentioned, their thoughts were struck with an inexpressible damp, and Mr. *Mawrice* waited, with a visible concern, and impatience pictured in his countenance, for the answer she should make. *Theodora* was, for a time, unable to speak, her shock was so great; but at last she broke silence, and addressed the person who brought these proposals in the following words.

I intreat, Sir, you will present my most respectful duty to my father; tell him, no one can be more sensible than I am, of his goodness; but at the same time acquaint his Lordship, that if he would give me his whole estate, on the same terms, I must beg leave to refuse it, as I now do this, for never shall the forfeiture of *nature*, prove the means of my *exaltation*. And who, that feels its soft pleadings, or has the smallest particle of humanity, could fly a *friend*, much less a good *mother* in distress? No, Sir! I never will do any thing that shall brand me with the name of ungrateful; it were purchasing an establishment at too dear a rate. I should rejoice at sharing my filial affections between my father and mother; but the former giving me no opportunity to shew him how much I love him, a double portion falls to the latter, of which it were ungenerous to deprive her, rendered too poor already, by the loss of a husband and two daughters, that she still sincerely loves. Tell my father, Sir, continued she, that his blessing, and the smallest triffle yearly, if permitted to share it with my mother, I should esteem an abundance; to which mark of his favour, my fond attachment to my parents is my only claim, not being vain enough to think I have any merit of my own, to entitle me to his smallest notice. But nature, partial nature, may perhaps in his breast, as in that of my mother, construe my defects into perfections, and once more enrich me with a *father's love*.

Here *Theodora* ceased speaking, none of her hearers having the least desire to interrupt her in her speech, had she continued it ever so long. A general silence ensued, in which, diffident of herself lest she had said any thing improper, she sat with her eyes fixed on the ground, in the greatest confusion; when Mr. *Mawrice*, at last recovered from the surprize her words had thrown him into, cried out, Good! and great God! Is it possible? Did you ever hear the like? So much love to her parents! such generosity! such gratitude! such sentiments! such – in short, I cannot speak what I think of thee, thou little wonder! thou magazine of good sense! Here is a pattern for you, my boys and girls, if you prove such blessings to me, I shall be too, too happy; and so saying, the good man burst into tears of joy and extacy, that choaked his words. A murmur of applause ran through the room, and *Theodora* unable to support such unmerited praise, was obliged to quit it. Now the worthy divine repeated those passages in her discourse that had most touched him, made the messenger promise faithfully to represent what he had heard in its own colours, as near as possible, and said if the Earl could withstand their force, he was either more – or less than man.

The negotiator now took his leave, to return to the Earl with his daughter's answer. By good fortune he found the opportunity; his lordship listened to him with attention, and seemed sensibly touched. By heavens, said he, I like her the better for her spirit: Why, she is my own self; she has more wit in her little finger, than all the children I ever had, put them in a lump together, except *Dick*. *Jack*, he promises to be a smart boy. Well, well, she shall not fare the worse for refusing my offer. I do love the girl, *Jack*; but hush, I believe there is some one listening: Do look, *Jack*. On this the other went to the door, and just at the instant his dear *Jago* coming in, he winks at the mediator, and almost in the same breath, says to the intruder, G-d damn the little b——ch, the true spirit of the mother, by G-d she must forsooth be at liberty to bestow what she has to her own liking, and share it with her mother and be damn'd to her; but, if that is the case she shan't have a shilling of mine. Never was mortal under a greater degree of astonishment than the spectator. *Jago* answered his Lordship, that it was no more than what he expected, but his Lordship was in the right to satisfy himself in making the experiment.

If the friend was surprized at this affair, what was the good doctor *Mawrice*, and the Earl's daughter, when they were made acquainted by him with it? *Theodora*, who was by this time extremely ill, gave a heavy sigh, and said, now I am certain, I have for ever lost my father; since he's afraid to acknowledge his own thoughts, or execute his own will, what can I expect, were I even so happy as to possess his love? Poor man, said Mr. *Mawrice*, I pity him with all my heart; for 'tis plain, he is given over into the hands of his enemies.

Theodora's illness not a little increased by the trouble of her mind, was at last obliged to yield, and thinking her last moments approaching, expressed a fond desire to breathe her last in the arms of her beloved mother; which Mr. *Mawrice* seeing, tho' griev'd at parting with one for whom he had conceived an affection little short of paternal, had every thing prepared for her departure, and sent his son to attend her with his own horses; after he and the worthy Mrs. *Bingley*, had done every thing they could think to relieve her, but all to no purpose.

Her favourite *Juno* still her constant attendant, beating the fields before her, in token of her gratitude for the kindness her mistress had shewn her; behold, she leaps up to the horses head to stop the carriage, which having effected, up flies the creature into the chaise, and drops a snipe into her lap, being the fruits of her labour. At this uncommon mark of sagacity and love in a brute, the good Mr. *Mawrice*, who was present, having come along with *Theodora* to conduct her a few miles in her way home, remarked every thing was sensible of her worth, but her father; even the brute creation, of which that dog gave a convincing proof.

They were obliged to make short stages, on account of *Theodora*'s indisposition, which increased to such a degree, that she could scarce endure the fatigue of the journey; and arrived at her mother's, so altered by grief and pain, that the Countess at sight of her was quite shocked and scarce knew her. The charming *Clytandre*, having delivered his charge into the proper hands, took a melancholy leave of the young lady, for whom he had conceived a tender regard, but never expecting to see her again; at the thought of which, as he afterwards confessed, he felt a pang at his heart, that he was at a loss how to account for; 'twas different from what he had ever felt for a sister, and as yet he was a stranger to the symptoms of the growing passion with which his breast was besieged, and which, 'tis probable, had he been but a few years older he would more readily have understood.

However he took the soft impression with him. He incessantly talked of *Theodora*, and would remind his father, and his aunt eternally of her, with an earnestness, and partiality that betrayed the secret impulse in his heart, to those who were better experienced in those matters than he possibly could be; in which they rather encouraged the young gentleman, than otherwise; well knowing of what advantage a well-founded first attachment is to a young man. For when the idea is engrossed by a deserving object, 'tis a sort of bulwark against inferior temptations, and prevents the youth from plunging into vices that he thinks will render him unworthy her he loves. Nay, it often serves to stir up an emulation to excel, in order to be more deserving of her favour; which was the case of young *Mawrice*, who from that time closely applied himself to study, on his father's saying that no one would have any chance in obtaining *Theodora*'s affections, but such as were perfectly accomplished, and whose sentiments corresponded with her own. This hint was sufficient to engage *Clytandre* to be all his father wish'd him to be.

In the mean time, the goal of his fond wishes was thinking of another world. The Countess, distracted on her daughter's account, had a consultation of physicians on her disorder, who declared in all their practice they had never met with a parallel case; that they knew not what to prescribe, that it wou'd be a miracle if she ever recovered, all the chance she had was her youth, and change of air; and thereupon advised the Countess to lose no time in taking her to *Bath*.

Theodora heard all this with the greatest composure of mind, and lifting up her hands and eyes to heaven, said, glory be to thee my God! then my misery will soon be at an end, and sure I should with patience bear whatever thou thinkest proper to inflict. Comfort my mother Lord! and enable her to bear the pangs of parting, 'tis but for a little time and we shall meet again in happiness. These words were like a dagger to the heart of her fond mother, who as expeditiously as possible, got every thing in readiness for their departure, tho' quite contrary to the inclination of *Theodora*, who wou'd not have had her put herself to such expence on her account, who she heard could not, without a miracle, recover; but the poor Countess was determined to do every thing in her power to preserve her only child, as she then call'd her; they therefore in a short time set sail for *Bristol*.

The disorder of this poor young Lady was dreadful; her head had open'd in the divisions of the skull, like a child in the rickets; in many parts of which, her forehead particularly, you could perceive the flesh, or rather skin, rise and fall, as tho' her brains were in a ferment, or boiling; she could not sleep, her tortures were so great, and if she happened for a few moments to doze, she waked with a shriek, and thought her eyes were pulling out of her head.

In this dreadful way was she, when they set sail, and when they arrived at *Bristol*, where they were recieved by a distant relation of the Countess's, who sent express to *Bath* for the first physician there, one doctor *N—*, to come immediately, and give his advice in this extraordinary case. The doctor with great humanity enquired into the disorder, and what it proceeded from. The Countess gave him a succinct account of her excursion to see her father; the usage she had met with, the pleuretic fever, her little attendance to it, and her trouble at her disappointment. The doctor, without the assistance of a gold headed cane applied to his chin, mouth or nose, which was somewhat strange, said, her complaint was in her mind, tho' it made these external appearances, and that all he could prescribe would avail nothing, unless there could be some means found to dislodge it from its dangerous post in the brain. The doctor gave these directions, first, that she should above all things never be left alone, but be constantly in sprightly, young company, that wou'd not permit her to think, he then asked, was she fond of dancing? the Countess answered she was remarkably so, when well, but now she discovered no propensity to any sort of amusement, she was in such excruciating pain. He replied, that did not signify; she must be taken where that amusement was, and if possible, prevailed upon to join in it. On this the Countess smiled and asked him, did he think she was bit by a tarantula? he said she had imbibed a poison far more subtle, and harder to be eradicated, and that was grief, that if she could be got to dance, it might cause a perspiration which would save her life; he then prescribed a trifling medicine, and ordered her feet to be bathed in warm water up to her knees, for an hour every night, to be kept to a gradual heat, after which to have them rubb'd well with a coarse cloth, and go directly after it into a warm bed.

These particulars are only related to shew the singular integrity of the doctor, who, contrary to the general practice of the profession, applied himself heartily to the disorder of his patient; nor disregarded the simplicity of his prescription, provided it proved effectual.

This prescription to a person, who was by no means fond of drugs, proved very agreeable, and next, being given gratis, for he refused a fee from the Countess tho' he came twelve miles on purpose, so enhanced his worth with *Theodora*, that she thought the advice coming from so good a man could not but bring a blessing with it; she therefore resolved truly to adhere to it, being desirous to shew her gratitude one time or other for such an uncommon piece of generosity.

Accordingly in a few days afterwards, the matter of the ceremony being previously apprized of their rank, they went to the *Long Room*, at the *Hot Wells*; a sprightly young templer having engaged *Theodora* at dinner, to be his partner in country dances, if she found herself able, having in the morning, as an addition to the other impediments in her way, got a violent pain in her great toe, which they jested with her about, and said, as the gout was hereditary in her family, she had surely got it. But her spirits were too low to bear their raillery, which at another time, she had been pleased with, and affected her to such a degree of weakness, as to occasion tears; however her mother pacified her, and her gay templar, who was happily for him, out of the scrape, soothed and flattered her into temper again; she in this mood arrived at the *Long Room*, where she seemed startled at the sight of so much company, and told her mother she wished she had not come.

She was dressed out, it is true; but from her colour, they might conclude she had come from the grave; her eyes had lost their little stock of fire, and seemed dead in her head, her face was swoln, and withal she had the greatest dejection of countenance; but behold the musick strikes up, hautboys, kettle drums and trumpets. Martial musick of all things in the world was her delight, it has an effect like electricity upon her whole frame. The master of the ceremony comes to take her out, to open the ball with Lord ——, son to the late earl of ——. Without hesitation she gets up, and dances as well as ever she did in her life. The Countess is astonish'd;

a murmur of applause runs through the room, with who's that? upon my word she dances finely. The Earl of —— asks Sir *Charles* —— who the young Lady is that dances with his son? Sir *Charles* looks earnestly at her, and says, if the Earl of *Volpont* has a daughter in the world, that is she; for since I was born, I never saw any two so like each other, save the difference of sexes, youth, and age.

The gentleman of the ceremony is call'd; and he telling who she is, Sir *Charles* says, I told you so, I could have sworn it. After she has danced, they both come up to her, compliment her on her performance, and tell her what had passed between them, on the likeness she bore to her father. The Countess is quite charm'd to see the alteration in her daughter; the *French* dances are done. Now we see her and her partner go to the head of the country dances. *Theodora* compliments Lord —— (who had taken out another lady to dance country dances) and his partner, with leading off the first dance, to bring her into practice. This the earl observing, comes up to his son, and desires him by no means to take the upper hand of *Theodora*; and so she is oblig'd to begin, whether she will or no, but does it with such spirit, that she attracts the notice, and gains the praise of all the spectators.

The men wish all their partners could dance as well, and the Ladies strive to imitate her; so that like a spirited leader of a band of musick, who can inspire a lifeless set of humdrums to make a pleasing concert between them by dint of example, she gives life to all around her. Happy for her, perspiration from her head alone becomes so violent, that she is obliged to supply the place of her necklace with a cambrick handkerchief, which she wets eight or ten times in the space of a few hours; when returning home, and punctually observing the rules laid down by the doctor, she gets a little rest. The Countess who sees the good effects of mirth, won't let her miss a day without giving her some diversion or other; by which means the pain abates; she regains her pristine looks; and her company, a certain antidote against low spirits, is coveted by every one.

Theodora's spirits and health being now perfectly restored, she applies her leisure hours to works of use and fancy. She invents fashions, being her own milliner, to save expences to her mother, whom she thinks at too much on her account already. The Ladies must all have the same of whatever she appears in; by which means the milliners sollicit the favour of her patterns, and acknowledge her taste is of more advantage to them, than any three of their customers. All the gentlemen are eager to compliment her with tea, and he is esteemed the happiest man in the room, at the head of whose table she deigns to sit, and form his party of her own sex; being sure then to have the highest in the room; the Countess of ——, and the Countess of *Volpont* generally sitting on either side of *Theodora*, together with the then beautiful Lady *Bellamont*; and so delighted did they seem with *Theodora*'s dancing that the card players would leave orders, to let them know when she came down the dance; at which times they would leave their games, come with the cards in their hands, and follow her down: In short, no creature could be more caressed, or greater attention paid to, than was *Theodora*, to the no small joy of the Countess her mother. As a specimen of this, the following extraordinary thing happened to her one night as she was dancing, when there were above twenty couple standing up; at the bottom of the dance she found a plain gold ring on the fourth finger of her left hand, which had been dextrously slipt on without her knowledge, by some one of the gentlemen, but by whom she never could discover, every one pleading ignorance.

For some time *Theodora* had mingled among the crowd, civil to all, but partial to no man. A first friendship indeed she had contracted with the most celebrated beauty there, a young Lady from *Barbadoes*, whose external attractions, tho' very great, were her smallest perfections, being endowed with a sagacity superior to her years, and a soul that fell little short of being truly Angelic; each discovering in the other what they liked, that liking presently ripened into the warmest friendship, which engaged a mutual confidence, and rendered them unhappy when asunder; when unavoidable to be seperate for a day or so, they would write twice or thrice to each other in that day, to render their separation bearable.

One night, when the Countess of *Volpont, Theodora*, and the charming *Adalaide*, for that was this young Lady's name, were returning from the *Long Room* to *Bristol*, the coach going very slow, and they chatting very agreeably together, they were all of a sudden stopt, close by the wall of *Brandon-Hill*, not five yards beyond a lamp, and a man wrapt up in a great coat, presented a pistol in at the coach window, close by the Countess's ear, crying in an unnatural hoarse voice, damn me, Ladies, no noise, your money, watches and rings. *Theodora*, who sat opposite to her mother, was close by the fellow, and was at first in the mind to beat down the pistol out of his hand; but then recollecting it might go off in so doing, without being in the least daunted, she said, my dear Sir, do you imagine we are such simpletons to be out at this time o'night with watches, or any thing of considerable value about us? Well then, replied he, be quick and give me your purses, or I must search. With this *Theodora* pulling off two or three bawbles she had on her fingers, he concluded undoubtedly, that she was going to give them to him, but how great was his surprize, when, instead of presenting them to the modest claimant, she clapped them into her mouth, saying, I will be sworn if you get these, you must first encounter the sharp weapons, by which they are now inclosed.

At this drollery he could not avoid smiling, and seemed with difficulty to forbear laughing; but intent upon business, it did not then suit with the austerity of his function to shew so much levity, so he was decently preparing to come into the coach, and rifle the Ladies pockets; when the Countess and *Adalaide*, willing to preserve their watches, &c. threw him their purses. On this acquisition, chinking them in his hand, in order it is to be presumed to make an estimate of what they contained, he said it will do; and then very politely put up the step of the coach, and shut the door too; during which the Countess who was greatly in fear, and willing to get quit of him; complimented the villain, and prayed him not to give himself so much trouble.

Theodora all this time was fretting herself that her companions had been so precipitate in their motions; still hoping to delay time, until some people had come up, when it would have been his interest to have fled without his booty. As soon as they were robbed, the coachman (who was afterwards found out to be in combination with him) drove off as fast as possible, tho' *Theodora* repeatedly called out to him to stop. *Adalaide* beginning to regret the loss of some valuable medals that were in her purse, together with twelve or fourteen guineas, *Theodora* determining in her own mind to pursue the robber, in the hopes she might secure him, and recover what he had taken from her mother and friend; the former of whom could but ill spare eight or ten guineas, the sum in her purse at this particular juncture.

Our heroine, therefore the moment the coach was stopped, by those who heard her cry out, darted from it like an arrow from a bow, and pursued the rogue almost as far as *Jacob's Well*, crying as she went, *stop thief*, and held him in view all the way, until the play breaking up, the voice of a female at that time of night, raised the curiosity of a parcel of gentlemen to see who it was; when a moon[37] that was lighting them along, being held up to *Theodora*, they were struck with respect of the person, and astonishment at the cause, admiring at a lady having courage to venture so far after one, who seeing himself thus closely pursued, might have turned and shot her. She entreated that they would turn back, and assist her, assuring them that the thief could not be far off, as she had never lost sight of him, until they came up; altho' he ran very fast.

They all agreed, however, that it would be to no purpose to follow him, as there were so many turnings and windings about *Brandon Hill*, to facilitate his escape; so *Theodora* was prevailed on to let them wait on her back to the Countess of *Volpont*, who was almost terrified to death at the danger she ran.

The next day, the coachman that drove them the night before absconded; and *Theodora* having said openly, that she should know the robber again, having taken particular notice of him, by the light of the lamp, as he stood between her, and it. They were requested to appear at the *Tholsel*,[38] to see two men who were taken up, on suspicion of having committed this and other robberies. Now the ladies began to tremble at the apprehension of bringing a poor wretch to condign punishment.

They notwithstanding complied with the request, and to their no small joy found that neither of the poor creatures in durance, were the man. They appeared all pale and trembling, and by their looks might have condemned themselves, had they bore any resemblance of the person they were suspected to be; but there was such a disparity in their height, bulk, and features, that the moment *Theodora* was desired to look on the prisoners, she cried out with a visible satisfaction in her countenance, they are innocent of this fact, neither of them, on my honour, is the man; on which their features instantly brightened up, and falling on their knees, they blessed God for their acquital, praying for the young Lady, that was under him, the means of saving them from ignominy; And she had the pleasure to see them, on her bare word, set at liberty.

She was now desired to give a description of the man; which she did very minutely; every particular of which, by order of the court, was set down in writing; and it was found out that had the gentlemen followed the young lady's advice, he had certainly been taken the night before; for one every way answering her description, came into a beer house, at *Jacob's Well*, quite out of breath, a few minutes after she was stoped in her pursuit. Twice after this *Theodora* met the very man, and imprudently, had it not been involuntary, each time cried out that's the man; and attempted, unassisted, the first time to seize him; but he still gave her the slip, and by out running her, escaped three times that punishment he deserved, but which had she considered she would not for the world have brought on his head.

This affair made a very great noise, the gentlemen extoll'd her courage to the skies, but her own sex condemned her without mercy, saying it was an exploit out of character. She has a very masculine spirit truly, cryed *Cœlia* – Lard! did one ever hear the like, rejoined *Prudentia*, for a young lady to run so far after a man, and in the dark too, I am sure, said *Iris*, I should have fainted at the sight of a pistol in the ruffian's hand. And so might one half of her sex, replied a gentleman, there are not many *Theodora*'s, as to courage, see here my girls what the news paper says of her. "As the Countess of *Volpont*, her daughter and another young Lady, were coming from the *Hot Wells* to *Bristol*, their coach was stopped by a single footpad, who presented a pistol in at the coach, and robbed them. The Countess's daughter got out and pursued the fellow for above a quarter of a mile, crying out, *stop thief*, all the way she went; notwithstanding which, the fellow made his escape with his booty. It were to be wished that all his majesties officers were endowed with the same heroic spirit of this young Lady." Come, Ladies continued he, I hope after this public applause, you will never find fault with the charming *Theodora* again.

Each hung her head and flirted her fan, in token of the envy with which she was filled on this occasion.

Now methinks, I hear my youthful reader cry, but when shall we hear of this same love affair that was long since promised us? Why, my good friend, I think your impatience very allowable; for let me see, who would think it? I protest *Theodora* is now somewhat of the antiquated order of maids; turned of twenty, Oh! shameful; and not to have been once thoroughly in love. How unlike to the common run of novels and romances? Why the heroine of one of those would have been over head and ears before she had well entered into her *teens*, and here is ours has quite and clean leaped over the magic number before she has acknowledged the power of irresistable love; I am almost afraid it will appear too late, and out of character, to introduce the promised scene; but hang it, I will run all risks to keep my word, therefore my dear, good natured reader, to have every thing in proper form, drop four or five years, and imagine *Theodora* to be of the very age you, yourself, could have wished her, and all will be right. *Fancy*, with most writers, being the adjuster of those matters, I only vary from them a little, in that they do themselves what I am bold enough to trouble my reader with.

Theodora was now turned of twenty, sixteen, ay! sixteen let it be, when crossing the drawbridge, she meets a smart young officer; he starts, stops short, and pulling off his hat, with a most bewitching grace, and a respect that shewed he knew who he spoke to, he address'd her, and requested the honour of attending her, as she had no servant with her. She answered, he had the advantage of her, she not having the honour to know him. That I have escaped your ladyship's notice, said he, is not to be wondered at; but to see you once, and to forget you, is a thing that I believe many beside me have found impossible? a compliment so genteel, unavoidably engaging *Theodora*'s attention, she raised her eyes, which she had not before done, to view from whence it proceeded, when encountering his, she beheld a modest confusion in his look, that plainly discovered his address was not the effects of impudence; which not a little prepossess'd her in his favour, and made her allow him to accompany her to *Adalaide*'s, whither she was going. In the way he seized the opportunity to make her acquainted with his name, and family, with which she had the pleasure to know her mother was extremely intimate, and therefore made no difficulty to present the young gentleman to her dear *Adalaide* and her mother, as one to whose family she was no stranger.

He waited until she had made her visit, and then insisted upon conducting her home; this she had not the least objection to, for she had already found a something in his conversation that pleased her, and when his eyes met her's, she felt an instantaneous throb at her heart, that she could not account for, not having till that moment experienced it; but it was both painful and pleasing, and to which, on repetition, she found such an increase, that she feared at last she had caught some dangerous illness, and long'd to be at home. When he took her hand to lead her across the street, she perceived that he was all in a tremble; at which, the weather not being cold, she could not avoid wondering, and being interested, without knowing she was so, in his preservation, she with an earnestness uncommon, asked, was he not well? He sighed, and gently prest her hand, but could not speak. When dreading that she had asked a question which was not proper for him to resolve, an involuntary sigh steals from her.

How happy should I esteem myself, said he, had I the vanity to believe I had any share in that sigh. I could not have thought you so cruel, said she, as to wish yourself the cause of pain or trouble to any one, and sighs always proceed from one or the other. Not always returned *Clementine*, your Ladyship must allow they sometimes arise from a softer incitement. What is that? said she. A tender impulse of the heart, that I fear you have, but wish you may not yet have felt, said he. Friendship and gratitude, returned she, are, in my opinion, the softest the heart can be sensible of, and those I promise you, I have felt in their most exalted degree.

But not *love*, said he, with some emotion. Why not, said she, I hope you do not imagine, I so ill perform the commands of God, as not to love my fellow creatures. But none particularly, I hope, said he. Yes, particularly, replied she, but pray, why am I so closely catechised? I beg pardon, if I have offended, said he, in a low and faultering tone of voice, turning pale; at which *Theodora*, alarmed, cried out, dear *Clementine*, are you ill?

By this time they had reached her lodging, and fortunately the Countess was abroad, on which she asked him in, and getting a glass of hartshorn and water immediately, she made him drink it, but the unhappiness she discovered at his illness, effected his recovery much sooner than the medicine. However, her words had stung him to the quick, and his at the same time puzzled her not a little, so that for some moments they sat together without speaking a word. At last *Theodora* broke silence, and said she wish'd her mamma was come home (tho' God knows quite foreign from her heart at the same time, but she said it just to introduce what she thought would relieve him from the doubts she had raised, by adding) that *one* that she particularly loved above all the world, at the same time giving a significant smile. This was enough for *Clementine*, he took the hint, and looking earnestly at her, he asked her, was that the only dangerous rival he had to encounter, she answered, that, that rival, little as he might esteem her, was of more consequence than he imagined, in the disposal of her liking.

Liking perhaps, said he, may be directed in its lukewarm choice; but love always makes its own, despising reason's cool advice. This is a doctrine I don't understand, replied *Theodora*, if not above being taught, said he, I shall take great pleasure to instruct you. A pretty master, I'll be sworn, said she, not older, if so old as myself. But what would you say, said he, if I told you, you first taught me? I first taught you! said she, how is that possible, I beseech you? Oh! *Theodora*, said he, it is ungenerous to trifle with me in this manner, you cannot be so ignorant as you pretend, of the meaning of my words. But if I must be plain, I adore you, and have done so, ever since I first saw you; I have often wished for an opportunity to tell you so; but could never find one until to-day; then wonder not, I seize it. You may impute the prematureness of the declaration I make, to the violence of that passion you have raised, together with the dread of never having the like opportunity again. Did I rank you among the common run of women, I should also dread the pride and vanity, together with the ambition of your sex, would prove my enemies; and make you resent that presumption that poorly qualified for it, aspires to your love; but after knowing my name, I need not tell you, I am a gentleman; and tho' a younger brother, yet my expectations are not inconsiderable; nor can your union with my family, in the least disgrace yours. May I not therefore hope, that when convinced of the sincerity of my professions, I may engage you in time to reward my love.

Indeed captain, said she, this attack is too sudden, I am not prepared to answer it, then, said he, in a rapture, I am by that permitted to conclude, I have no favoured rival in my way; upon my word, retorted she, you have no bad nack of construing my meaning to your own liking whatever. But – here she stopt short, and *Clementine* throwing himself at her feet, and seizing her hand between his, cryed, but what, my angel! Oh! proceed to pronounce my sentence, and give at once life or death to my hopes. Well then, I declare, said she, it were a pity to destroy so thriving a progeny, as your *hopes*; they on'y got birth a moment ago, and they seem already arrived to maturity: no, no, I would have you by all means nourish and rear them. My witty charmer, said he, then you bid me entertain them? certainly replied she; then said he, as a pledge of future favour, let me have the honour to dance with you to-night. Can you dance well? said she, do you yourself be the judge replied he. Agreed said she, when in came the Countess, who seemed a little surprised, at seeing a strange gentleman with her daughter; but *Theodora* immediately presenting him to her, and letting her know who he was, she behaved to him with great complaisance and respect, and began to ask him several questions about his family with all of whom she was very intimate.

Now *Theodora* being excluded from the conversation, had an opportunity to steal a look now and then, without being observed, at her lover; and at every look became more and more prepossest with the opinion that he was the very prettiest fellow she had ever seen in her life; but love is certainly one of the most partial views, we women can take a man in, that same urchin always turning the wrong end of the perspective to the defects of the beloved object: But magnifying his good qualities to the height of perfection. Thus looked *Theodora* at *Clementine*, therefore we wont abide by her description; but give such a portrait of him as he really deserved. He was not quite of age, tall, slender and perfectly genteel; with a pair of remarkable handsome legs, his face oval, an aquiline nose, eyes that had vast tenderness and expression in them, placid brow, good teeth, fair complexion, and light hair, add to this, a mind enriched with every virtue, and a heart untainted with vice.

Such was *Clementine*, who to *Theodora*'s great joy, she found her mother much pleased with. They went, as usual, in the evening to the long room, where the impatient *Clementine*, waited their arrival at the door, to have the pleasure of handing them from their coach.

Theodora as usual, opened the ball with lord —— the eyes of *Clementine* pursuing her in every movement, envious that any one should engross her so long from him, and the moment his lordship had handed her to her seat, the fond lover planted himself by her, at which she was not in the least displeased, nor yet, when he told her mother that she danced a minuet better than any one he had ever seen; scarce had he spoke, when he was summoned to display his excellence in that way; and fixed her in the same opinion of him, that he had formed of her. Both ardently wishing for the country dances to begin, that they might more particularly entertain each other.

What odd effects this same love has upon different complexions, *Clementine* and *Theodora* seem to have made an exchange of temper as well as hearts. He, rather of the serious cast, assumes a vivacity that adds innumerable graces to his person. She, who was all life and spirit before, wears a pensive air, and scarce dares to raise her eyes, to those of her partner's; tho', while unprejudiced in favour of those with whom she danced, she could look them full in the face, and favour them with her smiles. At his very touch in taking hands, she feels a soft emotion at her heart; if so sensible with gloves on; what must she be with them off. I think, I need say no more, to prove she is initiated into the soft mystery of that irresistable passion, which has vanquished those, who have vanquished worlds.

   He sues, she sighs,
   She looks, he dies.

Both strangers to dissimulation, he seeks not to destroy, nor she to conceal, the impression he has made; he openly declares himself her slave, and she freely acknowledges, she is sensible of his worth, and prefers him before all the world. Scarce a day passes, that they are not together, and in private company; though ever so many present, his station is at the feet of his beloved *Theodora*; the perfect respect he pays to her mother, shews his sincere regard to the daughter; he watches the Countess's eyes, and flies to execute her will, before she has well made it known. She love's him as her own son, but will have nothing to say to their union, tho' nothing she more sincerely wishes than to see him and her daughter one.

When the *Hot Wells* season is over, the town assembly begins, to which the Countess and her daughter are, by the two new appointed stewards, the very first invited. At these assemblies they have established rules, that one of the stewards always dance first couple, and the rest of the gentlemen draw for places, which rules their politeness to *Theodora*, broke through: for, on her first appearance there, one of those gentlemen, took her out to dance the first minuet; and, the *French* dances over, they asked her was she engaged with a partner? She answered in the affirmative, and naming *Clementine* as the person; when he went to draw, as the rest did, the steward told him that *Theodora*'s Partner, was exempted from following their rules, let him be whom he would.

On which he remarked that the *Bristol* gentlemen had paid her a greater degree of respect, than they were ever known to shew to any stranger, particularly nobility; and added, but it is no wonder, my angel! that all the world should pay homage to thy superiour merit. My dearest, *Clementine* replied she, what your partiality would attribute to my merit, I rather look upon to be the meer effect of their own innate goodness, and great humanity, treating me now with greater civility, on account of my distresses, than they perhaps would, could I appear in all that glare of grandeur I once did, and to which my birth entitles me.

Oh! my *Theodora*, said he, cease thus to charm me; least I should loose sight of thee as a woman, and adore thee as a divinity. Fye, *Clementine*, replied she, don't sink beneath a man, in commencing flatterer; and unkindly encreasing that vanity, that is already raised to too high a pitch, by thy love. Great God! said he, this is too much; my love, my life, my *Theodora*; how shall I ever be able to compensate this condescension? easily, said she, only by continuing to look so favourably on me as you now do, and ever blessing me with thy love. And before I cease to love thee, said he, may the icy hand of death, first close those eyes, that now so doat upon thee.

Now called to the dance, this little stolen tête a tête, was interrupted before *Theodora* could make a reply to the dear youth, other than with her eyes, whose well understood rhetoric, told him, how little her love was inferior to his own. In short, never were hearts, more interwoven than theirs; a separation in their waking hours was intollerable; though for ever of short duration, too often robbing their senses, of the needful refreshment of sleep; but drowsiness dare not approach their eye lids, while they could gaze upon each other; and sigh, and talk the short lived hours away, upon the subject of their promised future bliss.

Clementine, now grown impatient to possess the object of his wishes, presses *Theodora* to bestow her hand upon him; she would gladly wait a few months longer, until of age;[39] but, ah! how can she refuse the man she truly loves? impossible, his reiterated entreaties must at length prevail; she gives the wished for consent then hides her blushes in his bosom. The transported youth having caught her in his arms, the moment she had pronounced the soul enlivening yes. *Theodora*, now for once, tasted of unalloyed pleasure, in the joy this monosylable dispensed on her dear *Clementine*; he steals a ring from off the mistic finger, whereby to fit it, with one for the purpose; the day is fixed, and the place appointed, where the ceremony is to be performed, that is to unite those for ever, who are already one in fond affection and mutual love.

The morning, previous to their intended nuptials, *Clementine*, as usual, comes to enquire after the Countess's and his dear *Theodora*'s health, and as he is going out, says apart to her, I am just going to the goldsmith's for the ring, my love, don't forget to-morrow morning, eight o'clock; you know where, but I suppose I shall come in the evening to remind you. Oh! that tomorrow night were come, my *Theodora*, my wife, may I not call thee so? will not to-morrow make thee mine for ever? *Theodora*, though she knew not why, gave a heavy sigh, and said, I hope so: on which a tear instantaneously following, her beloved *Clementine* asked her what was the meaning of these dark presages, and with real concern said, he hoped she did not repent already? far be it from me, my dearest *Clementine*, said she, but alas! I fear it is too much happiness for one so unfortunate as I have been, to expect. The height of my ambition would be to call thee mine; and if to-morrow grants that blessing to me, fortune and I will then be friends; never will I complain of her again. He then rallied her for doubting of what was now of such a certainty, and giving her a tender embrace, bid her banish all such idle notions, for that the morrow's sun shou'd see them one.

The charming *Adalaide* being then at *Bath*; *Theodora*, had confided the secret of her intended marriage, in the breast of a young lady, who was then on a visit to her from *Bath*. *Clementine* came not in the evening according to his promise, but this she took no notice of, she return'd with the Countess and her new created confidant home; the latter was her bed-fellow, and when they were alone, *Theodora*, bursting into tears, the poor young lady stood all amazed at so odd a behaviour; and said, good God! my dear Lady, what is the matter? All this night have I been pained to the soul, to see the ill concealed conflict in your breast, have you any dislike to the engagement you are going to enter into? Do you not love *Clementine*? Love him! reply'd *Theodora*, yes! I do love him, even to distraction; and would prefer the meanest situation in life with him, to the sharing of a throne, with the greatest monarch in the world. Oh! *Maria*, soothe the anguish in my breast, nay, rather reprove the folly, which, though to-morrow is fixed upon to make us one, views that happiness at a great, and endless distance; my idle fears portend, my dear, it will never, never be.

Absurd to the last degree, cries the friend; I could not have thought it, that one of your understanding, and good sense, would be so industrious in creating evils, to torment your imagination. Fye! for shame, compose yourself, let us go to rest, a pleasing dream will chace these weak forbodings from your mind; and to-morrow morning will give certainty to crown your wishes. Would I were so near becoming his, that I most love; I should be mad with joy, instead of groaning thus in spirit, like an old devotee, preached into despair of God's mercy, by some fanatic leader:

And so saying, being by this time disencumbered of her garments, into bed the mad thing leapt.

In the morning, *Maria* roused *Theodora*, from her pillow, and hurried her to get dressed to go to the place of rendezvous, where she said she was sure *Clementine* was impatiently expecting her; she acquiesced with her friend's desire, and was with her at the place, at the time appointed, where they were met by the Parson, and father *Doner* by *Clementine's* direction; but no *Clementine* was there. On the arrival of the Bride, they seemed amazed that the bridegroom was not come. One hour elapsed, another, and no *Clementine* appears. They wonder, and every one seems vexed but *Theodora*, who wears a gaiety on her countenance that is, in reality, quite foreign to her heart, and says, it is all for the better; perhaps it were better miss than meet, and then apologizing for the trouble they had been at, she invites them all home to breakfast with her mother.

The Countess, by the time they arrive, is up, and receives them; but *Theodora* having cautioned them before-hand, not a word of what has happened is let drop: So it appears they met by accident in their morning's walk, and all is well. The Countess goes out, and the gentlemen taking their leave, *Theodora*, and Maria are left together: The brow of the latter clouded, can scarce raise her eyes to the former, who walks about the room, humming a tune, as if nothing had happened. At last she says, *Maria*. Well, says the other, in a very plaintive tone of voice, is not this a very fine day? No, says *Maria*, I think it the most disagreeable I ever saw. Why so, my dear, says *Theodora*, for my part I think the sun shines brighter than usual. O! *Theodora*, said the other, is it possible that you have so little sensibility, as not to be affected with what has happened? And is it possible, my dear girl replied she, that you should have so mean an opinion of me, as to imagine me incapable of bearing so trifling a disappointment. A trifling disappointment, exclaimed the other! call you that a trifle, to lose the man you love? I cannot lose, said *Theodora*, what I never had. It is true I loved him, nay, I will say more, I still love him, and perhaps shall ever love him, but am above letting him see it is in his power to give me pain; therefore, though I lose my life in the conflict, I am determined not to see him, or hear any excuse he can make; upon which, ringing the bell, the servant coming up, she ordered him never to admit *Clementine* again. The footman, amazed at the command, and not crediting his ears, replies, Not admit the captain my Lady? No, said she. So lifting up his eyes, in token of his wonder, he withdrew.

The whole day passed over, without seeing or hearing from him; and though *Theodora* concluded him to be one of the falsest creatures living, yet she felt a secret uneasiness, lest some evil had befallen him; but her pride was too great, to suffer her to make the least enquiry about him, or even to suggest to *Maria*, the favourable excuse her love would fain engage her to make for him. Never did a poor creature, suffer equal to what she did; though, to all appearance, she braved the disappointment she had met with a spirit truly magnanimous. What would she not have given, for a few hours to herself, to have given vent to her grief-swoln heart, without having any witness to her weakness? Surely her situation, is truly pityable; she, who hates dissimulation, strives to assume a smile, and laugh, and chat with her mother, and company that came that evening, while her mind is on a perfect rack of torture.

Simple *Theodora*, thus to conceal thy anguish; art thou not afraid, that the violence you offer to nature in so doing, may be of the most fatal consequence; that sickness, is the smallest evil you may expect; and that death may perhaps ensue? She knows all this already, but reconciled to either, she dreads neither. Life is an insupportable burthen, it is true, but still she submits to the will of heaven; nor will she fly in the face of Providence, by attempting any thing against that life, which he who gave it, has alone a right to take. In this state of concealed misery, *Theodora* and the rest of the family retire to rest; *Maria* tries to purloin her thoughts from the disagreeable subject, still further than she imagines they are strayed; though surprised at the seeming progress she has already made, in the extinction of so fixed [affection?] as her's appeared to be. Her head not much encumbered with care, nor her heart with pain, *Maria* scarce sinks upon the downy pillow, before she resigns her senses to the soft embrace of sweet invigorating sleep: Now all is still and hush; when *Theodora*'s sighs burst forth, and interrupt the awful silence; fearful to disturb her friend's repose, she steals with caution from her bed, and slipping on her morning wrapper, gropes her way into another room, where she gives herself up to the most poignant grief and bitter reflection.

O God, she cries, if *Clementine* be false, what man should ever be credited? Their words, their oaths, their very looks deceive; sincerity and love are nought but specious masks put on at will, to answer their malicious purposes, in making dupes of our credulity. Farewel to all the sex for ever; Reason, hereafter, shall steel my heart against their every attack; nor think, too lovely, perjured youth, that I will again once listen to, or yet believe thee: No, I have done with thee for ever. Here spoke female resentment; but love must have its turn, and she continues thus: Perhaps some accident has happened to him; he may be ill, he may be dead; forbid it heaven, forbid it love; Oh! my *Clementine*, my dear *Clementine*, thy *Theodora* then were wretched indeed.

In this manner did she pass the live-long night, angrily condemning, and fondly excusing the man who got the full possession of her heart; but the morning dawn appearing, and nature growing faint and weary, she went again to bed, prepossessed in the opinion least advantageous to *Clementine*, in which she slept a little, and then arose, her mind vastly calmed, by the indulgence she had given her grief over night.

It was yet early, and the Countess not up, when *Theodora* sitting by the fire in the dining-room quite alone, who should appear but *Clementine*? She just turned her head, on hearing the door open; and seeing him clap himself upon one knee, even at that distance, as much feared as though she had beheld a spectre, she cried, O God! and fled directly into her chamber, double locked and bolted the door; and throwing herself on the bed, wrapped up her head in the bed-clothes to prevent her hearing him, lest she should not have strength to resist those prayers and entreaties, which she judged, by his humiliating posture, he was prepared to employ for reinstating himself in her favour. In this disagreeable manner she remained until, almost stifled, she was forced to take breath; when hearing *Maria*'s voice at the door, begging to be admitted, she refused complying, unless assured that no one was there, but herself. She protesting solemnly there was not, *Theodora* opened the door for her friend; who saluted her with saying, that she did not think her Ladyship had such cruelty as she found she had, in withstanding the prayers, entreaties, and even tears of the unhappy *Clementine*; which had so affected her, that she feared she should not get the better of it, of a long time, though not so interested in his preservation as *Theodora* should be, if she ever loved him, or was endowed with that pity she always thought her possessed of.

All artifice, returned *Theodora*; I am glad I did not hear it, as I might, like you, have thought him sincere, and again have been deceived. If ever man was sincere, continued *Maria*, I believe he is. And pray what excuse has he invented, for his late behaviour? said *Theodora*. That he did not tell me, replied the other, but he seemed almost distracted, and vowed vengeance against somebody, whose name I don't remember, though he repeated it two or three times; but never did I see grief and anguish painted stronger in any one's face than that of poor *Clementine*; may heaven grant, he don't do some mischief to himself. No my dear, added *Theodora*, there is no fear of that; how finely should I have been imposed upon, had I not had the courage to fly the deceiver, before he had fascinated my senses to a belief of his innocence. O *Maria*, those men are subtle creatures; there is scarce one in a thousand, that can be depended upon. But won't you see him *Theodora*, will you condemn him unheard? replied *Maria*. I neither will condemn, or acquit him, said she, but see him I never will, if I continue in the same mind, I am now in. Which I pray God, returned *Maria*, you may not long do, lest it should prove too late to change it.

The Countess coming in, they changed their discourse. *Clementine*'s not coming to them as usual, greatly surprised that lady, which taking notice of to *Theodora*, she turned it off with a jest, and said, he perhaps was gone a courting; on which the Countess, looking with an air of severity at her daughter, said, she was sure if it was so, it must be her fault. *Theodora* reddened at this speech, which discovered the good opinion the Countess had of *Clementine*.

He wrote to her, she inclosed his letter back again to him unopened: in short, nothing could be more miserable than she rendered her lover, without being a whit the better by the cruelty she exercised towards him; she still loved him, and every day her resentment diminished towards him. *Maria* was ever reproaching her on his account; but what above all got the victory over her obstinacy, for it surely deserves no better name, was, seeing the dear youth, with arms a-cross, and pensive, walking every night before her windows, for the space of eight or ten nights; for so long (and that was a pretty while for a woman that loved as she did) she held her resolution not to admit him.

At first she avoided the windows, lest she should see him; by degrees she came to give a peep, now and then, at him; at last, to sit whole hours in expectation of seeing him; when one evening, as she was thus employed, he appeared, gazed up at her windows, and seeing him apply his handkerchief to his eyes, she without knowing what she did, cried out, Oh heavens! my dearest *Clementine!* – that is too much – I cannot bear it – *Maria* help me, and so saying, she fainted; the Countess being engaged abroad at cards, which *Theodora* always avoided as much as possible, *Maria* running to her assistance, immediately espied the cause, and left her to bring the right physician, as quick as possible; she notified to the lover the situation of his mistress, and he, borne on the wings of love, in an instant had her in his arms.

She remains so long insensible, that believing her in reality dead, he strains her to his panting breast, and glewing his lips to hers, he cries, And art thou gone my Love? Has thy gentle spirit taken its flight? Oh my dear *Theodora*, I will not long stay after thee! Why, charming maid, would'st thou not stay, to seal the pardon of thy wretched *Clementine!* She gives a heavy sigh, and almost inarticulately says, My dear *Clementine!* forgive – pardon – Oh! my life, my soul! cries *Clementine*, open thine eyes, my dear *Theodora*, and behold thy husband, who wishes not to live, unless to call thee his.

Theodora, at the sound of that beloved voice, revives; she opens her eyes, and views her *Clementine* upon his knee at her feet, as a criminal that waits his sentence if to live or die; while the tears run trickling down his pallid cheek; she views him attentively, and sees a change in his countenance, that well explains the trouble he has felt, since last she saw him. Alas! she cries, Is this my *Clementine*? 'Tis all, said he, that grief, at thy displeasure, has left of him. Love runs now with doubled force to her breast, accompanied by pity, and throwing her arms around his neck, she says, My *Clementine*, my only love, have pity, forget the usage I have given thee, and live to make thy *Theodora* happy.

True woman – angry at first, to a fault, and now condescending to a folly! You would not suffer your lover to exculpate himself of the crime he, to all appearance though innocently, lay under, and now you not only forgive him, without knowing he merits that forgiveness; but you take the fault upon yourself, and sue for his pardon, with whom you have been offended with some degree of reason; but as in fashions, so in our passions, we women are, to tell the truth, too apt to run a little or so into extremes.

There is an old saying, that was here truly verified, namely, "The falling out of lovers, is the renewal of love." This transient breach served to cement their affections still stronger, and to make great part of that reserve vanish, that *Theodora* had always preserved with her lover; though at the same time she loved him as her life. But the true way to preserve the respect due to us, is to keep these encroaches at a proper distance; for with some men, this melting tenderness which she discovered, thro' down right compassion to the altered looks of her *Clementine*, might have proved the means of her ruin; which I fear has too frequently been the unhappy fate of many a fond, believing, unsuspecting maid. The moments of tender reconciliation in such circumstances, being to the full, if not more dangerous than those on the eve of a marriage, which a certain author has very *feelingly* described. The anguish of the heart humbles its pride, the sudden transition from grief to joy, at regaining the beloved object, puts prudence off its guard, and when love has once been able to make us wrongfully criminate ourselves, to lighten the charge against the object of our wishes, whom we seek an excuse to pardon, there wants but a few ardent sighs, to waft the lover from liberty to liberty, until by the completion of his desires, he robs her of that innocence and virtue that was the fair foundation of his honourable pursuits; that lost, he flies the wretch he has undone. Like unto the swine, who, though the foulest of feeders, rejects the food it has contaminated with its own obnoxious breath.

Though *Theodora* possessed a moderate share of prudence, it was at this critical time so enfeebled, her love so great, and her innocence so unsuspecting, that there is no knowing how compleat his victory might have proved, had he not been possessed of the strictest honour, and that honour kept in due discipline by the presence of *Maria*, who was going to withdraw, but was prevented by the dear youth himself, who loved his *Theodora* too well, to depend on his own strength of resolution, in withstanding the temptations of privacy with her.

The transports of this young couple being a little subsided, *Maria*, in her usual droll way, after crying and laughing alternately at their well expressed pain and pleasure, addressed them in the following words: Well, I protest, this is as strange an affair as ever I knew; but though you, my good Sir, may be glad to slip your neck out of the halter; and you *Theodora*, are glad to be reconciled to your doating piece, without seeking any satisfaction for what has given you, to my knowledge, more pain than *Clementine* can ever make you amends for; yet I am a woman, and he not having it in his power to oblige me more particularly, at least for the present, than in gratifying that curiosity he has excited, I insist upon knowing the cause of this disappointment, that gave rise to a quarrel, which is now I think as unaccountably made up, as it was carried on, to a too great length on my conscience.

Theodora smiled at this interrogation; she wished to hear it as much as her friend, but was ashamed to ask, lest he could not give a sufficient reason, and thereby call her judgment in question, in which, love had totally cleared him already. *Clementine* looking upon her with an affectionate concern, said, How culpable must I have appeared in thine eyes, my angel? Alas! the thought of it pains me, but when you shall have heard how I was served, you will rather pity than condemn thy *Clementine*.

The day before that one, which I flattered myself would have rendered me the happiest man living, in making me the owner of a treasure that my soul pants after, I went to the goldsmith's, as I told you I would; I had got the ring, and was just coming out of the shop, twirling it round the top of my little finger, when I was met by a person that moment arrived from *Ireland*, who was very intimate with all my family; I was rejoiced at seeing him, esteeming him my friend, but he unfortunately 'spying the ring, asked me with impatience, what was that? I answered him, a pledge of endless love. In which, I hope, said he, you have no share. – I replied, Why not? Is it really for yourself, said he? Undoubtedly, I answered. – He asked me then who was the lady? This I refused to tell him, saying, it was a secret. He said, he could not think I could have any which I might not confide in him, or he expect to hear.

This reproach extorted the secret from me: Pardon me, my dear *Theodora*, for here was my crime; I should not have told the villain any thing about it. On my naming whose daughter you were, and that we were to be married early next morning, he started, and with extreme warmth, bid me have nothing to say to you, for the daughter of such a man as my *Theodora*'s father could never make me a good wife. I said, I was sure by this he did not know my *Theodora*; for if he did, he would be of another opinion; that I loved you, and thought it my greatest happiness that you had consented to be mine.

He then set forth every thing in the most disagreeable light to me, that though you might make me such a wife, as I, he feared vainly, flattered myself you would, yet it might prove my ruin; for your father, pardon me, my love, for repeating his words, was so bad a man, that he would seek every occasion to hurt me, and would exert his interest to stop my rise in the army, instead of facilitating it. All this, I said I would risk for my *Theodora*; so finding that his officious advice was bestowed to no purpose, he seemed to acquiesce with the choice my heart had made; said he longed to see the young lady to whom I was so lavish of praise, for it would seem flattery to tell my *Theodora* all I said of her: And asked me to dine with him, that we might drink to your health, and our mutual happiness.

I accepted his invitation, and little suspecting his dark designs, I went with him to his lodgings. After dinner, he proposed your health in half pint bumpers, which I could by no means refuse. He is one of those persons who pride themselves in being able to out-drink all his companions, to which not being used, I was soon intoxicated; and when so, I have reason to think, he used some illicit means to stupify my senses, for I fell fast asleep, when he had me put to bed, where I remained until twelve or one o'clock the next day.

When I awaked and found where I was, and what the hour of the day, I concluded what had passed in the morning, and was like one distracted; I do believe, had the villain been in the way, I should instantly have destroyed him; this he was aware of, and so escaped the punishment he merited from one he had injured in so tender a point. A false shame prevented my coming to you, which I certainly should have done; I searched every where I could think to find that scoundrel out, but all to no purpose: he concealed himself for a few days, and then set out for *London*, which I was but a day or two ago acquainted with. The day after this unhappy affair, I came here, you flew me, at which I felt a sorrow that I have not words to describe, but which I believe my looks sufficiently evince: your resentment was too justly grounded for me to condemn; but indeed, my dear *Theodora*, had it been of a much longer continuance, your forgiveness had come too late, to save the life of him, to whom it became burdensome, under your displeasure. Here *Clementine*, concluded his account; at which both *Maria* and *Theodora* wept, but the latter particularly, reproaching herself severely for so unjustly refusing to hear what he had to say in his own justification.

Happy at this eclaircissment,[40] and of course perfectly reconciled, the Countess found these lovers at her return home; in which seeming to feel some pleasure, and perceiving the alteration in *Clementine*'s countenance, she tenderly expressed her concern, asking had he been ill? then enquired the cause of his long absence, saying, she hoped he had not met with any thing in her behaviour to disgust him;

he answered, that so far from it, he was truly sensible of the unmerited attention her ladyship had ever shewn him, which he should ever remember with the warmest gratitude.

Theodora throwing herself at her mother's feet, and imploring her pardon, for attempting to bestow her hand upon *Clementine*, without asking her consent, informed her of what had past, from beginning to ending; at which, she appeared much affected. *Clementine*, now afraid that, on this information, the Countess might interpose her authority, to prevent his union with her daughter, so soon as he could wish, on account of her unhappy situation, he thought he would not let slip this favourable opportunity, to sollicit her approbation and consent to his happiness.

She told him, she had so great a regard for him, that did the disposal of *Theodora* depend entirely on her, she would rejoice, in making her the property of one so deserving as he was; but that was a thing she could not pretend to, while she was under age, and had a father living; that a very short time would make her, according to law, her own mistress, and then no blame could be laid to her charge by the Earl. She therefore thought it prudent to wait a little longer; they were both young, and the time would glide imperceptibly by, that was past in each others company.

There was too much reason in this advice, to admit of any contradiction; notwithstanding which, *Clementine* urged every thing he possibly could, to hasten that felicity, he promised himself, in the possession of her he loved; but the Countess remained fixed in her opinion; and he was obliged, at least in appearance, to acquiesce with it; though determined to try if he could not prevail on *Theodora*, to act contrary. But she, unwilling to disoblige her mother, would by no means consent to a clandestine marriage again; saying, that what she would have done, before the Countess was acquainted with it, she might hope for forgiveness in, but the case being altered, what was before in its nature innocent, would now be criminal, in becoming an act of disobedience, which she never yet having committed, she would not now begin to run counter to the wise counsels of so good a parent; nay it was what *Clementine* would not wish her to do, if he loved her.

Theodora in this was certainly right; but surely no poor creature ever suffered more by filial attatchment, than she had done, and was still ordained to do. In a few days after their reconciliation, the route came to the regiment, to which *Clementine* belonged; they were ordered abroad: this was like a thunderbolt, to the two lovers. *Clementine* now thought he had a right to *Theodora*'s hand: but alas! the Countess secretly rejoiced at the disappointment, that had prevented her loss of her daughter; whom she must have yielded up to a husband's superior authority, had *Clementine* then married her: there was therefore, no possibility of obtaining her consent; without which, *Theodora* would not yield to his fond entreaty. What was her situation? suspended between love and duty: to part with the man she loved, perhaps for ever, was death to her; then for his sake to quit a mother, who came to *Bristol* on her account only, and to leave her bereft of all comfort, was so unnatural, so ungrateful, that she could not bear the thought.

Wretched *Theodora!* One moment to see the dear youth on his knees, the picture of death, imploring thee to comply; next, the tender mother, with streaming eyes, asking thee, can you be so cruel, to leave her without the smallest consolation, to follow the fortunes of a young man, you scarce know a twelvemonth? Dreadful conflict! not yet determined! The day, the unfortunate, dreadful day, approaches: Cruel thou must be, or to lover, or to mother. Oh! heavens! Which way turn thee? How decide? The eve of the day arrives, that they must part. The Countess indulgent to their mutual torture, together with another Lady, sits up the whole night with them, which is past in sighs and tears. *Clementine* snatches up a prayer-book, and swears by that, he will never marry any other woman but herself: She promises to keep her love entire for him: They both agree to hold a constant correspondence, while separate. But hark! The drum beats –. He starts. She shrieks, and faints. Little better than herself, he does all he can to recover her. He clasps her to his bosom, bathes her face with his tears, and recalls her once more to life, and misery, who had been glad then to die in his arms. Again the drum beats – Cruel summons.

Oh! heavens! And must I leave thee, my *Theodora*? he cries. You cannot, you shall not leave me, she replies, *Clementine*, you are my husband, I will not stay behind thee. The officers, who know his situation, will not call him until the last minute: The men are mustered; ready to march, of which the drum again gives notice. *Clementine* attempts to leave her; but has not power to tear himself from the arms of *Theodora*, his beloved, his wretched *Theodora*; who clinging to him, rends the house with her cries, and vows before she will quit her hold, she will suffer to be torn piece-meal.

Two, or three of his friends come up to the room, where they are. She redoubles her cries, at seeing them, and entreats they will not take her husband, her dear, her adored *Clementine* from her. He strains her with fervour to his breast, and begs they will kill him thus; for dying with his *Theodora*, were preferable to living without her. This tragic scene affects every one present, that view the sufferings of the hapless lovers. But part they must, to hasten which, messenger after messenger arrives; another kiss, but yet another kind embrace, My love, My life, My husband, My wife, My *Theodora*, My *Clementine*, are a thousand times repeated.

But now they have recourse to force. *Theodora*'s friends hold her, while his tear him from her. She struggles, they are forced asunder. They break from their holders; they fly once more into each others arms; beseeching heaven to give them both death at once, rather than let them part: At last they are separated – And that for ever.

O! cruel, cruel fate, that those who love so tenderly, who seem alone formed for each other, should never, never, meet again! *Theodora* sinks motionless into the arms of those that cruelly tore her from her love. *Clementine* wants to fly to her assistance; but his brother officers hurry him from a sight which unmans him. Pale, trembling, and almost lifeless, he joins his corps; and they immediately march out of town.

Theodora goes from one fainting fit into another, in which way she remains for several hours; *Clementine*, at the first halt they make, sends an express to know how his *Theodora* does; with the following words of comfort to her:

"If my *Theodora* lives, let her ease the anguish of her *Clementine*, by a line from under her own hand. The thought of her unhappiness, enhances my sufferings to a degree I cannot express. O preserve that life, my angel, on which mine depends. We shall meet again, I hope, and be happy. Present my duty to our good, but cruel mother; sure I may call her so; for if she is thine she must also be his, who is and ever will be, my dearest life, thy affectionate Husband,
C L E M E N T I N E."

When *Theodora* received this note, she was just recovered out of a fit, that lasted so long, the Countess had almost given her over for dead, and began to wish she had consented to her union with *Clementine*, though she were never to have seen her child again, rather than thus to have been, as then she accused herself, accessary to her death. Never was cordial more reviving, than the above note was to *Theodora*, who, though quite weak, and low, sat up in bed, to write an answer to it, which contained the following words:

"Oh! my *Clementine*! thou Lord of my fond wishes, in no other would I be careful of a life, of which I am sick, but that you say you are interested in it. Now, but that we are commanded to bless and curse not, could I pour forth a thousand maledictions on the head of him, to whom I owe the pain I feel, in being separated from thee. Had not my ill stars directed him to be the means of our disappointment, I had now been happy in thy arms: But oh! that was, as I predicted, too great a blessing for me to expect. Pray heaven! my misfortunes may not pursue me to a still greater length, in making thee forget, that no one else can ever have a right to subscribe herself thy affectionate wife, but thy poor *Theodora*."

Two or three other expresses were sent off by *Clementine* to her, in the course of two, or three days march, conveying the most tender assurances of an invariable, and constant affection; to all which she made suitable returns: her mother, and her dear *Adalaide*, whose sympathizing soul shared in the distress of *Theodora*, did all they could to mollify her grief.

The Countess now having a desire to return to *Ireland*, and *Theodora* being informed by *Clementine*, that his regiment was to set sail for *Minorca* in a day or two, she pressed her mother to leave a place, which would, by constantly reminding her of the pleasure she had tasted in his presence, give daily increase to the pain she must endure in his absence; the Countess readily agreeing, they set sail the very day on which *Clementine* left *England*. They arrived at *Cork* in *Ireland*, their destined port; of which having acquainted her beloved *Clementine* before they left *England*, she in as short a time as could be expected, receives a letter from the dear youth, giving her the pleasurable account of his safe arrival at *Minorca*, with fresh assurances of the continuance of his love. She answers it in terms that leave no room for him to think her insincere; and scarce a month but she receives one, or two letters from him; so that in a short time she becomes reconciled to her fate.

On their arrival, the Countess accepted of a small house in a most romantic situation by the river *Lee*, with which a worthy friend of hers, named *Shaloon*, complimented her. Nothing in nature could be better suited to the turn of *Theodora*'s mind, than this rural retreat. The rocks impending over the smooth surface of a beautiful meandering river, clad by nature with a variety of shrubs, which hang over the wide mouths of hollow caverns, as if to hide the peaceful retreat of some poor wretched being, detached from all the follies of a busy, inconsiderate world. On the top of a stupendous hill, whose craggy sides are almost inaccessible, stands the beautiful ruins of a castle, or rather a fort, which in days of yore was a formidable redoubt: a few roods[41] from it, see an ancient church, whose thick and solid walls seem to defy the levelling hand of time. Beneath this hill, a cottage, neat but homely, near unto which there is a tuck mill,[42] whose awful stroke beats time to the melancholy murmurs of its forced stream. Over this, a little bridge is fixed, which affords a communication with an extensive common, whose verdant carpet, embellished with daizies, primroses, violets, and butterflowers, yields a delightful prospect to the contemplative eye, while the swelling river, cutting its way thro' it, adds amazingly to its beauty.

In this enchanting spot, they sit them down with vast contentment to pass the tedious moments by, until Providence thinks fit to mollify the rigour of their fate, one praying for a change in the mind of her lord, the other, that none may happen in that of her lover. But not the solitude of the place, the rusticity of their appearance, or the little desire they have for company, can save *Theodora* from the solicitude of admirers: she has three or four presently in her train; but scorning to hold those in durance, that she has it not in power to reward, she candidly informs each in turn, that her heart is not at her disposal, being the property of another, in whom her only hope of earthly happiness is entirely vested; therefore intreats they will not encourage the growth of a passion for one who can make no other return for their kindness but thanks.

I do not know how it was, but this ingenuity rather drew their liking more upon her; and though they desisted to importune, they nourished still a tender regard, little short of love for her; nor could they in their own mind avoid applauding that sincerity, that deprived them of the smallest hopes of success.

One of these gentlemen was the son of a worthy divine of noble family. This young gentleman, had not *Theodora* been prepossessed in favour of another, would have had an exceptionable claim to a preference, being endowed with every qualification of mind and person, to recommend him to her notice. He was intended for the church, for which he had accomplished his studies; joined to a solid judgment, he had a bright and lively wit, which he frequently exercised in the praise of *Theodora*.

He that stood next in the list of her admirers, was the son of that gentleman who had furnished the Countess with the little cottage in which they resided. This young gentleman was not by some years so old as the other, and was of a graver cast, than his years entitled him to. He was very ingenuous, and left nothing undone that could improve his understanding, or store his mind with knowledge; and so much in love with books as he was, it was in fact something extraordinary, that he gave any attention to the merit of *Theodora*; he was young, but sagacious beyond the expectation of those that converted with him; add to this a goodness of soul, that could not fail making the woman happy that made him her choice. However, *Theodora*'s was already made; had it not, the parson's son very probably would have fixed it. To distinguish one from the other, for the short time we shall have occasion to mention them, we will call Mr. *Shaloon*'s son, *Sylvius*, and the other *Lucius*.

With the Countess's consent, her daughter having gone to town with the sister of *Lucius*, at that young lady's request, and that of her brother, she staid at their house for two or three days; but uneasy at her mother's being alone, they could not prevail on her to stay longer; so her two admirers *Lucius*, and *Sylvius* attended her home; where they found no one but the two maids; a neighbour of their's at the other side of the River *Lee*, having prevailed on the Countess to pass the time that *Theodora* was absent with them, taking the footman with her, since which there had fallen such a quantity of rain, that the river was then unpassable. This giving the young lady some pain, her two humble servants offered to stay all night to protect her; but this she would by no means permit: So after dinner, they took their leave, and returned to town. *Theodora* had before she left town, got a letter from her beloved *Clementine*, if possible, more fond, and affectionate than ever: So that my gentle reader may imagine the time could not sit heavy on her hands, who could have read the welcome epistle, a thousand times over, without being tired. She read it, wet it with her tears, and kissed the dear paper dry again a dozen times; when the hour of rest approaching, after seeing all the doors and windows secured, ordering the maids to make their bed on the floor in her room, she retired, and they all went to bed.

Theodora had scarce resigned herself to a balmy slumber, when she was disturbed by the whispering of the two maids; who, on her enquiring the cause, answered, nothing my Lady? She again strove to rest, when a second time awakened by their whispers; she insisted that something was the matter; on which, they at last told her, they heard some one breaking into the house. Good God! said she, why did not you tell me before? and so saying leapt out of bed, though in total darkness; sought out a case of pistols that the father of *Sylvius* had lent her, with powder and shot, with which having loaded them, she claps one under her arm, and with the other in her hand, she unlocks her chamber door; at this the poor maids are frightened almost out of their wits, and beg she will shut it again. What, said she, do you think I will quietly wait their coming? No, no, I will go more than half way, to meet my nocturnal visitants. So saying, she sallies out, and they afraid to stay behind her, both at once lay fast hold of her by the shift, trembling so violently, that she has reason to fear they will pull her down. In this formidable condition, she steals softly down stairs, goes from one part to the other through the house, but hears, or sees, nothing; at last she recollecting a cellar under the maids-room, she opens it softly, perceives the window broke, and some people busied, to make their way into the house. Without discovering to her female pages *enchemise*[43] what she has seen, she shuts it again softly to, and locks it; after which she goes to the room over it, and opens the window, with vast precaution, cocks her pistol, points it downwards, and lets fly among the gentry below; on which they hear a confined scream, and great bustle, as if two or three were carrying off one, whom, she presumed, she had wounded.

She then calls out, if you have not enough stay, and you shall have a second part, to the same tune; but here I suppose, they begged to be excused; on which she shut the window, and went to the front of the house, from whence she fired the other pistol; then recharging both, she laid them by her side on a chair, went into bed, and slept perfectly sound; other than generally when her eyes were closed, *Morpheus* brought her dear *Clementine* to her view: But this made her rather try to sleep, than lie awake, to think of him; a thing between you and I, my gentle reader, that was of no small utility to her health; for the senses when awake, are apt to aggravate misfortunes, whereby, the distance between us and those absent, is magnified. But, a kindly dream removes the real space, and brings us together; sometimes to taste more pleasure in idea, than we ever did, or possibly can experience, in a personal intercourse.

Theodora was not up in the morning, before all her neighbours came to see the mischief, which they concluded, from hearing the repeated shots, was committed over night; but which to prevent, not one attempted. They no doubt expected to have seen nothing else but blood and slaughter; and were perhaps disappointed of the entertainment they promised themselves, in recounting the shocking, cruel, and inhuman murder of *Theodora* and her two maids. Let it be as it will, they found this little female garrison safe and well, at which they seemed greatly surprised; but how did they stare, when informed of the particulars, and saw the ground stained with blood, from the cellar window, through the little hamlet, into a large field, where they lost it? She was revered like a little goddess among them; her courage was spoke of, far and near. The poor honest folks, taking it in their heads, that they were no common robbers, that had tried to get into the house, but some one with intention to carry off their young Amazon, they never saw her go out alone, of which she was very fond, but two or three would follow her at a distance, or be at the inside or outside of the hedge nearest to her, with large oaken towels,[44] to rub any one down, that attempted to lay hold on her. The Countess was so charitable and humane amongst the poor, that they almost adored her: She was the physician-general of the place, and *Theodora* the surgeon; the first prescribing remedies, and the latter preparing them, and dressing their wounds.

Love, the *soul* of poetry, had now made *Theodora* dedicate great part of her time to the muses, and *music* being the food of love, not to let the passion starve, she played on the spinnet, and sung almost every day: *Sylvius* played on the violin, and frequently accompanied her; this helped to render the winter very agreeable. One tempestuous day, when it rained with uncommon violence, there came a miserable, tall, thin, almost drowned being, to the kitchen door: he spoke in an uncommon tongue, which the servants not understanding, one of them came into the parlour, to acquaint the Countess of it. *Theodora* went immediately out, and accosting the stranger in *French*, found he understood, and spoke it a little. He straightway presented her with a certificate, setting forth, That he was an *Italian* merchant, who was cast away, and all he had, lost in the shipwreck. She was touched with his miserable situation, and therefore invited him to dry and warm himself at the fire; when observing, that he had an extreme coarse shirt on, wringing wet, she ran up into her room, and tearing an apron up, added it to one of her habit shifts, which made it long enough; and bringing it down to the unfortunate stranger, begged he would take off his wet shirt, and put that on. This his extreme modesty not permitting him to do in public, the footman shewed him into his own room, where the stranger put it on, and came down so much altered for the better, that *Theodora* ran into her mother, and told her, she fancied he was some person of consequence; on which the Countess desired, she might see him; her daughter conducted him into the parlour, where he entered with a politeness, that confirmed them both in the opinion, that he was much beyond what the certificate set him forth to be. They had the cloth laid for him, and gave him the best the house afforded to eat and drink; after which he went to the spinnet, sung an Italian song with great taste, and accompanied it with the thorough bass.

Never sure, were creatures more astonished, than the Countess and her daughter, the latter of whom he offered to teach *Italian*; and began, with making her repeat the most passionate expressions of love to himself, and when she innocently repeated them, not knowing their meaning, he would look with a tenderness at her, that she thought vastly odd in a stranger. When supper came in, the Countess made him signs to sit down; every moment he seemed to brighten in their opinion: but night advancing, they began to be uneasy at his stay; the rain continued, they were loath to turn him out, and yet unwilling that he should stay in the house all night. They consulted together what to do, to extricate themselves out of the dilemma, into which their good nature had plunged them. *Theodora* advised her mother, to send him to the mill; and that she was sure, the people would let him, at her request, lie on the broad cloths, which made at one and the same time an excellent bed and bed-clothes. This advice being approved of, the gentleman, though with some reluctance, went to the mill; where he submitted to lie on the broad cloths, instead of a bed. It was extraordinary, that although the certificate recommended him to the charity of the well-disposed, yet when he put his breeches under his head, they appeared by the chink to contain no trifling sum of gold in them. What was still more remarkable, he had, under the shirt that *Theodora* gave him another many degrees finer, with laced ruffles to it, and beneath his main garments, a rich waistcoat. These were alarming circumstances, bordering somewhat upon the marvellous; to which, *Theodora* would hardly have given credence, had she not the next day got a glimpse of the lace, peeping out under the shirt she had given him; this however, only served to convince them still the more, that he was not the person he was represented to be.

The next day, this wonder creating personage, came into breakfast with the Countess and *Theodora*, without any previous invitation; he again played on the spinnet, and wanted *Theodora* to take another *Italian* lesson; but this she did not chuse: then he began to pay violent court to her in *French*, at which she was much displeased, and wished him gone, with all her heart; but to leave a place he seemed so much to like, he did not appear to have the least notion. Several that evening coming to see them, they no sooner understood their uneasiness, but they obliged the adventurer to decamp; and represented, how cautious they should be who they admitted, in so lonesome a place. The Countess struck with a panic, insisted *Theodora* should go with the company to town, and take a house directly, for there she was determined not to stay the remainder of the winter. All the company seemed pleased with this new resolve, but her daughter; who, grown in love with solitude, is unwilling to resign the sweets she tasted in it. But it was become a maxim with *Theodora*, never to dispute a parent's will; being, in her opinion, absolute over the inclinations of those, the authors of whose beings they were: She therefore obeyed, went to town, and took a genteel house, by her mother's desire, in her own name; so that now, we see her the titular owner of a house, for which she was unable to pay the rent, or provide. However, she got it tolerably furnished, and fitted up in a very short time, for the reception of her mother; who was frightened to town the very next day after *Theodora* left her, by their late extraordinary guest, who came to the house, the morning after he was driven thence, made signs that he wanted to see the young lady; but when they made him understand, that she was not at home, he began to storm, and betray the greatest rage, at this unexpected disappointment; giving the servants ocular demonstration, by the display of a handsome laced waistcoat, that he was of greater consequence than he seemed; and by an oath or two, that in his passion escaped him, shewed he was no novice in the *English* language; at which they were not a little alarmed; and he left them like one bereft of reason.

Having some hopes, it is to be presumed, that *Theodora* might return again that evening, he took his station under the shelter of an ever-green tree by the road side, and there took out a german flute, upon which he played with such attractive sweetness, that, as powerful as *Orpheus*, he gathered every rustic traveller, in a circle round him; but with this difference, the one gave, as story says, to things inanimate a motion, while this so fascinated the attention of the living, as to deprive them of all motion, and chain them to the spot. The plaintiveness of his notes setting loose the soft fountains of pity, while the copious stream of flooded grief poured down the sad musician's cheek.

This story soon flew to the Countess, who quite terrified, set out directly for town, and took up her abode with *Theodora*, at the house of her friend *Shaloon*, until the house was ready for them; in which, through her daughter's indefatigable endeavour, it was not long before they were settled much to their satisfaction; if any thing could be thought satisfactory to *Theodora*, while deprived of her dear *Clementine*, whose letters were her only consolation.

Now initiated once more a little into life, they were visited by many, and of course, the young lady, without wishing for it, made an increase to her conquests. She went to the assemblies, plays, and could not avoid sharing in many diversions; for which she had in a manner lost all relish; but her mother insisted upon it, and she was submissive. *Sylvius* frequently made little concerts at his house, for *Theodora*; to which he used to invite the best company, and the most capital private performers. One evening, at one of these musical meetings, he introduced a young gentleman, he had often promised them great pleasure in hearing; being, as he represented him, very excellent on the violin. *Mellidore*,[45] for that was his name being a foreigner, and speaking bad *English*, the stress of conversation with him lay upon *Theodora*, because an adept in *French*; which made him perhaps more particularly notice her than the rest. Let it be as it will, *Sylvius* asked him in *French*, if he thought he had told him too much of *Theodora*; he, with a politeness natural to his nation, replied, the original far surpassed the description. She exhibited her performance on the harpsicord, which *Mellidore*, with his usual compliance, greatly praised; and the evening being past agreeably, the Countess gave him an invitation to her house; which feeling himself interested in, he readily accepted; nor did he fail, in a day or two afterwards to pay his respects to her Ladyship, who received him with the greatest civility. This visit being frequently repeated, he at length got on a familiar footing; which, one evening, emboldened him in a distant manner, to penetrate into the state of *Theodora*'s heart; who, with her accustomed candour, told him her inclinations were fixed on the most deserving of objects; to whom her warmest affections were due. *Mellidore* seeming alone to be actuated by friendship or curiosity, no matter which, she seized the opportunity to launch into the praises of her beloved *Clementine*, whose name she sought not to conceal; but openly talked of him as a person destined for, and whom she looked upon as her husband. At all this *Mellidore* did not appear in the least uneasy, or dissatisfied; which, had *Theodora* any suspicion of his being interestedly inquisitive, was quite sufficient to remove it; but of which, not having the least apprehension, whenever they met, her love for *Clementine* was generally the topic of their conversation; and this indulgence was so very pleasing to her, that she was always glad to see him.

A letter now is expected from *Clementine*; but not coming, *Theodora* is inconsolable, lest any thing has happened to her beloved *Clementine*; she writes, waits the limited time for his answer; none comes; another month glides by, without bringing her the wished for pacquet. Now more than ever to be pitied is the wretched maid. But ah! what tongue can speak her anguish, horror, distraction, and despair, when she is assured, by one whose veracity cannot be doubted, that the false, inconstant, perjured *Clementine*, forgetful of his vows, his love, his truth, his honour, has given his hand to a Lady of good fortune in *Mahon*.[46] This comes like a dagger to her heart. Poor *Theodora*, this is not all, you must yet have a little more to fill up the measure of your woes. The villainous aspersions that were cast on thee, when thou camest from *England* first, must be again revived, and pursue thee hither. Cruel father, not only to listen to, and believe the wicked invectives thrown out against thy daughter, by her enemies, but even to propagate the scandal thyself. Alas! what shall she do? Where run to screen her from the sword of slander? From the pangs of hopeless love? This, I could have born, she says, had *Clementine* been constant – Unnatural father – Ungrateful *Clementine*! Then in a fit of wild despair, she runs, and catching up the prayer book, she swears, she will marry the first man that asks her, let him be who he would. To this, the first oath she had ever taken, her mother, and a woman servant are the only witnesses present; the Countess, though grieved to the soul, at her daughter's distress, reproves her for the rashness of the action; at the same time, soothing her extreme anguish, with all the tenderness of maternal affection.

While *Theodora* is in the extremity of grief, rage, and resentment, *Mellidore* pays her a visit; and being before-hand made acquainted with what had happened, without any further preface, he tells her that he had nourished a passion for her ever since he first saw her, on which, in regard to that confidence she had honoured him with, he had imposed silence: But now as the bar to his wishes was removed, by the marriage of *Clementine*, he could not be so great an enemy to himself, as to neglect the opportunity that offered, of asking her hand. *Theodora*, like one transfixed with wonder, is for a time struck speechless; but at last recovering herself a little, she, in a tone of voice, and with a look expressive of her resentment, asks him, what he had ever seen in her behaviour, to give encouragement to his presumption? He answers that love is a mere leveller of conditions; that he did not aspire higher than he was intitled to by birth, though fortune had frowned on his family; but his chief hope was, that he had not been too late in solliciting this happiness. Immediately recollecting the inconsiderate oath she had taken, of which she concludes he has had intelligence, she replies with haughty indignation, a rash vow is better broken than kept; that if he raised his hopes upon so weak a foundation, he was much to blame, as she was determined never to marry. Upon receiving this answer, *Mellidore* seems overwhelmed with the deepest affliction, declaring if she persists long in that resolution, he would not outlive her refusal, and so takes his leave.

Mellidore gone, the unhappy *Theodora* resigned herself up to the most bitter reflection imaginable: O God! she cries, how unfortunate am I! the only man upon earth, that I can love, has forsaken me, while the one I least thought of, lays claim to me, upon the strength of that despair, to which I was hurried by the loss of all I hold dear. O! *Clementine*, canst thou have peace of mind with the perjury of which thou art guilty? Is it possible, after the many solemn vows thou hast made me, to be ever and only mine; that you should give that hand and heart to another, to which I alone have right? But alas! crueller again is my father: Superior merit, superior fortune, might have tempted thy young heart to stray, and break through the weak charm with which an ill judged liking of me had bound thee: But Oh! what excuse can be formed for him, who breaks through the stronger ties of nature, and persecutes that which he is bound to protect? Thou, my heavenly Father, has kept my innocence hitherto untainted. Lo! thou my earthly father seek'st by the foulest calumny, to cloud the lustre of that virtue, from which thyself, wert thou endowed with parental feelings, might hope to atchieve some honour. To what a wretched alternative am I now driven by thy means? If I refuse *Mellidore*, I am foresworn – If I consent, I sacrifice my fortune to my conscience; nay! in fact, I do an outrage to my delicacy, and even virtue; for what is marrying a man we do not love, better than prostitution? I will fly him: – But then I must fly my mother too, – that mother for the love of whom I withstood all the pleading rhetoric of the perjured *Clementine*, assisted by my fond affection for the charming traitor. Well, no matter, she cannot say I fled her for a man, as many daughters undutifully have done; but to shun one, who unauthorized by her approbation, pursues me.

This resolve was no sooner formed, than *Theodora* sets about to accomplish it. She procures, unknown to any one, a compleat disguise, to fit her for the character of a servant maid, which she intended to assume, in order to gain admittance into some service, at a distance as great as she could get to, from the unlucky spot she was fixed in. She wrote an affectionate letter to her mother, to inform her of the true cause of her leaving her, beseeching her to rely upon her never doing any thing that might render her unworthy the honour of subscribing herself her affectionate daughter.

This letter being prepared, she determined the next morning to quit the house, before any one was stirring. It lay open upon the desk in her closet; when her mother calling for her in the hurry and perplexity of her thoughts, she took the key out of the door, imagining she had locked it, and went to the Countess; who detained her about some particular business, for a considerable time.

The servant who was by at her making the inconsiderate oath, on which *Mellidore* built his hopes, and who was intirely in his interest, actuated by an impertinent curiosity, in which an *Abigail* is seldom deficient, went in, and seeing the letter, took it up, and made herself mistress of its contents; at which, she was not a little surprized. Then casting her eyes about, she found a small bundle, containing nothing more than one of *Theodora*'s plainest gowns, and some linen, which was all the wardrobe she intended to take with her, save what she intended to beat her march in; which lay ready on a chair for her to put on. All this notable aparatus, together with the letter, she immediately removed, and put them up safe, in hopes that *Mellidore* would come before her young Lady could provide herself with more to answer her purpose. On *Theodora*'s return to her closet, she saw she had left it open; and presently found some body had been there, as she missed the letter she had left on her desk. She rung the bell, and *Abigail*, who waited what might ensue, appeared. *Theodora* with the utmost impatience, asked her who had been in her closet? She replied, she was; and instantly threw herself at her feet, implored her pardon for what she had done; which she assured her, was intirely owing to her affection for her, not being able to bear the thought of her putting in execution, what she had signified in her letter; that she perhaps did not perceive the dreadful consequences that might attend the step that she was about to take; to prevent which, the Almighty had no doubt given her the inclination to go into her closet, a thing she had never done before, though the door lay frequently open.

She begged she would consider the insults she would render herself liable to, from the meanest of the sex, while she endeavoured to fly the honest pursuits of a gentleman, such as *Mellidore*; that the capacity of a servant ill suited a lady of her high birth and pretensions, whose delicate texture could not undergo their laborious vocation; in short, that she was sure the Countess would break her heart if she left her; and she had not the least doubt, but *Mellidore* would destroy himself; so in persisting in her design, she would have the death of a mother that doated on her, and that of a gentleman that adored her, to answer for; after which, she need never expect to taste of the smallest happiness or peace of mind here, or hereafter.

Theodora was in such agitation of spirit, on this address, that she knew not what to answer, other than by her tears, which flowed in abundance. She one moment determined to throw herself at her mother's feet, and beg her protection against *Mellidore*; but then she thought if she did, the Countess would reproach her, for having, by her oath, given encouragement to his pretensions, and though she disapproved of the match, would look upon her as a perjured wretch in denying him. She then begged and implored her maid to keep her secret, and let her go; but her intreaties were in vain; they did not corespond with *Abigail*'s views; who declared, if she persisted, she would tell all to the Countess, whose authority she knew *Theodora* would not withstand. Twenty times was she on the point of acquainting her mother, but still restrained, by shame, or rather an irresistible fatality that hung over her. *Mellidore* came the next morning early, used all the rhetoric in his power, to persuade her into a compliance; when finding his entreaties were to no purpose, he left her with a wild despair pictured on his countenance; declaring he would never see her again. Her maid letting him out, returned to *Theodora*, in the greatest fright, and told her that she was sure her cruelty had made him form some desperate design against his life; to prevent which, she begged she would write only one line. *Theodora* was terrified to death at the apprehensions of what was suggested; to which his words and actions not a little contributed; so that scarce knowing what she did, she complied with her desire, and wrote, to beg *Mellidore* would, for her sake, not think of doing any injury to himself. This was sufficient encouragement; he was presently back again, and testified a joy, that not a little displeased her, in that it was founded on the certainty of his success.

He pressed her to name the day, that she would give him her hand; but this she positively refused, at the present; and he unwilling to incur her displeasure, disisted for that time. But his faithful agent neglected not a moment to sound his praise, and to persuade that she would be his death, if she longer resisted the completion of his wishes. The idea of *Clementine*'s falsehood had given her a dislike to all the sex in general, one of the greatest obstacles *Mellidore* had to surmount, even as great as the unceasing passion with which she was inspired. But then on the other hand, the scandals propagated to her disadvantage, rendered it absolutely prudent to put herself under the protection of a husband, who could assert her innocence, and screen her reputation from slander. The man she loved was now the property of another, which rendered an indulgence of that passion criminal, which was before her glory. While she remained in a single state, she found she could never conquer it; all the sex were indifferent to her; but the duty due to a husband, was the only counterpoise, as she thought, that could eradicate the love she had imbibed in her heart for the cruel, ungrateful *Clementine*. *Mellidore* having told her, that he intended taking her to *France*, as soon as she was his, pleased her; as by that, he seemed to have no pecuniary expectations from his union with her; but the quitting *Ireland* for ever, above all the rest, weighed with her most. In short, they were privately married; the day before which, *Mellidore* had previously secured their passage to *France*, entirely with the consent of *Theodora*; who wished then for nothing more, than to leave a country, in which she had experienced so much sorrow.

However, the knot was no sooner tied, than she felt the utmost compunction, for what she had done. All her love and duty for her mother revived with double force; nor was the idea of *Clementine* out of the scale. She would hardly admit *Mellidore* to give her a salute, before she fled to her mother, threw herself on her knees, and told her what had happened, in consequence of the rash and unadvised vow she had made; but withal added, that she had not admitted *Mellidore* to the smallest liberties, and that, as their marriage was clandestine, she had fulfilled her vow; and it rested upon her Ladyship, to annul, or make it good as she thought proper, it being entirely at her own option.

By this, my dear child, said the Countess, you bid me infer, that you do not love the man you are united to. Oh! madam, said *Theodora*, you knew *Clementine*, then judge. I pity you, my poor child, said she, with all my heart; but consider, my dear, how we are circumstanced: It is even better to abide by what you have done, than by disputing the validity of your marriage, call the malicious eye of the world upon us, and give our enemies a subject, that they are well inclined to handle to our disadvantage. I wish now, said she with a sigh, that I had consented to your leaving me for *Clementine*; it is to me you owe your present and future unhappiness: Forgive me my *Theodora*. Here the poor Countess burst into tears; which had such an effect on her daughter, that never were nuptials ushered in with greater pomp of real sorrow. In a short time after this, *Mellidore* came dressed out; but little thought that *Theodora* had discovered all to her mother. However, when he came, she ran to meet him, and prepare him for what he was to expect. As soon as he came in sight of the Countess, he prostrated himself before her, and intreated her blessing; which not readily giving, he expressed so much concern, that the humane Countess straight relenting, raised him from his knees, with her blessing, and forgiveness. She then advised to keep their marriage secret, till such time as it proved convenient to own it. *Mellidore* now observed, that *Theodora* had not informed her mother of their design of going to *France*; wherefore he mentioned it himself: but the Countess would by no means, consent to it, saying, That if they could consent themselves, to live as she did, she would share her small pittance with them, while she lived. The loss of *Theodora* she could not support, being the only comfort she had. This extreme kindness touched them to the soul, and made them instantly resolve to acquiesce with her desires.

The Countess having an extreme desire to see her two younger daughters, resolved to pay them a visit; not having the least apprehension, that they would treat her with any indignity, or refuse to receive her with all the duty and affection due to such a mother. This resolution was no sooner formed, than it was put into execution; and the Countess accompanied by *Theodora*, and attended by one footman, on horseback, set out in a one horse chaise, that *Mellidore* had borrowed, for the place of *Carina*'s residence. This was an indifferent sort of equipage, and simple retinue for the Countess of *Volpont*; who had once made such a splendid appearance, whenever she travelled. No adoring croud now graced her carriage wheels; the grand parade was over; the charm that attracted their notice was broken; no running footman now proclaims her approach, or French-horns salute her entry, into every town and village. But to this undistinguished manner of travelling, she is long since reconciled; happy in the company and conversation of *Theodora*, she finds the journey perhaps as agreeable, as when she shone in all the splendor, to which her rank entitled her.

All the way they went, they pleased themselves, with the idea of that joy with which *Carina* and *Eliza* who lived with her sister, would receive them; but towards the latter end of their journey, they met a small alloy to their pleasure; for being obliged to cross the country, to which they, together with the servant, were entire strangers, they were directed wrong, and led across some rocky mountains; where the wild inhabitants, never before having seen a carriage pass, seemed quite affrighted, and ran into their little hovels, like so many rabbits into a borough.

The impracticableness of passing the rude rocks seemed so great, that the Countess could not avoid betraying great terror. But they were far advanced; a few miles would surmount the difficulties before them; which to avoid, by turning back, they had many to encounter, that by experience, they knew were not much inferior; besides, they stood a melancholy chance of being benighted in a place, where they might as well hope to meet with a diamond mine, as the least accommodation.

The Countess seeing these difficulties surmounted, whereat she had been so much terrified, gave *Theodora* thanks with the most cordial affection; and said, she was as good a protectress, and as safe a guide, as she had met with in her life; in which opinion she had soon after reason to be confirmed. Night approaching, and the horses growing tired, the Countess asked the servant, whether he had given them their proper feed of oats in the morning.

"Touch a galled horse, and he will wince." The consciousness of his own villainy, made the fellow conclude, the Countess by this question, suspected him; on this he became very insolent, and cursed and swore; a thing they had never before heard him do, of consequence greatly alarmed the Countess; who through terror, made the wretch many concessions. Presently after, arriving at the foot of a steep hill, it was found necessary to relieve the poor horse, by the two ladies walking it up, which they both very chearfully submitted to: The servant led the chaise before them; when instead of stopping at the summit of the hill, the fellow went on; which not a little surprized them, and made them apprehend, he might perhaps take it into his head to let them prosecute the remainder of their journey on foot; but the Countess was utterly incapable of doing this, and no house was within many miles of them. All these circumstances crouded in an instant into the imagination of *Theodora*; but what more alarmed her than all, was, they had left the pistols in the chair; and had furnished him with an opportunity of turning their own arms against them. This idea was no sooner formed, than to prevent, if possible, the consequences, without apprizing the Countess of her intentions, like an arrow from a bow, she fled after the chair, which she presently overtook, and though it was going on at a pretty smart rate, without calling to the fellow, or stopping it, she leaped into the chair; and catching up the reins, suddenly stopped the horse, to the no small astonishment of the leader, who was not aware of her approach. Then assuming a tone of voice, that denoted her anger, she asked him, how he dared to go beyond the limits prescribed him by his lady? On this unexpected salute, his confusion was visible, and denied him the power of speech, for some moments; in which time, she turned about, and went to meet her mother; who was so fatigued, with endeavouring to hasten after *Theodora*, that she was quite out of breath, and scarce able to stand. However, the chair again turned, she helped the Countess into it, and returned to the spot where she had left the fellow, who began again with his impertinence.

Theodora perceiving the Countess quite terrified, and unable to exert her authority, took upon herself the task; and holding one of the pistols in her hand, told him, she had reason to think he had premeditated some wicked design against their lives, but that, as self preservation was the first law of nature, she would instantly prevent his having an opportunity to put it into execution, and insisted upon his immediately asking the Countess's pardon: which command he, through fear more than inclination, complied with; as he likewise did, with that of leading them; while his young Lady held herself prepared, to resent any injury that he might offer them, with the pistol ready cocked in her hand; which held him in such due discipline, that they got safe to their stage, though far advanced in the night; and that they had a dangerous ferry to cross, before they could meet with any tolerable accommodation; to which, they had a chance not to arrive that night, had not some gentlemen turned back out of their road, to shew them the way.

The next day they prosecuted their journey, and arrived in the evening, at *Carina*'s seat; but were not a little disconcerted, at finding the whole family gone to pass some days at the house of *Belmont* senior, the father of *Carina*'s husband. However, it being very late, the Countess thought she might make so free, as to take up her lodging in her daughter's house; to which the servants, on finding who the visitants were, had no manner of objection, but received them with the greatest joy; giving them a hearty welcome, to every thing the house afforded. This they imagined was no more than what was due to the mother and sister of their Lady, who they judged from their own natural feelings, would be pleased with what they did, and return home the moment she found who was there: for this reason, though late it was, they sent off an express on the best horse they had, to bear the happy tidings to the ears of *Carina* and *Eliza*. Through the extreme fatigue of the preceding day, the Countess and *Theodora* slept very soundly, and never once dreamed that they were unwelcome guests.

But let the reader judge of their surprize, and the resentment that must naturally have inspired the Countess, when the next morning, the express, who eagerly set off, returned abashed at the message with which he was charged; namely, that his Lady, and Lady *Eliza*, presented their duty to the Countess, and love to their sister, to acquaint them, that it was not in their power to see them, as they would by that incur the Earl's displeasure; and that they were even afraid, that he never would forgive their having let the Countess and *Theodora* sleep one night in the house, though they knew nothing of the matter, nor had given the least encouragement to such a rash scheme; being the furthest from their thoughts. Together with this dutiful and affectionate message, there came a private reprimand to the servants, for having given admittance to strangers, in the absence of their master and mistress, for which they should every one lose their places.

Never was consternation equal to that now reigning in this little besieged fortress; the domestics blushed for the ill behaviour of their superiors; nor could one of them have the cruelty to deliver this unnatural message to the Countess; whose noble aspect, and mild address, at once commanded and engaged their respect. *Theodora* first perceived the confusion that sat upon their brows, and suspecting the truth, from what she had herself experienced a couple of years before, she questioned one of the servants; and learning the cause of their dissatisfaction, conveyed the substance of it, in the most delicate manner she could, to her mother; who instantly exclaimed, that such words were well suited to a *Goneril* and *Regan*, but thank heaven, said she, I have my *Cordelia* too, as well as poor *King Lear*;[47] and with that looked tenderly at *Theodora*, the soft fountain of whose heart, was set loose and ran in chrystal streams from her eyes, at this kind expression of the Countess's love.

Come, madam, said she, let us begone from those unhospitable walls, to which you have done too much honour, in approaching them. No, replied the Countess, I will stay, if it were no more but to vex them. *Theodora*, who never yet knew what it was to contradict her, immediately acquiesced; saying, whatever was most agreeable to her, she had no right, or inclination to dispute. A thousand tender expressions, were the reward of this filial submission in *Theodora*, which fully compensated her loss of father and sisters.

In the midst of this endearing scene was the Countess and her daughter, when word was brought them, that Lady *Eliza* was arrived, with her sister's eldest son. All the Countess's resentment towards this young Lady now subsided; and she was received by the good Countess and *Theodora* with the most cordial affection; the joy they felt, at seeing a daughter and a sister, after an absence of upwards of four years, rendered the scene extremely affecting. The Countess and *Theodora*, alternately clasped *Eliza* and the little boy in their arms, in all the dumb eloquence of mingled tears; for words fell short of the transport that they felt; which when a little abated, they impatiently enquired, where was *Carina*, and if they should not see her also? But this *Eliza* informed them, was what they must not expect; and that had she listened to the advice of those she left behind her, she would not have come; but she thought it best, not to wait the return of an express that was dispatched to her father, with an account of the Countess's arrival, lest she should be commanded not to see her mother; and thereby aggravate her fault in his eyes; that her chief inducement in coming was, to entreat the Countess not to stay in the house where she at present was, as it might tend to all their disadvantages. What! replied the Countess, was it then your intention, to turn your mother and sister out, after the many risks they ran, in a long and dangerous journey; merely from a desire, of once more beholding those unworthy of their attention? If that was your design, we are not much beholden for this visit. I shall stay here, as long as it suits my conveniency; and then I will quit the residence of such unnatural brutes, without a single wish of ever seeing them more. *Eliza* seemed thoroughly sensible of these heart-rending words; and after making many successless apologies for what she had said, returned back from whence she came. – Where what effect her account had on *Carina*, &c. is immaterial to our story.

The Countess was presently visited by the best about the neighbourhood; among the rest, by one of *Carina*'s brothers-in-law, an agreeable young gentleman, possessed of the most amiable qualities, with one of the best of hearts; not a little prepossessed in favour of *Theodora*, not imagining her the property of another. The worthy and reverend Doctor *Mawrice*, *Theodora*'s respected friend and protector, formerly mentioned, no sooner heard of their being so near him, than he sent his charming son, the young *Clytandre*, to pay them his respects, with the good clergyman's best compliments, and an apology for not waiting on them himself, being then indisposed.

Near three years had so improved *Clytandre*, that he was scarce to be known; but though changed in person, his heart seemed not to have forgot the tender impulse with which *Theodora* had impregnated it, at an earlier date; this was demonstrated by the eager gaze, the tender sighs that stole from his soul. When he addressed her, he faultered, and when he touched her, a tremor seized upon his whole frame. He was with them some days before he could summon up a resolution to make a declaration of that sincere and lasting passion with which he was inspired. At length the charming youth found her alone in the garden, when modestly approaching her, he fell upon one knee, and said, I know not, divine *Theodora*, if I am pardonable for the presumption of which I am guilty, in declaring myself your slave. You gave the first impression my fond heart was ever sensible of; which your absence, instead of curing, has with my years increased. My extreme youth, when I first knew you, prevented my taking the liberty I now do, nor did I then, indeed, well know what caused my attachment. But this meeting gives me to understand, that if you prove cruel, I must for the remainder of my days be the most wretched of my sex.

Good God! *Clytandre*, cried *Theodora*, you astonish me, I have ever held you in the light of a beloved brother. Oh! change but the name of brother, said he, to that of the most ardent of lovers, still by thee beloved, and I shall be happy. That is a thing impossible, replied *Theodora*. Impossible! said he, but why should I wonder at that? – It was not for me to aim at the position of such perfection! – How daring were my hopes! – Forgive me, adored *Theodora*, my death – will –.

Here the lovely youth turned pale, and *Theodora* seeing him ready to fall to the ground, ran, in the utmost confusion, and catching him in her arms, laid her cheek to his, and bathed it with her tears. Was ever creature, she cries, so unfortunate as I? – Too sensible to the charms of an ingrate: – the image of the perjured *Clementine* still intrudes itself upon my rebel heart, contrary to the dictates of reason, and the duty I owe to another, then how unable am I to make the smallest return to this deserving youth? O, *Clytandre!* be contented with my friendship – more is not in the power of *Theodora* to give. Here he opened his languishing eyes, and fetching a deep sigh, said, you pity me, divine *Theodora*, but alas! may I not aspire to the possession of that heart, which to have acquired, I would have resigned all claim every other earthly blessing.

Too generous youth, interrupted *Theodora*, I am truly sensible how great had been my happiness, had the heart you set so high a value upon, fallen to the lot of one so truly deserving of a nobler prize. Heaven, I hope, has ordained you for some beauteous nymph, far more worthy your attention than the unfortunate *Theodora*; when you shall reflect with astonishment, that you ever bestowed a thought upon her, and joy that you escaped a destiny so cruel as those must share who are any way connected with her. But *Clytandre*, though my regard for you is too great to admit you as a lover, I cannot resign the son of Doctor *Mawrice* as a friend, nay, still nearer, a brother – for did not your father prove a father to me, when my own rejected me? Oh! *Theodora*, said he, would to God I had then been of an age, to have secured to my father the privilege of calling you daughter. – Why did I quit you? Alas! Why did I not wait upon your steps, and by my presence, and faithful services, have won that heart, that is informed with too much gratitude, to have been insensible to so ardent a passion as mine? But 'tis lost, for ever lost to me, as I am to all happiness in this world. – Do not say so, *Clytandre*, said *Theodora*, you have many happy days of hope, before you. Here the Countess opportunely came to *Theodora*'s relief, and tenderly upbraided her for her long absence, while *Clytandre*, unable to conceal his confusion, turned down a different walk.

Ever after this declaration, *Theodora* carefully avoided giving *Clytandre* any opportunity of speaking with her in private; but in public, shewed him the most particular respect, which the brother of *Belmont* observing with some concern, sought occasion to pick a quarrel with *Clytandre*, and one day in conversation, very abruptly contradicted him, while he modestly endeavoured to support his opinion; on which, words grew high between them, both at once starting from their seats, and it was with difficulty, they were prevented from coming to an explanation, that might in all probability, have proved fatal to one or both of them. But the Countess and *Theodora* interposing, the affair was happily made up, only with the loss of his company who imagined himself least favoured by her, who was the latent cause of their dispute.

Here they remained for near a fortnight, during all which time, neither *Carina* nor *Eliza* came near them, in perfect obedience to the command of their father. The Countess grew tired of a place, where she found herself so little welcome, and resolving to quit it, the young *Clytandre* intreated her leave to attend her on her journey back again, still flattering himself that the liking, which he imagined, *Theodora* had for another, might in time be surmounted by an unwearied pursuit. The Countess consented, and they set off, accompanied by this charming cavalier, who knowing the road perfectly well, they met with no obstacle in their way, and arriving safe on a Sunday morning, within twelve miles of their destined port, at a pleasant village, where the parson of the parish was one of the Countess's particular friends, she determined to rest a day or two at his house, where they were received with a warmth of friendship, that told them they were welcome; the hour of divine service drawing nigh, he invited them, if not too tired, to make up part of his congregation; this they readily agreeing to, they attended him to church.

Theodora having signified by letter to *Mellidore* the day they intended leaving *Belmont*'s, who should she cast her eyes upon, but him unexpectedly in the next pew to them? A conscious blush overspread her cheek, at seeing her husband so near; she thought, and not without some reason, that she perceived an uneasiness in his eyes, at seeing so charming a young man as *Clytandre*, so remarkably attentive to her; this a good deal disconcerted her devotion, and caused some perturbations in her mind, not very agreeable, but too visible not to be observed by those less interested in her, than *Clytandre*, who searched around with much anxiety in his looks, for the cause; when his eyes soon clashing with those of *Mellidore*, which were the moment before rivetted on *Theodora*, he did not hesitate to conclude him the person; on which the youth turned pale, his lips quivered, and stooping his head, he was very tall, he with vast eagerness demanded of *Theodora*, who the person was, in the next pew them, and at the same time described his dress. *Theodora* replied, it was a friend of theirs. – Yes, said he, with redoubled emotion, I thought as much: O God! and then laid his head against the side of the pew, to conceal the situation of his mind from the Countess, who demanded of *Theodora*, was *Clytandre* not well? Yes, – No, replied *Theodora*, Madam, were you speaking to me? Good God! said the Countess, what is the matter? *Theodora*, with that, signed to her to look about. This the Countess instantly doing, she received a low bow from *Mellidore*, that threw her into a confusion, little short of her daughter's.

Church being over, to the general satisfaction of all the four, *Mellidore* came up to them; *Theodora* and he saluted each other, with all the formality of distant respect; which policy, throwing a cloak over the first part of their emotion, *Clytandre* scarce knew what to think; he imagined he read a private intelligence in their eyes; but this their present behaviour contradicting, and being willing still to flatter himself, he inclined to think it was nothing but the mere effect of imagination. The good clergyman seeing that *Mellidore* was a friend to the Countess, politely invited him to dinner; and he seizing his opportunity, asked *Theodora* privately, who their charming companion was? when understanding he was the son of doctor *Mawrice*, of whom he had frequently heard the Countess and his wife make mention, he seemed a little satisfied; but *Clytandre*, who was watchful of *Theodora*'s every motion, felt more than can be expressed, at the liberty *Mellidore* took in whispering her; she saw his uneasiness, and immediately determined to make him the confident of her private marriage; hoping that when he found it impossible to attain to his wishes, he would summon up his reason, to conquer them. For this purpose, *Theodora* with a benign smile, invited *Clytandre* to take a turn in the garden; at which particular notice, he could scarce contain his transport, and the reader may imagine, if he was ever in love, did not hesitate one moment in complying with her request: This seemed the greatest favour she had ever done him, since his first declaration; never having furnished him with a second opportunity of conversing with her on the same subject. Looking on it as a favourable omen, he resolved to urge his suit; and was considering with himself how to begin, when both finding themselves sequestered from the view of any body, quite out of hearing, Dear *Clytandre!* and, My adorable *Theodora!* proceeded from their lips, at one and the same time; when he observing that she was going to speak, politely gave her discourse the precedency; and *Theodora* went on: "I perceive by the preamble, what the discourse is, that you were going to entertain me with; but it is absolutely necessary, you should suppress any wish you may have for me – I am about to tell you what demands more fortitude than I am at present mistress of; let us sit down on this seat, until I recover myself a little".

Here *Theodora* shewed the most visible marks of confusion, and *Clytandre* all pale and trembling by her side, waited the dreaded conclusion of the discovery she was about to make. She recited to him the story of her love to *Clementine*, the ungrateful return he had made, and the consequences attending it. At this account, the tender sympathizing heart of *Clytandre* felt the severest pangs – he gazed upon the suffering *Theodora*, whose wounds, being thus new probed, began to bleed afresh: She sighed, he wept, while she, all drowned in tears, gave over speaking; her voice quite lost in sorrow. *Clytandre* strove to speak, but could not for some moments; then, in a gust of frantic grief, involuntarily catching up her apparently lifeless hand, he bathed it with the tears of soft compassion; pressed it with fervor to his lips, which for a time remained glewed to it: then raising his eyes to heaven, and letting fall her hand, he clasped his hands, and cried, great God! how equal and how hard our fate! Oh! *Theodora*, you then know by woeful experience, the pangs of hopeless love; and needs must pity the undone *Clytandre*. Had that affection, bestowed with such profusion on the worthless *Clementine*, but fallen to my share, how happy had I been! – Nay, was there now a possibility of my obtaining thy heart, even after its ship-wreck, together with thy hand, I should not envy his having had the preference. But you are married: my ruined charmer, you are the property of another. Oh! cruel destiny, happy *Mellidore!* Where was I, when that rash vow was made, that authorized thy presumptuous hope? Why was I suffered to see her, since not at the time when I might have been successful in my love; But hold, we must submit to our fate. In lamenting my own miseries, I must undoubtedly augment thine, my first and only love, *Mellidore* is thy husband – and *Clytandre*'s love must now be all absorbed in friendship, in which he claims a share. He has done no more than what I, – what every one would have done, to have secured so great a blessing theirs, as the divine *Theodora*. Happy, happy, mayest thou be, thou loveliest of thy sex, while I, resigned to my hard fate, will, instead of the gown, take up the sword, and by braving death in the midst of danger, hope to find a cordial for my wounded heart in the peaceful grave. Here the big-swoln grief rendered the words of *Clytandre* inarticulate, his voice being choaked. You *Clytandre*, said *Theodora* would almost persuade me, there is sincerity in man; which after the treachery I met in *Clementine*, I began to doubt: But would you believe it, that in spite of all appearances, I still would think him innocent, and myself the aggressor? O! *Clytandre*, should I have been imposed upon, what will be my situation? Come, said he, you must not indulge such a thought, as it might cast a shade over the lustre of your actions, and render you deficient in conjugal affection; you, who have ever been so remarkable in filial love: With these words, *Clytandre* fetched a sigh, that seemed to proceed from his inmost soul, and proposed returning to the company; which she readily consented to, fearing their long absence might raise suspicion in the breast of one, whom she thought it her business now to please, in compliance with the duty due to a husband.

That their *tête a tête* had not been one of the most agreeable, was very perceivable by the redness of their eyes, which were much swoln. To conceal this, *Theodora* kept on her hat, and he pleaded a cold in his head. *Clytandre*, who had before been introduced by the Countess to *Mellidore*, now singled him out from the rest of the company in conversation, and payed him a more particular regard than to any other. Now the husband and lover of *Theodora*, in mutual confidence, communicated their sentiments and situations; *Clytandre* wished him happiness, yet owned he envied him the source from whence it must spring. *Mellidore* pitied his rival's pain, at the same time glorying that he engrossed to himself what alone could administer his cure. They were friends and enemies, for one and the same cause, and it is not improbable but *Clytandre* could have been glad that the Lycurgan laws[48] had been then established among them.

Here they passed a few days very agreeably, and then proceeded on their journey; at the end of which they arrived early the next day; where they were received with much joy by their friends, particularly *Theodora*, by her two humble servants, *Lucius* and *Sylvius*; the former having, in her absence, gone into orders, and commenced Divine. He made her an offering of his first sermon; which he dedicated to her, in hopes, no doubt, that he should, in time, convert her to a right way of thinking; at least in regard to himself. Indeed, had not her heart been prepossessed in favour of another, it would have proved a difficult task to withstand the attack of so much merit – joined to the partiality this young gentleman had for her, his many virtues, bright genius, and excellent understanding, being the fair foundation of a most distinguished character.

Now the Countess determined to make her daughter's marriage public, and for that purpose proposed to have them married over again; after which, she designed to retire into some part of the country, where the Earl of *Volpont* lived; to be on the spot, lest he should relent, and grow desirous of being reconciled with her; which she still, but vainly, flattered herself would be the case. Settlements were accordingly drawn. *Mellidore* generously resigned all that *Theodora* might ever expect, to her own disposal. The licence was obtained, the day fixed, and every thing prepared to leave the place, so soon as they were married. All these steps were taken with the greatest secrecy possible, in order to prevent the church being crouded. At early prayers our bride and bridegroom, in riding-dresses, as the least remarkable, went into the vestry-room, where they were met by their bride's men and maids. The charming *Clytandre* was *Theodora*'s father-doner; *Lucius* married them; hard trial surely, of a lover's patience but the fortitude of more than they was tried on this occasion. *Sylvius* was there, and another new made slave of *Theodora*'s, in canonicals, preached that morning. The church, though early it was, could scarce contain the people that crouded in to see them married. Poor *Lucius* seemed so affected, he was scarce able to speak; and when he went to give the ring to *Mellidore*, he trembled so, he had like to have dropt it from his convulsed hand.

Clytandre gave her away, as a fond parent might do a favourite child, who, through a religious frenzy, is obstinately bent on immuring herself within the awful walls of a cloister; and *Sylvius*, no doubt, cursed his stars, for having introduced *Mellidore* to *Theodora*. After they were married, bidding a tender adieu to all esteemed friends, they set out in company with *Clytandre* and the Countess, for the house of the parson, where they had been before. Here they were again received with the greatest demonstration of joy. All the people of fashion about came to congratulate the new-married couple: The doctor, kept open house for them; and the whole week was passed away in diversions. They had a ball every night, at which the bride was *Clytandre*'s constant partner, in preference to all the young beauties present; nor did *Mellidore* seem in the least offended, or dissatisfied.

The Sunday following, they went in grand procession to divine service, all elegantly dressed, and made no indifferent figure, it is to be presumed, in a country church. The parson preached a sermon, entirely on the duties of the married state, and directed his discourse particularly to the young pair. The clerk, not to be behind-hand, gave out the psalms that are sung on the marriages of the royal family; for which kindness, the man knew what he was about, *Mellidore* gave him a piece of gold; at the sight whereof his bows and scrapes shewed how much he was delighted. Here they staid near a fortnight; when, with much difficulty, the worthy parson and family let their sojourners depart in peace, enriched with a thousand blessings.

Bless me, what a track of paper has my pen ran over! Why, on my conscience, my dear reader, I believe we must wish our heroine, together with the Countess of *Volpont*, the happy *Mellidore*, and the gentle *Clytandre*, a good journey, and have done with them – or, perhaps, instead of two volumes, we shall have three or four.[49] – Hang it – I am sorry too – for I think we might have made something more of the story still. *Theodora*'s *pêtit ménage*, in a rural life, her domestic cares – how the Earl and Countess of *Volpont*'s quarrel ended – what became of *Jago*, &c. &c. – In short, as the silk-worm spins its vitals, to adorn the gay, so would I gladly have extended my ideas, to please my kind reader, had I it in my power. But if they are not tired of my nonsense, why they have only to command me to reassume my pen, and go on – No, no, not to the enormous length of a Sir *Charles Grandison* neither; nor yet to that of a *Tristram Shandy*[50] – though perhaps you may say, I went something on that plan, by delaying so long to bring my heroine into play. But I will assure you, my dear friend, *whosoever thou art*, (Dear me! why did I not introduce this romantic saying before now?) that I do not think the example worthy imitation. I rather took the hint from a good, honest country mason, who told me, if ever I wanted to raise an edifice, to be sure to lay a solid foundation. Or, to shew you I understand something of the œconomy of a table, the first course is substantial; and to those who come with keen appetites to this entertainment, it may be acceptable; while such as are of a more puny and delicate texture, may wait for the second, and pick a bit where they like; or, *a la mode Francoise*, if they choose a desert, – why, – I protest they must wait for it till next year: – when I shall endeavour to provide somewhat of the bitter, sweet and sour, – in a variety of incidents, that may alternately actuate the human passions – and prove sufficient to fill a third volume. – I therefore, for the present, must bid my kind, indulgent reader a tender adieu! while I flatter myself with the pleasing idea of our meeting again, and enjoying an agreeable *tête a tête* in the flowery-field of imagination.

END OF THE SECOND VOLUME.

Notes

1. Variant spelling of anchorite, meaning a religious recluse.
2. A woman's riding habit with a cape and buttons down the front.
3. Correctly, Rocinante. The name of Don Quixote's horse in Cervantes' great work.
4. Captain Macheath is a roguish highwaymen from John Gay's *Threepenny Opera* (1728).
5. A real club notorious in eighteenth-century Britain and Ireland for its celebration of rakish excesses, most active between the 1740s and the 1760s.
6. The Queen's Basin, a reservoir. Theodora is following the path of the Queen's Walk.
7. *French*. With his hat off.
8. If this episode is based on a real incident, given that the princess involved was an adult (and apparently not a married woman, as Princess Amelia would have been by this point), it was likely Caroline or Mary.
9. George II.
10. Ann Simpson was granted a pension of 100*l* by the crown in January 1745 at the request of Lord Chesterfield, which was doubled a few years later.
11. A bad-tempered, argumentative woman.
12. "A familiar appellation for a sailor: perhaps abbreviation of tarpaulin" (*OED*).
13. A derogatory term for a British person who acquired vast wealth in India.
14. A character from Richard Steele's 1722 sentimental comedy *The Conscious Lovers*.
15. Du Bois uses "only" here to mean one alone or singly, i.e. one-ly.
16. I.e. cupid.
17. *Latin*. In the form of a pauper, meaning that she did not have to pay the usual court fees.
18. This likely refers to the suit Ann Simpson brought against Richard Annesley to the House of Lords in 1748, which was withdrawn at her request, "the earl having offered her an accommodation" (*Journal of the House of Lords* 31).
19. A screech-owl or barn owl's piercing cry was popularly thought to be a dark omen.
20. If Musgrave is correct regarding his identification of the Garden sisters as the Gunnings and the Lord Lieutenant as William Stanhope (see notes below) then this is likely an allusion to the celebrations held on 30 October 1748 for King George II's birthday. The ball hosted that evening by Viscountess Petersham famously saw the debut of the beautiful Gunning sisters, Maria and Elizabeth, who would become the belles of London society in the 1750s (Robins 28). Du Bois thus places her mother and her younger self at one of the most gossiped about events of mid-eighteenth century Ireland.
21. The Irish Parliament sat every second year from autumn to early summer.
22. Musgrave identifies the Lord Lieutenant in question as William Stanhope, 1st Earl of Harrington. Harrington was indeed a widower, his wife having died giving birth to his twin sons in 1719.
23. *Incognito*.
24. A fabric made of cotton or silk.
25. The Lord Lieutenant's remark regarding Theodora's "patriotic" dress is an allusion to the Irish patriot movement of the mid-eighteenth century, which fought against crippling restrictions placed on Irish trade by the British parliament, particularly textiles; see Padhraig Higgins.

26 Musgrave identifies "Maria Garden" as Maria Gunning, later Countess of Coventry, the famous Irish beauty who died young at twenty-eight of lead poisoning from the makeup she wore every day.
27 The central figures in the 1709 love poem "Henry and Emma" by Matthew Prior.
28 A watch-paper was a piece of ornamented paper placed inside a watch case in order to protect the mechanism from dust and damage.
29 In *The Case of Ann Countess of Anglesey* (Appendix B), Du Bois dates an incident in which she was attacked while attempting to visit her ailing father to November 1760, which would be about a decade later than the timeline presented in *Theodora*. The author may of course be conflating more than one event or there may have been more than one such incident.
30 Du Bois is referring to Sancho Pan*za* (rather than Pan*cho*), the squire to Don Quixote in Cervantes text of the same name.
31 Du Bois is likely referring to the marine clock invented by John Harrison (not "Harris") in the 1730s, which solved the longitude problem in seafaring.
32 Smelling salts.
33 If this is a version of the episode in which Du Bois attempts to visit her father and is menaced by his attendants and her half brother, that also appears in "A True Tale" (Appendix A) and *The Case of Ann Countess of Anglesey* (Appendix B), then this version considerably elides the more disturbing elements of the story related in those previous texts, particularly in *The Case*.
34 A fast pace in horse-riding somewhere between a canter and a gallop.
35 In the Book of *Daniel*, the prophet Daniel acts as advisor to the aged King Nebuchadnezzar.
36 From Shakespeare's *Henry VI*, act v, scene vi.
37 "A globe-shaped gaslight" (*OED*).
38 A local municipal building.
39 The 1754 marriage act made it illegal for young people under twenty-one to marry without their parents' consent. Du Bois appears to have forgotten that she had reduced Theodora's age to sixteen.
40 Properly, éclaircissement, meaning an enlightening explanation.
41 A unit of area equal to one quarter of an acre.
42 A mill designed to pound wool in order to clean it and improve its quality, producing at the end of the process a worsted fabric.
43 *French*. In their nightgowns.
44 *Slang*. "Oaken towel, also simply towel, a stick, cudgel" (*OED*).
45 Peter Du Bois, a musician and Du Bois' husband.
46 Mahón, Spain. The capital of Minorca.
47 In Shakespeare's *King Lear* (1606), the king relinquishes his throne to his two selfish daughters Goneril and Regan who mistreat him when he is in their power. He punishes his third daughter Cordelia for her unwavering honesty, but she remains loyal to him, nonetheless.
48 Lycurgus of Sparta instituted a system in which all male citizens were equal.
49 No further volumes of *Theodora* were published.
50 *The History of Sir Charles Grandison* (1753) by Samuel Richardson has seven volumes, while *The Life and Opinions of Tristram Shandy, Gentleman* (1759) by Laurence Sterne has nine.

Appendix A

"A TRUE TALE" FROM *POEMS ON SEVERAL OCCASIONS* (1764)

NATURE had form'd *Anglesus*[1] full of Grace,
Both as to Understanding, Form and Face;
A pleasing Wit, quick Penetration, and
Such jocund Humour, as wou'd Mirth command,
He wedded with a Fair and spotless Maid,
In blooming Youth and Innocence array'd;
Obtain'd a Fortune to his Wish; nay more
Than he cou'd then expect, for he was poor
In point of Fortune, altho' nobly born;
But lovely *Anna*,[2] might a Crown adorn,
So was the Fair-one call'd; and many a Swain
Strove for her Love, whom *Anglesus* did gain.
Some Years they liv'd, in Happiness and Peace,
And Heaven bless'd their Marriage with Encrease,
Three Daughters (out of Seven) gave them Joy,
But both were anxious to obtain a Boy.
Tho' these sweet Pledges, he wou'd often swear,
To his fond Heart, were equally as dear.

Soon to a Title and a great Estate
Anglesus' succeeded, by the will of Fate.[3]
His lovely Wife, and infant Daughters shone
In all the Pomp, that Grandeur cou'd put on;
At Court, at ev'ry public Place appear'd,
Admir'd by all; by ev'ry one rever'd.
But who'd on human Happiness depend;
This short-liv'd, glitt'ring Scene was soon to end.
Transient Felicity! – *Anglesus* grew
Unkind to *Anna*; sigh'd for something New;
Beheld a Tenant's Daughter with Desire,[4]

DOI: 10.4324/9781003150794-6

APPENDIX A

Nor scrupled to indulge the guilty Fire.
Tho' mean the *Nymph*, and common to Mankind
She gain'd an Empire o'er his fickle Mind;
Contriv'd such Schemes, and us'd such subtile Art,
She soon, alas! Occasion'd them to part.

The faithful Wife, the tender Mother view,
Now exil'd from her Lord, and Children too;
To his Inconstancy a Victim made,
Forsaken, comfortless, to Want betray'd.
Her hapless Daughters now, like tender Plants,
The Sun-shine of a Parent's Kindness wants;
From Place to Place, the wretched Suff'rers tost,
By Heav'n unless preserv'd, had sure been lost.
Dorinda now (the eldest of the Three)[5]
Began to feel the Force of Misery;
Mourn'd her sad Fate, to be expos'd to Woe
Ere her weak Years, the Task cou'd undergo.
Scheme after Scheme was for her Ruin laid,
But Virtue guarded still the tim'rous Maid;
Attempts prove fruitless, cautiously she trod,
Entrusting still her Innocence to GOD.
The pow'rful Guardian, watchful on her side,
Preserv'd the Maid, who sought Him for her Guide.

The King to *Anna*, bless'd his Mem'ry be,
A Pension gave; and, when at Liberty,
The anxious Mother to her Children came,
Shelter'd their Youth, and rescu'd them from Shame.
But *Anglesus* the younger Two retakes,

(Some three Years after) and the First forsakes.

Dorinda, proudly scorn'd each flatt'ring Tale
To lure her from her Mother none prevail:
By Nature bound, by Gratitude and Love,
Blest in a Mother, she'd a Daughter prove.
Retir'd and quiet from the World's Turmoils,
They liv'd together, no domestic Broils
Imbitter'd Life, for peacefully they dwelt,
When our *Dorinda* some Emotions felt
For a young Foreigner,[6] whose gentle Mind

Seem'd for her Happiness alone design'd.
To the fond Impulse of her Heart she yields,
Marries the Youth, and both fair *Anna* shields.
The tender, kind, good Mother takes a Pride,
That for the happy Pair she can provide.
A lisping Offspring gave their Joys Encrease;
And promises Delight that ne'er can cease.
While gentle *Anna* loves them as her own;
And ev'ry Action makes her Virtues known.

When Vice once gains Dominion o'er the Mind,
She reigns a Tyrant, by no Laws confin'd.
The hood-wink'd Reason, no clear Object views,
Who hath no Choice, can ne'er pretend to chuse;
But as directed, still his Fate pursues.
Old *Anglesus*, a Slave to Woman's Art,
Lives from the World and Virtue, quite apart.
Nurtures a spurious Race, his Fortune spends
In base Obscurity and has no Friends,
Save such as Favours want, or yet incline
T'assist his Folly, in each black Design.

Nature worn out, enfeebled by Disease,
Burdened with numerous ill-spent Days;
At length a violent Fit o'erpow'rs his Frame,
The instant Danger, Doctors strait proclaim.
While ev'ry Face of his Dependants wear
A sort of Sorrow, that denotes their Fear.
Distraction, Horror, sits upon each Brow;
Each dreads he's lost, his rich Protector now.
Report spreads wide; the interesting News,
Which each repeats, with his own private Views;
But all conclude it must, of Course, elate
His injur'd Family, to hear his Fate.

The Tidings come, unwelcome to their Ears,
Their Eyes o'erflow, with sympathetic Tears.
The yet most-lovely *Anna* mourns her Lord,
Dorinda's Grief won't let her speak a Word,
But silent sits; at length the Storm gives Way;
And she in Sobs, her Sorrow doth convey;

Her ev'ry Word proclaims her filial Love,
And doth her Duty and Affection prove.
Her eldest Son she presses to her Heart,
Anglesus, dearest Love, will soon depart;
He never saw thee, my sweet lovely Boy,
Nor ever felt, a kind Grand-father's Joy.
Tho' from our fond Embraces, long he's stole,
May-hap he mourns us, with his fleeting Soul:
Now calls my Mother, now repeats my Name;
Wou'd see us both, but can't his Wish proclaim.
For ah! my Love, we've Enemies around,
Wou'd quickly smother the unwelcome Sound.
Indeed, Mamma, says the dear prattling Boy,
Were I with old *Anglesus*, I'd employ
My little Arts to make him fond of you;
And if I cou'd succeed, he'd love me too.
True, my dear Creature, cou'd he once but see
Thy pretty Face, he'd soon be Friends with me.
Then on her Knees she falls, I've one Request
Which if refus'd me, I shall ne'er have Rest,
My dearest Mother, grant me it – ah! do,
And you, my Husband! gratify me too.
Permit me, of my Father to obtain
One parting Glimpse, and happy I'll remain:
Nature and Conscience, now may take my Part,
Awake his Tenderness, and turn his Heart.
To gain his Blessing, ere he quits this Life,
To reconcile him to his injur'd Wife;
Wou'd be such Extacy of Bliss to me,
I'd wish no greater 'tween Eternity.
Soft'ned at length, the kind Permission giv'n,
They recommend her to the Care of Heav'n!
And each, by Turn, fast hold her in their Arms,
Beseeching God! to shield her from all Harms.
Dissolv'd in Tears – they parted – swift she flew
T'experience Villainy of deepest Hue.
Sh' obtain'd the sight, so earnestly she sought,
But at the Hazard of her Life 'twas bought.
The cruel Father imprecating lay,
Disowning Nature, order'd her away;
Tho' to Appearance, ready just to go,
And pay that Debt which all to Nature owe.
A num'rous Throng of Ruffians now surround
The sad *Dorinda*, prostrate on the Ground.

His base-born Son,[7] a Pistol e'en presents,
Behind her Head; but watchful Heav'n prevents
The Fiend from executing his Intents.
They pull and drag her, tear her Hands and Cloak,
Nay dare uplift their own to give a Stroke:
Force her from Room to Room, then down the Stairs,
Nor heed her piteous Cries, nor flowing Tears.
Some, more humane, now shook indeed their Head
As they pass'd by, but nothing still they said.
(Scarce two Months past a dang'rous Lying-in,
Such cruel Usage surely was a Sin.)
Now driv'n from the House, *Dorinda* sate
And humbly warm'd her at the Kitchen Grate.
While ev'ry Word, was followed by a Sigh,
Behold her Woes draw Tears from ev'ry Eye.
Her Servants now are ty'd, her Horse's Ear
Inhumanly cut off: 'tis much they spare
Dorinda's Life, whom thus they seem to hate
With Spleen, uncommonly inveterate.
Forc'd now to walk along the dirty Road,
Her Legs scarce able to support their Load;
They bring her Pris'ner to th' adjacent Town,
Where her unhappy Fate's no sooner known,
Than all lament the Usage she receiv'd,
They wept in Secret, and in Secret griev'd:
But none dare openly express their Grief,
Nor, tho' she fasting was, bestow Relief.
Faint, hungry, cold and comfortless she sate
The whole long Night, bemoaning of her Fate;
No Bed whereon to lay her weary'd Head,
By Grief and Sorrow she alone is fed.

The wish'd-for Morn but slowly doth appear,
The Horrors, of the Night encrease her Fear;
The beating Rains, the Winds dread hollow roar,
And heavy Clouds, you'd think her Fate deplore.
The tardy Morn, at length, bestows his Light,
Behind the Clouds, bright *Phœbus* hides from Sight.
His Course near run, when see *Dorinda* brought
To a bleak Park – Oh! Ill surpassing Thought!
There kept, there threat'ned, fright'ned to Despair,
Her Screeches rend the terrified Air.
At last exhausted, Limbs benumb'd decline

Their usual Office, and on Earth recline:
Unanimated now, she breathless lies,
While all repeat, too sure, alas! she dies:
Recall'd, she treads the Scene of Woe again,
And frantic raves, and calls on Death in vain:
The pale-fac'd Moon, the twinkling Stars admire;
Whilst she in Fancy grasps, th' exalted Fire;
Calls on her Husband! Mother! Infants! Friends!
Then cries alas! I've none – none Comfort sends;
Thus madly raving she by two is led,
Racing one Moment, sinks the next as dead.

A second Morn brings Life and Spirits too,
And she gains Leave her Journey to pursue.
Her Servants Pris'ners kept, behind remain;
While she a well-affected Town* doth gain.
They soon o'ertake her with their savage Guard;
Who narrowly escap'd their due Reward:
Th' enrag'd Inhabitants together rose,
And their *Dorinda*'s Enemies oppose.
Fierce Anger blaz'd in each resenting Eye,
And Stones, in Show'rs, at her Oppressors fly.
Is this, cry'd they, for Duty a Reward,
This a Return for such a Child's Regard?
A Child, which once he doated on so much,
Can we believe our Eyes, his Nature's such,
That to so dutiful a Daughter, he
Can so unnatural a Father be?
May we but see the Day, when we may take
Dorinda's Part, for her lov'd Mother's Sake.
With Hands uplifted, Heav'n then implor'd
To turn the harden'd Heart of *Anna*'s Lord.
Thus disappointed, quite abash'd, return'd
The sad *Dorinda*, who this Trial mourn'd;
Deeming it Rashness, her Attempt to move
A Father's Tenderness, so void of Love.
The sole Result of it was only Pain,
And Madness nearly had o'er-turn'd her Brain.
The troubl'd *Anna* listens to her Tale
With pain'd Attention, nor can long conceal

* Ferns, in the County of Wexford.

APPENDIX A

The rising Tumults, struggling in her Breast;
But Sighs aloud, and Tears she long supprest
Burst forth in Torrents – while *Dorinda*'s Lord
Smothers his Grief, and utters not a Word.
At last, within his Arms he folds his Wife,
And cries, I'm happy, they have spar'd thy Life;
But ah! my Love, what need had you to go,
And willingly thus plunge yourself in Woe?
Thus leave your Mother, little Babes and me,
In Search of naught, but Inhumanity;
Thy Father's Heart, alas! too hard'ned grown,
Denieth Pity, even to his own:
But I, susceptible of all thy Charms,
Ne'er wish another in those faithful Arms.

Since this, behold, *Dorinda* fearful flies
Her once-lov'd Cottage, where her Treasure lies;
Self-preservation orders them to part,
And she forsakes them, with an aching Heart,
Comes up to Town, in search of some Relief,
And to her Friends discovers all her Grief.
They Pity her – condemn the lawless Man,
And joy she scap'd the Dangers which she ran.

But now, to sum up all *Dorinda*'s Woe,
Anglesus really dies,[8] 'twas order'd so,
Offended Heav'n! wou'd no longer see
A Man absorb'd in Vice and Infamy:
His Talents buried, his Genius cramp'd,
And by base Influence, each Virtue damp'd.
What Pity, that those Qualities divine
Shou'd be exhausted in a Life supine?
That Intellectuals, bright and shining shou'd
Have lost their Force, nor sought the public Good;
But ev'n a Scourge to his right Offspring prove,
While those of *Devilyn*,[9] engross'd his Love.

Thus liv'd *Anglesus*, dup'd by Woman's Art;
Who when he dy'd, to shew her real Heart
A black Compound, of full Ingratitude
(Which she had then no Power to elude)

191

She disrespectfully his Corps interr'd,
And some few Guineas to his Fame preferr'd.
Laid in a shallow half-dug Grave, behold!
The great *Anglesus*, strip'd of all his Gold;
No Mourners, no Attendants in the Dark,
With scarce a Link, he's hurried thro' his Park,
His Body, on his Coach's-body laid,
Within a Coffin, of a Fir-tree made;
The horrors, of a black and gloomy Night,
Set the poor Horses in such sad affright,
That thro' the rustling Trees they took their Flight,
And like t'have left in Pieces the Remains
Of poor *Anglesus*, mangled on the Plains.
His Soul, in Conflict, on his dying Bed
Recogniz'd all his Errors, oft, he said,
He wrong'd his Wife, his Children; then implor'd
From Death a Respite, of th' Almighty Lord!
That He, in some Sort, might those Crimes atone,
For which his Conscience did incessant groan:
He mourn'd that Life he had so long mis-spent,
But most of all, their Suff'rings did lament.
The vicious *Devilyn* to Virtue lost,
Wou'd at his Bed-side, still maintain her Post;
And like a Fiend, tormented him ere dead,
Constr'ing to Folly, ev'ry Thing he said.
Her own curst Int'rest the Decision gave,
My Lord, says she, indeed does only rave;
He knows not what he says, thus his Distress
She strove to heighten, not to make it less.
But ere he dy'd, some nine Years, as they say
She o'er his Mind, obtain'd so great a Sway,
That tho' already marry'd, (to her Shame
Be't spoken) she obtain'd the shadowy Name
Of Wife,[10] altho' he had no Right to give
That Name to any one, and *Anna* live.
But, so infatuated was he grown,
He fear'd her Pow'r, and quite forgot his own.
His Will, or rather her's, she next has done,
And leaves th' Estate to her ill-gotten Son:
Whom in it she stiles L—d, her Daughters too
She titles Ladies, what won't Cunning do?
The artful Wretch obtains whate'er she craves,
Then as a Tyrant, to her Dupe behaves.
Thus she, who once wou'd to his Foot-men yield,

APPENDIX A

Becomes his Queen, and doth his Sceptre wield;
Exerts a Power, by few Wives assum'd,
Or rather none, it is to be presum'd.

To Law! voracious Law, fair *Anna* now
Must have Recourse, it cannot disallow
Her Right, which on it's own Foundation lies,
And can't be deaf to Truth's distressful Cries.
Dorinda and her Sisters too appeal
To Truth and Justice, these must strait prevail
O'er Vice and Perjury, for sure in vain
Distressed Virtue never can complain,
Where soft Compassion, well is known to reign.

Notes

1. Richard Annesley, Earl of Anglesey and Dorothea Du Bois' father.
2. Ann Simpson, Du Bois' mother.
3. Richard became Lord Altham on the death of his older brother, Arthur Annesley, in 1727 and Earl of Anglesey in 1737 on the death of his uncle.
4. Juliana Donovan, later Countess of Anglesey.
5. Du Bois was the eldest daughter of Richard Annesley and Ann Simpson.
6. Peter Du Bois, a French musician and Du Bois' husband.
7. Arthur Annesley, son of Richard Annesley by Juliana Donovan, who claimed Richard Annesley's titles on his father's death. However, while the Irish House of Lords granted him the title of Viscount Valentia, a House of Lords committee decided that due to the questions around his legitimacy, he had no right to the title of Earl of Anglesey. He was later made Earl Mountnorris.
8. Richard Annesley died in 1761.
9. I.e. Juliana Donovan.
10. Richard Annesley married Juliana Donovan publicly in 1752, but in order to legitimise their son Arthur upon Annesley's death, Donovan claimed they had held a previous, secret marriage ceremony in 1741, the witnesses to which had all since died. The British House of Lords did not accept the legitimacy of the certificate she produced.

Appendix B

THE CASE OF ANN COUNTESS OF ANGLESEY, LATELY DECEASED . . . (1766)[1]

Lawful Wife of RICHARD ANNESLEY,

Late Earl of ANGLESEY,

AND

of Her Three Surviving DAUGHTERS, Lady DOROTHEA, Lady CAROLINE and Lady ELIZABETH, by the said EARL.

Deliver me not over into the Will of mine Adversaries: for there are false Witnesses risen up against me, and such as speak wrong.
Psal. xxvii. ver. 14.

London: Printed in the Year 1766

Introduction

THE Disadvantages I labour under by being unable to make that Appearance my Birth and Pretensions intitle me to, lays me under the Necessity of publishing an impartial State of my Case, in order to undeceive the Public, who have been prejudiced against me, by the malicious Reports, base Insinuations and industrious Machinations of an Enemy, who fights me with my own Weapon, and possessed of what of Right belongs to me and Family, can cut a Figure and mingle amongst the Great, whence Oppression, Poverty, and Wrongs exclude me.[2]

'Tis a severe Stab to that filial Duty and Affection I have ever retained in my Breast, to be obliged to expose to Light, the Errors of a Father, that I tenderly loved, and have even run the risque of my Life, to rouse from that Lethargy of Vice he sunk into, by the evil Counsel of those wicked People under whose Influence he fell after his Separation from my Mother, and who Leech-like sucked away his Sense and Cash, and undermined his Honour. That Attempt, pious and warrantable as it was, in a dutiful Child, has been basely misrepresented, and such villainous Falsehoods propagated in regard thereto, that I find it incumbent on me to give a full Detail of the whole Affair, in Vindication of that Honour, that is dearer to me than Life. In a Book of Poems, which my Necessities obliged me to publish, by Subscription, some few Years ago, I gave a poetical Account of this Transaction,[3] which now, in simple Prose, I shall submit to the Inspection of the judicious and impartial.

In November 1760, I was informed my Father, *Richard* the last Earl of *Anglesey*, lay dangerously ill; Nature wrought so powerfully in my Breast, as to determine my endeavouring to see that dear deluded Father, in hopes the sight of a Child, he once dearly loved, might be a Means of recalling him to a Sense of his Duty, and a Desire of Reconciliation with his Family. It was certainly very great Rashness in me, to venture myself in the Hands of Enemies, with whom he was surrounded, whose inveterate Hatred I had before experienced, and particularly at a Time, when my Spirits and Strength were greatly impaired by Child-birth, having lain-in about seven Weeks before of my sixth Child. With great Difficulty I prevailed on my Mother and my Husband, to consent to my taking this hazardous Step; but this Point gained, after recommending myself to the Protection of Almighty God, I set out for the Family Seat, at *Camolin-Park* in the County of *Wexford*, attended only by an old Man, and a Foot-Boy of thirteen Years of Age, who rode before me. I lay that Night at a Town within two Miles of my Father's, and well convinced that, if known, I should have no Chance of seeing him, I ordered Matters so, as to be there early the next Morning, when concealing my Face, and knowing the Situation of my Father's Bedchamber, I made my Way to it, without the least Difficulty or Obstruction, but alas! found a Female Companion with him, from whom I could hope for little Lenity. – She started when she saw me enter, and discover who I was, by throwing myself on my Knees at my poor Father's Bedside, and, with Tears, implore his Blessing, – No one but such as have the same Feelings I have, can conceive the tender Agony that seized my Soul, on seeing the Change Time had wrought in the Author, under God, of my Being. – But who can describe my Astonishment and Grief, at hearing him utter the most shocking imprecations against his Child; – a Child that loved him as her Life, and would have sacrificed it to his Preservation and Conversion. – How shall I repeat it? He called for his Pistols to shoot me! – Self preservation, they say, is the first Law of Nature – therefore, seeing Mrs. *Donovan* make towards a Closet where I formerly knew Fire-Arms hung. – I started to my Feet, and charged her, at her Peril, not to harm me, as she certainly would suffer for it, if she did, as many knew of my coming, and for what Purpose, which was no other than to obtain a Father's blessing before he died. After a few more Altercations not worthy Repetition, she rang the Bell, when a number of ill-looking Wretches, who dishonoured the Name of Servants, appeared; Mrs. *Donovan* ordered those, her Ruffians, to seize and drag me out of the Room, vainly imagining that, if I could obtain a few Moments longer Stay in his Presence, my Father's Heart would relent, as his Anger seemed to subside; on finding myself thus attacked, I drew a small silver-mounted Pistol from my

Pocket, which I blush to say was, with its Fellow, unloaded; and only meant to keep those Ruffians, I expected to meet, at a Distance. A Cry, equalling that they describe the wild *Indians* to give, was set up at the Sight of this formidable Weapon. Presenting the harmless Bugbear alone at my ferocious Assailants, I bid them not lay Hands upon me, or expect the Consequences. At first they obeyed through Fear, but finding I did not fire, they pressed in upon me; three Men all at once laid hold on it, and had Strength and Valour sufficient to wrest it out of the Hand of a weak Woman; but not without leaving that Hand in a gore of Blood. While those attacked me in Front, others endeavoured to strangle me behind my Back, by pulling my Cloak, and had effected their Intention, were I not under the Banner of an all-wise all-powerful Being! who ordered the strings to break; I was again saved by the same Hand! who intimidated the Heart of Mrs. *Donovan*'s Son[4] from letting off a Pistol, which he courageously held cocked at the back of my Head, and occasioned his meeting with a severe Rebuke from an ignorant Pantry-Boy, whom he desired to shoot me, the Boy telling him, *"you may do it yourself, I have no Mind for the Gallows."* After this, they hurried me down the Stairs into the Hall, took my other Pistol from me, but not before I unscrewed the Barrel, and shewed them there was nothing in it. Then it was my humble Lot to be obliged to sit in the Kitchen, where I was an Eye-witness to such Things as gave room for this Reflection, *that where Vice presided, Order, Regularity, and Plenty were banished.* My Servants were threatened with a Gaol, together with their unfortunate Mistress, they were pinioned like Thieves, and by the Order of the young Lord,[*] as they called Mrs. *Donovan*'s Son, they inhumanly cut off the Ear of the innocent Horse I rode, though the poor Brute could not possibly be deemed an Accessary in my Offence, had my Intention even been Criminal. They then obliged me to walk two Miles in the deep Road, to the Village of *Camolin*, where they would have lodged me in the Watch-house; but a compassionate Ale-seller, who was also a Butcher, suffered us into his House, though at his Peril; for an Express was sent before me to forbid any one, on pain of Displeasure, to give me a morsel of Bread, though I should offer ever so much for it. That Night I was forced to sit up with my own Servants, the lowest of my Father's, who were set as Spies over me, and a parcel of Constables as Guards to prevent our Flight. The next Day the Companions of my Woe, were sent for to the Parkhouse to be examined; and about Four o'Clock in the Afternoon, I was also sent for. Happy at the Thought of once more seeing my dear missed Father, though in such shocking Circumstances, I readily obeyed the Summons: But oh! Words are too faint to describe the Sufferings I went through. They brought me, indeed, within Sight of the House, but the Heavens were the only Roof I was suffered under; exposed to the Inclemency of a cold frosty Night, expecting Death from behind every Tree, till at length Nature, unable to support me longer, I sunk under the

---

[*] Who now stiles himself Earl of Anglesey, &c. &c.

Weight of Cruelty and Oppression heaped upon me, and fell into violent convulsive Fits. I in that Situation remained till Eleven o'clock at Night; a Delirium seemed to have seized my Brain, and my dangerous Symptoms having frightened my Tormentors from a Continuance of their Persecutions, I was carried to a Blacksmith's House, whose Wife had the Humanity to take me in, and lay me in a Bed; to which charitable Act I owe my Life.

The next Day, they again wanted to take me to *Wexford* Gaol, with my servants, but the Town of *Ferns*, sensible of my cruel usage, rose in my Defence, and rescu'd me from the hand of Persecution. This is the Truth, as I shall answer it to my God! of an Affair that has been so industriously misrepresented, and so scandalously reported to my Disadvantage, as to render those cool in my Interest, who pitied, and were inclined to relieve my Distress. To say, I attempted to commit the horrid Crime of Parricide; – threatened to shoot my Father! held a Pistol to his venerable Head! Oh! Horror, horror! no! I would as readily have spilt my own Heart's Blood, as have hurted a Hair in his Head – three Affidavits are still to the fore, relative to this Affair, – namely, my own, and those of my two Servants who are still alive, and which verify the Truth of what I have here asserted. I can never be sufficiently thankful for my miraculous Preservation, when the Hand of Providence so visibly protected and brought me through the imminent Dangers that, for two Nights and near three Days, surrounded me, notwithstanding the dangerous Consequences thereof to my Health, for my long fasting had such an effect upon me, that for some time after, I fainted at the Sight and Smell of any kind of Nourishment, vomited Blood, and got such a severe Cold, as to ulcerate my Gums, occasion the Loss of a Tooth, and throw me into a violent pleuritic Fever; and to this Day, am subject to a dreadful pain in my Leftside, which I expect, sooner or later, will be my Death. But this suffering is not thought sufficient by my implacable uncharitable Enemies; who not only keep me out of my indubitable Rights, but take every method possible, to undermine me in the Esteem of the World, to make those who have and would serve me, withdraw their salutary Assistance; in order, I suppose, to verify their own generous Boasts, viz. "*We don't value her, she can never be able to recover any Thing, as she has not wherewith to buy* Bread *for her and her Children.*" It is true, I am reduced to those straits, – and by whose means? Theirs, who robbed me of a Father, and with-hold what I have the justest Claim to, and which would place me, far above Want or being a Burthen to my Friends. But 'till Heaven thinks fit to mollify my untoward Fate, I must submit, and do the best I can, to stem the Tide of Adversity into which I am innocently plunged; and flatter myself, my grievous Situation, immergent Wants, and that Charity so conspicuous in these Nations, will entitle me to the Notice and Protection of the humane Public, to whom I submit the following State of a Case, which I hope, will merit their Attention, and intreat their Pardon for so long ingrossing it by so melancholy a subject as the foregoing, but which I found absolutely necessary in vindication of my *Character*.

APPENDIX B

King-Street,
Golden-Square.

DOROTHEA DU BOIS.

THE

CASE

OF

ANN Countess of ANGLESEY, &c.

IN the Year 1727, the Honourable *Richard Annesley*, the youngest Son of *Richard* Lord *Altham;* Dean of *Exeter*, who had been an Ensign in the Army, but was struck off the Halfpay in the Year 1715, and was then destitute of any Fortune or Subsistence whatever, being at *Dublin*, and passing for a Batchellor, made his Addresses to Miss *Ann Simpson*, the only Daughter of Mr. *John Simpson* a wealthy and reputable Citizen; she at that Time being no more than fourteen or fifteen Years of Age. After many Solicitations, (her Mother and most careful Guardian having died some time before) he at length prevailed on her to be privately married to him, without the knowledge or consent of her father, who was highly displeased with her on that Account.[5] But *Arthur* Lord *Altham*, Elder Brother of the said *Richard*, having interposed his good Offices for a Reconciliation, they were again, at the requisition of her father, and of the said Lord *Altham*, who insisted upon it, married in a public Manner, by the Reverend *Henry Daniel*, then Curate of St. *Catherine*'s, by a Licence taken out of the Consistorial Court of the Diocese of *Dublin*, who indorsed a Certificate of the Marriage on the back of the Licence. Mr. *Simpson*, her Father, thereupon was not only reconciled to them, and took his said Daughter and her Husband into his Favour and Family, but gave the said *Richard* a considerable Portion with her, and supported them for some Years after their Marriage, suitable to their Rank, which was attended with an extraordinary Expence, on account of the said *Richard*'s having, by the death of his Elder Brother, which happened soon after his Marriage, assumed the Title of Lord *Altham*; and from the Time of the said Marriage they lived publicly together as Man and Wife under the Denomination of Lord and Lady *Altham*, and as such were universally deemed, reputed, and universally received and treated by all their Acquaintances.

In the Year 1729 *Nicholas Simpson*, a Relation of her Father, filed his Bill in Chancery against the said *Richard*, then Lord *Altham*, and *Ann* Lady *Altham* his Wife, to be relieved against a promissory Note, perfected by the said *Nicholas* to them or one of them; to which Bill they put in a joint Answer taken upon Honour, by the Name and Stile of *Richard* Lord *Altham* and *Ann* Baroness of *Altham* his Wife, wherein the said *Richard* acknowledged his Marriage with the said *Ann*, which Bill and Answer are of Record in that Court.

APPENDIX B

On the Death of Mr. *Simpson*, Father of the said *Ann*, which happened in the Year 1730, he by his Will charged his Estate with an Annuity of 20*l* a Year to his said Daughter during her Life, for her sole and separate Use, independant of her Husband, under the Stile and Title of the Right Honourable *Ann* Baroness of *Altham*, and bequeathed a Legacy of 100*l* to the said *Richard*, under the Denomination of *Richard* Lord *Altham* his Son-in-Law; 10*l* to the said *Dorothea Annesley*, their Daughter; which two last Legacies, the said *Richard* not only received, and applied to his own Use; but soon after, in the Year 1733, having Occasion for Money, he prevailed upon his said Wife to sell the said Annuity of 20*l*. a Year, to one *William Mackenzie*, and to join with him, for that Purpose, in a Deed, and in levying a Fine to the said *Mackenzie*; which Deed and Fine were accordingly executed and acknowledged by him, and the said *Ann* his Wife, at the Bar of the Court of Common Pleas, by their then Stile and Title of *Richard* Lord Baron of *Altham*, and *Ann* Lady *Altham*, his Wife, as appears by the said Deed and Fine both remaining of Record.

In the Year 1737, *Arthur* Earl of *Anglesey* dying without Issue, the said *Richard* became possessed of his Honours and Estate, both in *England* and *Ireland;* and thereupon, he and his said Wife were introduced and received at the Lord Lieutenant's Court, as Earl and Countess of *Anglesey*, and the said Lady *Dorothea* and her Sisters, as the Daughters of an Earl, and were universally acknowledged by his Grace the Duke of *Devonshire*, then Lord Lieutenant, and his Duchess, and all the Nobility of the Kingdom, at Court as well as at all other Places, as such, and took their Rank and Precedency accordingly.

In the same Year 1737, soon after the Death of the above mentioned *Arthur* late Earl of *Anglesey*, great Contests having arisen between the said Earl *Richard* and one *Charles Annesley*, concerning their respective Rights of Succession to the said Earl *Arthur*'s Estate, they came to an Agreement to divide the same; and thereupon indented Articles of Agreement, dated the 6th of *June* 1737, were entered into, and executed between them, whereby, among other Things, it was agreed, that if either of them should happen to die without Issue, the Survivor and his Heirs should succeed to the deceased's Share of the Inheritance, and they were reciprocally impowered by said Articles of Agreement, to charge their respective Shares with a Jointure to each of their Wives, and with a certain Sum of Money. The said Earl *Richard* particularly, was thereby impowered to charge his Share with 25,000*l*. and also with 2000*l*. a Year for his Widow, in lieu of Jointure.

Soon after these Articles were entered into, Earl *Richard* having discovered, that he had been greatly imposed upon by the said *Charles Annesley*, who had no Manner of present Right, refused to carry the same into Execution; whereupon fresh Disputes arose between them, and each of them filed their Bill in the Court of Chancery, the Earl to set the said Articles aside, and *Charles* for a specific Performance of the same.

Pending those Suits, the Earl, who had levied Fines, and suffered Recoveries of all, or the greatest Part of the said Estates, being in *November* 1740 seized with a dangerous Illness, and being desirous to make Provision for his said Wife, and

Daughters by her; he in execution of the Powers vested in him, by said Articles, executed a Deed of Settlement, dated 14th *November* 1740, between himself of the one Part, *Simon Bradstreet*, Esq; afterwards Sir *Simon Bradstreet*, Baronet, and *William Colthurst* of the City of *Dublin*, Gent. of the other Part, as Trustees, reciting the several Fines and Recoveries of all the Estate whereof he stood seized; and declaring by the said Deed, that all the said Fines and Recoveries so levied and suffered between him and the said Parties, should enure to the only proper Use of the said Earl, his Heirs and Assigns for ever, but subject nevertheless to, and charged with the Payment of 2000*l.* a Year for his said Wife, in case she should survive him to be paid on every 25th Day of *December*, and 24th of *June*, from his Decease, during her Life; and also, charged with 10000*l.* to his eldest Daughter, Lady *Dorothea*, at her Age of eighteen Years, or Day of Marriage, which should first happen, with lawful Interest for the same till paid, for her Maintenance and Education; and with the further Sum of 8000*l.* to his second Daughter Lady *Caroline*, and 7000*l.* to Lady *Elizabeth* his youngest Daughter, also payable at their respective Ages of eighteen, or Marriage, with the like Interest for the same, till paid, for their Maintenance and Education; and in case any of his said Daughters should happen to die before the Age of twenty-one Years, or Marriage, that her or their Share or Shares should go to the Survivor or Survivors of them.

Immediately after the Execution of this Deed, the said Earl *Richard* delivered it into the Custody of Mr. *John Simpson*, his Brother-in-Law, for the Use of Lady *Anglesey*, his Wife, and his three Daughters, but would not suffer the same to be registered, but kept a profound Secret, pending the above mentioned Suits betwixt him and *Charles Annesley:* lest the said *Charles* should take Advantage thereof, as tending to corroborate the said Articles, which he was then endeavouring to set aside.

Hitherto the said Earl *Richard* had always lived in great Harmony with his said Wife, and took great Care of the Education of his three Daughters by her; but having soon after, in her Absence, contracted a Familiarity, and criminal Intercourse with one *Gillin* alias *Julian Donovan*, the Daughter of one *Richard Donovan*, who sold an unlicensed Kind of Ale, called *Shebeen*,[6] in a Cabin, in the Village of *Camolin*, where his Lordship's Men Servants usually frequented, often at very untimely Hours, and sometimes stayed out of the Family whole Nights, for the sake of the said *Gillin*'s Company; he from thence forward began to treat his said Countess and her Children, with great Indifference and Neglect; and was at length, by the contrivance of the said *Julian Donovan*, and the wicked arts of one *John Ians*, a Surgeon, her Confederate, prevailed upon not only to treat them with great Cruelty, and totally to abandon her and his hapless Children to absolute Want, but to break open her Escrutore[7] and rob her of all her Writings, particularly of the above mentioned Deed of Provision for her and her said Daughters, which had been delivered into her own Custody some time before by the said *John Simpson* her Brother. But happily for her, and her unfortunate Children, the original Draft of the Deed, as settled by Sir *Simon Bradstreet*, hath been since acknowledged, and the due Execution of the said Deed proved by the Witnesses.

This *Ians*, who was a Sort of Agent for and Dependant on his Lordship, was intrusted with most of his secret Transactions, and on that Account had great Influence over him; but having some time before been detected by the said Countess in defrauding his Lordship of several considerable Sums of Money, he swore Revenge against her, and not only took this Method of satiating his Malice, but pursued it still further, by persuading his Lordship that he might easily obtain a Divorce; and the said Earl being overpersuaded by *Ians* and his Accomplices, was so weak as to attempt it; and for that Purpose he and *Ians* his Agent offered considerable Bribes to several People, to swear something Criminal against her, as a Pretence for his Separation, and thus cruelly abandoning her and his Children. But the People to whom they addressed themselves, being too conscientious to accept of such infamous Proposals, he at length, by the Contrivance of the said *John Ians*, and one *Jack Hatton* an Attorney, found out an abandoned Wretch called *Mary Egan*, who was at that Time a Prisoner in *Wexford* Gaol for Felony, and who upon a Promise of being bailed and brought to *England* by his Lordship, and of being made his Lordship's Housekeeper, and thereby avoid being tryed for that Offence, and by Promises of other Rewards, was prevailed upon by the said *Hatton* to swear such an Affadavit as he dictated to her. She was accordingly bailed out of Gaol, and brought immediately over to *England* by his Lordship, and was for some Time kept at his House in *Duke Street* St. *James's*; but upon her being disappointed of the other Promises made to her, she disclosed this whole Scene of Iniquity to several Persons, particularly to Mr. *John Giffard*, one of his Lordship's Attorneys; and her Declarations relative thereto, being afterwards reduced into an Affidavit, was sworn before a Master in Chancery, and transmitted to *Cæsar Colclough*, Esquire, Knight of the Shire for the County of *Wexford*, in order to be communicated, by him, to the other Gentlemen of that County, in Vindication of the unfortunate Lady's Character from the wicked Aspersions cast upon her by the said Earl and his Accomplices.

In the Year 1741, the said *Ann* Countess of *Anglesey*, being thus forlorn and totally destitute of any Subsistence, she by the Advice of Doctor *Boulter*, the then worthy and virtuous Lord Primate of *Ireland*, with whose Family she was in great Intimacy, instituted her Suit in the Consistorial Court of the Diocese of *Dublin*, against the said Earl *Richard*, for Cruelty and Adultery with the said *Julian Donovan*; and upon Confession of his Marriage with the said Countess *Ann*, in his personal Sentence, she obtained an Order against him for an interim Alimony of Four Pounds a Week until a full Answer should be pronounced in the said Suit; and further, that the said Earl should pay her Costs to that Time, and her future Costs in the Cause.

The said Earl having been served with a Monition[8] to obey the said Order, and having declined to perform the same, Sentence of Excommunication was pronounced against him, and having still continued in his Obstinacy, he was, after all the due Forms had been used, declared an excommunicated Person, and so remained till his Death; and Application having been made to the then Lord Chancellor for a Writ, *de excommunicato capiendo*,[9] to take the said Earl into Custody,

APPENDIX B

and the Chancellor having declined to grant it, on account of his Privilege of Peerage, her Suit in that Respect proved ineffectual; and her sole Support, and that of her Children, from thence forward to her Death, which happened in *August* 1765 was a Pension of 200*l*. a Year upon the *Irish* Establishment, which his late most excellent Majesty was graciously pleased to grant her, on the Representation of the Earl of *Chesterfield*,[10] then Lord Lieutenant of that Kingdom, of the Cruelty and Hardship of her Case.

The said Earl *Richard* and his Accomplices finding themselves defeated in their – Scheme of obtaining a Divorce, thought proper to try some other Method. He therefore, in the Course of the abovementioned Proceedings in the consistorial Court, (having first in vain applied to his late Majesty for a *noli prosequi*[11] on account of Bigamy) set up another Marriage, *prior* to that of his Countess, with one *Ann Phrust*[12] of the County of *Devon* in *England*, who died some short Time before, as appears by one of his Answers to the Libel of the said Countess of *Anglesey*, which was the first Notice she ever had of any such Marriage; but, on the contrary, if the said pretended Marriage had any real foundation, the same was all along concealed from her with the greatest Care and Secresy till that Time. And it is particularly to be observed with relation to that pretended Marriage, that some short Time after the said *Richard* became Earl of *Anglesey*, the above named *Ann Phrust*, who had never in the least claimed him as her Husband, or given the least Notice to Lady *Anglesey* of her *prior* Marriage, if any such was really solemnized, wrote him a Letter from *Biddeford* in *Devonshire* to *Ireland*, to claim an Alimony; and that his Lordship was so alarmed at this Letter, and so industrious to conceal it from his Countess, who by this Time had been introduced at the Lord Lieutenant's Court, and complimented by all the Nobility of the Kingdom as Countess *of Anglesey*, that he immediately wrote to one *William Henderson* his *English* Agent, a most pressing Letter, requesting him to go immediately to *Biddeford*, and silence that Woman let it cost what it would, lest her Pretensions should make a Noise, and come to Lady *Anglesey*'s Ears.

Henderson thereupon immediately proceeded to *Biddeford*, and entered into an Agreement with the said *Ann Phrust*, in Consideration of 3500*l*. to execute an Instrument, whereby she disclaimed the said Earl as a Husband, and covenanted thereby never afterwards to molest him on that account; which Instrument was afterwards delivered to his Lordship, and, if not destroyed, must now be in the Hands and Possession of the said *Julian Donovan*. By these iniquitous Means the said *Ann* Countess of *Anglesey* was kept totally in the Dark, and under an invincible Ignorance of the said pretended Marriage, and of the Fraud and Imposition put upon her for a great while after the Execution of the said Instrument, and until after she had exhibited her above-mentioned Libel in the Year 1741, in the Consistorial Court of the Diocese of *Dublin*, upwards of fourteen Years after her Intermarriage with the said Earl, and after she had bore him seven Children, of which the abovementioned three Daughters are still alive.

It is also to be observed, that his Lordship in his Defence on the above-mentioned Suit in the Consistorial Court, having set up his said *prior* Marriage with the said

Ann Phrust, in order to give the better Colour to that Allegation, produced a Copy of a Writing unwitnessed, which he pretended was given him by *Ann Simpson* his Countess before her Inter-marriage with him, purporting, as he alledged, her Knowledge of his having another Wife in *England*, and promising never to molest him on that account; but being required to produce the Original, which he could not comply with as no such Writing was ever executed, his Plea, in that respect, was rejected with Costs. He however some Time afterwards produced another Writing of the same Purport, which he pretended to be the Original, and of the Hand-writing of his said Countess *Ann*, signed by one Witness, who as alledged was dead some Time before, which in like Manner was also dismissed with Costs, as not being of the Hand-writing of the said *Ann Simpson* his Wife, altho' alledged so to be, and so a third Time still with Costs.

In the same Year 1741, the said Earl, after he had totally deserted his Wife, took the said *Gillin Donovan*, with whom he had secretly kept up a criminal Intercourse from the latter End of the Year 1740, into his House, in the Character of a menial Servant, in which Condition she continued for seven Years; during which Time she had several Children by him, and, among others, a Son called *Arthur*, who was born in *July* 1744, and who now pretends to be intitled to the Honours of Earl of *Anglesey*; by which Means, and the Arts of her Confederates, she some Time after gained so great an Ascendancy and Influence over him, as to have the chief Management of his Affairs left to her, whereby she accumulated large Sums of Money to herself; but she never was able to prevail on him to suffer her to assume the Title of his Wife until the Year 1752, long after the Birth of the said *Arthur* and her other Children,[13] when, thro' old Age, and a vicious Course of Life, his Intellects being greatly impaired, he became totally lost to all Sense of Honour and Shame, and married the said *Gillin Donovan*, tho' the said *Ann Simpson*, his Countess, was then, and for several Years after, alive, and the said Suit in the Consistorial Court still subsisting: To which may be added, the strong Desire he always expressed of having a male Heir, which co-operated powerfully with the Artifices of the said *Julian Donovan*, and her Confederates, not only to induce him to take this absurd Step, but also to acquiesce in their trumping up a Certificate of a Marriage, alledged to have been solemnized in 1741, which, from all Circumstances, must be a mere Forgery and Imposition.

This Marriage of *Sept.* 1752,[14] if it can be called one, was performed at *Camolin-Park*, by one *Laurence Neal*, a profligate, suspended Clergyman, brought from a distant Country, without either Licence or Publication of Banns; the said Earl, and the said *Donovan* being conscious that no Bishop or Surrogate in the Kingdom would grant a Licence for that Purpose, nor any Clergyman of Character or Reputation in the Country where they lived, perform the Ceremony. And tho' the said *Julian Donovan*, in order to secure her Jointure, and to legitimate her said Children, now pretends, that she was married to the said Earl by the said *Laurence Neal*, in *September* 1741; yet it is notorious to the whole County of *Wexford*, and more particularly to the Neighbourhood of the several Places where his Lordship resided, to the Servants who then lived in his Family, and to all People of any

APPENDIX B

Credit, who were in the most intimate Connections with him, some of whom he consulted in all his Affairs, that no such Marriage was ever heard of in 1741, but on the contrary declare, that the said *Julian Donovan* was always deemed and reputed in the Family and the Country round it, to be no other than a kept Mistress at best, and her said Children Bastards, and that they were treated as such, and declared to be illegitimate by the said Earl himself, to several Persons of Credit, till some short Time before the Year 1752, that he conceived a Scheme of leaving a male Heir to inherit his Honours and Estate, and for that Purpose, consistent with himself, endeavoured, by preparatory Speeches, various Arts and Contrivances, to collect a Number of seemingly concurring Circumstances, in order to make his spurious Issue by *Donovan* pass for legitimate Children, contrary to his former Declarations; besides, several of the Servants, who were then in the Earl's Family, and out of the Reach of the Influence of Mrs. *Donovan*, and other People of Credit, declare, that *Laurence Neal*, the Parson, was not at *Camolin* in *September* 1741.

As a further corroborating Proof, that this Marriage of *September* 1741, is a mere Fiction, lately set up by Mrs. *Donovan*, on purpose to legitimate her Children, and secure to herself a Jointure, it is to be observed, that she at different Times, since their Birth, lent several Sums of Money to divers Persons, and took Securities for the same, in her own Name of *Julian Donovan*, and more particularly, that she lent to *Francis Annesley*, of *Ballysax*, in the County of *Kildare* Esq; a considerable Sum of Money, and took a Bond and Warrant of Attorney to confess Judgment for the same, in her own proper Name of *Julian Donovan*, which Judgment was accordingly entered in his Majesty's Court of Exchequer in *Ireland*, against the said *Francis Annesley*; and the said Debt, with the Interest and Cost, being afterwards, in the Year 1751 [illegible] paid by the said *Francis Annesley*, she not only signed a Receipt, but executed a Warrant of Attorney, to acknowledge Satisfaction on the Record of the said Judgment, in her own proper Name of *Julian Donovan*; and Satisfaction was accordingly entered thereon in Trinity Term 1751, which also remains of Record in that Court.

The said *Julian Donovan*, towards the Decline of the said Earl's Life, by her Arts gained an entire Ascendancy over him, insomuch, that all the later Transactions of his Life were governed by her and her Confederates, who now alledge, that the said Earl, notwithstanding the Sentence of Excommunication in Force against him, did on the 7th of *April* 1759, execute his last Will and Testament,* by which, (amongst other Things), he bequeathed to her the said *Donovan*, by the Title of his dear and well beloved Wife, *Juliana* Countess of *Anglesey*, a Rent Charge of 1000*l*. yearly, payable out of his Estate in *Great Britain* and *Ireland*, and all the personal Estate he should die possessed of, which was to be in full of all Thirds. And to his lawful Wife by the Name of *Ann Simpson*, with whom he received a very considerable Fortune, he bequeaths a Legacy of 10*l*. only,

---

* As he was under Sentence of Excommunication, he was incapacitated by law to make a will or bequeath a personal estate.

expressed to be in full Satisfaction of all Claims which she could pretend to, and to his eldest Daughter, Lady *Dorothea*, by the Title of his natural Daughter *Dorothea*, 5s. in full of all Claims, *&c.* which last mentioned Legacies, seem to have been artfully inserted in the said pretended Will, by the Means and Contrivance of the said *Julian Donovan* and her Accomplices, to insult the said *Ann*, Countess of *Anglesey* and her Children; and, in order to be afterwards pleaded in Bar to their just Claims under the said Deed of the 14th of *November* 1740, which they are now suing for in the Court of Chancery of *Ireland*, and where Execution of the said Deed has been proved and acknowledged.

The 14th of *February* 1761, the said Earl died under the above-mentioned Sentence of Excommunication; and the said *Julian Donovan* soon after his Death, possessed herself of all his personal Estate, under Colour of the said pretended Will, amounting to upwards of 20,000*l.* and immediately thereupon *Ann*, Countess of *Anglesey* his Wife, entered Caveats in the Prerogative Courts of *England* and *Ireland*, to oppose the Probate of the said pretended Will; and Administration to be granted thereon to the said *Julian Donovan*: In consequence whereof a Suit was commenced in both the said Courts by the said *Julian Donovan*, and by the said *Ann*, Countess of *Anglesey*, concerning the Validity of their respective marriages; both which Causes are still depending in the said Prerogative Courts. But, alas! the Contest hitherto hath been very unequal, not in Point of Justice on the Part of the said Countess *Ann*, but in Point of Ability to proceed; one of the Parties, *namely*, the said *Julian*, wallowing in Riches, acquired in the above-mentioned infamous Manner, which enabled her to retain a most extraordinary Number of the greatest Counsel at the Bar, and the other oppressed with Poverty and Distress, unable to retain any, or even to undergo the necessary Expences of vindicating her just Rights, or defending herself against the Attacks of such an opulent Adversary. Nor are her unfortunate Children, who now have the same Causes to support, in Defence of their own Legitimacy, in a better, but a far more deplorable Situation since her Death; and to crown their Misfortunes, the Suit between their deceased Mother and the said *Julian Donovan*, concerning their respective Marriages; has unhappily fallen under the Cognizance, of a person, who is at the same Time of standing Counsel for their opponents in all Causes, and Judge of the said Prerogative Court in *Ireland* where that Suit is depending; and who in the Course of the Proceedings has all along discovered such manifest Partiality in favour of Mrs. *Donovan*, his Client as at length became so glaring, as to oblige their Mother to appeal to *England*, to his Majesty in his Court of Chancery for a Commission of Delegates; which Appeal is still depending. Nor was his Partiality, in his Capacity of Attorney-General, less conspicuous in favour of his other Client *Arthur Annesley*, the said Mrs. *Donovan's* Son, in the Dispute between him and *John Annesley* Esquire, concerning the *Irish* Honours of Viscount *Valentia* and Baron *Mountnorris*, to whom their respective Petitions were referred.

The said *John Annesley* claimed these Honours as descended to him by Right of Inheritance, on the Death of *Richard* late Earl of *Anglesey*, without any legitimate Issue Male; and he, in Support of his Petition for that Purpose, produced a great

APPENDIX B

Variety of Evidence, to prove, from the general Voice of the Country, where the said Earl resided, – from the Testimony of Servants who lived in his Family – from his Lordship's own Declarations to several People of Credit, his Relations and intimate Friends – from the Circumstance of his being married long before to the said *Ann Simpson*, his Countess, who was then alive, and from other Evidence, some of which are Matters of Record, that the pretended Marriage of the said Earl with the said *Julian Donovan*, in *September* 1741, upon which the Legitimacy of her said Son *Arthur*, the other Claimant, is solely founded, (in case the Marriage of the said Countess *Ann* should not be established) was a mere Fiction, and consequently, that all the said *Donovan*'s Children were spurious, as they were all born before her Marriage in the Year 1752.

The said Attorney General, notwithstanding the variety of the above mentioned Evidence, and the great Importance of the Contest betwixt the Parties in this Case, as tending in its Consequences to divest one of them of a Right of Inheritance to a Peerage, and the three unfortunate Daughters of the said Earl by his said Countess *Ann Simpson* of their Legitimacy; and notwithstanding the still remaining doubtfulness of the Case, wherein the Honour of the *Irish* Peerage was deeply concerned, has nevertheless taken upon him to conclude his Report and Opinion thereupon absolutely, in favour of one of the contending Parties his Client, without taking any special Notice, as he ought to have done, of the Contest then and now still subsisting in his own Court, concerning the Matrimonial Rights of the said *Ann* Countess of *Anglesey* and the said *Julian Donovan*; which is of such a Nature, that without a previous and final determination thereof, the Right to that Peerage could not be legally determined.

And it is also to be observed that this Report, which concludes so absolutely in favour of one of the Parties, is contrary to the Policy of our Laws, and to the general Practice in like Cases, founded upon the most vague, uncertain, and most dangerous Kind of written Evidence, *namely*, upon Affidavits of mean obscure Persons, taken in different corners of the Country, by one or other of the Party's interested, or their Agents, without the Presence of any Person in behalf of the adverse Party to controul them; such sort of Evidence in its own Nature is every way insufficient and inconclusive, and is never relied upon even in the Determination of the meanest and most insignificant Cause, and far less in a Case of this high Nature, on the Determination whereof, the most essential Rights of so many Persons depended. And it is also to be observed, that several of the Affidavits upon which Mr. Attorney in his Report lays the greatest Stress, are suspicious and liable to strong Exceptions; namely the Affidavit of the said *Julian Donovan*, who is a Party every way deeply interested; that of *John Ians* the Surgeon, whose malevolence to the Countess *Ann* was publicly known, and whose Character and Veracity was otherwise liable to many objections. And the same may be said of the other Witnesses, who have given any material Evidence in support of the Marriage of *Julian Donovan* in *September* 1741.

It is in like manner to be observed, that the Evidence given by *Ruth Coxon* in favour of Mr. *John Annesley*, was so very material to disprove the pretended

Marriage of the said *Julian Donovan* in *September* 1741, that they had no other way of avoiding the force of it, but by procuring a set of low lived illiterate Papists, most of whom are Persons of bad Character themselves, to make Affidivits tending to impeach hers; although what these People have sworn against her, is clearly repugnant to the offices she had been employed in about the said Earl's Family, and to the Trust reposed in her by him as well as by his Countess *Ann Simpson*, in committing the Education of their Children to her Care in their early Infancy; and afterwards by the said Earl's sending for her to *Bray* in the Year 1741, after he had abandoned his Countess and taken the said *Julian Donovan* into keeping as a Concubine, to be in his Family, to instruct the said *Julian* how to dress and behave herself. Moreover, her Character would have been supported by several Persons of Worth and Veracity, particularly by the Evidence of the Clergyman of the Parish of *Bray* where she resided, who not only voluntarily granted her a Certificate of her Sobriety and good Behaviour, in contradiction to the Affidavits sworn against her by those wretches, but would have given Evidence of the same, had not the said *John Annesley* by an inexcuseable Neglect of his own interest omitted it, as well as many other material Things, which would have strengthened his Case, and invalidated that of his Adversary.[15]

This neglect of his proceeded partly from his too great Confidence, that the Evidence, which he had laid before the Attorney General, was sufficient, to render the Question concerning the Illegitimacy of his Adversary, and the nullity of the pretended Marriage of his Mother in the Year 1741, certain, or at least doubtful; and it was more than sufficient to authorize the Attorney General to report it as such; and to advise, as is always done in all contested Cases of that Nature and Importance, its being referred to the House of Lords of *Ireland*, or some other Tribunal vested with competent Jurisdiction, to enquire thoroughly into the Matter, where both Parties would have an opportunity of supporting their Case by the fullest Evidence; and he was the more confirmed in this his Opinion, as it was well known an Attorney General has no competent Jurisdiction to enable him to report finally on such a Case. For that Officer of the Crown is vested with no judicial Power, and could not, by any compulsive Process, compel Witnesses to appear before him, to be examined and cross-examined, *viva voce*, upon Oath; nor could he even tender them an Oath, his Office being only ministerial and not judicial. Therefore this unhappy Man, *John Annesley*, relying on this established and invariable Doctrine, and never suspecting that the Attorney General would take upon himself to report finally in Favour of either Party, in a Case of such Importance, and at the same Time so doubtful in itself, on Account of the great contrariety of Evidence laid before him, and not in the least doubting but that his Report would have been such, as to lay a Foundation for a Reference from his Majesty to the House of Lords, where he would have a fair Opportunity of supporting his Case, and of establishing the Character of his own, as well as of making just Objections to the Characters of his Adversary's Witnesses. He therefore omitted to take the proper Steps, to enforce its being referred to that honourable House, in which the Honour of the Peerage was deeply interested, to make thorough Enquiry into the Matter in Question.

But be that as it may, it is very amazing that Gentleman, in summing up the Evidence on each side of the Question, should so far forget himself as slightly to pass over the first and most material Consideration to be taken Notice of in it, and upon which in a Manner the Determination of that Peerage wholly depended; *namely*, the prior Marriage of the said Countess *Ann Simpson* with the said Earl *Richard*, by barely making a cursory mention of it, and without any Evidence or Foundation, expressing a Doubt whether they were at all married; and this notwithstanding that the said Countess had long before proved her Marriage in his own Court, as Judge of the Prerogative, and that so many public Instances and Proofs of their Marriage were known to him; – such as the Earl's own Acknowledgments of his Marriage with her, their cohabiting publickly as Man and Wife for a course of fourteen Years; joining with her as his Wife in Answers in Chancery, and in levying Fines, which are Matters of Record; his settling a Jointure on her as his Wife, her being publickly acknowledged as Countess of *Anglesey*, and her Daughters as his legitimate Children, as well by the Duke of *Devonshire*, the then Lord Lieutenant, and his Duchess, as by all the Nobility of both Sexes in the Kingdom, all which must have been known to that Gentleman as matters of public notoriety.

It is also very extraordinary, that he should by his said Report, put the Credit of the Record relative to Mrs. *Donovan*'s taking Securities from *Francis Annesley*, and executing a Power of Attorney to acknowledge Satisfaction to that Gentleman in her own Name, in Competition with the Affidavits of the said *Julian Donovan*, and of *Ians* the Popish Surgeon; whose Character he was not unacquainted with, and giving those Affidavits the Preference to these Records But it is still the more extraordinary in a Person of his Knowledge of Law, as it is a received Maxim, that no Person can be admitted to aver against a Record of their own Act and Deed, and much less a Person who had it in her own Power to refuse executing those Deeds; for if she was really married in *September* 1741, as pretended, she in that Case had nothing to fear from her Refusal to execute them. But how are her pretended Scruples in this point and the affected Difficulties she pretended to make to execute a Receipt in her own Name to the said *Francis Annesley*, consistent with many Letters voluntarily wrote by her in her proper Name of *Julian Donovan*, for several Years after *September* 1741.

Upon the whole, this Report is liable to so many Objections, on account of its laying the greatest Stress upon every minute Circumstance that could in the least favour his Client *Arthur*, and either slightly passing over or not mentioning many Circumstances that were favourable to the said *John Annesley*, that it would be taking up too much of the Reader's Time to enumerate them. The Public in general in *Ireland*, as this Affair was circumstanced, are amazed, and at a loss to find by what Means the said *Arthur* could procure a Writ for his Admittance into the House of Lords, upon the bare Report of the Attorney General only. For it was the Opinion of some eminent Lawyers of both Kingdoms, at the Time this Affair was depending before the Attorney General, that he could make no final Report to preclude either of the Parties. And it is the general Opinion since the Report hath been made, that instead of concluding it so absolutely as he has done in Favour of one of the contending Parties, he ought, as is always done in the like Cases, where a contrariety of Evidence appears, to have concluded his Report, that the Matter referred to him by the said Petitions was of so high and important a Nature, the Contrariety of Evidence laid before him so great, and the Matter in Question so complicated with the Contest, concerning the respective Marriages of the Countess *Ann Simpson* and *Julian Donovan* with the said Earl *Richard*, and his Powers as Attorney General so circumscribed, that he could not take upon him to make a final Report. That he therefore apprehended, that a Matter of such Importance as a Right of Inheritance to a Peerage, claimed by each of the contending Parties, could not be legally determined in a summary Way upon such inconclusive Evidence as he had before him; nor otherwise than by a full and open Trial, either in the House of Peers of *Ireland*, or some other Tribunal vested with competent Jurisdiction, to try and determine the Matter in a judicial Way: That by such a Trial all Parties would have an Opportunity of a candid Hearing, of examining and cross-examining Witnesses, *viva Voce*, upon Oath, and of the Assistance of many able and impartial Judges; and then to have concluded with his Opinion, that his Majesty might be advised to refer the Matter of the Petitions to the House of Lords.

If such a Reference had been recommended to his Majesty, there can be no Doubt but he would have been graciously pleased to have ordered it, more particularly as no Man can, by the Laws or Constitution of these Kingdoms, be ousted of his Right, and more especially of a Right of Inheritance to a Peerage such as this was, without a legal Trial. And such a Trial in this Case was the more necessary, as many Gentlemen of Honour and Probity, who thought it improper for them, on Account of their living in the Neighbourhood of the said *Arthur* and his Mother Mrs. *Donovan*, voluntarily to appear in Favour of the said *John Annesley*, but would nevertheless, if legally called upon, either by Summons or Subpœna, have given very material Evidence for him.[16] By all which it plainly appears, that the said *John Annesley* has been deprived of the Testimony of many valuable Witnesses in support of his Claim, by this unprecedented Method of proceeding. Besides, Mr. Attorney General ought, in his said Report, to have taken very particular Notice of the Contest still subsisting in his own Court, as Judge of the Prerogative between the said Countess *Ann Simpson* and *Julian Donovan*, concerning the Validity of their respective Marriages, which was so intimately connected with the Contest about these Honours, that there can be no final Determination of the one without that of the other. For whether Mrs. *Donovan's* Marriage of *September* 1741, was real or not, her Son cannot be intitled to these Honours, if the Marriage of the Countess *Ann Simpson* should be established, which many able Council are of Opinion it must; as her Case is, in every Respect, exactly similar to that of Mrs. *Campbell* in the Suit with Mrs. *Kennedy*, which was determined a few Years ago, upon an Appeal in the House of Lords of *Great Britain* in Favour of Mrs. *Campbell*, and with great Justice.[17] For if a Woman, under a prior Contract of Marriage, knows that her Husband has imposed upon and married another, as in the present Case, and if she does not claim him as her Husband, or acquaint the abused Person of it, but, on the contrary, contributes to the Fraud by a voluntary and concerted

Concealment, and thereby not only suffers the other by such Concealment to be stripped of her Fortune and Character, but her innocent Offspring to be branded with the Imputation of Illegitimacy, what Woman in such a Case can possibly be safe? But at any rate, Mrs. *Donovan* was highly to blame, for she acted a base and unjust Part with her Eyes open. She knew that the Countess *Ann Simpson* was married to the said Earl *Richard* many Years; that he received a large Fortune in Marriage with her; that he had many Children by her; and that she was publickly acknowledged by him and the whole Kingdom as his Countess; she also knew that a Suit was depending in the Consistorial Court of the Diocese of *Dublin*, for Cruelty, and Adultery with herself, as well as to establish the said Countess *Ann*'s Marriage with the said Earl, notwithstanding which, she in the Year 1752 married him: whereas she ought at least to have waited the Event of that Suit, and to know whether she could legally do it or not. From all which it is evident, that the unhappy Countess *Ann Simpson*, and since her Death her unfortunate Children, who now have the Burthen of supporting their own Legitimacy, are manifestly injured by this very extraordinary Report; as Mr Attorney has thereby taken upon him to pre-judge their Cause, by taking the Validity of the pretended Marriage of the said *Julian Donovan* therein for granted, which was the very Thing in Question in the said Prerogative Court, of which he himself is Judge, and that, pending an Appeal from him to a Court of Delegates in *England*, and before the Merits of the Case was heard in either Court. The fatal Consequence whereof is, that they are already precluded in the Kingdom of *Ireland* from maintaining their Legitimacy, and making a proper Defence, or even calling in Question the Marriage of the said *Julian Donovan* with their Father in that Kingdom; as such a proceeding might be construed into a breach of Privilege, after the Admission of the said *Julian*'s Son into the *Irish* House of Peers.

Many other Observations equally material might be made on this very extraordinary Report, which are reserved for a future Opportunity, in case that Gentleman should venture to support his Report or Conduct in the management of it. One Thing, however, cannot but be taken Notice of, to shew how far Prejudice and Prepossession may get the better of the best Understandings, and of that Impartiality to be expected in a Judge; and that is, that from the Beginning of this Contest, and during the whole Course of the Proceedings before that Gentleman, he constantly complimented his Client *Arthur*, the Son of Mrs. *Donovan*, with the Appellation of Earl of *Anglesey*; and his Antagonist, though the first who petitioned, with that of Mr. *Annesley* only.

In August 1765, the said *Ann* Countess of *Anglesey*, after struggling in the above-mentioned Suits against many Acts of Cruelty, Injustice, and Oppression on the Part of the said Earl her Husband, and of the said *Donovan* and her Accomplices, died of a broken Heart, leaving her three Daughters by the said Earl without any Provision or Support, other than their Right to the Arrears of her Jointure, and the Portions allotted for them by the said Earl their Father, by the said Deed of the 14th of *November* 1740, which is most unjustly witheld from them by the said *Donovan* and her said Son, and which they are now contending for in the Court of

Chancery in *Ireland* as before mentioned. The Case of Lady *Dorothea* the eldest in particular, whose sole Dependence, and that of her six small Children, was on the Support she received from her Mother out of her Pension, is most deplorable, as they are by her Death left destitute of every Kind of Subsistence, and of the Means of prosecuting her just Right, or even of defending her Legitimacy, by establishing the Marriage of her mother, which is now depending in the Prerogative Courts of both Kingdoms, unless the kind Hand of Providence should move the Hearts of some compassionate Persons to enable her to vindicate and support the same.

P.S. *My great Inability to obtain the necessary Assistance, in the compiling those Truths I have conveyed in the foregoing Case, which demanded a better Head and clearer Understanding than mine, to put it in an advantageous Dress, will, I flatter myself, meet with that Indulgence and Allowances, my Sex and Distresses may intitle me to, from the compassionate, generous and humane.*

Dorothea Du Bois

Notes

1. Ann Simpson died in 1765.
2. Juliana Donovan styled herself Countess of Anglesey while Du Bois' mother Ann Simpson was still living. If Richard Annesley's marriage to Simpson was legitimate, as Du Bois believed, then Donovan had no right to the title, and her children (including Arthur Annesley, who claimed to be Annesley's heir) had no right to their titles either.
3. "A True Tale" from Du Bois' *Poems on Several Occasions*, reproduced in Appendix A.
4. Arthur Annesley, Du Bois' half brother, later Viscount Valentia and eventually Earl Mountnorris.
5. From 1707 it was illegal in Ireland for a girl under eighteen to be married without her parents' consent, while abduction for the purpose of forced marriage (as appears to be the case from Du Bois' account) was punishable by death.
6. A "shebeen" (an anglicisation of the Irish "síbín") denotes both an unlicenced alehouse and an unlicenced ale.
7. A type of writing desk also known as an *escritoire*, particularly fashionable in the early decades of the eighteenth century.
8. A formal notice from the ecclesiastical court not to take a specified action.
9. *Latin*. The seizing of an excommunicated person.
10. The Earl of Chesterfield is listed among the subscribers to Du Bois' *Poems on Several Occasions*.
11. *Latin*. Correctly "nolle prosequi," meaning to not want to pursue. The term is used in law to convey that prosecution will not be sought.
12. Richard Annesley married Ann Prust or Phrust in 1715 but left her soon afterwards.
13. This was the conclusion of the committee of Rights and Privileges of the British House of Lords, which declined to recognise Arthur Annesley's claim to the Earldom of Anglesey on the grounds that the evidence for his parents having married secretly in 1741 was questionable.
14. Du Bois is mistaken in the month of her father's marriage to Juliana Donovan, which occurred in October rather than September of 1752.
15. The upholding of Richard Annesley's marriage to Ann Simpson would have had the effect of automatically ruling the marriage between him and Juliana Donovan unlawful and thereby rendered his rival claimant, Arthur Annesley, illegitimate, but this was just

APPENDIX B

one avenue through which John Annesley might have claimed his title. It would also have meant ceding a considerable portion of his inheritance to Du Bois and her sisters. For these reasons and others, John Annesley was probably not as exercised about this issue as Du Bois.

16 These "Gentlemen of Honour and Probity" did not, however, materialise for the House of Lords trial Du Bois had so desired in 1770–71.
17 Du Bois cites a 1747 case in the Scottish courts in which a Mrs Kennedy sued a Mrs Campbell for the recognition of her prior marriage to Mr Campbell and produced a certificate, which he had signed, in which he promised to marry her. The court did not uphold the marriage in part because she had not raised the issue over the twenty years during which Mr Campbell had cohabited publicly with Mrs Campbell.

BIBLIOGRAPHY

Primary sources

An Abstract of the Case of the Honourable James Annesley, Esq; Humbly Submitted to the Consideration of All Disinterested Persons, and of All Lovers of Justice and Truth. Dublin, 1754. July 2021. https://link.gale.com/apps/doc/CW0124071079/ECCO?u=dublin&sid=bookmark-ECCO&xid=612306d9&pg=50.

Calendar of Home Office Papers of the Reign of George III: 1766–1769. Vol. 2. London, 1879. *Google Books.* August 2020. https://books.google.ie/books?id=1ZBnAAAAMAAJ&pg=PP9#v=onepage&q&f=false.

Du Bois, Dorothea. *Advertisement.* London, 1767.

———. *The Case of Ann Countess of Anglesey.* London, 1766. *Google Books.* August 2021. https://books.google.ie/books?id=JS9cAAAAQAAJ&pg=PA1#v=onepage&q&f=false.

———. *The Divorce, a Musical Entertainment, with Music Composed by Mr. Hook.* London, 1771.

———. *The Lady's Polite Secretary, or New Female Letter Writer.* London, 1771. *Eighteenth Century Collections Online.* August 2020. https://link.gale.com/apps/doc/CW0112595204/ECCO?u=dublin&sid=bookmark-ECCO&xid=6bff4bb4&pg=1.

———. *The Magnet, a Musical Entertainment, as Sung at Marybone Gardens.* London, 1771. *Google Books.* January 2021. https://books.google.ie/books?id=MZciDIN4s-YC&source=gbs_navlinks_s.

———. *Poems on Several Occasions by a Lady of Quality.* Dublin, 1764. *Eighteenth Century Collections Online.* August 2020. https://link.gale.com/apps/doc/CW0111525207/ECCO?u=dublin&sid=bookmark-ECCO&xid=92d3d1b2&pg=1.

———. *Theodora, a Novel.* 2 vols. London, 1770. *Google Books.* Accessed August 2021. https://books.google.ie/books?id=rZXMdeB9DK4C&pg=PP1#v=onepage&q&f=false.

The Freeman's Journal. Dublin, 1764–74. *Irish Newspaper Archive.* Accessed January 2021. https://www.irishnewsarchive.com.

Hays, Mary. *Female Biography: Or, Memoirs of Illustrious and Celebrated Women, of All Ages and Countries: Alphabetically Arranged.* Vol. 4. London, 1803. *Google Books.* January 2021. https://books.google.ie/books?id=jJgMAAAAYAAJ&pg=PP5#v=onepage&q&f=false.

Haywood, Eliza. *Memoirs of an Unfortunate Young Nobleman Returned from a Thirteen Years Slavery in America, Where He Had Been Sent by the Wicked Contrivances of His Cruel Uncle.* London, 1743. Google Books. January 2021. https://books.google.ie/books?id=ZE-oLHQ-N7UC&pg=PP1#v=onepage&q&f=false

Jacob, Alexander. *A Complete English Peerage, Containing a Genealogical, Biographical, and Historical: Account of the Peers of this Realm*. London, 1766. *Eighteenth Century Collections Online*. August 2020. https://link.gale.com/apps/doc/CW0101371501/ECCO?u=dublin&sid=bookmark-ECCO&xid=f522a349&pg=1.

Journals of the House of Lords: 1 GEO. I–19 GEO. III, 1714–1779. Vols. 20–35. London, 1796. *Eighteenth Century Collections Online*. August 2020. https://link.gale.com/apps/doc/CW0106256359/ECCO?u=dublin&sid=bookmark-ECCO&xid=0f4d2b89&pg=300.

Minutes of the Proceedings Before the Lords Committees for Privileges on the Claim to the Title of the Earl of Anglesey. Dublin, 1772. *Google Books*. January 2021. https://link.gale.com/apps/doc/CB0130216431/ECCO?u=dublin&sid=bookmark-ECCO&xid=887ab622&pg=1.

Minutes of the Proceedings Before the Lords Committees for Privileges upon the Several Claims to the titles of Viscount Valentia, &c. Dublin, 1773. *Google Books*. January 2021. https://books.google.ie/books?id=AU1gAAAAcAAJ&pg=PA1#v=onepage&q&f=false.

Review of *Theodora, a Novel*, by Dorothea Du Bois. *The Monthly Review*. Vol. 43. London, 1770. *Google Books*. August 2020. https://books.google.ie/books?id=FJIzHB9DGeMC&pg=PR1#v=onepage&q&f=false.

Review of *Theodora, a Novel*, by Dorothea Du Bois. *The Critical Review, or, Annals of Literature*. Vol. 29. London, 1770. *Google Books*. August 2020. https://books.google.ie/books?id=k7oPAAAAQAAJ&pg=PP5#v=onepage&q&f=false.

Smollet, Tobias. *The Adventures of Peregrine Pickle*. London, 1751. *Eighteenth Century Collections Online*. August 2020. https://link.gale.com/apps/doc/CW0113059663/ECCO?u=dublin&sid=bookmark-ECCO&xid=79d68300&pg=1.

The Trial in Ejectment Between Campbell Craig, Lessee of James Annesley Esq., and Others, Plaintiff, and the Right Honourable Richard Earl of Anglesey. Dublin, 1744. *Google Books*. August 2020. https://books.google.ie/books?id=VpNaAAAAYAAJ&pg=PP9#v=onepage&q&f=false.

Young, Arthur. *A Tour in Ireland, with General Observations on the Present State of That Kingdom in 1776–78*. Vol. 2. London, 1780. *Eighteenth Century Collections Online*. August 2020. https://link.gale.com/apps/doc/CW0103089596/ECCO?u=dublin&sid=bookmark-ECCO&xid=3f74b12a&pg=1.

Secondary sources

Barnard, T. C. *The Abduction of a Limerick Heiress: Social and Political Relations in Mid-Eighteenth Century Ireland*. Irish Academic Press, 1998.

———. *A New Anatomy of Ireland: The Irish Protestants, 1649–1770*. Yale UP, 2004.

Carpenter, Andrew. "Poetry in English, 1690–1800: From the Williamite Wars to the Act of Union." *Cambridge History of Irish Literature*, edited by Margaret Kelleher. Vol. 1. Cambridge UP, 2006, pp. 282–319.

Ekirch, Roger A. *Birthright: The True Story That Inspired Kidnapped*. Norton, 2010.

Fens-de Zeeuw, Lyda. "The Letter-Writing Manual in the Eighteenth and Nineteenth Centuries: From Polite to Practical." *Studies in Late Modern English Correspondence: Methodology and Data*, edited by Marina Dossena and Ingrid Tieken-Boon van Ostade. Peter Lang, 2008, pp. 163–92.

Griffiths, Anthony. "Sir William Musgrave and British Biography." *British Library Journal*, vol. 18, 1992, pp. 171–89.

Hand, Derek. *A History of the Irish Novel*. Cambridge UP, 2011.

Higgins, Padhraig. "Consumption, Gender, and the Politics of 'Free Trade' in Eighteenth-Century Ireland." *Eighteenth-Century Studies*, vol. 41, no. 1, 2007, pp. 87–105.

Kelly, James. "The Abduction of Women of Fortune in Eighteenth-Century Ireland." *Eighteenth-Century Ireland/Iris an Dá Chultúr*, vol. 9, 1994, pp. 7–43.

———. *That Damn'd Thing Called Honour: Duelling in Ireland 1570–1860*. Cork UP, 1995.

Luddy, Maria and Mary O'Dowd. *Marriage in Ireland, 1660–1925*. Cambridge UP, 2020.

McBride, Ian. *Eighteenth-Century Ireland: The Isle of Slaves – the Protestant Ascendancy in Ireland*. Gill & Macmillan, 2009.

McVeigh, Simon. "Calendar of London Concerts 1750–1800." *In Concert*, 2014 [Dataset], https://doi.org/10.25602/GOLD.00010342

Mitchell, Linda C. "Entertainment and Instruction: Women's Roles in the English Epistolary Tradition." *Huntington Library Quarterly*, vol. 66, no. 3–4, 2003, pp. 331–47.

Power Thomas P. *Forcibly Without Her Consent: Abductions in Ireland, 1700–1850*. iUniverse, 2010.

Prescott, Sarah. "Archipelagic Literary History: Eighteenth- Century Poetry from Ireland, Scotland and Wales." *Women's Writing, 1660–1830: Feminisms and Futures*, edited by Jennie Batchelor and Gillian Dow, Palgrave, 2016, pp. 179–201.

Robins, Joseph. *Champagne and Silver Buckles: The Viceregal Court at Dublin Castle, 1700–1922*. Lilliput Press, Ltd., 2001.

Schirmer, Gregory A. *Out of What Began: A History of Irish Poetry in English*. Cornell UP, 1998.

Walle, Taylor. "'These Gentlemens Ill Treatment of Our Mother Tongue': Female Grammarians and the Power of the Vernacular." *Tulsa Studies in Women's Literature*, vol. 36, no. 1, Spring 2017, pp. 17–43.